Religion and Latin America in the
Twenty-First Century

SALALM Secretariat
Benson Latin American Collection
The General Libraries
The University of Texas at Austin

Religion and Latin America in the Twenty-First Century: Libraries Reacting to Social Change

Papers of the Forty-Second Annual Meeting of the
SEMINAR ON THE ACQUISITION OF
LATIN AMERICAN LIBRARY MATERIALS

Rockville, Maryland
May 17–21, 1997

Mark L. Grover
Editor

SALALM Secretariat
Benson Latin American Collection
The General Libraries
The University of Texas at Austin

ISBN: 0-917617-59-2

Contents

Religion in Mexico

Religion in Brazil

Religion in the English-Speaking Caribbean

Afro-Brazilian Religions

Religious Syncretism and the Latin American Indian

The Library of Congress and Global Resources

Latin American Biography and Collections

Preface

Few regions of the world have undergone dramatic and major change to the extent that Latin America has during the past few years. As a result of political reform, military dictatorships have given way to democracies in many countries of the region. Economic adjustments have led to unprecedented growth and development and greater participation in the world economy. And emerging social movements have the potential to significantly alter Latin American culture and society.

In addition, unexpected change has occurred in the area of religion in Latin America. In a region long considered predominantly Catholic, Indian and African religions are becoming more prominent than ever before. Folk Catholicism, historically an indication of religious pluralism, is gaining attention. But by far the most significant change in Latin American religion during the past twenty years has been the growth of Evangelical Protestantism and its Catholic counterpart, the Charismatic movement. Within a few years, Evangelical Protestants will likely outnumber Catholics in many Latin American countries.

The challenge for librarians is to meet the needs of patrons doing research about a region that is undergoing such rapid change. Historically, there has been a lag of several years between events in Latin America and library resources pertaining to those events. Despite the increasing availability of electronic resources, most of the work being published in the United States on Latin American religion is based on research conducted at least ten years ago. Given this time lag, how can libraries provide patrons with the research materials they need in order to understand contemporary events in Latin America?

The forty-second annual meeting of SALALM, held in May 1997 in Rockville, Maryland, focused on religion in Latin America. The participants examined Catholicism, Protestantism and Evangelicalism, Afro-Latin religions, and indigenous religions. A common theme of the presentations was that Latin America is indeed pluralist when it comes to religion. As Dr. Edward Cleary, one of the keynote speakers, has pointed out, the religious change that is occurring in Latin America

> is neither simply the expansion of Protestant religion nor losses by the Catholic church but a reorganization of religion that cuts across organizational lines in response to structural changes. Religion grows or declines

or reshapes itself in a context of changing socioeconomic conditions and political arrangements.[1]

The common assumption has been that as Latin America modernized, religious fervor and faith would diminish. The responses to a 1997 survey in Brazil suggest that modernization has had the opposite effect. According to the survey results, 99 percent of all Brazilians believe in a God, and 43 percent of those questioned had actually gone to some type of church, temple, or religious center during the week before the survey.[2] Recent studies in Mexico and other parts of Latin America show similar results.

The papers in this volume reflect the rapidly changing nature of the study of religion in Latin America. The papers examine the changing political relationships between church and state; the present-day role of Evangelical churches in the political arena; historical Protestantism; new religions that challenge the system; and religious syncretism. Several papers emphasize the need for librarians to stay in touch with events in Latin America.

I am indebted to the committee chairs and panel organizers for their help in organizing a successful meeting. I am immensely grateful to the six host institutions: the Library of Congress Hispanic Cultural Society, Hispanic Division, and Directorate of Acquisitions; the Oliveira Lima Library of The Catholic University of America; Maryland College Park Libraries; and the Latin American Studies Center, University of Maryland. I would like to express particular appreciation to Terry C. Peet, chair of the Local Arrangements Committee, and to the members of his committees. The success of SALALM XLII was due in large part to their hard work and dedication. A final note of thanks to my children, Tony and Sylvia, for their understanding.

Mark L. Grover

NOTES

1.   Edward L. Cleary, "Evangelicals and Competition in Guatemala," in Edward L. Cleary and Hannah Stewart-Gambino, eds., *Conflict and Competition: The Latin American Church in a Changing Environment* (Boulder, Colo.: Lynne Rienner Publishers, 1992), p. 167.

2.   "Crer em Deus, hoje," *Veja* (April 2, 1997), pp. 96-100.

The Catholic Church in
Latin America

1. Crisis, Conflict, and Change: Contemporary Latin American Catholicism

Edward L. Cleary

Attending the Latin American Studies International Congress for the first time in 1972 was a profound personal disappointment. I found virtually no presentations on Latin American religion. Cole Blasier, later Chief of the Hispanic Division of the Library of Congress and then my mentor, explained that for social scientists to be interested in a topic, it had to be able to change. Catholicism was considered a monolith and unchanging, and Protestantism in Latin America was regarded as insignificant.

Twenty-five years later, as we approach a new century, countless books and periodicals have traced changes in Latin American religion. This paper emphasizes four themes: the vitality of religion; the special case of Mexico; religion, democracy, and the economy; and Catholic–non-Catholic relations.

Vitality of Religion

Anticlericalism, the withdrawal of Spanish clergy after independence in the 1820s, and the lack of native clergy left an apparently dying church in many countries.[1] Forty thousand Catholic missionaries could save it, wrote Maryknoll writer John Considine in 1946.[2] The Vatican mounted a vigorous response and a large missionary crusade began in the early 1960s.[3] Despite this effort, however, in the majority of Latin American countries more than half the clergy came from other countries.

Regrettable as having foreign clergy is, the missionaries served as transmitters of reform in parish life and schools, created radio schools, delivered health care, and enlivened faith through lay movements such as the Cursillos de Cristiandad. Thousands of lay persons became catechists and leaders of small communities. This renewed family religious life is apparent in the remarkable increase in the number persons entering the priesthood and religious life.

Between 1972 and 1994 the number of seminarians increased 300 to 1,000 percent in most Latin American countries (Table 1). Many of these students are older, with work experience, and now attend theology classes within Catholic universities. Seminary walls could not contain the numbers—as many as 1,000 in Guadalajara—and new seminary residences have been built almost everywhere.

Table 1. Latin American Seminarians, 1972–1994

Country	1972	1994	Increase (%)
Argentina	306	2,015	559
Bolivia	49	539	1,000
Brazil	939	6,772	621
Chile	111	761	586
Colombia	738	4,285	481
Ecuador	92	741	705
Paraguay	63	301	378
Peru	90	1,357	614
Uruguay	25	69	176
Venezuela	120	963	702
Mexico	2,264	6,762	199
Costa Rica	61	279	357
El Salvador	34	323	850
Guatemala	69	562	714
Honduras	16	105	556
Nicaragua	45	192	327
Panama	22	206	836
Cuba	49	60	2
Dominican Republic	51	551	980
Haiti	41	223	444
Puerto Rico	49	126	157

Sources: *Statistical Yearbook of the Church 1994* (latest year for which statistics are available); *Catholic Almanac 1975.*

One could interpret the large increase in seminarians where Pentecostalism flourishes, such as in Brazil, Chile, and Central America, as an indication of a generalized religious revival in Latin America rather than a marked decline in Catholicism.

Further, interviews with seminarians in Bolivia, Chile, Paraguay, and Central America point to large numbers being attracted by the church's involvement in society and by intense small community experience.[4] Having discovered what they describe as the beauty of Christianity as adults, a number of seminarians were eager to join in evangelization efforts. The amazing growth of seminarians has occurred almost universally (see Table 2).

Table 2. Major Seminarians and National Populations
in Latin America, 1994
(In Rank Order)

Country	Seminarians (Number)	Population (Millions)
Brazil	6,772	154
Mexico	6,762	93
Colombia	4,285	34
Argentina	2,015	34
Peru	1,357	23
Venezuela	963	21
Chile	761	14
Ecuador	741	11
Guatemala	562	10
Dominican Republic	551	8
Bolivia	539	7
El Salvador	323	6
Paraguay	301	5
Costa Rica	279	3
Haiti	223	7
Panama	206	3
Nicaragua	192	4
Puerto Rico	126	4
Honduras	105	6
Uruguay	69	3
Cuba	60	11

Sources: Data for seminarians from *Statistical Year-book of the Church 1994* (latest year for which statistics are available); national population data are from *Catholic Almanac* 1997.

In contrast to precipitous declines in other Western countries, the number of religious sisters has increased in Latin America, where they now total some 127,000.[5] More mobile than priests or laity, nuns are found almost everywhere. They serve as pastoral associates, teachers, and community workers in interior Amazon regions. Their numbers and activities compare favorably with the missionary outreach of Pentecostal clergy.

Greater participation by lay men and women has been the strongest sign of renewal in the Latin American Catholic Church. Lay movements have affected the lives of millions of persons. Laypersons have assumed ministries in the church in ways unknown before the Second Vatican Council (known as Vatican II), including preaching, prayer groups, Bible study (a novelty for Catholics before 1965), and community and pastoral service. Religious sisters and laity carry out functions previously reserved to priests, such as saying Mass in remote regions and impoverished urban areas.

In the spirit of Vatican II renewal, one Latin American innovation stands out—Christian Base Communities (CEBs). These small groups of men and women meet regularly to read and study Scripture, increase their knowledge of Catholic beliefs, and reflect on their lives. The groups' small size allows participants to learn leadership skills and fosters active involvement of all members, a preparation for participatory democracy.

Thirty years of experience with small Christian communities have left a trail of publications as well as many questions. Let me summarize. First, small Christian communities are voluntary organizations that rise and fall according to the enthusiasm of authorities and members. But they are not fads. Some 60,000 to 80,000 groups flourish in Brazil alone. Second, the alumni of these groups are found everywhere, such as in human rights groups and neighborhood improvement associations. Participants learned a social Christianity that was gravely missing in Latin America in the 1960s. Last, the liveliness of the Latin American church expresses itself as social Christianity. Theirs is the faith that does justice, the church that serves the world. Although a minority, this group of Catholics has transformed a sector of the church from otherworldly to thisworldly.

Progressive/Conservative Cleavages

The thisworldly progressive tendency of the religious and lay leadership in the church has diminished. In a series of country studies in religion and politics Hannah Stewart-Gambino wrote: "The space available to the progressive sector is in many ways more constrained and its boundaries less clear; however, conditions in Latin America ensure that this progressive sector will not disappear."[6] Indications that the progressive church will continue under modified leadership can be found in Brazil where Catholic laity and priests are abundantly present in social movements and where the institutional church is forging new church-state relations.[7] The opening of more space for progressive leadership has also occurred at the Conference of Latin American Bishops.

Given the passive quality of many Latin American Catholics, the major organizational thrust has to be enlivening the religious sentiments of Catholic laity. Toward this end, the church has employed several strategies: establishing parish groups for special needs, evangelization programs directed from the international and national levels, and specialized lay movements. Among the latter, lay movements of revitalization gained the most attention. Pre–Vatican II movements include Catholic Action and Cursillos de Cristiandad; the Christian Base Communities constitute the premier Vatican II movement. Recent influential lay movements in Latin America include Opus Dei, Focolari, and other communitarian groups, and the Charismatic Renewal. Ralph della Cava has identified some twenty "new movements" of Catholic laity. Most originated in Western Europe, appeal primarily to urban middle-class men and women, abhor secularization, and are devoted to personal (not social) spirituality.[8]

Shifting from a grassroots perspective to institutional church, one may characterize the changes as immense. At mid-century the Latin American Catholic Church had almost no modern organizational structures. Vast dioceses with a minimal corps of administrators existed as they had for decades, even centuries. Then the Vatican created new dioceses, often tripling jurisdictions in a short time. Rome also chose progressive, creative, and energetic persons as bishops. Archbishops, such as Arns, Lorsheider, Romero, and McGrath, emerged as world leaders, some with accomplishments of such merit that they were considered candidates for pope.

For scholars and for the church the most important structures to emerge over the last fifty years are CELAM (Consejo Episcopal Latinoamericano) and the Conference of Latin American Bishops.[9] After 1955, for the first time the bishops had a means to speak, often with significant influence, as a collective body, particularly in the areas of international affairs and national politics. Latin American bishops regularly elect leaders for CELAM. Headquartered in Bogotá, CELAM operates an active publishing enterprise.

The main orienting events of the Latin American church have been carried out by CELAM, with the Vatican, as episodic events at Medellín (1968), Puebla (1979), and Santo Domingo (1992).[10] [An intercontinental event of unknown value, the Synod of the America (sic) in Rome, will take place in November–December 1997.] The Medellín conference illustrated the application of Vatican II reforms to a specific world region. In preparing for the Medellín conference, Latin American theologians emerged in the Latin Americanization of the church south of the Rio Grande. A major expression of contextualizing theology[11] became known as liberation theology.

Since I have written extensively on liberation theology elsewhere,[12] I wish simply to note here that its central theme, option for the poor, remains the central conviction of thousands of Catholics who internalized Vatican II in the Latin American way. Moreover, men and women trained in liberation theology are fostering women's theology and midwifing the birth of indigenous theology, a theme that will grow in importance.[13]

Popular Religion and Vulnerabilities

On balance, renewal does not affect all Catholics. Many practice traditional forms of Latin American Christianity, generally referred to as popular religion, the religion that women and men create in their homes in the absence of priests.[14] Several studies have examined internal beliefs and external practices, such as home shrines, private devotions, and pilgrimage.

Nevertheless, the Catholic Church in Latin America has weaknesses, manifest most clearly in comparison with the rise in the number of Pentecostals, Mormons, and other non-Catholic Christians in Latin America. First, the church lacks adequate pastoral care. The shortage of priests and other pastoral workers leaves families unattended in remote areas and thousands out of touch with the church in inner city slums.

In their study of a Bolivian colonization project, Thomas Greaves, an anthropologist at Bucknell University, and his associates interviewed all twenty families in the project. One by one they said they were Pentecostal or *evangélico.* At the end of the road the researchers found the last family. The man of the house came out and said boldly: "Soy católico y nunca van a conquistarme." (I'm Catholic and they're never going to get me.) In pointing out the weakness in some pastoral agents, Pope John Paul commented, "the faithful do not find . . . that strong sense of God that such agents should be transmitting in their lives."[15]

Second, the Catholic Church lacks consistent structures for evangelization and spiritual formation. Catholics have tended to rely on baptism and popular religion to support their religious lives. When outside groups offer Bible study, make heroic demands (sacrificial giving and avoidance of drink), and offer immediate opportunities for advancement within the organization, as Pentecostals do, the Catholic Church loses members.

Third, personal holiness is demanded and expected by classical Pentecostalism and some other non-Catholic groups. This *contra mundum* stance contrasts with the ritual conformity of some Catholics.

The Special Case of Mexico

Mexico has quickly emerged as a nation worthy of note because of the North American Free Trade Agreement (NAFTA) and internal changes affecting the practice of religion. Mexican churches recently acquired full juridical status after decades of state anticlericalism. A silent Mexican church has become increasingly vocal. There is a growing recognition of the distinct qualities of Mexican Catholicism. Because of secular education, the majority of Catholics are steeped in a nineteenth-century liberalism that opposes institutional church activism. Further, Mexican Catholics practice religion and attend services at a relatively high rate compared with other Latin American Catholics.[16] We are beginning to see the first systematic English-language studies of Mexican

Catholicism.[17] Last, more than 60 percent of Latin Americans in the United States are of Mexican descent. Understanding their religious backgrounds may soon gain the attention it deserves.

Religion, Democracy, and the Economy

The transnational character of Catholicism stands out in Latin America.[18] It is especially evident in two major socioeconomic and political issues: poverty and nation-building. The economic debate centers on what Latin Americans call neoliberalism, or market capitalism. Northern and Southern colleagues in the Americas often do not speak the same language. For example, the Jesuit provincials of Latin America (the most influential religious order in Spanish Latin America) recently prepared a major statement about neoliberal economics[19] which they wanted the Jesuit regional superiors of North America to co-sign. They did not. Gaspar LoBiondo, S.J., an economist, is attempting to broker an agreement on this statement through a North-South dialogue coordinated by the Woodstock Theological Center at Georgetown University.

The Catholic Church fostered the current movement toward democratization in Latin America.[20] Volumes in English, Spanish, and Portuguese describe and evaluate fledgling Latin American democracies. Therein one reads with alarm about the exhaustion of the oldest democracy in Latin America, Venezuela, or about the disappearance of political parties in Peru. Nation-building is the order of the day, but the language used is often that of civil society and human rights.

In my view, social movements, especially the human rights movements, are expanding and working hard to establish the rule of law.[21] Many Christian activists, who matured in Christian Base Communities or in families with a social Christian orientation, are working to establish civil society as the basis for democracy. Making democracy work and molding the economy to meet the needs of the majority will challenge all churches that seek social change.

Catholic–Non-Catholic Relations

Catholic–non-Catholic relations, a lively and contentious area, will become an ever more important issue in the next century. Latin American Catholics feel overwhelmed by the sheer number of churches registered at the various national ministries of foreign relations and worship—Adventists, Mormons, Pentecostals, New Age, eastern religions, and health-and-wealth gospellers, among others.[22] Mark Grover, president of SALALM, tells me that some Catholics have adopted two categories to describe non-Catholics—evil and most evil.[23]

From the viewpoint of the transnational Catholic Church, Vatican officials recommend seeing interchurch relations in global perspective. In that view, both Catholics and Pentecostals are the targets of complaints from Protestant and Orthodox religions previously controlled by the state, as in Sweden or the former

Soviet Union. Swedes and Slavs use the same arguments that Latin American Catholics use against foreigners.

During the Latin American Studies International Congress in Guadalajara in April 1997, Cardinal Juan Sandoval cited the vicious attacks against the Catholic Church by non-Catholics outside the Guadalajara cathedral.[24] Through the years the Vatican and the World Council of Churches have developed a joint statement on proselytism.[25] Latin Americans are just beginning to face this issue, which also affects Hispanics in the United States.[26]

Four aspects of the issue of proselytism stand out: (1) Pentecostals account for 75–90 percent of non-Catholic church growth in Latin America;[27] (2) Catholic and classical Pentecostals have engaged in formal dialogue in Rome and elsewhere since 1972;[28] (3) a few persons knowledgeable about dialogue are beginning to occupy important posts in Latin America;[29] and (4) aggressive proselytism and public insults are issues of public peace. If these issues are not resolved by mutual respect, religious conflicts will intensify.

In my opinion, it is no longer very helpful to view religion only from denominational perspectives. Studies of Presbyterians in Guatemala ignore the significant growth of Pentecostals. Large-scale studies of Pentecostalism in Latin America give the impression of great Catholic losses and overlook Catholic resurgences. Both Catholic and Pentecostal growth is taking place against a background of larger social forces. Views of religion in the next century will take into account Afro and indigenous religions as well.

This conviction leads me to look to the future in terms of religious pluralism. Like it or not, there is a wide-open religious market where Guatemalan Indians or Brazilian technocrats may shop.[30] Visit Guatemala's highlands or read Ana Guillermoprieto's account of Brazilian Afro religion practiced by millions of the middle class.[31] The conclusion for Catholic theologians and pastors may well be that of the noted Brazilian theologian José Comblin: religion in the twenty-first century will be a matter of free election.[32] One's family background will no longer necessarily determine one's religious identity. The American religious sociologist Joseph Fitzpatrick years ago described this change as the evolution from ascribed to achieved status.

Latin Americans who came to the United States were overwhelmingly Catholic, by inheritance, for there were few choices in their home countries. In the United States, however, they have the option whether to remain Catholic or not.[33] Now that choice is available to Latin Americans on their home soil. In a word, religious identity has become the result of a deliberate choice. That is the definition of crisis. As the Bolivian said, "I'm Catholic. Try as they might, they're never going to get me."

NOTES

1. For a Latin American appraisal from the 1950s, see *Tercera Semana Interamericana de Acción Católica: documentos* (Lima: Semana Interamericana de Acción Católica, 1953) and William J. Coleman, *Latin American Catholicism: A Self-Evaluation* (Maryknoll, N.Y.: Maryknoll Publications, 1958).

2. John Considine, *A Call for Forty Thousand* (New York: Longmans Green, 1946).

3. See Gerald Costello, *Mission to Latin America: The Successes and Failures of a Twentieth-Century Crusade* (Maryknoll, N.Y.: Orbis, 1979).

4. Interviews by the author, Guatemala and Nicaragua, July 1981; Central America, August 1988 and July 1989; Bolivia, Paraguay, and Chile, May–June 1989; Mexico, November 1994; Peru, May 1995; and Argentina, May 1996.

5. The 10,000-member increase in religious sisters from 1972 to 1994 underestimates actual growth in native vocations since many sisters from foreign counties returned to their home countries during this period.

6. Hannah Stewart-Gambino, "Introduction: New Rules, New Game," in Edward L. Cleary and Hannah Stewart-Gambino, eds., *Conflict and Competition: The Latin American Church in a Changing Environment* (Boulder, Colo.: Lynne Rienner, 1992), p. 16.

7. Clovodis Boff, "Uma análise da conjuntura da igreja católica no final do milênio," *Revista Eclesiástica Brasileira* 56 (March 1996): 125–149; and Edward L. Cleary, "The Brazilian Catholic Church and Church-State Relations: Nation-Building," *Journal of Church and State* (Spring 1997), 253–272.

8. Ralph della Cava, "The Ten-Year Crusade toward the Millennium: An Account of Evangelization 2000 and Lumen 2000," in Douglas A. Chalmers et al., eds., *The Right and Democracy in Latin America* (Westport, Conn.: Praeger, 1992), pp. 202–222.

9. Consejo Episcopal Latinoamericano, *CELAM: Elementos para su historia, 1955–1980* (Bogotá: Consejo Episcopal Latinoamericano, 1982).

10. Second General Conference of Latin American Bishops, *The Church in the Present-Day Transformation of Latin America in the Light of the Council,* vol. 1: *Position Papers* and vol. 2: *Conclusions* (Washington, D.C.: U.S. Catholic Conference, 1970); John Eagleson and Philip Scharper, eds., *Puebla and Beyond* (Maryknoll, N.Y.: Orbis, 1979); and Alfred T. Hennelly, *Santo Domingo and Beyond* (Maryknoll, N.Y.: Orbis, 1993).

11. Robert Schreiter's *Constructing Local Theologies* (Maryknoll, N.Y.: Orbis, 1985) is a useful introduction to a first contextual theological wave. Anthropologist Darrell L. Whitman provides a view of contemporary theory and practice in "Contextualization: The Theory, the Gap, and the Challenge," *International Bulletin of Missionary Research* 21: 1 (January 1997), 2–7.

12. Especially in Edward L. Cleary, *Crisis and Change: The Church in Latin America Today* (Maryknoll, N.Y.: Orbis, 1985), ch. 3, pp. 51–103.

13. Edward L. Cleary, "Birth of Latin American Indigenous Theology," in Guillermo Cook, ed., *Crosscurrents in Indigenous Spirituality: Interface of Maya, Catholic, and Protestant Worldviews* (New York: E.J. Brill, 1997), pp. 171–188.

14. See especially the publications of Jaime Vidal on Puerto Rican spirituality and various publications of the Mexican-American Cultural Center, San Antonio, Texas.

15. "Opening Address to Fourth General Conference of Latin American Bishops," [Santo Domingo], 326, 12.

16. See Roderic Camp, *Crossing Swords* (New York: Oxford University Press, 1997).

17. Ibid. In Spanish the works of Roberto Blancarte stand out, such as his *Historia de la iglesia católica en México* (Mexico City: Fondo de Cultura Económica, 1992).

18. Ivan Vallier completed one of the first analyses of the Catholic Church as transnational actor in "The Roman Catholic Church: A Transnational Actor," in Robert O. Keohane and Joseph S. Nye, eds., *Transnational Relations and World Politics* (Cambridge, Mass.: Harvard University Press, 1972). A more recent edited volume is Susanne Hoeber Rudolph and James Piscatori, eds., *Transnational Religion and Fading States* (Boulder, Colo.: Westview, 1997).

19. English translation made available through Woodstock Theological Center, Georgetown University.

20. See, for example, Samuel P. Huntington, *The Third Wave: Democratization in the Late Twentieth Century* (Norman: University of Oklahoma Press, 1991).

21. Edward Cleary, *The Struggle for Human Rights in Latin America* (Westport, Conn.: Praeger, 1997) and Cleary, "Brazilian Catholic Church."

22. See, for example, a first attempt by Bolivia's subsecretariat of worship: Marta U. de Aguirre et al., *El fenómeno religioso no católico en Bolivia: una primera aproximación* (La Paz: Ministerio de Relaciones Exteriores y Culto, 1995).

23. Interview, May 9, 1997. Grover, current chair of SALALM, has a son who is serving as a Mormon missionary in Argentina.

24. Session SPS 57 April 14, 1997.

25. Joint Working Group between the Roman Catholic Church and the World Council of Churches, "The Challenge of Proselytism and the Calling to Common Witness," *Information Service* [The Pontifical Council for Promoting Christian Unity] 91: 1–2 (1991), 77–84.

26. See Cecil M. Robeck, "Evangelization or Proselytism of Hispanics: A Pentecostal Perspective," *Journal of Hispanic/Latino Theology* 4: 4 (May 1997), 42–64.

27. A recent analysis of Pentecostalism is provided in Edward L. Cleary and Hannah Stewart-Gambino, eds., *Power, Politics, and Pentecostals in Latin America* (Boulder, Colo.: Westview, 1997).

28. Edward L. Cleary, "Protestants and Catholics: Rivals or Siblings?," in Daniel R. Miller, ed., *Coming of Age: Protestantism in Contemporary Latin America* (Lanham, Md.: University Press of America, 1994), pp. 210–213; see also John A. Rodano, "Pentecostal–Roman Catholic International Dialogue," *Mid-Stream* 31: 1 (January 1992), 26–31.

29. For a Brazilian view of the process, see Fernando Altemeyer Junior, "Globalization and Inter-religious Dialogue," *The Month* 258: 1551 (March 1997), 114–118; for a view of the issues and dialogue partners, see *Concilium* 1996/3, an issue devoted to the Pentecostal movement as an ecumenical challenge.

30. The metaphor of religious marketplace has severe conceptual limitations.

31. Ana Guillermoprieto, "Letter from Rio," *The New Yorker* (December 2, 1991), pp. 116–131.

32. Comblin made this argument at seminars in Chile and elsewhere during 1993.

33. Interview, Bronx, New York, March 19, 1981.

Catholicism and Politics

2. José Martí: Political Philosophy and the Catholic Church

Jack A. Siggins

The writings of José Martí cover a number of subjects ranging from literature and art to economics, sociology, and politics. Throughout his life in exile and out, as he traveled from one country to another, Martí never lost sight of his goal: complete autonomy for Cuba. Cuba was the first loyal Spanish garrison in the New World and remained among the last, as one by one the colonies broke away from the Mother country. By the time of Martí's birth, the Spanish world had broken apart almost completely. Even in the "ever most loyal" island of Cuba, Spain was forced to establish an army. For some two decades resentment against Spanish rule had been growing among Cuban citizens, particularly since the exclusion of the West Indian deputies from the Spanish Cortes of 1837. Around the country a feeling of political uneasiness prevailed.

Many Cubans, however, had observed the experiences of those sister countries which already had become independent from Spain, and the convulsions in those countries more than once served to curb Cuban emulation. Romantic aspirations and dreams of absolute liberty at any cost were balanced by a fear of the consequences of premature independence. As a result, the dominant anti-Spanish political movement in Cuba was conflicted between the radical ideal of autonomy and the more modest concept of annexation. In the nineteenth century, Cubans had already acquired a kind of historical inferiority complex, which inhibited their move toward self-determination. This was the political setting into which José Martí was born.

José Julian Martí was born in Havana on January 28, 1853, into a Spanish culture whose origins reached back for centuries. His parents were Spanish and they raised him in a land governed by Spaniards. He studied in Havana among Spanish children, speaking the Spanish language and studying Spanish culture. Martí's education and early training were also totally Spanish. At the age of 12, he came under the tutorship of Rafael María Mendive. Mendive introduced Martí to cultures of other areas of the world, in particular those of France, England, and the United States. He also made Martí aware of the political problems of Cuba. The Spanish government eventually became for Martí the symbol of human injustice and insult, and the expulsion of the intruders became his main goal in life.

Martí was thrown into an environment of increasing political tension. Throughout Latin America there was anarchy and political confusion, and as Martí matured, he saw around him in Cuba the remnants of a decaying Spanish empire. At an early age he began to see faults in the government and the need for Cuban independence. He became very much aware of the political split between the Cubans and the Spaniards.

Gradually, Cubans began to think about their rights, until in 1868, following a revolution in Spain in which Queen Isabel II was driven from the throne, the Ten Years' War erupted to establish Cuban independence. Martí did not delay in contributing to the doomed effort, and in 1871 at the age of 18 he was deported to Spain because of his revolutionary activities.

Strictly speaking, the two wars of 1868–1878 and of 1895–1898 constituted a single long process reflecting the gradual evolution in national psychology from annexation to independence. The first war, initiated by rural landowners, focused on the idea of annexation. The second war, however, more accurately represented the longings of the popular masses, and demonstrated that most Cuban citizens desired liberty and full independence. On the success of that demonstration depended the future political morality of the Cubans. The person who had the greatest part in preparing the Cuban citizens psychologically for the second war was José Martí.

In addition to rising political discontent, there was another fissure. Martí had been born at a time when a set of values and ideals was being developed entirely foreign to those of the "Spanish way of life." Whereas Spain had maintained her humanism while displaying a lack of interest in economic theory and technology, a new world of science, rationalism, and economics had developed in other Western countries. As a result, the Spanish world declined in power.

Out of this situation came the intellectual conflict of nineteenth-century Spain. Martí deplored the backwardness of Spain and her policy of colonialism. Through his education and travels he came in contact with liberal political philosophies prevalent in the United States and Europe, particularly in France, and decided to dedicate his life to securing complete independence for Cuba. As a result of his training and knowledge of the crisis in Cuba, Martí developed a political philosophy, or at least what might be called a doctrine of solutions to Cuban and Latin American problems. He pictured the New World as raw material from which could be constructed a Utopia.

Organization of the Revolution

Martí could not accept the Treaty of Zanjón which brought an official end to the Ten Years' War. His greatest single effort after 1878 was the founding and directing of the Cuban Revolutionary Party. This organization, comprising mainly exiles from the island, was largely a result of his patriotism and his unflagging ambition to free his homeland. The political philosophy of Martí became the philosophy of the Cuban Revolution, for most certainly it was primarily through his influence, both in action and in writing, that the Cubans were able to unite in a concerted war effort.

The major part of Martí's endeavors in this period was in the field of propaganda and organization. Beginning in 1880 and continuing to his death, Martí was in almost constant contact with Cubans exiled in New York. Through his writings in newspapers and numerous speeches, he managed to raise the spirits of the revolutionaries and to maintain independence as a common desire among them. He unmasked the maneuvers of the Spaniards to frustrate the Cuban separatist activities, warning of the dangers and keeping a close watch over the insurrection movement.

By the end of 1891, Martí generally was recognized as the leader of the revolution and director of the liberation movement. Invited by Néstor Leonelo Carbonell, president of the "Ignacio Agramonte Club," Martí went to Tampa, Florida, in November of that year. Out of this meeting of the two revolutionaries came the "Resoluciones Tomadas por la Emigración Cubana de Tampa" of November 28, 1891, which in turn was a prologue to the "Bases del Partido Revolucionario Cubano." The four general resolutions produced at Tampa were embodied later in the first three articles of the "Bases." They called for unity in action, assurance to the Cuban people of the good intentions of the revolutionaries, and the desire for the establishment of a republic under democratic methods without class distinction. On January 5, 1892, at Cayo Hueso, the presidents of the various Cuban separatist groups and other prominent revolutionary elements, such as the veteran patriot José Francisco Lamadriz, president of the "Convención Cubana," approved the "Bases" and the "Estatuos Secretos del Partido." Martí contributed significantly to the writing of these documents, and later they were unanimously approved by the Cuban and Puerto Rican exiles. Martí was elected "Delegado" of the Party.

But Martí could not entirely destroy his ties with Spain. The bonds reaching across the sea from the mother country to the island and Martí could not be easily broken. Martí's life in Madrid and in Zaragosa and his friendship with the Spaniards during four years of his life there were influences added to those of his family, environment, and training. While despising the tyranny in his homeland, Martí was still greatly influenced by Spanish culture. It was in Spain that Martí came into contact with the philosophical writings of Spanish thinkers in the latter half of the nineteenth century. In particular, he was influenced by those whose doctrine was constructed on an elaboration and amplification of ideas of the obscure German philosopher Christian Krause.

Krausists dominated the philosophical thought in Spain in the twenty years before Martí's arrival in the early 1870s. Probably the most active and outstanding of these writers was Julian Sanz del Río, whose influence was particularly strong from 1857 to 1869, the year of his death. It was during this period that the first generation of Krausists emerged. Krausism in Spain was a movement of Europeanization and renovation which continued to find expression in the works of the writers of the "Generation '98," such as Unamuno, Blasco-Ibáñez, Valle-Inclán, Azorín, Baroja, and others.

One of the doctrines adopted by Krause and the Spanish Krausists was that of "todo en Dios," to which the German philosopher adapted the term "panentheism." Panentheism is the synthesis in which is resolved the historical opposition between pantheism and deism; it combines the propensity of the former to make the world divine with the recognition by the latter of the independence of the moral acts of man. This belief in universal order, in the blending of the finite world with the infinite, and in the lack of contradictions of Nature influenced Martí a great deal especially in his opinion of the Catholic Church. Martí believed that there is a commonality about all things; that everything has the same objective; and that every man has within him the Creator. He believed in a central unity in events, thoughts, and actions. He also believed that by studying Nature through the means of science, man can improve himself and thus bring himself closer to the divine spirit.

Martí applied this universal order to his concept of social order, saying: ". . . el orden universal inspira el orden individual," and "Hay carácter moral en todos los elementos de la Naturaleza: puesto que todos avivan este carácter en el hombre, puesto que todos lo producen, todos lo tienen." [1] These words help to explain Martí's concern for social equality and social harmony.

Of all of Martí's writings, the essay most indicative of his philosophical thought is the one titled "Emerson," written in praise of the American writer Ralph Waldo Emerson. This North American writer exercised great influence on Martí, especially through his philosophy of transcendentalism. In this movement (in addition to many secondary characteristics) there is the firm belief that science can not reveal all of reality and that Nature and the Universe extend beyond the scheme which science describes and explains. Martí knew Emerson, admired him profoundly, and found in the North American an affinity of thought.

Liberty

Apart from his abstract concept of liberty, Martí believed in the basic freedoms of religion, education, thought, and the rights to work and own property. He was especially outspoken on matters of religion and recognized the effects the power of the church had on nations. Church and state, he believed, were two entities which should be considered as being separate: "Iglesia y Estado bien pueden ser dos poderes mutuamente respetuosos: el uno, juez de lo temporal; de lo incorpóreo el otro." [2] The Catholic Church dominated Latin America and

Martí realized the tremendous influence it had not only as a religion but also as a political power: "La religión católica tiene dos fases que merecen cada una peculiar consideración; es doctrina religiosa, y es forma de gobierno. . . ."[3] He disliked what Catholicism had become in Latin America, claiming "el cristianismo ha muerto a manos del catolicismo"[4] and "el infatigable plato católico; ¡[se] absorbe tantos ahorros de los pobres pueblos!"[5] To him, the Catholic Church was more of an oppressor than a benefactor.

But Martí was not opposed solely to the Catholic Church and Catholic religion. He protested against any religious dogma whose bases for existence were authority and fanaticism. No intelligent person, he believed, could accept a religion on such terms. He describes his concept of the perfect church this way:

> Una iglesia sin credo dogmático, sino con ese grande y firme credo que la majestad del Universo y la del alma buena e inmortal inspiran. ¡qué gran iglesia fuera! ¡y como dignificaría la religión desacreditada![6]

Martí objected to any religion, Catholic or Protestant, that attempted to dominate a country to the extent of expelling all other faiths. Each man should have the right to choose his own faith and to answer his own conscience: ". . . todo el mundo . . . tiene derecho a su plena conciencia; tirano es el católico que se pone sobre un hindú, y el metodista que silba a un católico."[7] Religion should be concerned solely with the spiritual needs of a man and should not become involved in secular matters. This was especially true not only in the field of politics and government but also in education, where he considered lay, rather than religious, education to be the only one that could guarantee freedom of thought. He wrote:

> One has no right to teach the Catholic religion, nor an anti-Catholic religion, in schools; either honor is not one of the religious virtues, or education will be sufficiently religious if it is honest. It is not proper for a teacher to claim as the only true religion, one which is held in doubt by the majority of the people, even if he shares it, or offend a religion to which, since the student follows it in free use of his judgment, he already has a right. Or is the Catholic Church so vapid and empty that it will crumble with the study of Nature and the teaching of human virtues? Or is it, perhaps, that it is against these virtues, that it fears them? Or has it come to so little that, although it be a divine doctrine, and therefore eternal, as its supporters affirm, this work of centuries cannot be sustained even by the prestige of tradition, or the influence exerted by solemnly lit churches on the imagination and the senses, the terror aroused in souls by the threat of damnation, its practice and reverence in all homes, or with the permission to teach its cult in schools to all boys and girls whose parents ask for it?[8]

However, it should not be inferred from such opinions that Martí was an atheist, or antireligious. He had a "scientific" faith, derived from the philosophers and writers he came in contact with, one which did not deny the place of reason and rationality in the world. Education was very important to Martí and it had several meanings for him. He saw it as a necessity in the successful operation of a democracy, believing that courses in Catholic or religious theology, rhetoric, and logic ought to be replaced by instruction in physics, mechanics, and agricultural development.

Martí's doctrine on science and education is based upon the assumption that the stability and contentment of a country could be furthered through the development of material wealth. By embarking on a vast program of education and technical training, Latin America, he believed, could reach the cultural level of Europe and the United States.

Martí associated freedom of thought very closely with freedom of speech. He argued that since an idea is not an entity in itself and no idea can come forth until it is expressed, then he who obstructs the expressions of thought "viola los fueros humanos, niega las facultades mentales, [y] rompe las leyes naturales. . . ."[9] He is referring here to the Spanish government and Catholic Church which controlled the Cuban newspapers and dictated political thought. The truth was permitted in Cuba, according to Martí, only when it was of relatively little importance to the government or the Catholic Church. The government and the church, he asserted, must not control the expressions of thought among the people. Cubans must not be deterred from revealing their opinions, oral or written, by fear of reprisal.

The basic freedoms Martí espoused were typical of the constitutionalists of the nineteenth century who affirmed the rights of man, not God, as their foundation and the liberty of the individual as their goal. Martí sought freedom for all Cubans through the revolutionary movement and through the permanent establishment of basic freedoms for each person. But Martí could only express opinions in writing and do very little in the way of concrete action. With no way of gauging his effectiveness, he often overemphasized his view. For this reason, his political thoughts sometimes have the appearance of moral sermons.

His greatness does not arise from events he participated in, but rather from the power of his message and his ability to move men to action. One story, perhaps apocryphal, reveals this power: After listening attentively to some of Martí's speeches, a humble Cuban cigar maker said: "At times we don't understand him well, but we would die for him."

NOTES

1. José Martí, "Emerson," *Obras Completas*, vol. I (Havana: Editorial Lex, 1953), pp. 1058–1059.

2. José Martí, *Obras Completas*, vol. II (Havana: Editorial Lex, 1953), p. 228. Hereafter cited as *Obras Completas*, II.

3. "Escenas Mexicanas," *Obras Completas*, II, p. 716.
4. "Francisco de Paula Vigil," *Obras Completas*, II, p. 85.
5. "Nuestra América: Guatemala," *Obras Completas*, II, p. 217.
6. *Obras Completas*, II, pp. 497–498.
7. "Federico Proano, Periodista," *Obras Completas*, II, p. 83.
8. Philip S. Foner, ed., *José Martí on Education* (New York: Monthly Review Press, 1979), p. 23.
9. *Obras Completas*, II, p. 826.

3. El rol de Evita en las relaciones del régimen peronista con la Iglesia Católica argentina

Eudoxio Paredes-Ruiz

Hemos elegido el nombre de "Evita", porque es el que ella prefirió para ser llamada por sus descamisados, y porque nos referiremos a su actuación como Evita en el proceso de las relaciones del régimen peronista con la Iglesia Católica argentina. Su ascensión desde Eva Perón a "Evita",[1] ella la tomó como un homenaje de "los humildes"de su patria y la usó para aislar su causa, identificándose con ellos en su breve vida.

En la Argentina de los años 40, con la irrupción del peronismo aparece el despertar de una nueva conciencia de derechos en una clase social tradicionalmente relegada. Evita contribuyó a este despertar con su directa intervención en los asuntos políticos y sociales del régimen. Su recurso fue su trabajo con los obreros y el pueblo, basándose en la doctrina del justicialismo que propendía a una "redistribución de los bienes del país para que haya así menos ricos y menos pobres",[2] tema que también era del dominio de la Iglesia Católica. El principio y el final entre el primer y segundo régimen, opuestos en lo que se refiere a sus relaciones con la Iglesia Católica, resultan de una interacción de mutuas reservaciones no precedidas por ningún otro gobierno en la historia argentina. Habiéndose iniciado en visible cooperación, terminan con la caída del régimen,[3] lograda por la alianza de fuerzas institucionales y la pasiva resistencia organizada y predicada desde los púlpitos.

El desarrollo de su trayectoria política en relación con la iglesia, desde su irrupción en la vida nacional argentina hasta su muerte, la presentaremos en tres etapas: etapa de confirmación y afianzamiento de su identidad católica; etapa de la convivencia político-católica; y etapa del distanciamiento institucional político/religioso.

Evita en el período de confirmación y afianzamiento de su identidad católica

En la vida política de Evita, su origen humilde, su pasado artístico y sus relaciones con Perón antes de su matrimonio, fueron estigmas que empañaban su figura y que la hacían daño para su rol como Primera Dama. Conociendo la enorme influencia que la Iglesia Católica tiene en la vida política de los pueblos, su primer objetivo fue captar la confianza y apoyo de esa institución a la vez que ejercía su influencia en ella como en toda la vida nacional. Su matrimonio eclesiástico fue el primer paso.

Unen sus destinos en ceremonia civil en Junín y religiosa en La Plata, pues no de otra manera habrían podido remediar la irregularidad de su unión que venía creando cuchicheos y desplantes por parte de la escrupulosa sociedad de aristócratas y militares de entonces. El matrimonio eclesiástico se realizó en la Iglesia de San Francisco de La Plata el 10 de diciembre de 1945.[4] Ambos comulgan con gran devoción. Eva Duarte es ahora la esposa legítima de Perón, ante la Iglesia Católica tan necesaria para los planes de su contrayente.[5]

Una vez formalizada su unión, Evita, como ninguna otra Primera Dama argentina, acompaña a su esposo en su campaña electoral a través del territorio nacional que lo lleva al triunfo en las elecciones del 24 de febrero de 1946.[6]

Inmediato a la inauguración del mando de Perón realizado en el Congreso el 4 de junio, como una introducción de su figura en el régimen, ella comienza un despliegue de actividades, seguidas en detalle por los medios de difusión.[7] En este período de asentamiento del régimen, Evita muestra una cuidadosa norma de conducta católico/política, especialmente en sus mensajes donde hacía evocación constante del catolicismo, en los conceptos de pueblo, pobreza y humildad por el lado de sumisión; y riqueza, arrogancia, explotación, tiranía por el combativo, que también eran temas tradicionales ligados a la labor pastoral de la Iglesia Católica.

Con las gestiones en pro de los derechos civiles de la mujer comienza a hacer notar su presencia política. Desde su primer discurso dirigido a las mujeres del 25 de julio 1946, tan sólo un mes después de la asunción del poder de su esposo,[8] repetía, tal vez con calculada intención, para no despertar recelos en organismos tradicionales, que el lugar de la mujer es el hogar, dentro del modelo de sumisión al esposo, y con su primordial rol de promover la moral cristiana dentro del catolicismo tradicional. Iniciando un concepto nuevo de feminismo,[9] con su influencia, logra hacer realidad las gestiones que organizadamente venían haciendo desde 1905 agrupaciones sufragistas y de derechos de la mujer, compuestas en su mayoría por damas de ancestro aristocrático.[10]

Su feminismo de sumisión al marido lo compendia diciendo: "De la misma manera que una mujer alcanza su eternidad y su gloria . . . dándose por amor a un hombre, yo pienso que tal vez ningún movimiento feminista alcanzará en el mundo gloria y eternidad si no se entrega a la causa de un hombre",[11] y lo propone simultáneo a la participación política dentro de los límites que impone el cristianismo: ". . . estamos hablando de la mujer cristiana, y del hogar asentado sobre esta base de sólida moral tradicional. . . . El sufragio femenino será la escuela cívica donde llegará a su máxima expresión la influencia protectora del hogar cristiano. . . . En el seno de la familia, no cabe el instinto ni la barbarie, sino la cruz bajo la cual nos engendraron".[12]

Alecciona a la mujer argentina a continuar en una conducta irreprochable, de acuerdo con los principios cristianos y los cánones de la Iglesia Católica. La frecuente insinuación de su fe católica en sus escritos y mensajes, la analogía y referencias de sus contextos con pasajes o personajes bíblicos, mantenían a las autoridades eclesiásticas con una dosis de confianza y cooperación con sus proyectos.

Sus mensajes en favor del sufragio femenino como su apoyo a la sindicalización de los trabajadores y sus intereses en sus relaciones con los empleadores y el Estado, no contradicen los principios cristianos. Desde fines del siglo pasado, con la influencia de la industrialización en la sociedad, la mujer entra a formar parte de la fuerza activa, y es cuando la iglesia teme perder la base de la fe y cultura cristiana. En 1891 la encíclica Rerum Novarum del papa de los obreros León XIII, alude a la condición específica de la mujer, educando a los hijos y propiciando la integridad familiar y el orden social.[13] Apoya las organizaciones obreras, así como la dignidad del trabajador y el salario justo.[14]

Ante la evidente correlación entre las ideas implícitas en los escritos y arengas de Evita en favor de los humildes, los pobres y los trabajadores, en contra de los ricos y los explotadores, y el pensamiento de la más alta jerarquía eclesiástica de finales del siglo XIX, la iglesia argentina no podía poner oposición a la política revolucionaria del régimen y, aunque sin romper con la clase privilegiada y sus tradiciones, más bien apoyó la ascensión al poder del fundador y promotor del justicialismo.

En sus discursos y mensajes se encuentran expresiones como: "Que el mundo se trunque en una gran familia bendecida por Dios";[15] ". . . mi labor es mitigar el dolor, estar al lado de los niños, de los que sufren, de los desposeídos . . . gracias a Dios tenemos hoy a un Perón . . .";[16] "En esta memorable hora de la paz del Divino Redentor, tregua cristiana de Nochebuena, quiero llegaros al corazón. . . . Estar simbólicamente con mis 'descamisados'. . . . La piedad cristiana nos ha hecho pensar en nuestros hermanos del mundo . . . sea nuestra meta y sea nuestra primera preocupación, imitando humildemente a Cristo, el corazón del hombre y el amor por el prójimo".[17]

Al mismo tiempo que hace consciente en el pueblo el daño causado por los "malos argentinos", no descuida promocionar su obra, su nombre y el de Perón: "Saben ustedes perfectamente que me he constituido en la más modesta pero entusiasta colaboradora del general Perón. . . . Siempre digo que prefiero ser simplemente 'Evita'. . . si ese 'Evita' es pronunciado para calmar un dolor en algún hogar de mi patria".[18] "Yo, una mujer de pueblo, doy gracias a Dios porque el General Perón y los descamisados me dan la oportunidad . . . cuando llevo un poco de alegría a aquellos a quienes la fortuna no los ha favorecido. . . . No olviden el daño que han hecho esos malos argentinos . . . diariamente estoy viendo en la Secretaría de Trabajo y Previsión las injusticias que durante cien años no sólo cometieron aquellos sino que ni siquiera trataron de remediarlas".[19]

Simultáneamente con su campaña en favor del sufragio, y en su afán de agradar a la iglesia, influencia en el gobierno para la sanción de la ley de enseñanza religiosa en marzo de 1947.

Entre junio y agosto de 1947 realiza su viaje a Europa.[20] Como España estaba en medio de una crisis que incluía la carencia de alimentos, Franco, con la esperanza de un acercamiento a Latino América y de solucionar el problema económico, se mostró entusiasta con su visita.[21]

Esta fue la oportunidad que tuvo Evita para su desquite de las humillaciones que sentía ser objeto por parte de la oligarquía argentina, especialmente las damas de la ex-Beneficencia. ". . . su comitiva era la de una reina. . . . Cuarenta aviones militares . . . escoltaban a Eva Perón cuando el DC4 de Iberia se posó en el aeropuerto madrileño . . . la noche del 8 de junio. . . ".[22]

Al día siguiente, Franco la condecora con la Gran Cruz de Isabel la Católica, encomiando su "preocupación social y la inquietud para los humildes que florece" en Argentina, así como "la gran obra de asistencia, reivindicación y dignificación de los trabajadores". En su agradecimiento ella dice: "Me entregáis Señor, la Gran Cruz de una condecoración que toma su nombre de la Reina Católica. . . . Sabéis el testimonio de su fe católica; me hacéis partícipe de su celo de gobernante; de sus triunfos; de su temple magnífico de mujer y de aliada de combate en la renovada estirpe y siempre fresco destino de ganar almas para la cruz y tierras para España".[23]

El 15 de junio al referirse a su gestión por el sufragio dice: "La Iglesia nunca ha prohibido ni disuadido a la mujer de que ejerza de médico o de diputado o de embajadora con tal que no abandone sus deberes esenciales . . . ".[24]

En Madrid como en toda España visitó barrios humildes y pronuncia discursos en los que su fervor religioso y principios de la moral cristiana están presentes. Deja Madrid el 15 de junio. En Granada visitó el camarín de la Virgen de las Angustias; reparte dádivas entre los gitanos; visita la tumba de los Reyes Católicos. En Sevilla el clero andaluz la designa "Camarera de honor de la Virgen" Macarena. En Barcelona, la última ciudad de su estadía en España, dicen que, en la noche del 24 de junio, Evita obvió el protocolo oficial para visitar barrios populares.

Todos los eventos de su itinerario eran cubiertos por los periódicos, especialmente por *La Prensa* y *Democracia* en Argentina, reproduciendo muchos de los artículos de la prensa europea, que aludían a su presencia en la España católica.

La sanción de la ley de enseñanza religiosa; un discurso que pronuncia por radio con el tema "El voto femenino y la enseñanza religiosa", en el que afirma sus convicciones católicas; y una misa "pro-itinerantibus" en la Catedral de Buenos Aires, prepararon el ambiente para convencer tanto a autoridades europeas, en especial del Vaticano, de su auténtica fe religiosa.

La visita a Italia, no tuvo el tono apoteósico por no haber revestido el carácter oficial de la española. Sin embargo, un objetivo cumbre de su catolicismo fue la visita que debía hacer al Vaticano. Previo a su visita, especulaciones de la prensa italiana eran reproducidas en Buenos Aires con referencia al tipo de recepción que le sería otorgada. El padre Benítez, enviado con anticipación, había logrado conseguir una audiencia con el Pontífice.

El 27 de junio su Santidad Pio XII recibió a Evita, en su biblioteca privada, a las 11 de la mañana, y le concedió una audiencia de 20 minutos, de acuerdo con el protocolo del Vaticano para reinas.[25] Para ese día Evita luce un severo traje negro, la cabeza cubierta con un velo, y como única joya la Gran Cruz de Isabel la Católica, recientemente concedida por Franco. En el patio San Dámaso fue recibida por el Secretario de la Santa Congregación del Ceremonial y como acompañante el príncipe Alejandro Ruspoli, Gran Maestro del Sagrado Hospicio. En el Salón San Clementino en presencia de altos dignatarios eclesiásticos recibe el homenaje de la Guardia Suiza. Afable y con voz "apagada y lejana" el papa habló a Evita, brevemente en español, encomió su labor social y le entregó un rosario.[26] Luego ella oró en la capilla del Santo Sacramento. Se dice que una acariciada intención de su visita fue la obtención del marquesado pontificio, título que había sido otorgado a sólo dos damas aristócratas, ex-presidentas de la Sociedad de Beneficencia.[27] Entonces corrían rumores de que el fracaso de los Perón en este deseo, se debió a gestiones secretas por parte del Episcopado argentino en colaboración con adversarios de Perón y en complicidad del Cardenal Santiago Luis Copello, Arzobispo de Buenos Aires y Primado de Argentina; sin embargo, fue éste quien apoyaba el trabajo de la Fundación, bendiciendo sus obras y manteniéndose cerca a los Perón; igual que Monseñor De Carlo, obispo de la Resistencia, muy cooperativo con la obra social de Evita, amigo de los Perón por lo que le llamaban "obispo peronista"; a diferencia de Monseñor De Andrea de actitud conservadora y opuesto al régimen, o de Monseñor Franchesqui que controlaba órganos de prensa católicos.[28]

La recepción que la Embajada Argentina organizó en su honor, un día después de su audiencia con el papa, contó con la asistencia de nueve cardenales y de varios dignatarios eclesiásticos y de la Corte Pontifical. En esta ceremonia recibió en nombre de su esposo la Gran Cruz de Gregorio el Grande, envío del papa.[29] Evita en todo momento, quizás imbuida también por el ambiente religioso de Roma y la gente que frecuentaba, hacía despliegue de acendrada piedad con sus visitas y oraciones en las iglesias, en la misa que se celebró en su honor en la capilla de San Antonio, y en sus reuniones con sacerdotes mayormente de la orden franciscana. En toda su gira por Europa trató de identificar su imagen con el catolicismo, tal vez con la secreta intención de cambiar la imagen que trascendía de rumores maliciosos de sus enemigos, los que, con el poder que más tarde adquirió, no impedirían realizar sus proyectos.

En París se dice que se entrevista con Monseñor Roncalli, futuro Juan XXIII, de quien pide sus bendiciones a sus proyectos de obras sociales.

Período de Convivencia Político/Católica

Si por el decreto del 7 de setiembre de 1946, y por su influencia, se intervino y liquidó los bienes de la Sociedad de Beneficencia,[30] asombrando a las damas oligarcas y especialmente a su presidenta la marquesa pontificia Adelia Harilaos de Olmos, rica terrateniente en estrecha relación con las más altas autoridades de la iglesia; su fervor católico desplegado en Europa, sus discursos, sus visitas a orfelinatos, su ayuda social, su fervorosa asistencia a eventos religiosos de relieve como el Congreso Mariano de octubre de 1947, y su vinculación con algunos de los respetables miembros de la iglesia, comprometía a la institución católica argentina a contemplar y dar legitimidad a su actuación.

A su retorno de Europa, con las observaciones de la realidad social, los honores recibidos en España, el Vaticano y Francia, se presenta con una considerable evolución y un estilo de actuación drástica tendiente hacia el monopolio del poder que incluye a organismos de la prensa. Ya desde enero de 1947, *Democracia* estaba a su servicio y exaltaba su imagen reportando, en un espacio cada vez mayor, la intensa actividad de su trabajo con las mujeres, los obreros y los pobres.[31]

El 23 de setiembre de 1947 se sanciona la ley de los derechos políticos de la mujer. En su discurso de victoria, que de por sí ya es promoción de su figura y del líder, es una arenga a continuar la lucha, con la fe puesta en Dios, la patria y Perón: "Alcemos, todas juntas, esa fe, e iluminemos con ella el sendero de nuestro destino. . . . Tenemos para conquistarlo y merecerlo, tres bases insobornables, inconmovibles: una ilimitada confianza en Dios . . . una Patria incomparable a quien amar . . . y un líder que el destino moldeó para enfrentar victoriosamente los problemas de la época: el general Perón . . .".[32]

Una vez coronada con el éxito sus andanzas por los derechos cívicos de la mujer, intensifica su trabajo con los gremios y con la ayuda social. Desde que la Sociedad de Beneficencia había dejado de existir, Evita venía desempeñando lo que la prensa peronista llamaba una "Cruzada de Ayuda Social",[33] no institucionalizada, nacida porque la "obligó la necesidad de los pobres" que habían sido receptores de la caridad de las "decadentes sociedades de 'damas de beneficencia' ".[34] Dos años más tarde, el 8 de julio de 1948, Evita consigue que por decreto supremo se creara la Fundación de Ayuda Social María Eva Duarte de Perón.[35]

Por el febril trabajo y el poder de su fundadora, esta institución llegó a ser "una empresa única en su género, dinámica hasta el dintel de lo caótico, generosa hasta el derroche, compulsiva hasta el chantaje, dispendiosa, indiscreta, unipersonal y . . . terriblemente eficaz".[36] En verdad, en su obsesión de reivindicación por las injusticias Evita llegó hasta el derroche: ". . . la 'obra social' del siglo que nos precedió fue así: frío, sórdido, mezquino y egoísta. . . . Por eso mis 'hogares' son generosamente ricos . . . más aún, quiero excederme en esto. Quiero que sean lujosos. Precisamente porque un siglo de asilos miserables no se puede borrar sino con otro siglo de hogares 'excesivamente lujosos' ".[37]

Ella dice que su labor "No es filantropía, ni caridad, ni limosna, ni es solidaridad social, ni es beneficencia. . . . Para mí es estrictamente justicia. . . ¡Yo creo que Dios muchas veces se ha avergonzado de lo que los pobres recibían en su nombre!"[38]

La Fundación, pues, comienza con un concepto de justicia que nada tenía que ver con la caridad. Define a su institución como una "acción que es del pueblo y que va directamente al pueblo". La ayuda que ella ofrecía no era la fría y burocrática de la Sociedad de Beneficencia, tampoco era del tipo paternalista ni jerárquico como viniendo de alguien superior; su ayuda más bien era de tipo fraternal inmediato ofrecido, sin trámites, por la "compañera Evita".[39]

Además de la ayuda que ella daba a los que la visitaban en las oficinas de la Fundación, se realizaron trabajos en el campo de la educación con 1,000 escuelas y 18 hogares escuela en el interior del país. Construyó policlínicos en Buenos Aires, y otros en muchos pueblos de todo el territorio nacional,[40] además, "Durante el Primer Plan Quinquenal fueron edificados 350 mil viviendas para obreros".[41] Esto sólo como una muestra que los historiadores de Evita dan de las realizaciones de la Fundación.

Así abarcó casi todos los aspectos de la vida nacional desde un convenio colectivo, una vivienda familiar, ajuares para novias, para niños, máquinas de coser, puestos en una escuela para mujeres con niños, alimentos, turismo infantil, etcétera.[42] En el sentimiento popular, lleno de desesperanzas y frustraciones para alcanzar un bien, la Fundación vino a ser la "institución milagrosa" guiada por Evita que hacía realidad sus ilusiones como nunca se hizo anteriormente.

Con las obras de la Fundación, Evita invade el terreno que era exclusivo de la iglesia y sus instituciones de caridad como asilos sanatorios y cosas por el estilo atendidos por sus órdenes religiosas femeninas. Pero su omnipresencia no excluye la convivencia político católica: el Padre H. Benítez es el consejero espiritual de la Fundación; él supervisa la labor de sacerdotes que ofician las misas en las iglesias levantadas en los barrios obreros y de las religiosas que trabajan en hogares, hospitales, etcétera.[43] Las instituciones en su inauguración eran legitimadas por la bendición del Cardenal Primado Santiago Luis Copello.

Otra institución de poder en sus manos fue el Partido Peronista Femenino (PPF), que surge con la obtención de los derechos cívicos de la mujer. Fue nombrada su presidenta desde su creación en julio de 1949. Unidades básicas, en forma de centros en toda la república, bajo un estricto código moral, fomentaban actividades hogareñas. Allí se enseñaban labores como costura, bordado, fabricación de flores, o cursos de secretariado.

El PPF debía tener como principio fundamental "la unidad en torno a la doctrina y la persona de Perón. Ellas sólo pueden tener un líder, un objetivo y un camino,"[44] aunque estaban bajo el absoluto control de Evita. La formación de este partido aumentó considerablemente la influencia de ella hasta llegar a un nivel de competencia con la de Perón, sobre todo si las bases del movimiento peronista eran el Partido Peronista Masculino, el PPF, y la CGT donde ella tenía gran influencia. La iglesia si bien no tenía razones para argüir sobre la conducta de vida moral del partido femenino y de sus miembros, cada vez veía con más recelo la creciente influencia de su presidenta.

Su incursión en asuntos laborales se institucionaliza en una oficina cedida en la Secretaría de Trabajo y Previsión, y con su influencia cambia la perspectiva sindical argentina. Es allí donde ella discute contratos sindicales y da audiencias a delegaciones de trabajadores, y ayuda en la resolución de problemas laborales:

> Desde el mirador de la Secretaría se ve todo el panorama sindical argentino. "Yo, que lo he visto en 1944 y 1945 desde un rincón del mismo despacho que hoy presido . . . solamente puedo decir tal vez cómo ha cambiado todo en este sector de mi Patria. . . . Así, como la sombra del Líder, es mi presencia en la Secretaría. Y a su sombra yo intento seguir el camino que él inició".[45] En la tarde de los miércoles en la Casa de Gobierno, ayuda a Perón con los trabajadores agremiados: "En esta parte de mi trabajo es donde puede verse con más claridad la verdad de ese papel humilde pero tal vez útil para mi pueblo. . . . Soy algo así como un camino por donde el pueblo humilde ¡el pueblo trabajador! llega a su presencia.[46]

Los discursos de Evita, con el pasar del tiempo, hacían cada vez menos referencias católicas, pero sí continuaban dando preeminencia al pueblo, a la doctrina justicialista y a sus obras. Sin embargo, en este período de convivencia ella logró mantener la aquiescencia de las autoridades eclesiásticas con sus demostraciones de fervor religioso, sus mensajes de contenido cristiano, el efecto material de su obra social en favor de los humildes, y el cuidado de la moral en el seno de las organizaciones lideradas por ella.

Distanciamiento institucional político/religioso

Parece que ambos actores, iglesia-estado, no admitían abiertamente un deterioro en las relaciones[47] mientras que con la ayuda de Evita el régimen se orienta hacia una creciente personalización y centralización de poder. Sus mensajes tienden a la exaltación del justicialismo, sacralizando la figura de Perón, de la que ella depende: ". . . yo no era ni soy nada más que una humilde mujer . . . un gorrión en una inmensa bandada de gorriones. . . . Y él era y es el cóndor gigante que vuela alto y seguro entre las cumbres y cerca de Dios".[48] Ahora las referencias religiosas y bíblicas están cada vez más asociadas a la figura del Líder, a ella misma y a su obra.

Su abnegación hacia los humildes con la solución inmediata de sus problemas tanto materiales como de confort espiritual, su servicio como intercesora entre Perón y los trabajadores, y el fanatismo y énfasis de sus discursos en sus convicciones en pro de la justicia social, le van edificando un lugar especial en el corazón de su gente que ansiosa de retribuirle su cariño y admiración la van ascendiendo con títulos de connotaciones místicas y virginales, tales: "Primera Samaritana Argentina" (3 de agosto, 1946); "Señora de la Esperanza" como lo asigna *Democracia* por primera vez el 25 de enero de 1947; "Abogada de los Pobres"; "Ada Buena de los Niños"; "La Compañera Evita"; "Ciudadana de América";[49] "Abanderada de los Humildes"; "La Mártir de los Trabajadores";[50] "Jefa Espiritual de la Nación" el 7 de mayo (su compleaños), 1952.[51] El 18 de octubre de 1951 es declarado "Día de Santa Evita".[52]

Mientras la iglesia tradicional ha tendido a mantener un catolicismo popular dentro de los marcos de la resignación y humilde aceptación de su destino de clase, riqueza y poder, la presencia de Evita proclamaba en nombre del justicialismo la revolución en proceso, e insinuaba la aspiración al cambio como un derecho, con la mejora de la situación social, política y económica, es decir cultivaba con sus arengas una nueva conciencia de derechos propendiendo a la incorporación de un pueblo relegado, con la complicidad de la iglesia, a una nueva ciudadanía política.

En octubre de 1950 asisten a la clausura del Congreso Eucarístico de Rosario. En esta ocasión Perón dejó traslucir la situación de distanciamiento con la iglesia, enfatizando que él aceptaba plenamente la divinidad de Cristo pero criticando al mismo tiempo a los que sólo por llenar las apariencias cumplen con la liturgia católica y enalteciendo la doctrina justicialista que trata siempre de respetar y cumplir las prácticas cristianas. Sin embargo, el delegado papal al congreso se manifestó complaciente y hasta hizo una visita a la Fundación.[53] Carmen Llorca, al referirse a Evita en esta ocasión, transcribe: "aunque ella era creyente decía. . . . 'Cuando yo quiero hablar con Dios, hablo yo, porque yo conozco a los intermediarios' ". Vemos por esta expresión la encubierta desconfianza, y el distanciamiento que ha ido germinando en ella con respecto a los "intermediarios".

Toda la espectacularidad de su obra social; todo el carisma que cultiva y mantiene con los trabajadores y el pueblo; su fértil pujanza; su febril trabajar, sin control de sus horarios;[54] la difusión de sus sacrificios y expresiones en pro de los pobres;[55] el aprecio manifestado en los honores y títulos que le confieren instituciones y países; todo ello despierta sentimientos profundos de negación entre el sector privilegiado, y de adoración y sacralización entre los humildes. El pueblo la considera redentora de sus sufrimientos y por tanto ya en vida comienza a verla con una aureola de bondad milagrosa y a designarla con adjetivos y expresiones de analogías bíblicas. Estos sentimientos van intensificándose en el poco tiempo de vida que le queda, especialmente con el concurso de los órganos de prensa que cada día enaltecían su "misión semisagrada". El gobierno mismo e influencias de la Escuela Superior Peronista, dirigida por Raul Mendé, contribuyen en este proceso de mitificación, parangonándola con la Virgen María por su labor de intermediaria entre los problemas del proletariado y Perón, "Redentor de los pobres . . . [cuyos] afanes . . . de dignificación de los humildes . . . [fue el] objetivo principal de su quehacer político . . .".[56] El conjunto de todas estas circunstancias influyen en el pueblo que le da un lugar dentro de sus devociones, independientemente de las prácticas religiosas tradicionales.

En diciembre de 1951, se publica su autobiografía, *La razón de mi vida*. Su contexto, intercalando expresiones combativas contra los privilegiados y la oligarquía, no es más que la promoción de la figura del Líder y su doctrina; de su propia imagen y de su labor con las mujeres, con los gremios y con los pobres. Es en esta obra donde se describe su labor de intercesora entre el pueblo y Perón, y donde la omnipotencia de Perón y su doctrina se igualan con la de Cristo. Su publicación provocó expresiones de alabanzas por parte de la prensa y las Cámaras, incrementando la lista de títulos y denominaciones en honor a su persona: "Esencia semidivina" de Eva Perón, "El nombre sagrado de Eva Perón", "Mártir del trabajo", "Alma y ejemplo de nuestra Argentina", entre otros.[57] Todo este aparato de alabanzas venía creando en las autoridades eclesiásticas sentimientos de rivalidad y desconfianza.

Al final de su vida escribe *Mi mensaje*, que por razones políticas de Perón, no se publicó sino hasta 1987. En el capítulo 20, titulado "Las Jerarquías Clericales", Evita abiertamente expresa su frustración y dura crítica hacia las autoridades eclesiásticas: "Entre los hombres fríos de mi tiempo yo señalo a las jerarquías clericales cuya inmensa mayoría padece de una inconcebible indiferencia frente a la realidad sufriente de los pueblos. . . . En ellos simplemente he visto mezquinos y egoístas intereses y una sórdida ambición de privilegio . . .". Denuncia a esas autoridades el "haber combatido sordamente a Perón, desde sus conciliábulos con la oligarquía". Les reprocha el "haber abandonado a los pobres, a los humildes, a los descamisados . . . a los enfermos . . . y haber preferido en cambio la gloria y los honores de la oligarquía"; y les reprocha el "haber traicionado a Cristo . . . y haber hecho todo lo posible por ocultar el nombre y la figura de Cristo tras la cortina de humo con que lo inciensan . . .".[58]

Cuando sabía que la muerte estaba cercana, no tuvo inhibiciones de expresar estos sentimientos reprimidos. Esta etapa de nota anticlerical en el ánimo de Evita, ha ido germinando con su progresivo fanatismo y convencimiento de que en las realizaciones, la doctrina justicialista aventajaba a la practicada por las autoridades eclesiásticas. Muerta Evita, las relaciones entre la iglesia y el estado se mantuvieron distantes con susceptibilidad y mutua desconfianza.

Es durante su gravedad y después de su muerte que se patentiza la animadversión que en el lado opuesto también se venía germinando. Así cuando todo tipo de celebraciones estaba suspendido, las mujeres de la ACA organizaron el 13 de julio en el Luna Park, celebraciones por el 50 aniversario de sacerdocio de Copello; el Instituto Superior de Cultura Religiosa llevó a cabo su cena de homenaje al jefe de la iglesia nacional. *Criterio,* revista católica bajo la dirección de Monseñor Franceschi, fue muy parca en mostrar entusiasmo por Evita y su obra, más aún, sólo una breve nota de duelo ante su muerte. Años más tarde, otros órganos bajo la dirección de Franceschi, dejarían ver el rencor que existía hacia ella.[59]

El conflicto comienza a materializarse en setiembre de 1955, con el estallido de la revolución en Córdoba el 15 de ese mes; ella ya no estaba. Se dice que con su poder de atracción de las masas, ella habría podido prevenirlo. Durante el conflicto la figura y la obra de Evita eran invocadas constantemente por el pueblo peronista como singular ejemplos de cristianismo. La violencia llega a su máximo con la quema y profanación de iglesias y conventos en Buenos Aires, que se adjudica al peronismo; triunfa la Revolución Libertadora con la caída de Perón, el 21 de ese mes. Un testigo que trabajó al lado de sus colegas católicos antiperonistas dice: "Oprimido por aquel inmenso mar de hombres y mujeres que festejaban la liberación . . . cerca del peristilo de la Catedral, oí llegar hasta mí, a través de los altoparlantes, frases que había dudado poder oír nuevamente". Se refiere al discurso de victoria de Lonardi, que dice: "Será mi preocupación constante mantener inalterable el respeto y la garantía de los derechos de la iglesia y la conciencia de todos, sea cual fuere su credo".[60] Fue la Iglesia Católica la que había triunfado, con el concurso de otras fuerzas.

Conclusión

Conociendo bien el tradicional peso de la iglesia en la sociedad y en los asuntos de la política de un país latinoamericano, Evita, pese a los prejuicios individuales e institucionales que tuvo que afrontar logró conseguir la cooperación de sus autoridades a fin de introducir en el país la política del naciente justicialismo.

Mientras Evita se impuso como misión la inmediata atención de las necesidades de los pobres con bienes materiales, la iglesia aún continuaba con sus predicas sobre la salvación eterna. Evita les daba realizaciones; la iglesia les daba esperanzas. El pueblo veía que la ayuda social de Evita era concreta, inmediata, y llegaba desposeída del concepto de clase que regían las obras de caridad; mientras que la que la iglesia ofrecía les parecía abstracta, remota y espiritual y siempre distribuida con la ayuda de miembros provenientes de la clase privilegiada.

Evita, por su influencia, contribuyó a enfrentar al régimen con una institución religiosa, íntimamente ligada a la vida política y social, cuyos miembros eran "funcionarios de una empresa permanente", y cuyo sistema de autoridad es estrictamente jerarquizado y centralizado, enraizada en garantías acordadas por el estado desde que los españoles la implantaron en América Latina.

El enfrentamiento no fue necesariamente originado por el conflicto doctrinario del justicialismo con el catolicismo, puesto que en esencia había una "cabal coincidencia" entre ambos.[61] Se debió, más bien, a un conflicto de instituciones timoneadas por individuos con sed de poder sobre el pueblo que representa el sector mayoritario dentro de la sociedad. Triunfó la iglesia por su carácter universal contra el estado de carácter nacional, y por su organización y sus mecanismos de apoyo altamente desarrollados entre las élites institucionales del país.

El proceso de deterioro de las relaciones fue tan gradual que los participantes parece que no se daban cuenta, hasta que fue muy tarde. Los líderes de la iglesia esperaban consideraciones especiales, porque pensaban que su antigüedad y tradición de poder e influencia en asuntos de estado, les daba ese derecho; igual los del estado, porque basados en la doctrina de su causa y en posesión del poder, pensaban que habiéndose ganado la voluntad de una inmensa mayoría entre pueblo y trabajadores, su influencia debía prevalecer.

Eva Perón, hasta su muerte, tuvo presente al pueblo que le otorgó el privilegio de llamarse "Evita"; por ellos luchó con un estilo nuevo de lucha política rebosada de fanatismo y de anhelos de justicia social que la llevó, con la trascendencia de su figura, a cumplir su acariciada esperanza de ocupar un lugar no "al pie del capítulo maravilloso que la historia ciertamente dedicará a Perón" como ella escribió, sino al mismo nivel o con más gloria.

La obra de Evita queda, su memoria es venerada entre las clases a las que trató de incorporar, con todos los derechos, dentro de la sociedad argentina. Han pasado ya 45 años y el interés en ella ha ido creciendo en todo el mundo. Y el pueblo argentino la sigue recordando, porque su liderazgo de realidades en su ayuda ha calado hondo en el alma de sus "descamisados" y no ha sido repetido. En el mausoleo de la familia Duarte en La Recoleta no faltan flores frescas todos los días y en muchos hogares del pueblo que ayudó, todavía se ve una estampa con su imagen que veneran no como a la Virgen María pero sí como intercesora de sus problemas.

NOTAS

1.   Eva Perón, *La razón de mi vida* (Buenos Aires: El Cid, 1982), cap. 17; " 'Evita' es una palabra mítica que no solamente provoca el cariño de sus partidarios, sino también el odio y la indignación de sus detractores". Juan José Sebreli, *Eva Perón, aventurera o militante* (Buenos Aires: La Pléyade, 1982), p. 62.

2.   Perón, *La razón*, p. 116.

3.   Ver Florencio J. Arnaudo, *El año en que quemaron las iglesias* (Buenos Aires: Pleamar, 1995).

4.   Según partida de matrimonio religioso, folio 297, expediente 2397, firmada por el cura de la Parroquia Fray Francisco C. Sciammarella. Ver Héctor Daniel Vargas and Roberto Carlos Dimarco, *Evita, casamiento en Junín* (Junín: Taller Gráfico Salido, 1995), p. 93.

5.   Crespo a este respecto dice que el matrimonio debió realizarse el 29 de noviembre y que "En la mañana de ese día, rodeada por su madre y hermanas, Eva . . . en la Iglesia de San Ponciano . . . espera en vano la llegada de Perón. Alguien ha prevenido al coronel que se atentará contra su vida en el templo. Dejando a Eva librada a sus propios riesgos, Perón no concurre a la ceremonia. El acto se verificará el 10 de diciembre . . . previas las precauciones de rigor". Alfonso Crespo, *Eva Perón, viva o muerta* (Lima: Studium, 1978), p. 156; ver también Sebreli, *Eva Perón;* y Jane Van Der Karr, *Perón y los Estados Unidos* (Buenos Aires: Ed. Vinciguerra, 1990), p. 42.

6.   Van Der Karr, *Perón y los Estados Unidos*, pp. 47–52; ver también Crespo, *Eva Perón*, p. 167; y Noreen Frances Stack, "Avoiding the Greater Evil: The Response of the Argentine Catholic Church to Juan Perón, 1943–1955" (Tesis de doctorado, Rutgers University, The State University of New Jersey, New Brunswick, 1976), p. 337.

7.   Para una muestra de la intensidad de estas actividades, ver Marysa Navarro, *Evita* (Buenos Aires: Planeta, 1994), p. 139.

8.   Realizado el 4 de junio, 1946.

9.   Ver Van Der Karr, *Perón y los Estados Unidos*, pp. 58–60.

10.   El Centro Feminista Manuela Gorrity, fundado en 1905 por Alicia Moreau de Justo; la Asociación Argentina de Sufragio, fundada en 1930 por Carmela Horne de Burmeister. Ver Navarro, *Evita*, pp. 186–191.

11.   Perón, *La razón*, p. 50.

12.   Discurso pronunciado el 26 de febrero, 1947, por L.R.A. Radio del Estado, en Eva Perón, *Discursos completos* (Buenos Aires: Megafón, 1985), vol. I, pp. 55–59.

13.   Lila M. Caimari, *Perón y la Iglesia Católica* (Buenos Aires: Ariel Historia, 1995), p. 217.

14. El Papa León XIII, en 1877 cuando aún era Cardenal Joaquín Vicente Pecci, publica una pastoral donde hace constancia de su preocupación social ante los progresos de la industria. Demuestra su amor a los trabajadores y lanza anatemas contra los patronos y los ricos, pero sí defendiendo la necesidad de la propiedad privada. En su encíclica de 1891, rechaza la solución socialista. Presenta como remedio la fraternidad de los hombres en la doctrina de Cristo. Esta "Carta magna de las reivindicaciones del proletariado" justifica el derecho de los trabajadores para asociarse en uniones laborales "a fin de constituir el más conveniente medio para obtener sus objetivos . . . para mejorar en lo posible sus condiciones de cuerpo, alma y propiedad . . .". *Enciclopedia Universal Ilustrada Europeo-Americana* (Madrid: Espasa-Calpe, 1920–1958), t. 29; Catholic Church. Pope, 1922–1939 (Pius XI) Quadragésimo anno (15 de mayo, 1931), *Encyclical Letter of His Holiness Pius XI* (London: Catholic Truth Society, 1931), pp. 13–14; Edward McLean, *Roman Catholicism and the Right to Work* (New York: University Press of America, 1985), pp. 13–14.

15. En su mensaje a la mujer española, Madrid, 15 de junio, 1947, en Perón, *Discursos,* vol. I, p. 99.

16. En su discurso a los obreros de la fábrica "Pandet", la ciudad de Resistencia, Chaco, 26 de octubre, 1947; ibid., vol. I, p. 137.

17. El 24 de diciembre, 1947; ibid., vol. I, pp. 161, 163; en este mensaje también hay una analogía con el pasaje bíblico de Juan 13: 34, 35; ver *Sagrada Biblia* (Barcelona: Herder, 1964), p. 1289.

18. Discurso del 24 de febrero, 1948, ciudad de San Francisco, Provincia de Córdoba; ibid., vol. I, p. 181.

19. En Lomas de Zamora, 26 de junio, 1948; ibid., vol. I, p. 240.

20. Ver Fermín Chávez, *Eva Perón sin mitos* (Buenos Aires: Fraterna, 1990), pp.107–127.

21. "En diciembre de 1946 . . . las Naciones Unidas . . . vetaba al gobierno de Franco el derecho de pertenecer a los organismos internacionales . . . los estados miembros retiraron sus representantes diplomáticos acreditados en Madrid . . . ". Crespo, *Eva Perón,* p. 198.

22. Crespo, *Eva Perón,* p. 202.

23. Palacio Real, Madrid, 9 de junio, 1947, en Perón, *Discursos,* vol. I, p. 91.

24. Perón, *Discursos,* vol. I, p. 98.

25. Navarro, *Evita,* p. 171.

26. Más tarde le dice a Perón: "El papa me pareció una visión. Su voz era como un sueño. . . . Me dijo . . . que tu política ponía en práctica . . . los principios fundamentales del cristianismo", Juan D. Perón, *Del poder al exilio,* p. 58, citado por Navarro, *Evita,* p. 171; ver también Chávez, *Eva Perón sin mitos,* p. 119.

27. Estas fueron Adela María Harilaos de Olmos y María Unzué de Alvear.

28. Caimari, *Perón y la Iglesia,* pp. 237, 239; ver también Carmen Llorca, *Llamádme Evita* (Barcelona: Planeta, 1981), p. 111.

29. Chávez, *Eva Perón sin mitos,* p. 119; Navarro, *Evita,* p. 171.

30. Creada el 2 de enero, 1823, por Bernardino Rivadavia; el 10 de julio de ese año se instala en el convento de los Mercedarios en la calle Reconquista, donde aún estaba en 1946; ver Navarro, *Evita,* p. 240.

31. Ella lo dice: "Mi trabajo en el movimiento femenino nació y creció, lo mismo que mi obra de ayuda social y que mi actividad sindical. . . . Nunca imaginé que me iba a tocar algún día encabezar un movimiento femenino de mi país menos un movimiento político. Las circunstancias me abrieron el camino", Perón, *La razón,* cap. 47.

32. Discurso del 23 de setiembre, 1947, en Perón, *Discursos,* vol. I, p. 124.

33. Navarro, *Evita,* p. 244.

34. Perón, *La razón,* p. 161.

35. Después, por decreto 20.268 del 25 de setiembre, 1950, se denominó Fundación Eva Perón. "La administración corresponde única y exclusivamente a su fundadora . . . quien la ejercerá con carácter vitalicio y gozará de las más amplias atribuciones que las leyes y el Estado reconocen a las personas jurídicas" según el artículo 7° de sus estatutos, citado por Crespo, *Eva Perón,* p. 233.

36. Ibid., p. 234.

37. Perón, *La razón,* p. 154.

38. Ibid., p. 136.

39. Sebreli, *Eva Perón,* pp. 81–82.

40. Navarro, *Evita,* pp. 249–250; ver también Tomás Eloy Martínez, *Las memorias del General* (Buenos Aires: Planeta, 1996), p. 50.

41. Crespo, *Eva Perón,* p. 259.

42. Ella nos da una idea de la amplitud de sus obras: "Derribamos jubilosamente los oscuros orfanatos para levantar las paredes blancas y alegres de la Ciudad Infantil, de los hogares escuelas, de los policlínicos, de los hogares de tránsito, de los hogares de la empleada y de ancianos, de la Ciudad Estudiantil, de las ciudades universitarias, colonias de vacaciones, maternidades, escuelas y comedores populares. Barrimos con nuestra escoba justicialista los ranchos y taperas y elevamos los barrios obreros, exigidos por la dignidad social de nuestras masas laboriosas. Desterramos la limosna para exaltar la solidaridad como obra de justicia" . . . . Perón, *Discursos,* vol. II, p. 262.

43. "Según Benítez, 62 sacerdotes y 122 religiosas (en su mayoría . . . de la orden de la Misericordia) tenían a cargo la asistencia religiosa de la Fundación" . . . . Caimari, *Perón y la Iglesia,* pp. 222, 243.

44. Navarro, *Evita,* p. 220.

45. Perón, *La razón,* cap. 20.

46. Ibid., cap. 24.

47. Ver Stack, "Avoiding the Greater Evil", p. 267.

48. Perón, *La razón,* p. 7.

49. Proclamada el 10 de setiembre, 1949, por el pueblo del Ecuador; ver Llorca, *Llamádme Evita,* p. 230.

50. Que surge del discurso de José Espejo del 17 de octubre, 1951, aludiendo al 31 de agosto pasado "Día del Renunciamiento" cuando dice: "Su renuncia tiene la grandeza de las actitudes de los mártires y de los santos", citado por Caimari, *Perón y la Iglesia,* p. 229.

51. El 7 de mayo, 1952, Delia Parodi, ante la Cámara de Diputados presenta un proyecto diciendo "que la acción y la obra de la Señora . . . la han colocado, a justo título en el orden espiritual . . . por lo que merece el título de Jefa Espiritual de la Nación". V. Actas de las Sesiones de la Cámara, citado por Llorca, *Llamádme Evita,* p. 218; ver también Alberto Ciria, *Política y cultura popular: la Argentina peronista, 1946–1955* (Buenos Aires: Ed. de la Flor, 1983), pp. 122–123; y Navarro, *Evita,* p. 311.

52. "El 17 de octubre la concentración es dedicada a Eva Perón a quien se le otorga la medalla peronista", Sebreli, *Eva Perón,* p. 144.

53. *Democracia,* 2 de noviembre, 1950, p. 1; 3 de noviembre, 1950, p. 3, citado por Stack, "Avoiding the Greater Evil", p. 277.

54. Alberto Bolaños, ex-gerente de la Fundación, decía: "No sabía de balances ni de situaciones financieras . . . sus quince horas de trabajo diarias no le daban tiempo para números". Crespo, *Eva Perón*, p. 234; ver también Van Der Karr, *Perón y los Estados Unidos*, p. 62.

55. En su mensaje del 24 de diciembre, 1948, dice: ". . . Abrazada a la patria, todo lo daré, porque hay pobres en ella todavía, porque hay tristes, porque hay desesperanzados, porque hay enfermos. Mi alma lo sabe, mi cuerpo lo ha sentido. Pongo junto al alma de mi pueblo mi propia alma. Le ofrezco todas mis energías para que mi cuerpo sea como un puente tendido hacia la felicidad común. Pasad sobre él, firme el paso, alta la frente, hacia el destino supremo de la patria nueva". Perón, *Discursos*, vol. I, p. 363.

56. José Leopoldo Pérez Gaudio, *Catolicismo y Peronismo* (Buenos Aires: Corregidor, 1985), p. 56.

57. Ver Ciria, *Política y cultura*, pp. 122–125; ver también Navarro, *Evita*, pp. 311–313.

58. Eva Perón, *Mi mensaje* (Buenos Aires: Ediciones del Mundo, 1987), p. 55.

59. Caimari, *Perón y la Iglesia*, p. 239.

60. Arnaudo, *El año*, pp. 221–222.

61. Pérez Gaudio, *Catolicismo*, p. 49.

4. The Mythology of Eva Perón: Saint or Sinner

Donna Canevari de Paredes

The Eva Perón period is a landmark in the history of Argentina and Latin America. It represented a new era for politics, social assistance, and women. It also heralded the development of a new popular cult and subtly changed the way some Argentines viewed the Roman Catholic Church. Latin America and Argentina in particular have produced a multitude of notable figures, but none has been the object of as much controversy as Eva Perón. No Latin American woman has elicited such extreme feelings of love and hate, either in life or death.

Since 1945 interest in Eva Perón has been significant, though between 1955 and 1970 that interest waned somewhat because Juan Perón was living in exile and the whereabouts of the corpse of Eva Perón was unknown. Interest in Eva Perón (and in Peronism) reemerged in 1971 with the "discovery" of her body, which had been "missing" for 16 years, and Juan Perón's return as president of Argentina in 1973. Upon Juan Perón's death in 1974, Isabel Perón became president and attempted to resemble Eva in all aspects. She ordered the return of Eva's body to Argentina. Peronism revived once again in Argentina under Carlos Menem beginning in 1989. In addition, the Tim Rice/Andrew Lloyd Webber musical *Evita* enjoyed tremendous success in London, New York, and Madrid, followed by the film version in 1996. All of these events contributed to a substantial quantity of research, writing, and mythology about Eva Perón.

This paper explores the three major myths about Eva Perón and examines their impact on popular religion. There are more complex myths about Eva Perón than about any other historical figure of modern times. Her life and achievements are remarkable by themselves, but for many they are less real than the fictional shapes into which they have been formed. There are two prominent but contrasting images of her: one as saint—the white myth; one as sinner—the black myth. A less well known myth is that of a revolutionary, occasionally referred to as the red myth.

The Saint

Within a month of Eva's death, the newspaper vendors' union put forward her name for canonization. Although this gesture was never taken seriously by the Vatican, it was not an isolated incident. The idea of her holiness remained with many Argentines and was reinforced by the publication of government-

subsidized devotional literature; the naming of cities, schools, and subway sta-
tions in her honor; the issuing of memorial medallions; the casting of busts in
her image; and the issuing of commemorative stamps. The time of the evening
news broadcast was changed from 8:30 P.M. to 8:25 P.M, the time she officially
"passed into immortality." Each month there were torch-lit processions on the
day of her death, similar to those that mark religious observances.[1]

Popular Catholicism played an important part in the manner in which Eva
Perón was perceived. The popular Catholicism of the Argentine people is oriented toward informal beliefs. Her persona and legend took on mythical pro-
portions. The process began while she was still alive, but quickly became
permanent after her death.

The mythification of Eva Perón was dominated by the figure of the Virgin Mary and was reinforced by the officially projected images of the Peronist
government before and after her death and by her own speeches and writings.
At a time when Catholic devotion to the Virgin Mary was at its apogee, the
Peronist line on the deceased Eva Perón was curiously similar to official church
imagery with respect to Mary. Like Mary, Eva was portrayed as a symbol of
perpetual and perfect virginity. Her role was "special": she was an intermedi-
ary between humanity/*el pueblo* and God/Perón, but her role was also deriva-
tive of and dependent upon a subservient relationship with a Christlike, male
figure. The "Santa Evita"/Virgin Mary parallel penetrated the very heart of popular beliefs. Like Mary, Eva was seen as the coredemptor of mankind/*el pueblo*.
The "civic altars" constructed at the time of her death typify this parallelism.
Altars to Eva Perón remain in many Argentine homes to this day.[2]

She and her legend acquired a litany of saintly titles: "Lady of Hope,"
"Good Fairy of Children," "Martyr of Labor," "Standard-bearer of the Poor,"
"Spiritual Leader of the Nation," and, of course, "Santa Evita." In a petition to
the Vatican after her death, the Argentine labor union proposed her immediate
canonization as "Eva of America."

On the first anniversary of her death, the newspaper *La Prensa* published
a story about one of its readers who claimed to have seen her image in the face
of the moon. More such citings were reported in the newspapers. Official publications stopped just short of claiming sainthood for her. From 1953 to 1955,
Argentine schoolchildren learned to read from an array of Peronist textbooks
sanctioned and supplied by the government, all of which virtually canonized
her.[3] One such school primer, *Un año más*, contains, among other lessons, this
prayer:

> Our little Mother, thou who art in heaven
> good fairy laughing amongst the angels...
> Evita, I promise to be as good as you wish me
> to be respecting God, loving my country;

taking care of General Perón; studying and
being towards everyone the child you dreamed
I would be; healthy, happy, well-educated
and pure in heart.[4]

In the numerous prayers, poetry, prose, and songs published by Eva's followers, the imagery of Mary is central. The parallelism extended even to the concept of her Assumption into heaven. An example is found is the following
poem:

God sent his preferred Angel to alleviate all the
    suffering and tears of this world.
And, one day, God, who saw his wishes fulfilled,
    ordered her return.
A Beautiful Angel, a model of goodness, of love,
    and of tenderness,
She spread her white wings and let herself be
    carried away.[5]

This phenomenon was not limited to the years immediately after her death.
Prayers and other such literary tributes continue to be offered.[6]

Juan Perón was content to utilize Eva Perón's saintly image to best advantage. From 1952 to 1955 he and his government used and enhanced the myth
and its effect on the masses to improve his own image both in the eyes of the
people and, initially, in the eyes of the church. Perón himself petitioned Pope
Pius XII to canonize Eva Perón and some historians claim that the church's re-
fusal to do so caused Perón to seek revenge against the church.

By 1954 the Argentine Catholic Church and Peronism were at odds and
engaged in a power struggle. The church cautioned Catholics against the Peronist
ideas of Christmas, for example, the celebrations of Christmas that were associated with the Evita cult. A church circular of December 2, 1954, forbade Catholics "to attend acts that pretend to have a religious character without having been
approved in advance by the [Church] hierarchy." By 1955, as a result of his conflicts with the church, Perón had done away with most religious holidays in
Argentina and had inserted into the national calendar such observances as May
7, Eva's birthdate, and July 26, the date of her death. In early 1955, after he
outlawed Catholic Action and further restricted religious teaching in the schools,
he offered newly elected members of Congress the option of taking their oaths
in the name of God or in the name of Eva Perón.[7]

Juan Perón used the Evita/Mary parallel for the rest of his life. In 1964,
while in exile in Madrid, he is quoted as saying: "I took with me when I left
Argentina, two mementoes. An image of the little Virgin of Luján, patroness of
my country, and this picture . . . my favorite one of Evita."[8] Nine years later, in
a public address given in Buenos Aires immediately after his third election to

the presidency, in October 1973, Perón again publicly evoked Eva's memory and asked for her saintly protection.[9]

Although most comparisons concern the parallel of Evita/Mary, Eva Perón has also been compared to other religious figures, such as Jesus Christ and Joan of Arc. The latter image led to the emergence of the myth of Eva Perón, the revolutionary.

The Revolutionary

The image of Eva Perón as a revolutionary developed in the late 1960s and early 1970s, after her death. For the Peronist left, Eva possessed the combination of intelligence, intuition, emotion, instinct, and decision-making skills that made her act *as if* under the tutelage of her husband. For the radical Peronists, her image was a saintly one. The myth of Eva Perón as revolutionary/saint is sometimes referred to as the "evitismo" of the Peronist left. Twenty years after her death, in the public demonstrations of the Peronist left, the chant became, "We feel it, we feel it, Evita is present."

This group of followers became known as the Montoneros, the Argentine guerrilla youth of the late 1960s and early 1970s. Their acceptance of the Eva Perón cult extended to claiming that she alone deserved the credit for the October 17, 1945, mobilization—a claim belied by all historical investigation of that event. The Montoneros believed that Peronism was a uniquely Argentine revolutionary movement, owing its dynamism to the intimate intercession between Perón and the people. If Juan Perón had appeared weak or had made mistakes or if the Peronist process had run into difficulties from 1953 to 1955, it was because of Eva's death. To the Montoneros, Eva Perón was a saintly figure who had dedicated her life to "serve my people, my fatherland and Perón."[10]

The Sinner

The enemies of Perón and Peronism used the same symbols and myths to show that Eva Perón was nothing but a common and evil woman. This saint/ sinner or virgin/whore polarity has served to compound the mythology surrounding her.

After the fall of Perón, the new government made it a crime punishable by imprisonment to possess photographs of Eva or Juan Perón or to use the expressions Peronism and Peronist. The Peronist party itself was also officially disbanded. The early post-1955 attempts to purge Argentina of Peronism by making Eva into a monster had the reverse effect and gave rise to what Peronists have called "the resistance." A real and persistent cult began with this resistance.

A pattern emerges in the images of the woman of the white myth and the woman of the black myth. The praises of one are the accusations of the other. Both concern her rapport with the uneducated masses. While followers of the white myth laud her as the incarnation of the modern mother of God, believers in the black myth denounce her as the negation of that very ideal. For Peronists her appearance, grace, wardrobe, and possessions were necessary and put the finishing touches on her perfect image. Seen with other eyes, she spent her entire life motivated by a futile struggle to obtain these same status symbols. Santa Evita received her due as a tribute to her spiritual leadership of the ignorant, childlike masses. The woman of the black myth exploited and mocked this blind, devotional response.

In *Eva Perón: Myths of a Woman*, J. M. Taylor explores the three myths from an anthropological perspective. The author devotes an entire chapter, "The Lady of Hope and the Woman of the Black Myth," to a discussion of two opposing versions of Eva Perón, both of which point out the exaggeration of the myths.

The "Lady of Hope" version of her death and legend, in abbreviated form, reads:

> Her death, which loomed before her immediately after the Renunciation, made her martyrdom incontrovertible. Her broken-hearted followers responded to the dead Eva in the only way appropriate to her saintly act: they worshipped her as a saint. They erected altars to her; offered her prayers; called her their Spiritual Chief, Saint Eva, and the Spiritual Protector. . . ; they believed in her miraculous powers and waited for her return.[11]

The "Woman of the Black Myth" version, in an abbreviated form, reads:

> Her followers were already in paroxysms of grief when their Evita was suddenly dead. The entire nation of Peronists threw itself into a delirium of mass mourning maintained with sacrifices to the dead Spiritual Leader of the Nation. Altars sprang up everywhere. . . . The bereaved populace offered pagan prayers and rites up to its heroine not only in their homes . . . but in public . . . and in the queue . . . where the mourners waited for the chance to bid Evita a last farewell at the side of her coffin. They transformed their wait . . . into an orgy of distorted forms of worship. . . . The myth of Eva began to grow, gripping the ignorant masses with unrelenting power. Her people heaped exaggerated praise on her . . . comparing her with Joan of Arc . . . Isabel the Catholic of Spain, and the Virgin Mary herself. . . . Motivated by mystical love, Peronism set out to construct the largest monument in the world in which to lay the embalmed body. The prayers and rites of mourners did not disappear as time passed, but began to crystallize around the myth as a cult. The working classes continued to intone "Santa María Eva who are in heaven. . . ." Meanwhile the corpse . . . held sway over the cult and its members. Peronists, believing a prophecy that those who possessed the remains would also hold power in government, prepared to do battle to protect the beautiful corpse. When it

disappeared . . . its power did not diminish. The danger grew that it could, by its reappearance, arouse the masses to a frenzy that would cause a turning point in Argentinean history.[12]

The Cult of the Corpse

The legend of the sinner contributed to the cult of the saint, which in turn contributed to the mythology of the revolutionary. And the latter was further fuelled by the cult of the corpse. The legend of the corpse remains important to all of the mythology about Eva Perón.

Various versions of her dying, death, and embalming, plus speculation about the fate of her remains, continued to circulate. The fact that for more than 20 years the body was officially unburied, and that for much of that time its location was unknown, was an important and disturbing issue for politicians and popular groups. As Taylor states:

> To some extent her continuing importance and popularity may be attributed not only to her power as a woman, but also to the power of the dead.
> . . . As a female corpse reiterating a symbolic theme as both woman and martyr, Eva Perón perhaps lays a double claim to leadership.[13]

None of the Argentine leaders who followed Perón wanted Eva's final resting place to become a focal point or shrine of any group. This meant that she could not be buried anywhere in that country, and because of the church's prohibition of cremation the authorities were reluctant to destroy the body. While the body remained at the Argentine labor union [CGT] headquarters from the time immediately after the funeral until shortly after the fall of the Perón government in 1955, the cult of the corpse flourished. Inside the union building an improvised chapel was erected around the body. Only a very select group, of course, was allowed to see the Madonna-like figure in white. The façade of the building remained covered with flowers and other tributes to Eva's memory and the rank and file faithful gathered regularly to say the rosary—for her or to her. A semifictitious version of this scene appears in *Santa Evita*, by Tomás Eloy Martínez:

> Although no one could see the corpse, people imagined it lying there, in a private chapel, and came on Sundays to recite the rosary and offer flowers. Little by little Evita began to turn into a story that, before it ended, kindled another. She ceased to be what she said and what she did to become what people say she did.[14]

By 1971, in a final attempt by the Montoneros to obtain information on the location of the body, the cult of the corpse and the myth of the revolutionary resulted in the death of then former president Pedro Aramburu. Beginning with Eva's own idea of embalming and the memorial which was to be built, the image of the saint was, at least for Peronists, further enhanced.

Conclusion

There is no simple way to determine which, if any, of the mythology about Eva Perón is most valid. I simply return to fiction and this brief excerpt from *Santa Evita*:

> It took me years to arrive at these central folds where I am today. . . . The characters sometimes spoke in their own voices and sometimes in other people's, merely to explain to me that what is history is not always historical, that the truth is never what it appears to be. . . . The same thing happens in the text as happens in life. . . . Evita was no longer the same . . . other peoples wishes and memories had rained down on her. Transfigured into myth, Evita was millions.[15]

NOTES

1. Nicholas Fraser and Marysa Navarro, *Eva Perón* (New York, 1980), p. 170.

2. A study of the Eva Perón/Mary parallelism is found in Noreen Frances Stack, "Avoiding the Greater Evil: The Response of the Argentine Catholic Church to Juan Perón, 1943–1955" (Ph.D. dissertation, Rutgers University, 1976), pp. 325–353.

3. For more on textbooks, see Alberto Ciria, "Angels and Demons," *Index on Censorship*, vol. 14, no. 6 (December 1985), pp. 46–49

4. Ana Lerdo de Tejada and Aurora Zubillaga, *Un año más* (Buenos Aires: Luis Lasserre, 1953), p.1. This translation is from Fraser and Navarro, *Eva Perón*, p. 170.

5. Elsa G. R. Cozzani de Gillone, *Mensaje de luz* (Buenos Aires: Angel Estrada y Cía., 1953), pp. 87–88. This translation is from Stack, "Avoiding the Greater Evil," p. 345.

6. In 1994 the Fundación Evita issued an untitled five-volume compilation of appreciative articles of all types, which contains a substantial quantity of poems and prayers published in the period following her death. Fundación Evita, [no title], 5 vols. (Buenos Aires: Fundación Evita, 1994). The five volumes are not numbered. The copy verified by the author is in the Biblioteca Nacional of Argentina.

7. See V. W. Leonard, *Politicians, Pupils and Priests: Argentine Education Since 1943* (New York: Peter Lang, 1989), pp. 144–155; David Rock, "Perón and After," in his *Authoritarian Argentina* (Berkeley: University of California Press, 1993), pp. 157–193.

8. This translation is from Stack, "Avoiding the Greater Evil," p. 326.

9. As cited in Tico Medina, "Impresionante acto de afirmación peronista," *ABC* (Madrid), October 20, 1973, p. 5.

10. See J. M. Taylor, *Eva Perón: The Myths of a Woman* (Chicago: University of Chicago Press, 1979), pp. 127–144; and the references to Eva Perón in Richard Gillespie, *Soldiers of Perón: Argentina's Montoneros* (Oxford: Clarendon Press, 1982).

11. Taylor, *Eva Perón,* p. 77.

12. Ibid., pp. 82–83.

13. Ibid., p. 148.

14. Tomás Eloy Martínez, *Santa Evita*, translated by Helen Lane (New York: Knopf, 1996), p. 13.

15. Ibid., p. 54.

5. All Humankind Is One: Archbishop Claret and Racism in Nineteenth-Century Cuba

Rafael E. Tarragó

Archbishop Antonio María Claret y Clará is known to non-Catholic Hispanics from negative references to him in works by Azorín and Valle-Inclán.[1] Catholics know him as Saint Anthony Mary Claret, a church reformer of the nineteenth century and founder of religious orders.[2] It is not well known that Claret y Clará was archbishop of Cuba from 1850 to 1857, where his reformist zeal caused the last major church and state conflict between the Catholic Church and the Spanish monarchy, on an issue which placed the church in the role of upholder of the notion that Europeans, Africans, and their descendants in America are children of God and, following the Catholic doctrine that all human beings descend from Adam and Eve, radically equal. This paper analyzes the activities of Saint Anthony Mary Claret as archbishop of Santiago de Cuba in the context of the Catholic Church and race relations in Cuba in the nineteenth century.

The Roman Catholic Church in Cuba, 1512–1898

Roman Catholicism was established in Cuba under the auspices of the Spanish monarchy. Early in the century sixteenth the Catholic monarchs (Ferdinand of Aragon and Isabel I of Castile) obtained a series of privileges and control over the church in Spanish America which came to be known as royal patronage (*patronato real*). As royal patrons the kings of Castile protected the church as the true church, collected tithes for ecclesiastics, and reflected church law in civil legislation. In exchange for this protection, and for their financial generosity, the kings of Castile were given the right to nominate bishops (who were duly accepted by the popes), kept a percentage of the tithes that royal officers collected, had the right to decide which papal decrees could be read in the pulpits of Roman Catholic churches in their domains, and who could settle in them as religious and priests, as well as who could receive holy orders. The Spanish Inquisition was autonomous from the monarchy, but it was also autonomous from the pope.[3]

Royal patronage worked to the advantage of both church and state during the sixteenth and seventeenth centuries, when the kings of Castile and the Indies (as Spanish America was called in those days) were princes of the House of Hapsburg without pretensions to dictate ecclesiastical legislation or to appropriate church property. Under the influence of Catholic clergymen like Fray

Bartolomé de Las Casas and Rodrigo Ruiz de Montoya, the Hapsburg monarchs passed laws for the protection of the conquered peoples such as the New Laws of 1542. With relatively few exceptions the monarchs and their successors of the House of Hapsburg did not force their will on the church. In exchange, they expected and obtained the support of priests.[4] Also in early modern times the activities of priests and the faithful as keepers of birth, marriage, and death records, as well as in education and social welfare, were welcome by the monarchy as an unsalaried civil service bureaucracy, and health and education personnel.[5] This relationship began to change under the kings of the House of Bourbon who reigned in the second half of the eighteenth century. Charles III (king from 1759 to 1788) forbade popular religious plays, dictated church decoration, implemented an educational reform geared to deprive educational institutions of their autonomy from royal control, and expelled the Jesuits (who taught in their schools that good kings ought to be obeyed, but that tyrants should be resisted).[6] Charles IV (king from 1788 to 1808) continued the policy of his father of direct interference in church affairs, and in 1804 passed a decree which was equivalent to a confiscation of church property in New Spain (present-day Mexico).[7]

Under the constitutional monarchy of the nineteenth century, royal patronage became more advantageous to the state than to the church. Roman Catholicism continued being the only religion allowed public expression in the domains of the Spanish monarchy (now limited to present-day Spain, Cuba, Puerto Rico, the Philippines, and a few territories in Africa and Oceania), but the Inquisition was abolished. In the years following the death of Ferdinand VII (king form 1808 to 1833), the last absolute king, church property was confiscated, religious orders were disbanded, and the number of people allowed to be ordained was restricted by the ministers of Queen Isabel II (queen from 1833 to 1868). A concordat was signed between the Spanish government and the Holy See in 1851 which stipulated that in compensation for confiscated church property in the domains of Spanish monarchy priests and bishops there would receive salaries from that government. This compromise deprived the Catholic Church in those territories from the actual autonomy derived from self-support. In the case of Cuba, Puerto Rico, and the Philippine Islands, this financial dependence of the church from a state that paid the salaries of her ministers made the latter appear as agents of the state. Before 1898 the Catholic Church had ceased influencing Cuban society.

Manuel Maza Miguel, S. J., has written a thorough and nonpolemical account of the history of the Roman Catholic Church in Cuba—"Iglesia cubana: cinco siglos de desafíos y respuestas" (*Estudios Sociales*, vol. 27, no. 95 [January–March 1995], pp. 65–111)—analyzing the diverse manifestations of the royal patronage; Reynerio Lebroc-Martínez has published an analysis of the impact of the church policies of the constitutional monarchy in Cuba—*Cuba, iglesia y sociedad, 1830–1860* (Madrid, 1976); and in the insightful monograph *El alma del negocio y el negocio del alma* (Santiago de los Caballeros, 1990) Manuel Maza Miguel, S. J., analyzes the dire consequences for the Catholic Church in Cuba in the latter years of sovereignty of the Spanish monarchy in the island of the *patronato real.*

Race Relations in Cuba, 1512–1898

By the middle of the sixteenth century Europeans from Spain had conquered and settled Cuba. The original population was decimated by war, forced labor, and disease, but it was not extinguished. It was, however, absorbed by the European immigration through miscegenation, and a law equating the rights of natives to those of whites, which coincidentally abrogated their "Indianness."[8] By the end of the eighteenth century there was no settlement of self-defined native Cubans in the island. The recognizable "racial" groups in Cuba were European and African. A census taken in 1774 listing population numbers by color and status shows 96,000 whites, 30,000 free people of African ancestry, and 44,928 slaves.[9]

During the first three hundred years of Spanish Cuba, slavery was not a major component of the Cuban economy. In those centuries tobacco, leather, and tallow were the significant Cuban exports. Tobacco growing and ranching are not labor-intensive operations; however, African slavery was introduced in Cuba by the European conquerors soon after their conquest (when the collapse of the native population, and the insistence of the royal administration in implementing laws forbidding their enslavement, made it a more reliable and nonproblematic labor force). In the Cuban tobacco farms and cattle ranches African slaves had certain rights, including that of self-purchase (*coartación*). Manumission was a common action among slave owners on their deathbed.

At the time of the Spanish conquest of Cuba the Roman Catholic Church allowed slavery as the result of just warfare, and assumed that those enslaved were warriors or conquered populations who had forfeited their freedom in exchange for their life. This was customary in the Mediterranean world, where the church developed as an institution. By the second decade of the seventeenth century some clergymen were having doubts about the morality of the enslavement of Africans, and in 1639 Pope Urban VII issued a bull condemning the African slave trade. In 1689 Cardinal Cibo, of the Society for the Propagation of the Faith, at the Vatican, commanded Catholic missionaries in Africa to preach against the slave trade.[10] Urban VII's bull of 1639, however, was never read in Cuba. Although in 1684 the Capuchins Fray José de Jaca and Fray Epifanio de Moiráns argued in Cuba against the enslavement of Africans and were exonerated by the Holy Office of the Inquisitions when they were brought before its tribunal, the Catholic Church never condemned slavery as an institution in the island.[11] Furthermore, the Cuban Synod of Priests assembled in Santiago de Cuba in 1681 decided that blacks and mulattos should not be ordained priests or admitted in the religious orders (unless dispensation were granted.) [12]

During the centuries when the Roman Catholic Church was influential in Cuba, Africans and their descendants in the island were held theoretically equal to whites in the sight of God. Any other position taken by the church would have denied the humanity of the indigenous peoples and the Africans and would have severely undermined the supremacy of the church.[13] But also in those centuries in the history of Spanish Cuba slavery was not a major component of the Cuban economy. In the last decade of the eighteenth century the French colony of Saint Domingue (present-day Haiti) experienced a slave uprising followed by the destruction of its sugar industry, and entrepreneurial members of the Cuban elites in Havana saw the development of the sugar industry in Cuba as an opportunity which should not be missed. Until that time the Spanish Crown had restricted the importation of slaves in Cuba, but the economically minded monarchs of the House of Bourbon reigning in the last quarter of the eighteenth century did not question the Cuban planters' requests for more "arms" to make Cuba into a revenue-producing "colony," and allowed the importation of African slaves in unprecedented numbers. The slave population in Cuba, which at the time of the 1774 census was 20 percent, by 1817 reached a high of 44 percent of the population.[14] This growth in the slave population was accompanied by a change in slave-master relations—the masters became less paternalistic and more exploitative.

The Catholic priests would have found it difficult to continue their preaching for slave rights under the new conditions in any case, but the anticlerical policies of the constitutional governments after the death of Ferdinand VII in 1833 deprived them of the means to do so. In those years legislation was passed condemning to banishment any priest or religious who criticized any royal legislation for being contrary to Catholic doctrine.[15] This type of legislation, and the experience of dislodgment and expulsion, in many cases accompanied by the burning of their houses, broke the spirit of most of the Catholic clergy under the Spanish monarchy. Only in certain regions of northern Spain did the clergy keep a strong sense of its mission and the popular support to show it. As Franklin W. Knight has said, "In the Spanish overseas territories the Church lost the enthusiasm and the dynamic spirit it had in earlier centuries, when it had searchingly helped to formulate the New Laws of 1542, and by 1842 it had become a pale ghost."[16]

It is not to deny that many priests owned slaves and may have treated them as badly as lay owners, to say that the church lost its political authority at just the time when a new class of slave owners had arisen, with less respect for the customary role of the church in society, and that this loss of political influence gave an impression of religious indifference to the conditions of slaves in the island of Cuba. In nineteenth-century Cuba the presence of priests was discouraged in plantations by their owners, and eventually by legislation. Given the labor requirements of the new plantation system, priests would have been unable to instruct in anything slaves who worked up to twenty hours during the harvest. According to Christopher Madden (who traveled in Cuba in 1838), only two estates in all Cuba allowed slaves to go to Mass on Sundays and feast days, and only in one plantation (Santa Ana de Aguiar, belonging to José de Luz, at Bejucal) did there seem to be a regular chaplain.[17] Efforts to bring missionaries to provide religious education for the slaves were rejected in 1847 by the Spanish government, for "it would be very difficult to reconcile the Catechism with the respect which is owed to property," and in 1866 Havana lawyer Rafael Azcárte—representative of white Cubans—opposed the sending of missionaries to Cuba to evangelize the slaves on the grounds that he believed that religious teachings in accord with the religion of Jesus Christ would arouse aspirations to freedom among the slaves and would be the cause of terrible disorders.[18] The ambiguous attitude of the Catholic Church to slavery in Spanish Cuba has been analyzed in historical context without apology by Manuel Maza Miguel, S. J.[19]

The theoretical oneness of mankind was upheld by legislation under the Spanish monarchy until the eighteenth century despite its hierarchical organization and its absolutist constitution. Legal inequality was justified on the grounds of function, but all estates had rights as well as obligations. Terminology such as "limpieza de sangre" (purity of blood) and the deprivation of access to a university education and to certain offices and honors for those who did not have it (descendants of Jewish converts up to the fourth Christian generation, and Africans and their descendants) misleads modern readers unaware that these were consciously legal terms and not biological concepts, as suggested by the fact that the legislation that upheld them also mentioned exceptions and waivers. In Cuba the monarch excepted many a loyal "moreno" (black) or "pardo" (mulatto) from his/her racial status. Despite legislation forbidding it, descendants of Africans attended Havana University and were ordained to the priesthood in Cuba before 1865, when the purity of blood restrictions were abrogated. [20] Interracial marriage was allowed, and after five generations of "marrying white," the offspring of an interracial union was "reputed" to be white. In her insightful monograph *Marriage, Class and Colour in Nineteenth-Century Cuba*, Verena Martínez-Alier analyzed the complexity and elusiveness of race relations in Spanish Cuba.

In 1776 the enlightened King Charles III passed a Pragmatic Sanction requiring parental permission for noble minors intending to marry beneath their social rank in Spain, and two years later had this law issued in his overseas domains. In October 1805 the Council of the Indies issued a *real cédula* (royal

order) on marriages between persons of known nobility with persons of African ancestry, stating that such marriages could not take place without permission from the governor or the viceroy. A royal order of May of that year was
even more restrictive, requiring permission from the highest authorities for the
marriage of persons of known nobility or known "purity of blood" (all those
reputed to be white) with persons of African ancestry. A decree of the viceroy
of Mexico in 1810 reinforced the restrictions of the May 1805 royal order.[21]
Article 403 of the Penal Code of 1848 established the penalty of imprisonment
and a fine of 50 to 500 *duros* for those clergymen who authorized marriages
forbidden by civil law.[22] In Cuba these restrictions contrary to the moral teachings of the Catholic Church persisted until 1881, when they were abrogated by
a royal order.

The complete abolition of slavery was decreed in Cuba in 1886, but this
momentous legislation did not end the racial prejudice fostered by a system of
slavery limited to persons of one race during almost four hundred years. Before 1776 there was opposition to interracial marriages in Cuba among people
of certain distinction or aspirations to social mobility, and after the abrogation
of the marriage laws those prejudices persisted. Consensual interracial unions
continued to take place among the working-class sector of Cuban society even
after legal restrictions to interracial marriages ceased. Most of these unions were
permanent, common law marriages. Legal restrictions to the activities of non-
whites began to disappear in Cuba after 1880; when the Spanish constitution of
1776 was implemented in the island all free subjects of the Spanish Crown were
declared Spanish citizens. It was as Spanish citizens that Afro-Cuban leaders
like Don Juan Gualberto Gómez, Don Martín Morúa Delgado, and Don Rodolfo
Fernando Trava y Blanco de Lagardere waged—from different political perspectives—the struggle for full civil rights for Cubans of African ancestry narrated
brilliantly by Aline Helg in her monograph *Our Rightful Share: The Afro-Cuban
Struggle for Equality, 1886–1912* (Chapel Hill, 1995).

Claret the Catholic Reformer

Antonio María Claret y Clará (1808–1870) was born in Sallent, a town
near Barcelona. His father owned a small textile mill, and during his adoles-
cence Antonio María considered following his father in the family business. He
went to Barcelona to improve his knowledge of textile manufacturing and design, and perhaps to acquire practical management skills, but at age 21 he decided to become a priest. After attending the diocesan seminary in Vich,
Catalonia, he was ordained in 1835, when he was 27 years old. For five years
he was undecided about how to live his priestly vocation—he considered becoming a Jesuit in 1839—but in 1840 he decided to become a missionary
preacher in Spain itself. [23]

Claret y Clará's success as a preacher and reformer in Spain resulted in his name being suggested to Queen Isabel II when she had to nominate an archbishop for Santiago de Cuba in 1850. After his return to Spain from Cuba, in 1857, to become confessor to the Queen, he inspired the aristocracy to undertake social work and he himself refrained from any direct interference in political life. In Spain he founded the order of the Sons of the Immaculate Heart of Mary, and in Cuba he supported the foundation of the Institute of Mary Immaculate by María Antonia París. According to Raymond Carr, Claret was a reformer interested in spiritual and moral issues, and not an opportunistic voluptuary.[24]

Archbishop Claret and Race Relations in Cuba

It is surprising that a zealous Catholic reformer like Anthony Mary Claret would be made archbishop of Santiago de Cuba in 1850, because by the middle of the nineteenth century the Catholic Church in Cuba had become notorious for the dearth of preaching, the ignorance of church doctrine by the majority of the faithful, and the scandalous life of too many priests.[25] Preaching had become limited to towns to a large extent because of the diminishing numbers of the clergy brought about by the closing of religious houses, as well as by the sharp decrease of Cuban vocations to the priesthood. It may be argued that the behavior of parish priests in small towns was a symptom of demoralization and disregard for the doctrines and the authorities of the church fostered by the attitude of state authorities after 1833 toward the sacred, the hierarchy of the church in Spain, and the authority of the pope as head of the church.

Warned about the Cuban situation, Archbishop Claret put together a team of missionaries before he left Spain to assist him in Santiago de Cuba, but the warnings that he had received did not prepare him for the conditions of his archdiocese at the time of his arrival in February of 1851. The seminary in Santiago de Cuba and Catholic institutions in the larger towns of the archdiocese had improved shortly before his arrival, but conditions in the small towns and in the countryside required a re-evangelization. The scandalous life of several priests demanded disciplinary action, and the immense number of couples with children living together without marrying was alarming. Accompanied by his missionaries, Archbishop Claret began a pastoral visit to the whole archdiocese, which took two years to complete but allowed him to deal personally with the disciplining of wayward priests, the re-Christianization of rural areas, and remedying the widespread disregard for marriage among the masses. In the first stage of his visit he married thousands of couples of all colors who had lived in concubinage, and soon came into conflict with state authorities. In a way that today many would consider arrogant and high-handed, preaching the paramountcy of the individual's spiritual salvation and the need for Catholics to live the moral teachings of the church, Archbishop Claret defended freedom of choice in marriage which in turn implied the ultimate equality of all human beings.[26]

On June 30,1851, the authorities of the town of El Cobre wrote to the governor of Santiago de Cuba complaining about interracial marriages being performed in the area under their jurisdiction, and the provincial governor reported the complaint to the governor general of Cuba, José Gutiérrez de la Concha. [27] The authorities in El Cobre and the governor of Santiago de Cuba were concerned about the reaction of white Cubans to Archbishop Claret's disregard of the marriage laws requiring previous permission from the civil authorities for the celebration of interracial marriages. The governor of Santiago de Cuba wrote the archbishop a letter requesting his verification of the complaints against him and telling him to limit the number of marriages between unequals which he celebrated. Archbishop Claret answered the governor's letter on July 15, 1851, saying that he did not consider a serious matter the marriages of a few white men with mulatto women by whom they had publicly acknowledged children. He wanted to do everything possible so that the people would not lose their beliefs and to prevent the corruption of public mores.[28]

After spending almost a year visiting the western part of his archdiocese, Archbishop Claret wrote to Governor General José Gutiérrez de la Concha on April 8, 1852, telling him that he was disturbed by the disproportionate number of unmarried couples and the impossibility of putting a rapid end to that situation because of the marriage laws. In this letter he calls it intolerable that civil laws force couples who want to marry to live in concubinage.[29] Indeed, the civil laws undermined the preaching of Catholic morality. During a visit of the archbishop to Bayamo the mayor of that city approached him in the company of three pregnant women and asked him which one he ought to marry.[30]

In order to put a stop to the widespread disregard for his pastoral authority Archbishop Claret took refuge in civil legislation himself and in fulfillment of the spirit of a royal order of December 21, 1787, recommending that prelates use spiritual sanctions against public sins such as concubinage. On August 10, 1852, he issued a ban of excommunication "ipsu facto incurrenda" (with the lifting of excommunication reserved to him) against all those who opposed the marriage of a couple without canonical impediments to do so. According to Verena Martínez Alier, the rage of the secular authorities and the white inhabitants of Cuba was unleashed by Archbishop Claret's excommunication of the Spaniard Agustín Villarrodona, who despite repeated exhortations by the missionaries refused to marry his concubine, the mulatto Joaquina Arriba. The same author, commenting on the words of a government official who compared the actions of the archbishop to those of the Inquisition, says:

> To interpret the missionaries' efforts as symptomatic of a revival of the Inquisition appears to indicate singular confusion in the minds of those

spreading the rumor, since it had been precisely the Inquisition's basic occupation to watch over the Spaniards' racial purity, while Archbishop Claret defended his missionaries against their imputed disregard for the laws on interracial marriage, arguing that "in view of the great numbers of couples living in concubinage it is not possible to pay much attention to the color." [31]

On September 28, 1852, the authorities of the town of Cauto-Embarcadero, in eastern Cuba, began an investigation of the activities of Fray Esteban de Andáin and of Father Lorenzo San Martí–both missionaries in Archbishop Claret's team—accused of subverting established race relations. Undaunted by the reprisals against his subordinates, the archbishop made a visit to San José de Guisa where he celebrated 200 marriages, but he also wrote to Queen Isabel II asking for her protection.[32] The archbishop needed protectors, because on September 26, 1852, the governor of Santiago de Cuba had written to Governor General Valentín Cañedo (who had succeeded Concha in that year) complaining that he and his missionaries were preaching the equality of the races. Complaints against him were sent to Spain, including one accusing him of having insisted that a white American in Cuba married his mulatto mistress. On January 24, 1853, Governor General Cañedo wrote to him as Viceregal Patron of the Church, telling him that wayward zeal could be cause of great harm. But the archbishop would not be silenced, and he wrote back to the governor general immediately, reminding him that bishops were independent of secular authority in religious matters.[33] This was a major conflict between church and state, which was diffused by the arrival in Cuba as governor general of Juan Manuel González de la Pezuela on December 2, 1853.[34]

Governor General Pezuela defended Archbishop Claret's activities, attributing the hostility against him to the Cuban clergy who rebelled against his measures to moralize its members, and to promoters of Cuban independence "who could not look on unshaken while he [the archbishop] gained popular devotion through his own devotion to the masses." Indeed, Verena Martínez Alier believes that Archbishop Claret's friendship with Governor General Pezuela and his overtures to the poor and to those of African ancestry earned him the wrath of white Cubans of both the annexationist and the reformist persuasion, noticing that José Manuel Mestre, defense lawyer of Antonio Abad Torres (who attempted to murder the archbishop in 1856), was a well-known Cuban reformist.[35] It is a fact that in his *Crónicas de Santiago de Cuba* (Santiago de Cuba, 1925), Emilio Barcardí y Moreau depicts Archbishop Claret as a mere loyal agent of the Spanish monarchy essentially interested in securing Spanish supremacy in Cuba.[36] Cuban identification of the archbishop as such may explain the absence of any reference to him in the classics of Cuban historiography such as Ramiro Guerra Sánchez's *Manual de historia de Cuba* (Washington, D.C., 1938), and

Raúl Cepero Bonilla's *Azúcar y abolición* (Havana, 1948), and the popular textbook *Historia de la Isla de Cuba* (New York, 1975) by Carlos and Manuel Márquez Stérling. The Jesuit Gustavo Amigó Jansen makes no reference to him in his seminal "La Iglesia Católica en Cuba" (*Razón y fé*, 137:603 [April 1948], 296–313).

On January 12, 1854, the judge of the Havana District Court dictated that Archbishop Claret and his missionaries had acted illegally by celebrating interracial marriages, and that the civil power had the authority to legislate on marriages, even in disagreement with ecclesiastical authorities, but he expressed his willingness to hear the opinion of the archbishop. On February 27, 1854, Archbishop Claret wrote to the judge of Havana District Court, arguing that the royal order and the edict which were the legal regulations for marriage did not forbid "unequal" marriages except if they were celebrated without a license, and that they did not apply to all "inequalities" but solely to those resulting between people of noble origin and those of color—choosing as law-binding the royal order of October 1805 rather than that of May 1805.[37] He concluded by saying that white commoners of the age should be allowed to marry freely. On April 24 of that year the Havana District Court decided to support Archbishop Claret's opinion, and Governor General Pezuela passed a new marriage regulation reflecting the District Court decision. White Cubans as well as Spaniards in Cuba interpreted the governor general's liberalizing legislation as an attempt to "Africanize" Cuba, and many years later (during the process of beatification of Archbishop Claret) Pezuela would refer to this law as the main reason for his recall on August 28, 1854.[38]

Governor General Pezuela was succeeded by José Gutiérrez de la Concha, who suspended the decision of the Havana District Court and reestablished the more restrictive marriage legislation based on the royal order of May 1805. This decision made him agreeable to white Cubans and Spaniards in Cuba alike. On October 26, 1854, an editorial in the major Havana daily *El Diario de la Marina* approved of this decision. The governor of Santiago de Cuba wrote to Archbishop Claret on November 7, 1854, reiterating the decision of Governor General Concha. This reversal in the archbishop's fortunes was dwarfed by the seriousness of the attempt on his life during a pastoral visit to the city of Holguín on February 1, 1856.

The perpetrator of the failed attempt was Antonio Abad Torres, a laborer from the Canary Islands settled in the Hoguín region. Archbishop Claret says in his autobiography that he saw Satan aid the assassin, but soon after the attempt the rumor spread that Torres had earthly instigators, and conspiracy theories developed implicating either disciplined Cuban clergymen or Freemasonry.[39] Governor General Concha ordered an investigation, and Abad Torres was duly tried and condemned to death. The officer who delivered the sentence in Holguín declared that he was convinced that the defendant had accomplices, but that it could not be proved. Abad Torres appealed the death sentence, and his appeal was defended before the Havana District Court by a well-known Cuban-born lawyer, José Manuel Mestre, whose defense merited being published in the Havana law journal *Revista de Jurisprudencia*.[40] The Havana District Court commuted Abad Torres's death sentence to one of ten years in a North African prison, and the judge who handled it expressed the same opinion as the Holguín officer, that the convict was an instrument.[41] During the process for the beatification of Claret in Vich (1904) a priest who had been pastor of a parish in Holguín since 1865 testified that it was common knowledge in that city and its surrounding area that Abad Torres had attempted to kill the archbishop because his concubine had left him on account of Claret's preaching on marriage.[42] After the attempt against his life in Holguín Archbishop Claret's zeal waned, and he may have felt relief when he was recalled to Spain in March of 1857.

The Legacy of Claret in Cuba

In practical terms the activities of Archbishop Claret revitalized the administration of the archdiocese of Santiago de Cuba and improved the mores and the training of the priests working there. By marrying 9,000 couples during his seven years in Cuba he legitimized thousands of children. As far as direct impact on social legislation—he failed. After the restoration in October 1854 by Governor Concha of the marriage laws to the "status quo ante," fewer permits for interracial marriages were granted per year. But his example may have inspired the bishop of Havana, Fray Jacinto María Martínez de Peñacerrada, to raise the issue of interracial marriage in 1867. He complained—like Claret—that the marriage laws were an obstacle to remedying what he saw as evil (widespread concubinage), pointing out that Concha's edict of 1854 was acquiring an absolutely prohibitive nature "with grave damage to the law of God, the morality of the people, to women . . . and even to the political regime of this country."[43] From 1864 to 1874 no licenses were granted at all.

Archbishop Claret had no impact on the debate over slavery going on during his years in Cuba. He did not campaign against the source of racial segregation itself. As Verena Martínez Alier has said, "He was more concerned with freedom from sin rather than with freedom from bondage."[44] He did not condemn the structure of slavery, but condemned the individual slave owners who did not fulfill their obligations toward their slaves and who did not respect the limited rights that the latter had under the laws of the Spanish monarchy. He accepted the accidental inequality between masters and slaves, but was adamant in his opposition to claims against the essential equality of all human beings in general and all baptized Catholics in particular. I choose the Aristotelian terms accidental and essential on purpose, because in this context they describe the acceptance by the archbishop of an amount of inequality under duress, and his obdurate upholding of what he believed inalienable rights essential for a human being to preserve his/her integrity, and for a Catholic to save his/her soul.

The archbishop chose his battles, and since his main concern was to bring souls to Christ he condemned those laws and habits in Cuba which he considered inimical to the spiritual welfare of the faithful. Hence his concern about the marriage laws which placed obstacles to the sacramentalization of the coupling on interracial couples, and about the opposition of masters to the preaching of Catholic doctrine to their slaves and to the observance of Sundays and feast days in their plantations. On the one hand, his sermons and pastoral letters did not preach social equality. On the other hand, those who complained that his preaching and that of his missionaries challenged the structure of slavery understood that his claim that all humankind is one would eventually sow doubts about its legitimacy. One of his biographers claims that he gave communion to slaves side by side with prominent citizens.[45] Another tells the anecdote that once the archbishop had reprimanded a slave owner for branding his slaves on the arm, and when the man countered that God had made whites to be masters and blacks to serve them, he burned before the man a sheet of white paper and another of black paper, and then asked if their ashes were different.[46] In his first pastoral letter (March 25, 1853) he said clearly that black slaves were rational human beings—answering a question that many in Cuba had posed to him—and that their obligation to obey their masters ceased if the latter demanded that they perform a sinful action—that in such cases slaves could not ought not to obey.[47]

NOTES

1. See Federico Gutiérrez Serrano, *Azorín y San Antonio María Claret* (Madrid: Editorial Alpuerto, S. A., 1979); Ramón del Valle-Inclán, *La Corte de los milagros* (Madrid: Espasa-Calpe, 1961), p. 77.

2. See Cristóbal Fernández, *El Beato Padre Antonio María Claret: historia documentada de su vida y empresas*, 2 vols. (Madrid, 1946); Daniel Sargent, *The Assignments of Antonio María Claret* (New York: The Declan X. McMullen Company, Inc., 1948); Fanchon Royer, *The Life of St. Anthony Mary Claret: Modern Apostle* (Rockford, Ill.: TAN Books and Publishers, 1985).

3. C. H. Haring, *The Spanish Empire in America* (New York: Harcourt, Brace and World, Inc., 1952), pp. 166–193.

4. Colin MacLachlan, *Spain's Empire in the New World* (Berkeley: University of California Press, 1988), pp. 1–66.

5. Salvador de Madariaga, *The Rise of the Spanish American Empire* (New York: The New Press), pp. 51–56.

6. Richard Herr, *The Eighteenth-Century Revolution in Spain* (Princeton: Princeton University Press, 1958), pp. 11–36.

7. D. A. Brading, *The First America* (Cambridge: Cambridge University Press, 1991), p. 569.

8.   Verena Martínez Alier, *Marriage, Class and Colour in Nineteenth-Century Cuba* (Cambridge: Cambridge University Press, 1974), p. 77; Hugh Thomas, *Cuba: The Pursuit of Freedom* (New York: Harper and Row Publishers, 1971), p. 21.

9.   Thomas, *Cuba,* p. 65 n. 23.

10.   See Richard Gray, "The Vatican and the Atlantic Trade," *History Today* 31 (March 1981), 37–39.

11.   See Manuel Maza Miguel, S. J., "Clero católico y esclavitud en Cuba, siglos XVI al XIX: ensayo de síntesis," *Estudios Sociales* (Santo Domingo) 23:79/80 (January–July 1990), 17–60.

12.   See *Sínodo de Santiago de Cuba de 1681,* Juan Garcis de Palacio, ed. (Madrid: Instituto Francisco Suárez, 1982).

13.   Franklin W. Knight, *Slave Society in Cuba during the Nineteenth Century* (Madison: University of Wisconsin Press, 1970), p. 106.

14.   Thomas, *Cuba,* p. 169.

15.   Reynerio Lebroc-Martínez, *San Antonio María Claret, arzobispo misionero de Cuba* (Madrid: Misioneros Hijos del Inmaculado Corazón de María, 1992), p. 541 n. 68.

16.   Knight, *Slave Society,* p. 111.

17.   Thomas, *Cuba,* p. 151.

18.   Martínez Alier, *Marriage, Class and Colour,* p. 55.

19.   Maza Miguel, "Clero católico."

20.   "R. C. que los pardos que ejerzan la medicina puedan concurrir a la enseñanza de anatomía" (June 21, 1793), in Richard Konetzke, *Colección de documentos para la historia de la formación social de Hispanoamérica, 1493–1810* (Madrid: Consejo Superior de Investigaciones Científicas, 1962), III:2, pp. 719–720; for the cost of being relieved of the restrictions imposed on people of African ancestry, see items 69 and 70 of "R. C. insertando el nuevo arancel de los servicios pecuniarios señalados a las gracias al sacar," in Konetzke, *Colección de documentos,* III:2, p. 783.

21.   Martínez Alier, *Marriage, Class and Colour,* p. 12.

22.   Ibid., p. 52.

23.   Lebroc-Martínez, *San Antonio María Claret,* pp. 76–78.

24.   Raymond Carr, *Spain 1808–1939* (Oxford: Clarendon Press, 1966), p. 286; for a depiction of Claret as an opportunistic voluptuary, see Gustavo Adolfo Bécquer and Valeriano Bécquer, *Los borbones en pelota* (Madrid: Ediciones El Museo Universal, 1991).

25.   See Reynerio Lebroc-Martínez, *Cuba, iglesia y sociedad, 1830–1860* (Madrid, 1976).

26.   Martínez Alier, *Marriage, Class and Colour,* p. 48.

27.   Lebroc-Martínez, *San Antonio María Claret,* pp. 192–193.

28.   Ibid., p. 195.

29.   Ibid., p. 196.

30.   Ibid., p. 198.

31.   Martínez Alier, *Marriage, Class and Colour,* p. 52.

32.   Lebroc-Martínez, *San Antonio María Claret.*

33.   Ibid., p. 220.

34.   Ibid., p. 248.

35.   Martínez Alier, *Marriage, Class and Colour,* p. 55.

36.　Emilio Bacardí y Moreau, *Crónicas de Santiago de Cuba* (Madrid: Breogan, I.G.S.A., 1972), III, pp. 481–485.

37.　Lebroc-Martínez, *San Antonio María Claret*, pp. 252–253.

38.　Ibid., p. 256.

39.　San Antonio María Claret y Clará, *Autobiografía*, 3d ed., José María Viñas and Jesús Bermejo, eds. (Barcelona: Editorial Claret, 1985), p. 85; Lebroc-Martínez dismisses the accusations against the Cuban priests Antonio Santiesteban and Angel Fonte in his *San Antonio María Claret*, p. 282 n. 254; Daniel Sargent implicates secret societies (in this context a code name for Freemasonry) in his *The Assignments of Antonio Claret*, p. 115.

40.　"Defensa de José Mestre," *Revista de Jurisprudencia* 1 (1856), 58–64, 120–127.

41.　Lebroc-Martínez, *San Antonio María Claret*, p. 287.

42.　Ibid., p. 288 n. 275.

43.　Martínez Alier, *Marriage, Class and Colour,* p. 54.

44.　Ibid., p. 53.

45.　Tomas L. Pujadas, C. M. F., *San Antonio María Claret, apóstol de nuestro tiempo* (Madrid: Ediciones de Cultura Hispánica, 1957), p. 79.

46.　Augustín Cabre Rufatt, C. M. F., *Evangelizador de dos mundos: vida anecdótica de San Antonio María Claret* (N.p.: Ediciones Mundo, 1977), p. 117.

47.　Lebroc-Martínez, *San Antonio María Claret*, p. 547.

Protestantism in Latin America

6. "Like a Mighty Pushing Wind": The Growth of Protestantism in Contemporary Latin America

Virginia Garrard-Burnett

Conventional wisdom holds that Latin America has always been inextricably "Catholic" in religion, culture, and worldview. Nevertheless, Protestantism has been, arguably, the single most important social movement to sweep through the region in this century. This claim may appear extreme, but consider the following: there are more members in one metropolitan Pentecostal church in Guatemala City than there are Catholic priests in the entire country. In El Salvador ten times more people converted to Protestant churches during the 1980s than were killed during that nation's civil war. There were more Protestants in Nicaragua during the Sandinista decade than there were members of Catholic Christian Base Communities (CEBs). Or ponder this: one recent study found that 10,000 Brazilian Catholics abandon the church *per day*, mostly to become Protestants.[1]

One hundred years ago there were around 50,000 Protestants in all of Latin America, a figure made up nearly exclusively of foreigners—English Anglicans, German Lutherans, and the occasional wandering Mennonites—who happened to live and worship in that part of the world. In 1995 a reliable study estimated that 40,000,000 Protestants were spread across Latin America, the vast majority of whom belonged to independent Pentecostal denominations.[2] While some nations claim sizable Protestant populations, such as Guatemala (around 1.3 million Protestants), Brazil (just under 20 percent of that nation's enormous population), or Chile which is around one-quarter Protestant, others such as Mexico had fewer than 10 percent Protestants overall according to the 1990 national census. But even in the case of a highly "Catholic" country like Mexico, deep pockets of Protestantism can be found in critical areas: Chiapas, for example, is nearly 40 percent Protestant, while some indigenous *municipios* claim nearly total Protestant homogeneity.[3] A similar pattern is evident for a Catholic citadel like Ecuador, where, though the nation is less than 3 percent Protestant overall, nearly the entire populations of several northern Andean villages have converted to the Mormon church.[4]

What is perhaps most remarkable about this movement—and it does seem fair to refer to Protestant conversion as a social as well as a religious movement—

is that it has virtually all happened since 1960, during a period when many social scientists were distracted by other types of social and political currents—Marxism, authoritarianism, dependency theory, praetorianism, developmentalism, even radical Catholicism—that seemed to many outside observers to be more intellectually engaging and perhaps even more "authentic" to the Latin American experience than Protestantism. Yet, hidden in plain sight, Protestantism has engaged many more ordinary Latin Americans than have any of these other "isms." Neglect of the topic perhaps stems less from its impact than its aesthetic. As David Stoll, a prominent writer on the topic, has remarked, "No one who loves Latin America goes there to see nondescript little concrete churches with loudspeakers blasting out 'Onward Christian Soldiers.' "

And indeed, Protestantism does have a strong North Atlantic or at least North American cachet. As we will discuss, the implications of conversion are indeed great in societies where a Catholic worldview has long prevailed. Moreover, Protestantism was introduced into Latin America by forces that have been traditionally hostile to the totality of the Hispanic experience—it is perhaps not insignificant that British pirates taken before the Spanish colonial Inquisition two centuries ago were tried as heretics rather than for their crimes as thieves, rapists, and murderers.[5]

But the Protestant presence in Latin America—the invasion of the sects, as it is often called by hostile observers—really began in the second half of the nineteenth century, when North American and British missionaries of historical denominations such as the Methodist and Presbyterian churches came to the region bearing a message of salvation that was deeply imbedded in the cultural norms and behaviors of Victorian society and wrapped in the flag of political imperialism. While Liberal and Positivist leaders in the late 1800s often welcomed Protestant missionaries as harbingers of modernity and as a counterbalance to Catholic political power—as evidenced by Benito Juárez's sub rosa remark that North American missionaries might "teach Indians to read rather than light candles"—it is little wonder that the population at large tended to vigorously reject both the foreigners and their alien (and for them alienating) message. Only those most marginalized from society—drunkards, habitual adulterers, general ne'er-do-wells—"only those who have nothing whatsoever to lose by associating with us," in the words of one Presbyterian missionary writing from Guatemala, converted in those first decades. Even by 1960, the missionary movement seemed to have largely failed as not a single country in Latin America counted more than a handful of native (that is nonforeign) Protestants—in every case, less than 10 percent—in its national census.

But the religious landscape of Latin America changed dramatically over the course of the next decade. The decade of the 1960s is a pivotal era in the Protestant story in Latin America as it is in so many things. In the wake of Castro's victory in Cuba in 1959 a new type of missionary from North America began to operate in Latin America, promoting Protestantism as a "spiritual alternative to communism." In the early 1960s a variety of new nondenominational Protestant agencies usually based in Latin America but often financed from the United States began elaborate "salvation campaigns" across Latin America. The largest of these was a group called Latin American Mission (LAM), which, along with its imitators, utilized for the first time the latest in advertising and telecommunications techniques to proselytize, including stadium-size revivals, door-to-door evangelism based on market research as well as faith, extensive use of radio, and, to a lesser extent, television. (It is worth noting that this saturation marketing came at a time when the Catholic Church was suffering from a severe shortage of clergy, meaning that even a handful of lay evangelists could generate a bigger pastoral presence than a single Catholic priest. For example, as late as 1964 Guatemala had only 470 priests to serve a nation of over 4 million Catholics.)[6] Because of a favorable convergence of sociological, political, and even spiritual factors, the efforts of such interdenominational agencies quickly bore fruits, and by the middle of the decade, for the first time, locally run Protestant churches began to sprout in urban slums and rural villages of Latin America.

This effort coincided with the massive social and political dislocations that uprooted so many countries in the region during the same period: the beginnings of guerrilla warfare and counterinsurgency, militarization, developmentalist programs, and internal migration, which one anthropologist has referred to as "A bombardment of twentieth century forces."[7] Added to this were profound changes within the Mother Church: the Second Vatican Council (Vatican II) and the emergence of liberation theology, which within Latin America transformed ordinary Catholics from fatalists to activists and shifted the focus of the church from the hereafter to the here and now. An additional aspect of Vatican II little noticed in Latin American scholarly circles at the time was a new spirit of ecumenism: it was in the documents of the Council that the Roman Catholic Church first recognized Protestants as "separated brethren" instead of heretics. For future converts the distinction was critical, for it inadvertently provided a means by which Catholics could expose themselves to other faiths without fearing the loss of their place in the Kingdom of Heaven.[8]

The radicalization of the Catholic Church in the 1970s and 1980s has led many to the not-incorrect assumption that the growth of Protestantism is tied inextricably to politics: at the most facile level, this model pits Catholic progressives against conservative evangelicals who are backed by money and support from the Christian right in the United States. There is ample evidence of this sort of collusion, the most notorious example taking place in Guatemala in the early 1980s. There, the born-again general Efraín Ríos Montt, claiming he ruled by the will of God and with substantial financial support from the 700 club, presided over an eighteen-month scorched-earth sweep of the highlands to rout out those whom he called "the Anti-Christ, the communists." Ríos Montt's crusade left as many as 30,000 dead, most of the victims Indians and many of them Catholic activists.[9] In a case such as this, Guatemalans could hardly be blamed for assuming that there was a modicum of safety in Protestant churches, which as a rule tended to subscribe to the biblical injunction to "Submit to the authorities in power" and to shun political action of any kind.[10]

Although Guatemala presents the specific case, a reasonably large body of literature draws direct parallels between political behavior and religious affiliation, suggesting that the lure of Protestant churches in the post-1960s period has to do primarily with furthering U.S. Cold War–era political interests, channeled through the conduit of U.S. and domestic conservative Protestant agencies. Yet to my mind, this explanation, though based on more than just a kernel of truth, raises some important issues. First is the question of agency: in this interpretation, Latin Americans are passive agents of their own religious destiny. The sense is that Latin Americans are "empty vessels" into which foreign religious and political notions can easily be poured—an idea not in the least borne out by the much-chronicled resiliency of popular religion throughout Latin America's history from the colonial period onward. Second is the issue of contextual relativity: there is an implicit notion that Protestant religion when transferred to the Latin American context retains the same focus, style, and associations that it has in North America or Northern Europe. By this definition a member of the Assembly of God in Atlanta thinks, believes, and acts like a member in highland Guatemala, who is like a member in the Amazon, who is like a member in Buenos Aires, who is like a member in Seoul, Korea, ad infinitum. Despite the increasing homogeneity of global culture, this is hardly likely given the subdermal level at which religious beliefs operate. One need only look at Catholicism to see how even a faith that has gone to great pains throughout its long history to maintain orthodoxy has nonetheless undergone fundamental changes in alternative cultural milieus.

One thing that is significant about the development of the new Protestant churches in Latin America during the 1960s and into the 1970s was not their size or number—indeed, during this early period, Protestant conversion was still something of a novelty, and congregations were typically small enough to meet in a house or storefront—but that for the first time Protestant churches were being established, pastored, and attended exclusively by local converts, without the controlling paternalism of missionaries. These actocronous churches quickly took root, and as they branched out Protestantism in Latin America began to assume a more Latin face.

This is not to say that even now Protestantism in Latin America is completely autonomous from North American Evangelicalism: to the contrary, many

Latin American churches, especially those that draw their congregations from the urban middle and upper classes, are cheek and jowl with the beliefs and worldviews of North American Christians, especially those of politically conservative evangelical fundamentalists. At the same time, many other Latin American *congregaciones evangélicas*, perhaps even the majority, do not claim missionary origins. Most church growth in Latin America since the 1960s has not been in established, historic denominations but in small splinter churches that have only minimal or no ties at all to the doctrinal orthodoxy or structures of traditional Protestant denominations. They are, by design, local in pastorate, custom, and belief, insomuch as the pastor is usually the product of his own experience and revelation rather than of formal theological training in some faraway seminary.

The establishment of a new church or even brand-new denominations requires only three essential elements: a leader with a revelation; a congregation of at least one who believes in his revelation; and a place in which to meet.[11] Indeed, by the 1980s Latin American churches had become what might be called counterdenominational; they tend to be highly localized, schismatic, and dictated by personal revelation and charisma rather than separated from one another by formal theological differences. Such churches tend to be theologically idiosyncratic, to a degree that sometimes startles outsiders, who often mistake the austerity of the small houses of worship—which may have no more adornment than a large cross, a loudspeaker, and perhaps some Bible verses painted on the wall, but certainly no accouterments like candles or statues, which most Latin American Protestants would consider idolatrous—for orthodoxy. Yet given the latitude and heterodoxy of the beliefs that are called "Protestantism" in Latin America, it should not surprise us too much when Mayan Presbyterians believe that Jesus is rain-giver and vanquisher of evil eye, or when Quichua Pentecostals perform an *acción de gracias* when piercing the earth to plant their corn.[12] This is not to declare that Protestantism in undergoing syncretism—at least not yet—but rather to put forth the simple proposition that Latin American Protestantism is informed by the local views of the ineffable, not by the Ur-images and archetypes of ancient Europe and the Middle East.[13]

Protestant churches almost everywhere in Latin America differ from their North American counterparts on another central point as well—they are almost universally Pentecostal. To be a Pentecostal is not to belong to a particular denomination but to subscribe to a particular body of belief which places great emphasis on the power of the Third Entity of the Trinity, the Holy Spirit, as described in the Book of Acts. Pentecostals believe they must receive "baptism in the Holy Spirit" which is typically manifest by such "signs and wonders" as "speaking in tongues" (glossolalia), miraculous healing, and spirit possession exhibited through dance, shouting, song, or more exotic forms of ecstatic behavior.

Pentecostalism is by no means unique to Latin America; it has its roots in the bitter debates that fractured Western Christianity at the end of the last century, as modernists and fundamentalists wrestled with the issues of the "higher criticism" of biblical texts and the rationalization of faith and science brought to the fore by Darwin's writings on the origin of man. As a highly emotional practice and a transcendental system of belief, Pentecostalism provided a tonic to those who shunned the modernists' efforts to quantify faith through science.[14] Although Pentecostalism in the United States has historically been prevalent among subaltern groups such as poor whites, rural southerners, and African Americans, it is one of the fastest-growing varieties of Christianity in the United States today, where it now draws increasingly from the affluent middle class.[15] Even so, the growth of Pentecostalism in the United States can not begin to compare with its growth in Latin America, where more than 80 percent of all Protestants are Pentecostal.[16]

The specific appeal of Pentecostalism raised the larger issue of Protestant growth in Latin America at this particular point in history. Some of the earliest scholarly writing specifically on the phenomenon in Latin America is based, not surprisingly, on the work of the early sociologists of religion, Emile Durkheim and Max Weber. The historiography makes particular reference to Durkheim's understanding of how Protestantism serves as a bridge toward secularism as a society becomes more complex and even more important to Weber's explication of the "elective affinity" between the rise of Protestantism and the development of capitalism.[17]

One of these important Latin American case studies is Christian Lalive d'Epinay's *Haven to the Masses*, an examination of Protestantism among immigrants to urban Chile in the late 1960s, in which he suggests that the small evangelical congregations with their personalistic and often dictatorial pastors served the dubiously comfortable function of "replicating the authoritarianism of the old hacienda system."[18] The other pioneering study published slightly earlier is Emilio Willems's *Followers of the New Faith*, an analysis of Protestants in both urban and rural Chile and Brazil. Willems posits that Latin American converts are most likely to be found among people on the cusp of economic transition, such as from agrarian to urban society or in the throes of transition in twentieth-century capitalism.[19]

Lalive and Willems remain the godfathers of a series of subsequent studies which have described Protestantism's appeal to people displaced by economic transition, in both urban and rural settings, from this determinist view. For example, Roberts has described how new immigrants from the country utilize Protestant churches as voluntary organizations that enable them to save money and insulate themselves from social ills such as alcoholism and abuse; Annis demonstrates how Indian converts free themselves from the "milpa technology," which permits them to save and enter more fully into the capitalist economy, allowing them to raise themselves, in the phrase used by one of his informants, "del suelo a cielo."[20] An interesting twist on the idea of economic efficacy is Cecilia Mariz's study in which she argues that among Brazilian favela dwellers, Protestant (and specifically Pentecostal) religion does not offer any particular material advantage, but it does provide believers with certain new psychological strategies and attitudes that help them cope with the reality of their poverty.[21]

In 1990 two new studies appeared, which directly challenge this rather strict economic determinist paradigm. These two important, though in many ways very different, books, David Stoll's *Is Latin America Turning Protestant? The Politics of Evangelical Growth* and David Martin's *Tongues of Fire: The Explosion of Protestantism in Latin America,* seek to examine Protestant growth in Latin America from the inside out.[22] Their approach is to understand the kinds of comparative advantage that conversion offers believers from a cultural point of view. Martin makes a particular attempt to understand the kinds of changes—both positive and negative—that may occur if the fabric of Latin American societies is rewoven and overshot with religious pluralism. These two books spawned a series of monographs that have focused on specific aspects of conversion and its cultural impacts. Elizabeth Brusco's (wittily titled) *The Reformation of Machismo,* for example, examines how family relations in Colombia are reformed when one member (usually the wife) converts, with attention to how family resources improve overall when the husband stops drinking alcohol as part of his own conversion.[23] Andrew Chesnut, in an already controversial study of the Assembly of God in Amazonia, *Born Again in Brazil*, takes the gender argument even further, suggesting that in the highly sensualized context of contemporary Brazil, Pentecostal worship assumes a highly intimate and even erotic quality—this is based on the comments of local informants who describe their relationship with God in terms normally associated more with *eros* than *agape*.[24]

Elsewhere, a variety of studies examine how Protestantism affects community relations. Historically, the effect of conversion on community and family life has tended to be divisive in the extreme. While Eric Wolf's trope of the "close corporate community" may be passé, there is little dispute that the "traditional community" as an integrated social system did once define the countryside of much of Latin America, but it has now largely ceased to exist in most areas. For some, Protestantism is one of the key culprits in this decline: that is, when people exit the system of *costumbre* that tends to be constructed around Catholic (or what participants consider to be Catholic) rituals and beliefs, they also abandon the historical patterns of living in that community.[25] This abandonment may manifest itself in material ways—Annis, for example, suggests that Mayan women who are Protestant are not as likely to wear the elaborately

woven huipiles that have long been the index of Mayan identity. In the case of
Chiapas, moreover, the perception among traditionalists is that Protestants represent such a negative and divisive threat to the traditional "way of being" that
they are systematically and violently run out of town, filling the slums of San
Cristóbal and, some say, the ranks of the Zapatistas.[26]

The abandonment of traditional "ways of being" may well be manifest in
ways that indicate fundamental shifts in worldview. According to Annis, Protestant women did not stop wearing huipiles outright, but they were much more
likely to wear those embellished with simple cotton embroidered flowers, instead of the much more labor-intensive ones with ancient motifs woven directly
in the cloth. The reason? The thousand-year-old woven designs no longer carried any religious value for Protestant women. In most broader contexts Protestants do not typically participate in the kinds of rituals that have historically
defined community identity: they do not attend fiestas; they do not drink; they
do not belong to religious brotherhoods. They may be systematically excluded
from community life, but, even more important, they exclude themselves. As
David Martin has noted for Protestants and Pentecostals in particular, "[The
church] is its very own fiesta."[27]

In my book *Protestantism in Guatemala: Living in the New Jerusalem*, I
venture to suggest that one of the reasons why Latin Americans are choosing to
elect this new identity as Protestants is that the old identities that once desig-
nated one's place in life have given way over the course of the twentieth century. At least in the case of Guatemala, ancient verities, though not always
appealing, placed one solidly and inextricably within a static context which
seems veritable no longer: the patron is gone, the cofradía powerless, the young
are abroad, and snow peas are planted in the milpa. Even the Catholic Church,
the locus of eternal truth, has changed. In such a context, Protestant churches
can provide a new locus of meaning and identity: the new community is one of
the *hermanos* and *hermanas*, which is both geographically smaller and meta-
physically larger than the community of old.[28]

In aesthetic terms this probably does reduce some of Latin America's ex-
oticism for North Americans. Nevertheless, it is important to realize that for most
Latin American converts it is within the local setting that Protestantism is understood, contextualized, and, indeed, valued. David Martin has written that
Protestantism, rather than being the Americanization of Latin religion, is the
Latinization of American religion.[29] Though this is an interesting proposition,
it is perhaps a premature and glib assessment. The movement is so new to the
region that I would add a cautionary note: in a cultural sense, Protestantism yet
may flame like a fire that heats and purifies, or that burns and destroys. But it is
instructive to close with the reflection of Vitalino Simalox, a Mayan activist and
Presbyterian minister, recognizing that his words can apply to a broader Latin

American context. " . . . Cristianizar no se puede ser equivalente de occidentalizar," he wrote:

> El Cristianismo ha de respetar a todos los pueblos. . . . Ha de tratar de ser griego con los griegos, guatemalteco con los guatemaltecos, y maya con los mayas. Y esto en todos planos de la creación cultural (1 Cor. 9). [De decir menos] . . . se menosprecia y se marginan los valores objetivos y subjetivos de las culturas mayas en nuestro medio.[30]

NOTES

1. Eugene L. Stockwell, "Open and Closed: Protestantism in Latin America," *Christian Century* 112:10 (March 22, 1995), 317. The estimates of Protestant membership come from P. J. Johnstone, *Operation World*, 4th ed. (Bromley, Lent, England: STL Books and WEC International, 1986), p. 62, as quoted in David Stoll, *Is Latin America Turning Protestant? The Politics of Evangelical Growth* (Berkeley: University of California Press, 1990), pp. 335–336.

2. Stockwell, "Open and Closed."

3. Estados Unidos Mexicanos, *Resumen general tabulados complementarios; XI censo general de la población y vivienda 1990* (México: Instituto Nacional de Estadística, Geografía e Informática, 1993.) The regional estimate comes from Rev. Raúl Ruiz, the Methodist bishop of Chiapas, who estimates that some 980,000 Indians in Chiapas have converted or been born into Protestantism over the past twenty years. See David Luhnew, "Protestant Indians' Lands Taken: The Other War Waging in Chiapas," *The San Francisco Chronicle*, January 21, 1994.

4. For the purposes of this study certain groups which claim many adherents in Latin America such as the Church of Jesus Christ of Latter-day Saints (Mormon Church), the Seventh Day Adventists, and the Jehovah's Witnesses will be classified as non-Catholic Christian groups, but not as Protestant, and as such are largely outside the scope of this paper. Webster's dictionary defines "sect" as "a dissenting or schismatic religious body," a definition which, given the autonomy, high level of organizational structure, and well-established theology of all three of these groups, suggests that they do not merit this designation. Sources on Ecuador include Stoll, *Is Latin America*, p. 333, and Gregory Knapp, unpublished religious mapping project on Ecuador.

5. Gonzalo Baez-Camargo, *Protestantes enjudiciados por la Inquisición en Iberoamérica* (México: Casa Unida Publicaciones, 1960).

6. Richard N. Adams, *Crucifixion by Power: Essays on Guatemalan National Social Structure, 1944–1966* (Austin: University of Texas Press, 1970), pp. 137, 284.

7. Sheldon Annis, *God and Production in a Guatemalan Town* (Austin: University of Texas Press, 1987).

8. See Philip Berryman, *The Religious Roots of Rebellion: Christians in Central America's Revolutions* (Maryknoll, N.Y.: Orbis, 1984).

9. See Ricardo Falla, *Massacres in the Jungle: Ixcan, Guatemala, 1975–1982* (Boulder, Colo.: Westview, 1994).

10. See Enrique Domínguez and Deborah Huntington, "The Salvation Brokers: Conservative Evangelicals in Central America," *NACLA* 17:1 (1984), 2–36.

11. The use of the male pronoun is intentional. While women do often take active roles in Protestant worship in Latin America, they very rarely serve as pastors.

12. David Scotchmer, "Symbols of Salvation: A Local Mayan Protestant Theology," *Missiology: An International Review* 17:3 (1989), 293–310.

13. See Gary H. Gossens, *Symbol and Meaning Beyond the Closed Community: Essays in Mesoamerican Ideas* (Albany: Institute for Mesoamerican Studies, State University of New York, 1986).

14. See Donald Dayton, *Theological Roots of Pentecostalism* (New York: Oxford University Press, 1987).

15. See Harvey Cox, *Fire from Heaven: The Rise of Pentecostal Spirituality and the Reshaping of Religion in the Twenty-First Century* (Reading, Mass.: Addison-Wesley Publishing Co., 1995).

16. See Edward L. Cleary and Hannah Stewart-Gambino, *Power, Politics, and Pentecostals in Latin America* (Boulder, Colo.: Westview Press, 1997).

17. Emile Durkheim, *The Elementary Forms of the Religious Life* (New York: The Free Press, 1915); Max Weber, *Protestantism and the Spirit of Capitalism* (London: Allen and Unwin, 1930).

18. Christian Lalive d'Epinay, *Haven to the Masses: A Study of the Pentecostal Movement in Chile* (London: Butterworth Press, 1969).

19. Emilio Willems, *Followers of the New Faith: Culture Change and the Rise of Protestantism in Brazil and Chile* (Nashville: Vanderbilt University Press, 1967).

20. Bryan R. Roberts, "Protestant Groups and Coping with Urban Life in Guatemala," *American Journal of Sociology* 73 (1968), 753–767; Annis, *God and Production*.

21. Cecilia Loreto Mariz, *Coping with Poverty: Pentecostals and Christian Base Communities in Brazil* (Philadelphia: Temple University Press, 1994).

22. Stoll, *Is Latin America;* David Martin, *Tongues of Fire: The Explosion of Protestantism in Latin America* (Oxford, U.K.; Cambridge, Mass.: Basil Blackwell, 1990).

23. Elizabeth Brusco, *The Reformation of Machismo: Evangelical Conversion and Gender in Colombia* (Austin: University of Texas Press, 1995).

24. R. Andrew Chesnut, *Born Again in Brazil: The Pentecostal Boom and the Pathogen of Poverty* (New Brunswick, N.J.: Rutgers University Press, 1997).

25. See Duncan Earle, "Authority, Social Conflict and the Rise of Protestant Religious Conversion in a Mayan Village," *Social Compass* 39:3 (1992), 379–389.

26. Diego Ribaldeneira, "In Mexico's South, a Religious Divide: Non-Catholics, Seen as a Threat to the Social Order, Are Expelled from Majority Maya Towns," *The Boston Globe,* February 2, 1994.

27. David Martin in Virginia Garrard-Burnett and David Stoll, eds., *Rethinking Protestantism in Latin America* (Philadelphia: Temple University Press, 1993), p. 285.

28. Virginia Garrard-Burnett, *Protestantism in Guatemala: Living in the New Jerusalem* (Austin: University of Texas Press, 1998).

29. Martin, *Tongues of Fire,* p. 282.

30. Vitalino Simalox, "La evangelización y la cultura," address to the Conferencia de Iglesias Evangélicas de Guatemala, Programa de Asesoría Pastoral, June 1988.

7. La Iglesia Evangélica en el Perú: una aproximación socio-política

Carlos Alberto Acuña Ramos

Contra todo pronóstico, los evangélicos en el Perú han asumido en los últimos tiempos un protagonismo en materia de participación política que ha despertado el interés, no sólo de aquéllos que profesan una fe evangélica, sino de científicos y analistas sociales. Y es que en materia religiosa, América Latina se presenta como un continente en el cual la religión no ha perdido su carácter movilizador de las conciencias de las personas para la acción social y política, sino que, por el contrario, éstas se refuerzan e inspiran en utopías de carácter religioso que resultan significativas para el poblador de estas tierras, tanto en la vertiente católica como protestante del cristianismo. En el presente trabajo intentaremos hacer un breve panorama del horizonte de la relación entre evangélicos y política, a partir de una serie de investigaciones y trabajos previos referidos al caso peruano.

Haciendo un poco de historia, podemos señalar que la presencia protestante se inicia con el período de la independencia peruana del dominio español, a comienzos del siglo XIX. Desde esos tiempos la presencia de los primeros misioneros protestantes no estuvo desligada del acontecer político y de las relaciones con las personalidades que iban marcando el curso de la historia de la república, como en el caso del misionero escocés Diego Thomson, invitado por el libertador José de San Martín para realizar un programa de educación para la nueva nación, a partir del sistema lancasteriano y el uso de la Biblia como libro de texto. Asimismo, siendo el protestantismo, en un primer momento, un culto que no tenía legalidad como religión tolerada o permitida en el contexto nacional, los primeros misioneros estuvieron mucho más próximos a las ideas liberales de muchos políticos que no veían con buenos ojos el carácter tradicional del conservadurismo político peruano y que veían más bien en el trabajo misionero de estos misioneros, la posibilidad de acceder a la modernidad y el desarrollo que acompañaba el trasfondo cultural de la mayoría de ellos. Este mismo espíritu acompañó el desarrollo de los esfuerzos primero por la tolerancia y luego por la libertad de cultos que estuvieron dirigidos por políticos liberales que consideraban éste un supuesto fundamental de toda nación independiente y civilizada. El caso del misionero ítalo-uruguayo Guillermo Penzotti, encarcelado por el gobierno peruano por la difusión de sus ideas protestantes, fue uno de los detonantes finales en la afirmación de la libertad de cultos en el Perú.

71

Ya bien entrado el presente siglo, encontramos una Iglesia Evangélica nacional pujante, que en la medida que avanzaba en la difusión de su mensaje experimentaba un proceso de indigenización tanto en su liderazgo como en su estilo de encarnar los valores del Evangelio. Ejemplos de este fenómeno a mediados del siglo XX fueron los esfuerzos de las denominaciones pentecostales y la Iglesia Evangélica peruana, como primera denominación de carácter nacional en el país. En la medida que esta Iglesia Evangélica iba echando raíces en nuestras tierras, algunos miembros de su liderazgo consideraban que la acción social y la acción política no podían estar ajenas de la misión de los cristianos en el mundo.

Es así como, a través de diferentes canales, los evangélicos comenzaron a manifestar sus inquietudes en estos campos: participación en la vida social y cultural del país vía colegios evangélicos de alto nivel de enseñanza como el anglo-peruano, fundado por el misionero presbiteriano John A. Mackay, o como el colegio "María Alvarado", fundado por las misiones metodistas. También participaron en la obra social y de promoción humana, a través del compromiso cristiano de muchos que asumieron la expresión de su fe poniendo sus profesiones al servicio de aquéllos que menos tienen—trabajadores de la salud, ingenieros, abogados, entre otros. Encontraron un canal de proyección social a la comunidad a través del trabajo de algunas organizaciones para-eclesiásticas que comenzaron a desarrollar un ministerio en nuestras tierras.

Desde el campo en sí de la participación política en la línea de los partidos políticos, encontramos en esta época las experiencias de dos líderes evangélicos vinculados con el APRA, un movimiento político de clases medias y sectores populares que bajo la inspiración de Víctor Raúl Haya de la Torre, y que bajo una ideología radical, con la propuesta de contextualización de una forma de marxismo latinoamericano, logró convocar la atención de los evangélicos Pedro Ferreira y Pedro Arana quienes en 1950 y 1979 respectivamente participaron en sus filas en justas electorales que los llevaron a convertirse en los primeros evangélicos peruanos que llegaron a ser senadores y miembros de la Asamblea Constituyente. Y esto, podríamos decir, a pesar de su compromiso evangélico.

Y decimos "a pesar de su compromiso evangélico" porque desde el término de la Segunda Guerra Mundial, nuestro país vivió una época en que la llegada de misioneros provenientes de un contexto más bien norteamericano, influenciados por la discusión teológica con el "Evangelio Social" de cuño liberal, y condicionados por una situación de "guerra fría" con la entonces Unión Soviética, influenció en la iglesia a mirar con mucho recelo cualquier atisbo de compromiso social y político de parte de los evangélicos.

Se comenzó a construir la idea de sentido común que el "buen creyente evangélico" no participa en las cosas del mundo, de las cuales la acción política era definitivamente una de ellas. Esto llevó a satanizar cualquier tipo de participación política de líderes evangélicos, peor aún si se trataba de un partido político de influencia radical. Sin embargo, estos primeros líderes evangélicos que hicieron su aparición en instancias oficiales y responsabilidades de gobierno no utilizaron su identidad evangélica como una forma de conseguir adeptos, ni su campaña política descansó en acentuar su filiación religiosa. En todo caso, esto aparecía como parte de su vida privada y no fue un elemento detonante en su llegada al poder.

Pero, a partir de 1980, y seguramente inspirados por el éxito político de los anteriormente nombrados, una ola de conciencia política se despertó en varios líderes evangélicos, especialmente en sectores de clase media y profesionales que comenzaron a ver que la participación en esta faceta de la vida nacional no tenía que transcurrir necesariamente sólo por partidos de izquierda en nuestro país. Se comenzó a construir la idea que se podía ser conservador en teología y en política y participar de esta manera formando frentes y agrupaciones de carácter evangélico, que como tales comenzaron a organizarse a partir del espacio eclesiástico. Tales son los casos de movimientos como el Frente Evangélico (FE), AMAR o UREP que convocaron a profesionales evangélicos que se unieron en el momento estratégico que ellos consideraron con organizaciones de raigambre en la política peruana en el ala derecha como el Partido Popular Cristiano.

En este segundo momento de la participación política de los evangélicos, las iglesias todavía ven con ojos sospechosos este tipo de actividad. Si bien el hecho que los nuevos movimientos estén vinculados a una ideología más capitalista favoreció la aceptación, o por lo menos la disminución del prejuicio, sin embargo las iglesias, especialmente las más tradicionales en la defensa de su espiritualidad, no creían todavía que evangelio y política eran dos cosas compatibles.

La década de los 80 nos dejó un saldo en el ambiente evangélico de consolidación de la comprensión de la misión de la iglesia como misión integral a través de la obra realizada por instituciones como la Asociación de Grupos Evangélicos Universitarios del Perú (AGEUP) entre una nueva generación de estudiantes y profesionales evangélicos que no tenían como objetivo de vida simplemente adaptarse acríticamente a su sociedad sino buscar una acción transformadora, y la labor del Concilio Nacional Evangélico del Perú (CONEP), que de una otra forma van creando conciencia social entre los miembros de las iglesias. Frente a este desarrollo en la comprensión misiológica, no existió de parte de esta otra visión no-conservadora sobre la realidad, una articulación política de manera orgánica que permitiera al creyente pasar del discurso a la acción comprometida. Esta debilidad creó una falta de modelos reales que los miembros de las iglesias pudiesen observar. El prejuicio conservador de parte de los evangélicos peruanos en este tiempo colaboró para que la cultura política y la construcción de una ideología no pasara de una élite intelectual que no lograba impactar en el sentido común de las personas de las iglesias.

Es así como arribamos a 1990 donde cambios sustantivos ocurren con relación a nuestro tema planteado. Cambios que tienen que ver con la composición misma del campo socio-religioso protestante en el Perú, y cambios en las formas políticas que comenzaron a elaborarse en esta última década. En el campo socio-religioso asistimos a la formulación hegemónica de la propuesta del movimiento carismático al interior de las Iglesias Evangélicas en general, que les lleva a asimilar una propuesta de espiritualidad que era distinta con respecto a la propuesta tradicional de espiritualidad por lo menos en las siguientes cosas:

1. El centro del anuncio evangélico no estaba tanto en el llamado al arrepentimiento y el perdón de pecados en el nombre de Jesús, sino un llamado al hombre contemporáneo a probar la receta Jesús a sus problemas cotidianos: falta de salud, crisis económica, sufrimiento, etc.

2. El nivel de exigencias éticas tan rigurosas en la espiritualidad tradicional que habían formado una actitud de negación hacia las cosas del mundo se transforma por una voluntad de apertura hacia la perspectiva del disfrute y del gozo legítimo de las cosas de este mundo.

3. Bajo los influjos de la teología de la prosperidad los evangélicos comenzaron a aceptar que era parte del designio de Dios que a ellos como "hijos del Rey" les correspondiera ocupar los cargos públicos más importantes en las esferas de gobierno en el Perú.

4. Asimismo, los evangélicos carismáticos enseñaron a la Iglesia Evangélica a cuidar los aspectos de forma en sus presentaciones: saber hablar ante un micrófono, usar adecuadamente los medios de comunicación, cuidar la apariencia externa del predicador, mostrar a través de la vida misma de los creyentes que la alternativa evangélica no sólo es la mejor en términos religiosos, sino incluso en términos sociales: los evangélicos bajo la influencia de los movimientos carismáticos llegan a "ser alguien" bajo los criterios de la sociedad en general.

Esta cosmovisión religiosa favoreció la aparición de la intrepidez evangélica en materia político partidaria, aunándole a esta participación el criterio de eficacia. Si los evangélicos iban a participar en política era para ganar, Dios estaba con ellos. Esto, por supuesto, causó mucho impacto y redefinió la relación evangélicos–participación política de una manera drástica. Antiguos predicadores que habían condenado ésta, ahora decían que siempre habían enseñado que era necesario que los creyentes estuviesen involucrados desde la perspectiva de ser sal y luz. Los personajes bíblicos invocados ahora para legitimar esta participación estaban relacionados con Daniel en el destierro de Babilonia y con José como el eficiente funcionario del faraón en Egipto.

Como podemos ver, estos cambios desde el plano socio-religioso tuvieron que ver con la participación política de los evangélicos en las elecciones de 1990 y luego en 1995. No olvidemos que en el primer caso son muchos los candidatos que resultaron beneficiados con los votos de feligreses evangélicos como de los que no lo eran. Esto último estuvo relacionado con los cambios que se produjeron en materia política al interior del país y por qué no decirlo, a nivel del nuevo orden internacional.

La caída de los "socialismos realmente existentes", la crisis de lo institucional y de las utopías sociales; el auge de la informalidad a nivel de todas las áreas de la vida; la crisis de los partidos políticos tradicionales; la necesidad de un gobierno que asumiera la victoria del neoliberalismo como sistema en el mundo; y el auge de una cultura pragmática que se concentra en los resultados antes que en los medios acompañan la explicación en términos sociopolíticos, de la participación política evangélica en la década de los 90. En el nuevo escenario los evangélicos encontraron una situación de vacío que supieron aprovechar para ofrecer al público en general no una fórmula de gobierno y un plan de trabajo altamente elaborado. Los evangélicos centraron su discurso en los temas de la honestidad, su falta de experiencia política previa (lo que permitía suponer un posible nivel mayor de credibilidad), y el hecho que Dios estaría actuando en beneficio de la nación a través de ellos.

Esta formulación tuvo diferentes resultados en 1990 y 1995, respectivamente. En 1990 bajo la fuerza de lo novedoso, los evangélicos lograron llegar al poder incluidos dentro del movimiento que llevó al actual presidente del Perú, Alberto Fujimori, a la silla presidencial. Hay discusión en torno a la importancia que debe asignársele a la presencia evangélica en el éxito de la campaña electoral. Los especialistas discuten si éste puede ser considerado un argumento principal o secundario. En cualquier caso estamos ante la realidad que en la década de los 90 estamos discutiendo el impacto político de la práctica de un grupo religioso en el quehacer nacional.

Es así que repentinamente, en las elecciones de 1990 la propuesta evangélica abarcó una identidad política indefinida. Bajo el espectro de Cambio 90, todavía no se sabía si se encontraría la vieja propuesta del populismo o una receta de modernización de la economía con el consiguiente costo social. En este primer momento, los evangélicos se presentan en toda su dimensión de garantes morales de una propuesta y de una persona, en el marco del discurso que cuanto menos experiencia en política tenga el gobernante, más posibilidades hay que sea un buen presidente.

En este contexto de indefiniciones programáticas las pugnas entre el poder central y el sector evangélico no se hicieron esperar. Una vez llegado a la presidencia, Fujimori no tenía mayor necesidad de los evangélicos. Las luchas internas se agudizaron para 1992 cuando muchos evangélicos comenzaron a alejarse del régimen, mientras que otros se mantenían fieles al mismo produciéndose una fractura que terminaría con la eliminación de más del 50% de los líderes evangélicos que estuvieron en los orígenes de la campaña de 1990. Las iglesias por su parte, no aprovecharon esta oportunidad de estar en contacto con el poder político para adquirir mayor experiencia y criterio. Por el contrario se mantuvieron en una actitud de expectativa con respecto a lo que los políticos evangélicos podrían conseguir en beneficio de ellas para realizar mejor su trabajo misionero, pero no fueron nunca conciencia moral para sus propios líderes que estaban participando en estos cargos dentro de la vida nacional. En general, la iglesia toleró y hasta se entusiasmó con la participación política, pero nunca estuvo convencida que esa era también parte de su función espiritual y cristiana dentro de nuestro país.

Para 1995 el panorama electoral desde el campo evangélico había cambiado substantivamente. Desde la experiencia de las confrontaciones con el poder político, dos bloques se habían formado al interior del panorama evangélico. Por un lado, existía un sector de líderes que decidieron continuar en la arena política con una vocación de oposición al gobierno de Fujimori bastante evidente. Algunos evangélicos asumieron como un asunto de conciencia el intentar limitar los poderes cada vez más concentrados alrededor de una sola figura, la presidencial. Otros, por el contrario, se mantuvieron fieles al régimen, ocupando nuevas responsabilidades dentro de los planes de Fujimori.

En el medio de esta confrontación, las Iglesias Evangélicas han mantenido su discurso de neutralidad política, aunque siempre han simpatizado con aquellos que se encuentran en el poder. Además, cabe señalar, después de la campaña electoral de 1990, muy pocas Iglesias Evangélicas pueden argumentar el asunto de la neutralidad. La mayoría de ellas directa o indirectamente estuvieron activas en dar una palabra frente al hecho que por primera vez en la historia de nuestro país y en la historia del protestantismo en el Perú, los evangélicos se habían organizado para participar políticamente, y ya no desde un discurso que toleraba la fe evangélica, sino desde uno que empleaba el discurso religioso para mediatizar contenidos políticos.

Para finalizar, es bastante discutible si como conclusión de esta experiencia podemos extraer la idea que ha habido un desarrollo progresivo de la conciencia política de los evangélicos en nuestro país. Lo que hemos asistido en esta última década tiene más relación con el campo de las oportunidades aprovechadas por un grupo socio-religioso (el evangélico) en un contexto en el que quisieron instrumentalizar el poder político con objetivos religiosos y al final fueron instrumentalizados por un gobernante que utilizó con mucha habilidad la fuerza carismática, la trayectoria y el reconocimiento moral que la sociedad les concedía al pueblo evangélico para llegar al poder. Una vez conseguido este objetivo, los evangélicos podían ser innecesarios y hasta peligrosos.

Los líderes que participaron en estas justas electorales demostraron una vez más, salvo honrosas excepciones, las consecuencias de una mala formación en el área de las ciencias sociales, y en algunos casos muy penosos la crisis de fe tan temida ante las tentaciones del poder político. La improvisación, falta de información, el ridículo y el escándalo no han sido algo totalmente ajena de la evaluación superficial de esta primera experiencia masiva de presencia evangélica en el poder político.

Asimismo, se pudo apreciar que los esquemas teológicos demasiado rígidos y conservadores que han caracterizado a los evangélicos desde 1950 en adelante, mostraron una vez más sus limitaciones para dialogar con el mundo de la cultura y la sociedad en general. Las buenas intenciones o los buenos deseos de muchos de los que participaron en esta aventura política se estrellaron rápidamente con la realidad de una situación estructural para la cual no estaban preparados para hacer frente por lo que sólo quedaron como alternativas la frustración, el acomodo fácil o la inacción. Como todos sabemos, cualquiera de estas alternativas resulta mortal para una participación política eficaz en un país como el nuestro.

La iglesia, por su lado, demostró no estar interesada en la práctica política, aunque eventualmente pueda estar muy entusiasmada con el protagonismo que se desprende del hecho que uno de sus miembros resulte elegido para una responsabilidad de trascendencia. Asimismo, el tema del interés y el esfuerzo de los evangélicos por mejorar el status social de sus propias condiciones ha promovido que la iglesia vea en la participación política, no un campo de misión en donde tiene que destinar recursos, tiempo y esfuerzo, sino una oportunidad de aprovechar los males de la clásica política criolla peruana, dejando de lado la oportunidad de cumplir su función salinizadora en este campo.

Sabemos que una vez producido este encuentro final entre evangélicos y política resultará muy difícil el fin de la relación. Creemos con muchos otros analistas que la pregunta actual y con miras al futuro no será ya la vieja pregunta acerca de si los evangélicos debemos participar o no en política sino que la pregunta más bien será acerca del cómo debe darse esta participación. Hay demasiadas cosas en juego del tipo de respuesta que podamos ofrecer. No sólo el testimonio o prestigio de la iglesia como institución y de sus miembros como participantes está de por medio, sino que creemos estar ante una oportunidad por medio de la cual Dios mismo puede ensanchar nuestros reducidos supuestos a la hora de hacer misión y hacernos abrir los ojos ante estas nuevas fronteras de trabajo evangélico, fronteras a donde antes no habíamos logrado llegar.

8. Three Mennonite Colonies and the Indigenous Communities in the Central Chaco

Georgette M. Dorn

This essay explores the history of the first and three largest Mennonite colonies in the Paraguayan Chaco (Menno, Fernheim, and Neuland), their contribution to the development of this forbidding region, and their relations with the indigenous population. These colonies became an important dairy- and cattle-producing center in Paraguay.

The first group of Mennonite colonists arrived at Puerto Casado in the central Chaco on December 30, 1926. These 1,765 conservative Mennonites of the Chortitzer and Sommerfeld branches, also known as Alt Kolonie Mennonites, came from Manitoba, Canada. They were descendants of Dutch and German dissidents, spoke Low German, and were part of a migration of Mennonites from Russia to Canada in the 1870s and 1880s. They went to Canada because there they were granted exemption from military service (which Czar Alexander II had withdrawn from them) and the right to operate their schools in any way they desired. Thirty years later these "Russland" Mennonites left Manitoba when the Canadian government enacted a series of uniform education laws requiring that the language of schooling be English and that the Canadian flag be flown. In 1919, when the government finally forbade German-language schools, the Mennonites explored sites for emigration to Mexico and South America, seeking a place that would allow them to "live in the world but not of it."

The Mennonites were Anabaptists (Wiedertaeufer), who had separated from Ulrich Zwingli's reform movement in Switzerland because of a conflict over the doctrine of infant baptism. They were followers of Menno Simons (1496–1561), a former Dutch Catholic priest turned reformer. Anabaptists and Mennonites practiced baptism by immersion in water and based their theology on the Bible, which guided the authority and discipline of their church. Accustomed to persecution and suffering for their faith, they believed their reward would come in the next world. Mennonites recognized governments as part of God's scheme, but believed their mission was to pacify and pray for society. Their most basic tenet was conscious objection to bearing arms (in their view only God could take lives) and they refused to take oaths. Mennonites believed in brotherhoods of believers, a universal priesthood, and that preachers should be elected by their congregations.[1]

At the turn of the twentieth century Paraguay actively encouraged European immigration in order to develop the rural sector. Consequently Paraguay granted the Mennonites "special legal freedom" so they might "live in the world but not of it." Mennonites were guaranteed the right to religious freedom; to establish, maintain, and operate schools; and to administer their property and inheritance. They were allowed to prohibit the sale of alcoholic beverages within 5 km of their villages and were given exemption from military service and from all taxes. Paraguay also promised to admit future Mennonite immigrants.[2] Since they were excellent farmers Mennonites played a pivotal role in the agricultural development of the region during the ensuing years.

The vast, untamed, semiarid, alluvial plain of dense bush and intermittent savannas, known as the Chaco Boreal, is the frontier of Paraguay. Located west of the Paraguay and Pilcomayo rivers forming the region's borders with Brazil and Argentina, respectively, the Chaco does not have a natural demarcation boundary with Bolivia—which became the principal cause of the Chaco War (1932–1935). The Paraguayan Chaco continues to be one of the least inhabited areas of South America. Because of its extreme heat and heavy rains, European immigrants call this forbidding land of exotic flora and fauna *infierno verde* or "drunken forest" (because of the prevalence of the *palo borracho* tree).[3]

After arriving in Puerto Casado in 1926 the Mennonites discovered that the land they purchased had not been surveyed. Consequently they had to wait a year and a half before settling the colony. During that time they endured hardships such as a severe typhoid epidemic which cost nearly 200 lives. Finally, in April 1928, after complex financial arrangements were completed, they moved to their new lands and established the Menno colony. Villages were laid out in the German *Strassendorf* (village street) style with homes on each side of a straight road. The inhabitants plowed the fields and raised crops.

In their search for freedom, Mennonites in Paraguay faced a complex intercultural dynamic. They were a foreign element within a core culture (Spanish, Catholic, and indigenous). The Mennonites interacted most frequently with the mixed culture of the indigenous groups who were attracted to their colonies. They faced dealing with indigenous people even though what they most wanted was isolation in order to live a peaceful agrarian life.[4]

The colonists encountered about 200 indigenous Lengua, nomads camping in the area chosen for one of the colony's villages. Although the Lengua and the Chulupí (a subtribe of the Ashluslay) had learned farming from Franciscan missionaries in the Puerto Casado area, they clung to a "boundless nostalgia for the open field, for the limitless waste"[5] and a seminomadic way of life. However, curiosity drew the Indians to the new settlers. They referred to the newcomers as "straw hats." The Lengua and the Chulupí trusted the Mennonites more than the Paraguayan soldiers in the area, especially during the Chaco War. One Mennonite remarked that the "Indians could see us even though we couldn't see them."[6] The Lenguas' first contacts with the colonists consisted of bartering fruits for rice and flour. Soon the Mennonites began hiring them to clear the bush, cut wood, and farm.

Principal crops cultivated by the Menno colony included cotton, kafir, peanuts, corns, and beans. Cattle raising and dairy farming were also major sources of income. Menno was the most theologically conservative of the three colonies discussed here and also had the highest birth rate. By 1950 the population of Menno had tripled and by 1977 it reached 6,352.[7]

In 1929 a new group of settlers immigrated to Paraguay. Chaos, collectivization of farms, and persecution of Mennonites in the Soviet Union in the 1920s prompted the remaining Russian Mennonites to seek and, after a long struggle, secure official permission to emigrate to Paraguay. With help from the Mennonite Central Committee of the United States, 1,500 Mennonites arrived in the Chaco by way of China, and 378 migrated via Germany between 1930 and 1932. Many perished during the arduous journey from China.[8] These new arrivals founded the Fernheim colony, as well as numerous villages, near Menno. This group was more sophisticated than the earlier immigrants who founded Menno. With a more skilled and educated population, the new colony rapidly became prosperous.

A main reason why Fernheim immigrants decided to remain in the Chaco rather than re-immigrate to Canada was the presence of the Lengua, Toba, and Sanapá Indians whom they wanted to help and convert. The colonists built villages for the indigenous population in an effort to settle them and attempted to stop the custom of infanticide, which the Toba practiced. By 1932 the sect had founded an organization called Licht de Indianern (Light of the Indians) for the purpose of converting the native population. However, because of the Chaco War no evangelization took place until 1935.[9]

Shortly after the establishment of the second Mennonite settlement, the Chaco War became a disruptive and often frightening experience for the colonists, who were pacifists and refused to bear arms even in self-defense. The raging conflict was even more unsettling to the recently arrived Fernheim colonists, who had suffered hardship during the wars in the Soviet Union. The colonists did, however, have some involvement in the conflict. They cared for the wounded in their hospital at Filadelfia and tried to shield the indigenous population from the soldiers and harm's way. The Lengua were often caught in the cross fire between the warring armies. Historian David Zook believes that the establishment of prosperous Mennonite colonies might have been a factor in triggering the conflict between Paraguay and Bolivia over a poorly demarcated boundary area because the colonists demonstrated the desirability of the desolate area.[10]

The third Mennonite migration to the central Chaco occurred after World War II and also came from the Soviet Union. More than 30,000 Mennonites chose to retreat with the German army in 1943. However, the Russian army recaptured about 20,000 of them and sent most to Siberia. In Germany young Mennonite men were drafted into the army. After the end of World War II and with help from the Mennonite Central Committee, the German-Russian Mennonite refugees had no choice but to go to Paraguay. Initially, 786 settlers arrived by ship from Germany by way of Buenos Aires and founded the Neuland colony in 1947. By 1950 Neuland had 2,497 people. Farming operations were more difficult for these families because many were fatherless as a result of the war. The settlers in Neuland had also been reluctant to relocate to Paraguay and were discouraged by life in the Chaco. Many returned to Germany. As a result, Neuland constantly lost population.[11]

Each colony was officially incorporated and registered as an autonomous legal entity, under Ley 514 of Paraguay. Each had its own constitution and statutes and was governed by a mixed system of theocracy and democratic government. Each colony was governed by an *Oberschulze* elected by the male colonists. Welfare, education, health, and public utilities were handled by an *Amt* or administrative organization.

To expedite agricultural production and commerce, the Fernheim colony started a cooperative, promptly adopted by the Menno colony. These cooperatives became an important factor in the economic success of the Mennonite colonies. They bought and sold the crops produced by the farms and became purchasing agents representing the colonies in the capital city of Asunción. They also served as centers for the social life of the colonies. Eventually, after some twenty years, the cooperatives were criticized for being too large and inimical to private enterprise and were eliminated. Nevertheless, they represented an important factor in the economic success of the colonies.[12]

The church was powerful in all the colonies. Membership in the Mennonite church was 97.8 percent. Church membership was granted after instruction in Mennonite dogma, and baptism and marriages could only be performed between church members. The Menno colony was the most theologically and socially conservative. Here the church exerted control over all the activities of the community. Its form of government was modeled after the old Mennonite colonies in Russia. The Fernheim and Neuland colonies incorporated a more diverse group of Mennonite branches, such as the Evangelical Mennonite Brethren, the Mennonite Brethren, and the General Conference Mennonites. These groups held their meetings in Filadelfia. Fernheim and Neuland stressed education of the young more than the Menno colony, where grade school education was deemed sufficient. In all three colonies family life was of paramount importance.[13]

The Mennonites attempted to instill their values and way of life in the indigenous communities whom they encountered and attracted to their villages. The principal indigenous groups who came into contact with the Mennonite colonies were the Lengua, Chulupí, Sanapaná, Toba (Guaicuru), and smaller numbers of Ayoreo, Angaité, Tapieté, and Guarani. According to the *Censo de la población indígena*, massive indigenous migration to the central Chaco occurred because of the availability of work in the Mennonite colonies, "the most dynamic area of the Chaco."[14]

The establishment in 1955 of two villages at Salve Yanga became the first indigenous agricultural settlement. There some worked on the farms, while a growing number worked as carpenters, tanners, and in other small industries. Four additional indigenous agricultural settlements followed: La Esperanza (1962), Campo Largo (1963), Campo Alegre (1964), and Pozo Amarillo (1966).[15]

Mennonite leaders organized a Comité Ejecutivo de los Establecimientos Indígenas in 1961 to oversee the settlements and provide technical guidance and assistance to the indigenous agricultural villages and settlements. The Mennonites' economic and social work with the indigenous population was completely separate from their missionary efforts. The indigenous villages were built to resemble the Mennonite towns with a school and houses along both sides of a main street. The villages were surrounded by farmland and grazing areas. Land titles were officially transferred to the indigenous villages once each became duly incorporated under the Asociación de Servicios de Cooperación Indígena Menonita and recognized by the Paraguayan government.

The indigenous agricultural settlement of Salve Yanga began with 240 Lengua families and by 1988 included 1,296 people living on 5,965 hectares of land. Although many followed the Mennonite religion and social customs, the community was able to retain some of its traditional culture, such as matrifocal family structure. The inhabitants work mainly in agriculture and raise cattle. Members of the village cooperative work in groups of 20 to 40 on the commonly held farmland and keep track of the work performed by each member. Cattle raising is also carried out within the framework of a cooperative modeled after the Mennonite cooperatives. Some of the townspeople also work outside of their village for extra earnings. Salve Yanga has the most important hospital used by the indigenous population, where they can also receive training in nursing and laboratory technology. Salve Yanga is governed by a religious leader as well as a traditional civil one, a system the Lengua call "líderes de todas las estirpes."[16] The other indigenous agricultural settlements functioned in the same fashion as Salve Yanga.

The indigenous population was familiar with cooperatives, primarily related to hunting and fishing, before they came into contact with the Mennonites. The Mennonites established a variety of indigenous cooperatives in the villages. Cooperative stores supplied farm equipment and other machinery. The trading cooperatives bought the products of the land and range as well as manufactured goods and sold them to other areas in Paraguay. In addition to indigenous agricultural settlements, there were also indigenous labor camps around Menno, Filadelfia, Fernheim, and Neuland. By 1976, 9,599 members of indigenous groups had settled permanently in the areas around the Mennonite colonies.

Between 1961 and 1981 improvements in the transportation infrastructure, such as completion of the Trans-Chaco Highway, markedly upgraded the economic situation of the Mennonite colonies. The Mennonites also made great strides in technical agriculture and cattle raising. Furthermore, urban centers such as Filadelfia and Loma Plata became active hubs of industry and trade.

Mennonites form the largest non-Catholic religious group in Paraguay. Although not great in number, they have had considerable impact on economic development in Paraguay. The indigenous people living in agricultural settlements within the Mennonite areas and those living in the indigenous labor camps all have to abide by Mennonite social rules and regulations. One of the Mennonites' greatest achievements has been the improvement of the health of the indigenous population working in the colonies. In addition to well-equipped hospitals and health centers in Filadelfia and Loma Linda, each indigenous agricultural settlement and some of the labor camps have health and dental centers. As a result, cases of tuberculosis, endemic among the Lengua and Sananapá, decreased markedly. Regarding education, there were 8 indigenous students in the Mennonite colonies in 1937 and by 1973 the number had increased to 1,242.[17] The Mennonite population of Paraguay continues to be an important influence on the country.

NOTES

1.   Walter Quiring, *Russlanddeutsche suchen eine Heimat; die deutsche Einwanderung in den paraguayischen Chaco* (Karlsruhe, Germany: Heinrich Schneider Verlag, 1938), pp. 18–36, 40–50; Rudolf Plett, *Presencia menonita en el Paraguay* (Asunción: Instituto Bíblico Asunción, 1980), pp. 32–64; Calvin W. Redekop, *Strangers Become Neighbors: Mennonite and Indigenous Relations in the Paraguayan Chaco* (Scottdale, Penn.: Herald Press, 1980), pp. 27–30.

2.   Paraguay, Laws, Statutes. Ley 514, 26 de julio, 1921, and Ley 914, 30 de agosto, 1927, provided for Mennonite migration. *Diario Oficial* further amplified the benefits of Ley 514; Martin W. Friesen, *Neue Heimat in der Chaco Wildnis* (Asunción: C. W. Friesen and Chortitzer Komitee, 1987), pp. 114–130.

3.   Friesen, *Neue Heimat*, pp. 73–130; Redekop, *Strangers*, pp. 27–30.

4.   Joseph Winfield Fretz, *Pilgrims in Paraguay: The Story of Mennonite Colonization in South America* (Scottdale, Penn.: Herald Press, 1953), pp. 16–19; Redekop, *Strangers*, pp. 95–97.

5.   Juan Belaieff, *Handbook of South American Indians* (Washington, D.C.: Smithsonian Institution, 1946), v. 1, p. 373.

6.   Redekop, *Strangers*, p. 97.

7.   Redekop, *Strangers*, pp. 107–110; Fretz, *Pilgrims*, pp. 16–19.

8.   Hans Duerksen, *Fernheim 1930–1980: Documento ilustrado sobre la vida de una colonia en el Chaco. Bildbericht ueber das Leben einer Siedlung im Chaco* (Filadelfia: Administración de la Colonia Fernheim, 1980), pp. 3–4.

9.   Fretz, *Pilgrims*, p. 229; Redekop, *Strangers*, pp. 98–102; Duerksen, *Fernheim*, pp. 1–4; *50 Jahre Kolonie Fernheim; ein Beitrag des Entwicklung Paraguays* (Asunción: Impr. Modelo, 1980), pp. 39–95; Quiring, *Russlanddeutsche*, p. 59.

10.   David H. Zook, *The Conduct of the Chaco War* (New Haven, Conn.: Bookman Associates, 1960), p. 34; Peter P. Klassen, *Die Mennoniten in Paraguay*, Bd, 2, *Die Begegnung mit Indianers und Paraguayern* (Bolanden-Weierhof: Mennonistischer Geschichtsverein, 1988), pp. 18, 53, 58, 61, 88, 93; Redekop, *Strangers*, p. 58. Interesting firsthand Mennonite accounts during the Chaco War can be found in *Kaputi Mennonita: arados y fusiles en la guerra del Chaco,* 2d ed. (n.p., 1976).

11.   Fretz, *Pilgrims*, pp. 38–48; Redekop, *Strangers*, pp. 102–104, 107.

12.   Fretz, *Pilgrims*, pp. 153–159; Redekop, *Strangers*, pp. 105–110; Peter Klassen, *Die Deutsch-völkische Zeit in der Kolonie Fernheim, Chaco, Paraguay, 1933–1945* (Bolanden-Weierhof: Mennonitischer Geschichtsverein, 1990), pp.105–106.

13.   Redekop, *Strangers*, pp. 106–123; Fretz, *Pilgrims*, pp. 88–95.

14.   *Censo y estudio de la población indígena del Paraguay 1981,* 1st ed. (Asunción: Instituto Paraguayo del Indígena, 1982), pp. 90–91.

15.   Wilmar Stahl, "Establecimientos agrícolas indígenas en el Chaco central: un estudio de cambio social guiado," *Suplemento Antropológico* 9:1–2 (1974), 112–121; *Los ayoreos, nuestros vecinos: a la misión del norte chaqueño*, David Hein, ed. (Asunción, 1990), p. 11.

16.   Miguel Chase-Sardi, Augusto Brun, and Miguel Angel Enciso, *Situación sociocultural, económica, jurídico-política actual de las comunidades indígenas en el Paraguay* (Asunción, 1990), pp. 84–86.

17.   Ibid., pp. 129–133.

9. Documents of Protestant Religious Missions to Latin America: Their Potential for Nonreligious Research

Karen Lindvall-Larson

My interest in Latin American missions grew out of my childhood as a "mission-ary kid" in El Salvador. As a Latin American Studies librarian I have watched with interest the recent increase in publishing on the history and growth of non–Roman Catholic Christian missions in Latin America. The impact of Protestantism in Latin America is evident in virtually every aspect of life, reflected in the hundreds of books and articles that have appeared in recent years. Increasing numbers of schol-ars are turning to the documents contained in mission archives for insights into all aspects of Latin American life. This paper (1) discusses mission records as sources of information on the communities where missionaries worked; (2) briefly outlines the history of these missions in Latin America; (3) describes the variety of mission archives available; and (4) provides some details on three missions to Latin America and the resources available for their study.

An excellent starting point for anyone planning to use mission records for research is the 1996 publication *Missionary Encounters: Sources and Issues.*[1] It presents research papers from the "Workshop on Missionary Archives" held at the School of Oriental and African Studies in London in July 1992. Discus-sions at this workshop responded to "practical issues about the location, acces-sibility and comprehensiveness of records, but also showed how such sources could be approached and used by scholars working in different disciplines with different aims."[2] The introduction makes the important point that "Reading mission archives and publications requires skills that differ from those used in the examination, translation and deconstruction of the official discourse of the colonial power."[3] The biases and often real strengths provided by this different world vision are described in the introduction and in many of the papers. The papers themselves provide models for using mission records to conduct research in a wide variety of fields including gender studies, anthropology, political sci-ence, education, and church history. While this book focuses on British Protes-tant missions in Africa and Asia, the research lessons learned are readily transferable to U.S. missions to Latin America.

Detailed histories trace the efforts of a variety of missions, in Latin America in general and in specific countries. A search under "Protestants" or

"Missions" subdivided geographically yields a wealth of information in major library catalogs and databases. *Tongues of Fire: The Explosion of Protestantism in Latin America* has an excellent bibliography.[4] It is also particularly useful because it includes references to the Latin American missions of the Mormons, Seventh-Day Adventists, and Jehovah's Witnesses, which are often excluded in works on Protestant missions, although the author believes their development has followed similar patterns. *Coming of Age: Protestantism in Contemporary Latin America* provides a sample of the range of topics currently being researched.[5] For the purposes of this paper, I found Roger S. Greenway's "Protestant Mission Activity in Latin America" useful.[6] It provides a succinct history beginning in the early nineteenth century and describes seven successive (and overlapping) waves of activity, each with its own particular evangelistic strategies and results.[7] They are (1) Bible distribution and translation; (2) missions to the Indians; (3) Protestant immigrants; (4) mainline Protestant churches; (5) faith missions; (6) Pentecostalism; and (7) electronic media. Greenway describes each wave, giving a social, historical, and political structure for each that is useful for scholars seeking to understand the mission records generated for each period.

Locating mission archives has become easier in recent years. In addition to consulting the reference tool *Subject Collections*[8] under the terms "missionaries" or "missions," one can also locate information on the World Wide Web. The Moravian Church, which first sent missionaries to the Caribbean in the 1700s and has a major presence in Honduras and Nicaragua, has a Web site.[9] The Summer Institute of Linguistics Web site includes a wealth of information on its activities.[10] The Archives of the Billy Graham Center at Wheaton College contain materials on the efforts of North American Protestant evangelicals throughout the world, including interviews, papers of individuals, and records of organizations, including foreign mission boards.[11] The Archives homepage includes online guides to many of the collections. The Missionary Research Collection at the Burke Library of Union Theological Seminary includes "tens of thousands of books, pamphlets, periodicals, reports, minutes, archival materials, etc. . . . [which] constitutes an invaluable record of Protestant missionary activity throughout the world, and provides a fascinating array of materials related to the geographic, sociopolitical, religious, and cultural settings in which this activity occurred."[12] The *Dictionary Catalog of the Missionary Research Library* provides access to many of these, including indexing the more than 800 missionary magazines being received at the time of publication.[13] Another rich collection is the Day Missions Library, the Yale Divinity School Library's "collection of mission and Third World Christianity documentation."[14] I have listed here only a selection of the many missions-related sites on the World Wide Web.

In the last portion of this paper I briefly describe as examples of mission records the resources for research on the missionary activities in Latin America of three specific groups: the Church of Jesus Christ of Latter-day Saints, the Presbyterian Church in the U.S.A., and the Assemblies of God.

Missionaries of the Church of Jesus Christ of Latter-day Saints turned their attention toward Latin America in the nineteenth century; their efforts resulted in a Latin American church membership (as of January 1, 1997) of 760,000 in Mexico, 370,000 in Central America, 90,000 in the Caribbean, and 2,100,000 in South America.[15] F. LaMond Tullis's *Mormons in Mexico: The Dynamics of Faith and Culture* is a carefully documented history of the earliest missionary efforts.[16] His extensive use of church archives provides invaluable information on the variety of resources available. Mark Grover discusses those collections in "The Latin American Library Collections of the Mormon Church" and describes in detail the resources available.[17] He comments that these are particularly rich because a "significant aspect of Mormon doctrine and practice is an unusually heightened sense of its own history. This preoccupation with the past has resulted in an almost fastidious attention to the creation, maintenance, and preservation of both institutional and personal records."[18] He recommends the L.D.S. Church Archives in Salt Lake City, Utah, for research on Latin American missions because they include institutional records such as minutes of meetings, financial reports, historical summaries of individual units within the church, and statistical reports, in addition to personal papers, diaries, and recorded interviews.

With the publication on microfilm of its extensive archive of worldwide missionary correspondence and reports from 1833 to 1911, the Presbyterian Church in the U.S.A. has made available an enormous wealth of information on Protestant missions in Latin America.[19]

> The Presbyterian Church in the U.S.A.'s foreign missionary enterprise in the nineteenth century was responsible for the establishment of indigenous churches, a variety of educational facilities, hospitals, orphanages, seminaries, and other institutions, that reflected the church's educational, medical and evangelical ministry. . . . The vast majority of material is incoming correspondence from the mission field and outgoing correspondence from the Board headquarters. Other primary sources include: receipts of sale; inventories of supplies (food, tobacco, sundries, etc.); diary accounts, sermon manuscripts; minutes of board meetings; annual reports on mission work; and personal and field reports, including information on the number of newly organized churches, ordained ministers, and members, as well as on average attendance.[20]

The earliest letters are from Argentina (1854) and Brazil (1860), with later nineteenth-century reports from Chile, Colombia, Guatemala, Mexico, Peru, and

Venezuela. The calendar reel has a detailed description of each item indexed. Accounts include descriptions of daily life, political events, women's sewing circles, and interaction with political figures, and detailed accounts of slavery and its abolition in Brazil. There are many accounts of single females who served as Presbyterian missionaries in Latin America, mirroring similar participation by single women in other missions.

The Assemblies of God is the largest of all Protestant groups in Latin America,[21] with 17,422,758 members and adherents as of May 1997.[22] Gary B. McGee has published *This Gospel Shall Be Preached: A History and Theology of Assemblies of God Foreign Missions,* which gives a detailed picture of the goals and achievements of the Foreign Missions Department from its foundation through 1989.[23] Lusia Jeter de Walker has published *Siembra y cosecha: reseña histórica de las Asambleas de Dios,* a history of missions in Mexico, Central America, Argentina, Bolivia, Chile, Paraguay, Peru, and Uruguay.[24] Much of the information in her book is gleaned from missionary interviews and reports. The Archives of the Assemblies of God in Springfield, Missouri, is the repository of the personal papers of veteran missionaries from throughout Latin America and has a growing collection of recorded interviews.[25]

There is an interest within the various missions in preserving their rich histories in Latin America and throughout the world. We need to express to them our support for their efforts and our recognition of the importance both to their constituents and to the scholarly community of keeping records that document their many contributions to the countries in which their missionaries serve.

NOTES

1.   Robert A. Bickers and Rosemary Seton, eds., *Missionary Encounters: Sources and Issues* (Richmond: Curzon Press, 1996).

2.   Ibid., p. 2.

3.   Ibid., p. 3.

4.   David Martin, *Tongues of Fire: The Explosion of Protestantism in Latin America* (Oxford, UK; Cambridge, Mass.: Basil Blackwell, 1990).

5.   Daniel R. Miller, ed., *Coming of Age: Protestantism in Contemporary Latin America* (Lanham, Md.: University Press of America, 1994).

6.   Roger S. Greenway, "Protestant Mission Activity in Latin America," in Daniel R. Miller, ed., *Coming of Age: Protestantism in Contemporary Latin America* (Lanham, Md.: University Press of America, 1994), pp. 175–204.

7.   Ibid., p. 177.

8.   *Subject Collections* (New York: Bowker, 1993).

9.   http://www.moravian.org/

10.   http://www.sil.org/

11.   http://h-net2.msu.edu/~local/manuscripts/arch-digest.html

12.   http://www.uts.columbia.edu/lib_int.html

13. New York (City), Missionary Research Library, *Dictionary Catalog of the Missionary Research Library, New York,* 17 volumes (Boston: G. K. Hall, 1968).

14. http://www.library.yale.edu/div/missions.htm

15. http://www.lds.org/Global_Medial_Guide/Membership_Distribution.html

16. F. LaMond Tullis, *Mormons in Mexico: The Dynamics of Faith and Culture* (Logan: Utah State University Press, 1987).

17. Mark Grover, "The Latin American Library Collections of the Mormon Church: An Introductory Examination," in *Proceedings from the 37th Annual Meeting of the Rocky Mountain Council on Latin American Studies: February 2–4, 1989, Las Cruces, New Mexico* (Albuquerque: RMCLAS, 1991), pp. 143–149.

18. Ibid., p. 144

19. *Presbyterian Church in the U.S.A., Board of Foreign Missions Correspondence and Reports, 1833–1911* (Wilmington, Del.: Scholarly Resources, 1996).

20. *Presbyterian Church in the U.S.A., Board of Foreign Missions Correspondence and Reports, 1833–1911, Guide to the Scholarly Resources Microfilm Edition* (Wilmington, Del.: Scholarly Resources, 1996), p. 4.

21. Miller, *Coming of Age,* p. 189.

22. Noted in phone call to Assemblies of God Foreign Missions Department, May 7, 1997.

23. Gary B. McGee, *This Gospel Shall Be Preached: A History and Theology of Assemblies of God Foreign Missions* (Springfield, Mo.: Gospel Publishing House, 1986–1989).

24. Luisa Jeter de Walker, *Siembra y cosecha: reseña histórica de las Asambleas de Dios* (Deerfield, Fla.: Editorial Vida, 1990–1992).

25. Archives of the Assemblies of God, 1445 Boonville Avenue, Springfield, Missouri 65802–1894.

Religion in Mexico

10. Hacia una tipología de la participación política de los evangélicos mexicanos

Rubén Ruiz Guerra

La cuestión religiosa ha estado presente a lo largo de la historia de México. De una u otra manera, religión, iglesia y clero se han manifestado (y han tenido participación importante) en diferentes períodos y momentos definitorios en la conformación de este país. Por ello se podría decir, sin temor a equivocarse, que estudiar la construcción de México y de lo mexicano implica, necesariamente, enfrentar el problema de lo religioso, de sus características, de sus manifestaciones y de sus implicaciones. Curiosamente, hasta hace pocos años, el tema había sido abordado de una manera incompleta y sesgada. Incompleta porque se había dado énfasis al estudio de las relaciones entre la iglesia y el estado (una de las caras del asunto) dejando de lado otros elementos que son definitorios de la religiosidad, tales como creencias, formas de culto, implicaciones éticas de las creencias, etcétera. Sesgada porque, normalmente, esos estudios habían partido de la apología o el ataque de la iglesia institución y la religión institucionalizada.[1] De esta manera, la construcción de instrumentos útiles para comprender el fenómeno religioso como tal ha sido extremadamente difícil y tardía en comparación con el desarrollo de otros campos de estudio de las ciencias sociales en México.[2]

Un problema más para la cabal comprensión de la religiosidad ha sido, y esto opera para todos los países latinoamericanos, la visión totalizadora que permea su estudio. No es casual ni anecdótica la identificación de lo mexicano con lo católico. Desde los albores de la vida independiente del país hasta la actualidad se extiende una larga cadena de pronunciamientos hechos por religiosos, políticos y académicos en este sentido.[3] Esta actitud, por supuesto, plantea obstáculos para la comprensión de otra de las características del fenómeno religioso: su multitud de facetas. Esto afecta, por supuesto, la comprensión de las diferentes heterodoxias que se pueden presentar en el universo de lo cristiano (pensemos en los protestantismos) o en los mundos "árabe", judío o de las iglesias paracristianas. De esta manera, a pesar de que en México han existido iglesias protestantes por más de un siglo (la que reclama orígenes más remotos es la bautista, organizada en Monterrey, Nuevo León, en 1864), su comprensión como fenómeno integrante de la sociedad mexicana sólo se ha dado hasta muy recientemente.[4] Y todavía son frecuentes las descalificaciones públicas de las disidencias religiosas por parte de clérigos y de algunos académicos. Pero, además esto tiene repercusiones en la comprensión del mundo católico mexicano. Estudios de la religiosidad popular o de las religiosidades características de otros grupos sociales como los criollos en la época colonial (que es necesariamente la de la jerarquía de la iglesia) son más bien recientes. Y todo esto, como lo podemos imaginar, agrava los problemas para entender las características y el significado de estas expresiones de religiosidad.

Por lo que se refiere a nuestro tema, podríamos decir que, a pesar de que existe una larga lista de trabajos sobre historia del protestantismo mexicano, nuestro conocimiento del tema está "en pañales".[5] Y aquí parece reproducirse el mismo patrón de los estudios del catolicismo mexicano. Se ha avanzado al señalar algunas ideas acerca de su papel político, pero la historia de su religiosidad está todavía por hacerse.[6] Lo que habremos de intentar en este trabajo es, siguiendo la misma línea de interpretación fundamentalmente política, apuntar algunas hipótesis que permitan vincular formas de religiosidad con acciones políticas concretas. Buscamos, sí, identificar algunos comportamientos de los protestantes mexicanos y marcar sus continuidades y rupturas, pero intentamos encontrar en sus creencias y conceptos elementos que expliquen lo que muchas veces ha aparecido, y así ha sido interpretado, como comportamientos contradictorios o, al menos, paradójicos.

Hay evidencia suficiente para pensar que existen tres modalidades bien diferenciadas de comportamiento político protestante en México. Su gestación ha correspondido a diferentes momentos históricos del país, pero se han mantenido vigentes e interactuantes hasta la actualidad. Primero se dio una etapa de participación política por medio de la prédica y la práctica de valores, que alcanza su máxima expresión durante el siglo XIX, pero que se mantiene como denominador común de la presencia de las iglesias protestantes en la vida social del país. Luego se presentó una etapa de activa participación política individual, que es muy clara a partir de los últimos años del siglo XIX y que, con matices, también sigue presente hasta nuestros días. Y por último, se presenta una participación de tipo institucional que ha cobrado particular importancia durante los últimos cinco o seis años.

La primera modalidad surgió cuando todavía no existía, hablando en sentido estricto, un protestantismo mexicano,[7] y se deriva de las propuestas de transformación de la sociedad por parte de políticos ilustrados y liberales. Ésta, que podríamos denominar propuesta "reformadora",[8] nos habla de que los valores de la moral cristiana pueden, y deben, tener un correlato en la creación de una moral pública moderna. Desde esta perspectiva, hacer del hombre alguien responsable, respetuoso de la ley, participativo, educado, honesto, trabajador, ahorrativo y muchas cosas más, es posible a través de la práctica de un cierto tipo de religiosidad.[9]

En la América Latina del siglo XIX, el ejemplo más claro de esta posición tal vez haya sido el de Vicente Rocafuerte, quien es considerado uno de los "fundadores" de la nación ecuatoriana y que llegara a representar a México en Inglaterra.[10] Rocafuerte fue uno de los principales promotores de la idea de construir la modernidad en las sociedades latinoamericanas. Su propuesta de creación de una nación pasaba, entre otros aspectos, por la defensa de las instituciones republicanas, de la libertad de comercio y de empresa, y del fortalecimiento del estado sustentado en la vigencia de la ley. Para lograr todo esto proponía la creación de una moral social moderna. Piedra angular en este planteamiento fue su *Ensayo sobre la tolerancia religiosa*,[11] publicado originalmente en México en 1831. El trabajo, que tenía una buena dosis de crítica en contra del gobierno mexicano del momento, planteaba la necesidad de establecer la pluralidad en la sociedad. Uno de los instrumentos para ello, proponía Rocafuerte, debía ser la competencia de instituciones religiosas, lo que abriría posibilidades a la aceptación de las diferencias sociales. El principal resultado "social" (y no meramente "religioso") de esta apertura habría de ser un cambio en el hombre por medio de un proceso educativo. Capacidades como la lectura y la escritura, el conocimiento de los derechos y las obligaciones civiles, la interiorización de pautas de conducta y valores morales y la creación de nuevas actitudes económicas encontrarían, según este autor, el vehículo ideal en la competencia de las religiones. El tono del texto, y sus resultados prácticos (Rocafuerte fue juzgado —y finalmente absuelto— por delitos de imprenta), hacen pensar en que la posición de su autor era, por decir lo menos, favorable al protestantismo.[12]

Este planteamiento habría de tener continuidad a lo largo de todo el siglo XIX y se mantuvo vigente con enorme fuerza en el protestantismo mexicano hasta los años 1930. Además del momento ya descrito, esta actitud alcanzará manifestaciones muy importantes en 1856–1857, cuando surgió un intento de los liberales (que habían llegado al poder unos pocos años antes) para crear una iglesia nacional[13] y con el surgimiento de las iglesias evangélicas como tales a partir de 1870.

Estas nuevas organizaciones tenían un proyecto social y político claro. No se planteaban, de ninguna manera, un aislacionismo o el refugiarse de un mundo que les era hostil. Su idea era transformar al mundo, pero no por medio de una prédica que implicara una política específica, sino como resultado de un cambio en los valores de la gente por medio de la educación. Este cambio incluía, sí, el conocimiento de los derechos y de las obligaciones del individuo, el cultivo de valores democráticos, republicanos y federalistas y otros meramente políticos, pero estaba sustentado en un cambio de ciertos elementos fundamentales que otorgaban seguridades a los individuos que los asumían: la creencia en un Dios personal que no necesita de intermediarios para manifestar su amor por el individuo; la existencia de mecanismos accesibles sencillos para vincularse con la divinidad, tales como la lectura de la Biblia; la posibilidad de ejercitar las capacidades intelectuales y aplicarlas a la experiencia religiosa por medio de ejercicio del libre examen; la eliminación de clericalismo y sus posibles demandas pecuniarias elevadas; la buena administración de los bienes que Dios entrega al hombre, etcétera.

Quienes optaban por este camino optaban por ser diferentes en lo religioso. Y lo hacían proponiendo, a la vez, un nuevo modelo de hacer política, adoptando principios políticos modernos. Su propuesta descansaba, entre otras cosas, en el principio de la separación de la iglesia y el estado. Para ellos no era lo mismo predicar que hacer política. Ejemplo claro de esto fue la posición del predicador Emilio Fuentes y Betancourt, liberal cubano exilado en México, quien fuera pastor (y hasta director del seminario y de la publicación periódica de los metodistas mexicanos), quien como editorialista de *El Monitor Republicano* (tal vez el diario liberal más importante del México decimonónico) criticaba algunas medidas administrativas del gobierno de Manuel González, pero que en ese mismo lugar sostenía que no se debía hacer del púlpito una tribuna política. Una cosa se debe hacer notar, Fuentes y Betancourt sí buscaba hacer del diario liberal un instrumento para comunicar sus convicciones relativas a la búsqueda de una nueva manera de hacer política, una manera permeada de sus valores que tenían que ver con el mundo de lo religioso, tales como la honestidad y la responsabilidad.[14]

Este tipo de actitudes, aunado al contexto social del cual surgieron las bases de los grupos protestantes de entonces (sectores sociales en transición ubicados en los estratos bajos y medios de la sociedad), produjo algunas manifestaciones políticas significativas dentro del protestantismo mexicano.[15] Cabría señalar que esas manifestaciones se dieron a título personal y marcando una separación clara entre filiación religiosa y participación política activa, lo que generó lo que podríamos calificar como un segundo tipo de participación protestante en la vida política del país.

Estas manifestaciones se dieron de una manera muy clara en la lucha revolucionaria de 1910–1920. Si bien es cierto que un número significativo de protestantes, particularmente pastores y aun ministros extranjeros, se involucró en los hechos que convulsionaban al país, los dirigentes de las iglesias, a pesar de tener simpatías por el movimiento armado, marcaron claramente que participaban a título personal, y en ciertos momentos se dio el caso de negar pasados y militancias protestantes.[16] De esta manera, la memoria histórica nos habla de la participación de protestantes como Pedro Flores Valderrama, Benjamín N. Velasco, Victoriano D. Báez, Pascual Orozco, Ignacio Gutiérrez, Aarón y Moisés Sáenz, etcétera, no del papel de la iglesia presbiteriana, o de los bautistas o del metodismo en la lucha. La participación se daba, pues, a título individual, pero estaba permeada de valores que se habían adoptado conscientemente al realizar el acto de "conversión". De esta manera, se trataba de llevar al ámbito de lo social y con un lenguaje "laico", aquello que se había experimentado en el nivel de lo personal por medio de la experiencia religiosa.

Este modelo de participación sigue siendo vigente hasta nuestros días aunque con algún matiz que puede ser importante. Muchos de esos revolucionarios protestantes se identificaron con los "gobiernos de la revolución" y participaron en ellos. Los dirigentes de los grupos protestantes también se sintieron identificados con una "revolución hecha gobierno" que negaba personalidad jurídica a las iglesias. Así, mientras se llegó a presentar un clima de conflicto, que condujo a una guerra religiosa (la de los cristeros) entre católicos y gobierno, los protestantes pudieron pasar el momento sin demasiados problemas. Una vez que los gobiernos posrevolucionarios se acercaron a la iglesia católica, la situación de los protestantes se hizo más endeble, al grado de tener que enfrentar épocas de marcada intolerancia tanto religiosa como social durante los años 40 y 50. En estas condiciones, los grupos protestantes, extremadamente pequeños en términos numéricos, se encerraron en sí mismos y buscaron protección en el estado, quien lo más que les ofreció fue un nivel mínimo de tolerancia. Cobraron entonces un papel significativo los vínculos que se habían podido construir con aquellos individuos que se habían incorporado al aparato estatal. Para los evangélicos se hizo más importante el estado que en alguna medida les garantizaba la existencia y los individuos que podían hacer efectiva esa garantía. Los protestantes dieron relevancia a figuras como Tomasa Valdés de Alemán, madre del presidente Miguel Alemán (1946–1952), la cual era una "simpatizante" metodista, o Eva Sámano, esposa del presidente Adolfo López Mateos (1958–1964), de familia presbiteriana y educada en una escuela de la misma denominación, quienes podían servir como intermediarios entre "los protestantes" y el estado. Dentro de este mismo esquema se fue formando una nueva generación de "políticos evangélicos", gente que seguía las mismas vías de incorporación al aparato del estado que cualquiera otra persona en el país, pero que, circunstancialmente, pertenecían a algún grupo evangélico. Esta generación había aprendido muy bien aquella idea de la separación de la iglesia y el estado. Lo religioso (y algunos de ellos lo eran profundamente) estaba en su vida privada y el quehacer político en la vida pública.

Este conjunto de actitudes produjo lo que se ha interpretado como una posición apolítica y de apoyo incondicional al estado.[17] El protestantismo, desde esta perspectiva, había sufrido mutaciones. De una vocación inicial de participación y/o crítica, se había pasado a encerrarse en sí mismo y a buscar apoyo en el gobierno. Con el paso de los años, el desgaste del modelo económico y político de los regímenes posrevolucionarios, el surgimiento de nuevas generaciones protestantes y un incremento significativo de éstos en términos numéricos, esta postura varió un poco. Empezaron a surgir nuevos individuos con ideas de participación política que ya no era ni necesariamente acrítica al sistema y que tampoco buscaba "encerrar" sus valores religiosos en su vida privada. Se dio, entonces, el surgimiento de políticos como Humberto Rice, perteneciente a una familia congregacional importante, quien llegara a ser secretario general del Partido Acción Nacional, ubicado a la derecha del espectro político, o como Evangelina Corona, lideresa del primer sindicato mexicano de costureras, quien llegara a ocupar una diputación por el Partido de la Revolución Democrática, de centro-izquierda, ambas las principales fuerzas de oposición al partido dominante. Esta nueva generación ya habla abiertamente de la necesidad de llevar sus valores, los evangélicos, al mundo de la política, pero actuando, siempre, bajo el esquema de participación individual.

Con los cambios en la relación iglesia-estado cristalizados en la reforma a la constitución mexicana y la creación de la Ley Reglamentaria de Asociaciones Religiosas y Culto Público, hechas en 1992, la participación política de los protestantes ha variado.[18] En primer lugar las iglesias han recuperado personalidad jurídica y, con ella, presencia pública. En segundo lugar, el estado les ha reconocido representatividad social y, con ella, calidad de interlocutores. En tercer lugar, al percibir estos cambios, ellas se saben con legitimidad y, por lo tanto, con la capacidad de expresarse públicamente. Esto ha dado origen a una nueva forma de participación política protestante, que para las generaciones actuales había sido desconocida: la institucional. Ya las iglesias protestantes, que han crecido en número y en presencia social de manera significativa,[19] se sienten habilitadas para hacer pronunciamientos públicos; ya el estado ha establecido mecanismos para comunicarse y entenderse con ellas; ya han surgido organizaciones paraeclesiásticas que se presentan como voceras de hasta "17 millones de evangélicos mexicanos", y son escuchadas; ya se ha llegado a plantear la conveniencia de crear un partido político evangélico.

Esta situación es, a primera vista, inédita. Y en muchos sentidos lo es. Nunca en la historia del protestantismo mexicano sus organizaciones se habían sentido facultadas para expresar públicamente su manera de comprender la realidad. Nunca como ahora estos grupos habían sido interlocutores del poder. Pero no podríamos decir con igual certeza que no hubieran existido intentos de participar institucionalmente en la vida política de la nación. Justamente a raíz de la participación protestante en la revolución mexicana y en otros procesos de magnitud similar en el resto de América Latina, y ante el proceso de construcción de los nuevos estados allá por los años 20, el protestantismo latinoamericano se planteó la necesidad, la posibilidad —y un proyecto para hacerla real—, de participar en la conformación de estos países.

El instrumento para realizar esta tarea fue el Consejo de Cooperación en América Latina (CCAL), organismo interdenominacional encabezado por un misionero que trabajara en México durante la revolución: Samuel Guy Inman. El proyecto partía de varias ideas fundamentales: era necesario que el protestantismo "tomara carta de naturalización" en Latinoamérica; ya existían cuadros e infraestructura significativas que podían ser aprovechadas para dar una nueva proyección al protestantismo en la región; los resultados de los trabajos anteriores, si bien reconocibles, no eran ni con mucho los deseados ni los deseables. Se trataba, sin embargo, de dar un nuevo lenguaje laico a preocupaciones religiosas. No se trataba, solamente, de evangelizar. Se intentaba hacer que los valores sociales del evangelio permearan la sociedad toda, aunque no fueran nombrados como tales. Se buscó, entonces, "formar el carácter" de estas naciones. El mecanismo considerado idóneo para realizar esta tarea fue la educación. La racionalización de los recursos ya existentes, la creación de circuitos educativos y la transmisión de ideas y valores fueron las tareas a emprender. Tal vez el ejemplo máximo de este esfuerzo fue la publicación de *La Nueva Democracia*, una revista mensual que sirvió de instrumento de comunicación entre muchos y muy diversos elementos de la intelectualidad latinoamericana de la época, y que viera su "edad de oro" durante los años 20 y 30.

El intento tuvo resultados valiosos. Fue, fundamentalmente, un buen espacio para el debate intelectual y la promoción de buenas relaciones entre los países americanos. Y resultó en una mayor visibilidad política del protestantismo en la región. Esto llegó a tal grado en el caso mexicano, que los evangélicos llegaron a plantear de manera pública su ideal de nación. La consecuencia de tal actitud fue la desilusión de los que habiendo participado de una manera o de otra en la vida política del país y habiéndose mantenido vinculados activamente con sus iglesias, sintieron de su participación política.[20] Al revisar su actuación posterior da la impresión de que se sintieron "usados". Ilustrativo de esta actitud fue en este sentido el cambio de "tono" en los documentos del Consejo Nacional de Iglesias Evangélicas entre 1934 y 1938.[21]

Así, es cierto que el protestantismo sufrió mutaciones. Se convirtió en una minoría pasiva que si bien no desarrolló una acción concreta, consciente, de creación de valores políticos, sí sirvió para cultivar dos elementos fundamentales para construir una democracia. Primero, en una sociedad corporativa, que ha sido y sigue siendo corporativa, en general, en estas iglesias se ha mantenido una cultura de la participación y la responsabilidad individuales. No existe en estas iglesias, en lo político propiamente dicho, un comportamiento corporativo.[22] Segundo, en una sociedad que durante muchos años ha buscado su identidad en una imagen monolítica, borrando las diferencias existentes en su seno, la mera existencia de estas iglesias ha sido una defensa de los principios de la pluralidad y la tolerancia.[23]

Al mediar los años 60 y 70 se presentó una situación que es necesario señalar. Con el surgimiento de nuevas generaciones en el liderazgo protestante y con el impulso a ciertas teorías sociológicas, tales como la de la dependencia y su corolario en la teología de la liberación y el consecuente replanteamiento de "lo social" en el mundo cristiano, surgió en el seno de las iglesias protestantes históricas un movimiento que buscaba una mayor participación institucional en el mundo de la política. Las iglesias fueron sacudidas en buena medida por estos movimientos. No se puede decir que estos movimientos hayan tenido una base social importante al interior de las iglesias mismas, y su impacto ha quedado más bien circunscrito a algunos círculos de intelectuales vinculados con la religión que han desarrollado proyectos interesantes de concientización política.[24]

En la actualidad, como ya se dijo, encontramos una situación inédita: existen organizaciones protestantes que buscan hacerse presentes en el mundo de la política y no sólo en el mundo de lo religioso. De alguna manera buscan hacer oír su voz en asuntos que hasta hace poco tiempo ellas mismas habían considerado como ajeno. Me parece encontrar, al menos, dos tendencias en esta actitud. Una de ellas, la más notoria, es la de aquellos que se presentan como los voceros del mundo evangélico y que son reconocidos como interlocutores por el estado. Éstos, a pesar de que no parecen tener un sustento real y efectivo en "sus bases", se han pronunciado abiertamente en asuntos de interés público que no les atañen directa y necesariamente. La otra tendencia es la de aquellos dirigentes que tienen conciencia de que existen y que son legítimos y que, por lo tanto, tienen derecho a ser reconocidos como entidades sociales. Sus pronunciamientos se refieren más bien a cuestiones que les tocan directamente, tales como problemas de intolerancia.

Como hemos visto, la presencia política del protestantismo en México es algo que ya tiene larga historia y que presenta diferentes modalidades. Tal como hemos tratado de mostrar, han existido tres modelos diferentes de participación, pero todos ellos tienen como elementos fundamentales una recuperación del papel del individuo tanto en lo teológico como en lo social; en la búsqueda de la "exportación" de sus valores, del universo meramente religioso al social y político y en la adaptación de sus posturas políticas al contexto ideológico del momento, buscando siempre, y de alguna manera, la posibilidad de desarrollar su quehacer en la sociedad.

NOTAS

    1.   Mariano Cuevas, *Historia de la iglesia en México*, 3a. ed. (El Paso, Tex.: Revista Católica, 1928); Alfonso Toro, *La iglesia y el estado en México: estudio sobre conflictos entre el clero católico y los gobiernos mexicanos desde la independencia hasta nuestros días* (México: Talleres Gráficos de la Nación, 1927).

2. No habremos de abundar en este trabajo en las razones de este "retraso". Baste en este momento señalar que la "secularización" del pensamiento mexicano, producto del conflicto sostenido entre la iglesia y el estado en los años 50 y 60 del siglo pasado, y su recrudecimiento en los años 20 y 30 del actual, tiene mucho que ver en este asunto. Cfr. Rubén Ruiz Guerra, "Liberalismo y religión: una primera aproximación" (mecanoscrito). Ha sido en los últimos siete u ocho años que han aparecido textos fundamentales para el estudio del fenómeno religioso en México. Citamos, prácticamente al azar, algunos de los principales. En historia colonial, tal vez el campo de la historiografía mexicana, en general, que más desarrollo ha tenido, tenemos los textos de Oscar Mazín, *Entre dos majestades: el obispo y la iglesia del Gran Michoacán ante las reformas borbónicas, 1758–1772* (México: El Colegio de Michoacán, 1987); Antonio Rubial, *El convento agustino y la sociedad novohispana* (1533–1630) (México: Universidad Nacional Autónoma de México, Instituto de Investigaciones Históricas, 1989); William B. Taylor, *Magistrates of the Sacred: Priests and Parishioners in Eighteenth-Century Mexico* (Stanford: Stanford University Press, 1996). En estudios de caso que han sido muy importantes descubriendo temas y marcando metodología de trabajo se pueden citar: Jean Pierre Bastian, *Los disidentes* (México: Fondo de Cultura Económica, El Colegio de México, 1989); Manuel Ceballos, *El catolicismo social: un tercero en discordia* (México: El Colegio de México, 1991); Roberto Blancarte, *Historia de la iglesia católica en México* (México: Fondo de Cultura Económica, 1992).

3. Cfr. Rubén Ruiz Guerra, "Religiosidad, modernidad e identidad: algunas consideraciones a partir de la experiencia mexicana decimonónica", *Cuadernos Americanos* 70 (1998), 64–72. Para revisar algunos de los pronunciamientos académicos relevantes en este sentido véase Gilberto Giménez, *La iglesia católica y las sectas en reciprocidad de perspectivas* (México: CIESAS, 1989); Andrés Antonio Fábregas, *El estudio antropológico de la religión* (México: SEP/ Programa Cultural de las Fronteras, Consejo Nacional de Fomento Educativo, CIESAS, 1989).

4. Tal vez el aporte más interesante de los textos de Bastian sea que hacen ver el carácter endógeno de los protestantismos. Esto aparece por primera vez, paradójicamente, en Jean Pierre Bastian, "La penetración de las sociedades religiosas norteamericanas en México, 1872–1876", *Taller de Teología* (México) 14 (1984), p. 30, idea que cobre singular importancia en *Los disidentes*.

5. La historiografía sobre el tema ha sido pródiga en los últimos años. De un inicio algo "lento", marcado por la tesis doctoral de Deborah Jo Baldwin, "Variation within the Vanguard: Protestants and the Mexican Revolution" (Ph. D. diss., University of Chicago, 1979) y los trabajos de Bastian, contamos con los de María Eugenia Fuentes Bazán, "El metodismo en Tlaxcala" (Tesis de Licenciatura, Universidad Nacional Autónoma de México, Facultad de Filosofía y Letras, 1992); Abraham Téllez, "La introducción del protestantismo en México" (Tesis de Licenciatura, Universidad Nacional Autónoma de México, Facultad de Filosofía y Letras, 1987); Rodolfo Casillas, "Una nueva aurora para las utopías religiosas en México", *Cristianismo y Sociedad* (México); Carlos Mondragón, "Protestantismo, panamericanismo e identidad nacional, 1920–1950", en Roberto Blancarte (comp.), *Cultura e identidad nacional* (México: Fondo de Cultura Económica, 1994); Felipe Vázquez, *Protestantismo en Jalapa* (Jalapa: Universidad Veracruzana, 1993).

6. En un nivel inicial, para el caso mexicano, el único trabajo de este tipo es el de Rubén Ruiz Guerra, *Hombres nuevos: metodismo y modernización en México, 1873–1930* (México: Casa Unida de Publicaciones, 1992).

7. Con esto queremos decir una práctica religiosa que, fundamentada en tres principios básicos (sólo la gracia de Dios da la salvación, sólo la fe en Cristo la hace accesible al hombre y sólo existe la escritura como camino de comunicación entre el hombre y Dios), tiene una concreción en una estructura eclesial determinada.

8. Estamos conscientes de que hemos sustituido el término protestante por el de "reformador". Con ello hemos intentando ampliar el sentido de nuestro concepto, refiriéndonos

entonces a la búsqueda de una religiosidad "moderna" (algo que creemos está presente en la formación de las iglesias protestantes) al igual que en movimientos renovadores que han surgido desde el mismo siglo XVI al interior del catolicismo.

9. Una manera de interpretar esta posición, referida, claro está, al caso europeo, pero que proporciona un rico esquema interpretativo, es la que encontramos en Ernest Troeltsch, *El protestantismo y el mundo moderno* (México: Fondo de Cultura Económica, 1951).

10. Cfr. Rubén Ruiz Guerra, "Hacia una cultura de la tolerancia", en Leopoldo Zea, *La cultura latinoamericana* (México: Instituto Panamericano de Geografía e Historia, Fondo de Cultura Económica, en prensa).

11. Vicente Rocafuerte, *Las revoluciones en México: ensayo sobre la tolerancia religiosa* (México, Bibliófilos Mexicanos, 1962).

12. En realidad el ecuatoriano era un católico practicante y devoto fiel de la Virgen del Rosario, aunque pugnaba por una racionalización de la práctica religiosa y por la vuelta al "verdadero espíritu evangélico".

13. Con frecuencia se cita una frase del Benemérito de las Américas, Benito Juárez, quien se dice aseveraba que los mexicanos debían hacerse protestantes para dejar de gastar sus ahorros en cirios y en fiestas religiosas y con ello hacerse ahorrativos. Por otro lado, Ignacio Manuel Altamirano, uno de los máximos exponentes del nacionalismo literario de esa época, nos plantea ese tipo de modernidad religiosa en su *Navidad en las montañas*. Fue en ese momento, a raíz de la promulgación de la Constitución liberal de 1857, que surgió un grupo religioso —que se separó de la iglesia católica— denominado de los Padres Constitucionalistas, organización que sería la matriz de las iglesias protestantes mexicanas que surgirán unos pocos años después. Cfr. Ricardo Pérez Montfort, "Nacionalismo, clero y religión durante la era de Juárez", en Laura Espejel López y Rubén Ruiz Guerra, *El protestantismo en México (1850–1940)* (México: Instituto Nacional de Antropología e Historia, 1995), pp. 39–76.

14. Cfr. "Emilio Fuentes y Betancourt, un liberal religioso en el México porfiriano", en *Quadrivium*, no. 7 (Toluca: Universidad Autónoma del Estado de México [UAEM], Centro de Investigación en Ciencias Sociales y Humanidades).

15. Son estas manifestaciones, precisamente, las que sirven a Bastian para estructurar su modelo explicativo. Este autor sostiene la hipótesis, que es la más difundida acerca del tema, de que los protestantismos de ese momento son el brazo religioso del liberalismo en la búsqueda de implantar su proyecto de nación. Cfr. Bastian, *Los disidentes,* particularmente pp. 213–262.

16. Véase, por ejemplo, *Actas de la vigésimo séptima Conferencia Anual de la Iglesia Metodista Episcopal en México, celebrada en el Templo Metodista de la ciudad de Orizaba del 23 al 27 de febrero de 1911. Publicadas por orden de la conferencia y aprobadas como el registro oficial de sus deliberaciones y acuerdos* (México: Imprenta Metodista Episcopal, 1911), p. 128.

17. Jean Pierre Bastian "Las mutaciones del protestantismo latinoamericano", en Tomás Gutiérrez Sánchez, *Protestantismo y cultura en América latina: visiones y perspectivas* (Quito: Cehila-Clai, 1994), pp. 115–135; Luis "Lindy" Scott, *Salt of the Earth: A Socio-Political Study of Mexico City Evangelical Protestants (1964–1991)* (México: Ed. Kyrios, 1991).

18. El estudio de la iglesia y la religión ha conocido un "boom" en los últimos años. Ya previo a estos cambios, habían salido al público textos fundamentales para el conocimiento del tema, pero la reforma constitucional propició un enorme número de publicaciones sobre el tema. Como ejemplo de ello citamos solamente Roberto J. Blancarte (coord.), *Religión, iglesias y democracia* (México: La Jornada Ediciones y Centro de Investigaciones Interdisciplinarias, UNAM, 1995).

19. En algunos municipios de la república, específicamente en el estado de Chiapas, los protestantes han alcanzado proporciones de más del 30 y del 40 por ciento de la población. Cfr. Rodolfo Casillas, "La prisa equívoca", *Este País* (México), no. 38 (mayo de 1994.)

20.   Tal vez el ejemplo más claro de esto sea el de Gonzalo Báez Camargo, quien de haber participado en la lucha armada (y ser condecorado por haber sido herido en campaña) y de defender activamente al gobierno de Calles al intentar explicar que no había persecución religiosa en México durante la Cristiada, llega a rechazar los medios directos de transformación de la sociedad y se centra más en transformaciones culturales que en acción política. Ciertamente, "don Gonzalo" continuó leyendo el "Pulso de los tiempos" hasta su muerte, pero su acción se ubica más como "intelectual" independiente que como "vocero" o "representante" de algún sector del protestantismo mexicano.

21.   Consejo Nacional de Iglesias Evangélicas.

22.   Mucho se habla de cacicazgos que negocian con el poder. El único estudio sobre la existencia de un "voto protestante" en México indica que no hay tal. El trabajo de Luis Scott, a pesar de algunos problemas metodológicos evidentes, muestra que los electores protestantes votan de acuerdo con los mismos patrones que el resto de la sociedad. Cfr. Scott, *Salt of the Earth*, pp. 72, 100.

23.   Carlos Monsiváis, "Cultura y minorías religiosas en México", ponencia presentada en el IIo. Encuentro Iglesias y Sociedad Mexicana, México, 13 de febrero de 1993. También "El protestantismo ha hecho progreso, pero todavía tiene zonas conservadoras, sostiene el escritor Carlos Monsiváis", *El Faro* (mayo–junio de 1994), pp. 81–83. Un análisis desde esta perspectiva en Rubén Ruiz Guerra, "Protestantismo y democracia en México: estudio de tres casos", en Blancarte (coord.), *Religión, iglesias y democracia.*

24.   Cfr. Raúl Macín, "Los protestantes y los movimientos populares", en *Religión y política en México* (México: Siglo XXI, 1985).

11. TESIUNAM: A Database for Supporting Scholarly Research in Religion

Filiberto Felipe Martínez-Arellano

The National Autonomous University of Mexico (UNAM) is the most important institution of higher education in Mexico. The university comprises 17 schools, in which over 250, 000 students are enrolled in undergraduate and graduate programs, along with 41 research institutes and centers.

At most Mexican higher education institutions, undergraduate and graduate students are required to complete a dissertation or thesis to receive their diploma. According to university regulations, all UNAM students must submit a copy of the dissertation to the Central Library. UNAM has created a database of these dissertations in CD-ROM format, called TESIUNAM (an acronym formed by the Spanish word for dissertation, *tesis,* and the initials of the university, UNAM). Now in its second edition (1997), the database includes over 240, 000 records covering the period 1914 to September 1996 and constitutes an important tool for supporting scholarly activities in different fields. In addition to UNAM, other Mexican universities, including El Colegio de México, Instituto Autónomo de México, and Universidad Pedagógica Nacional, also add dissertation records to the database. In total, dissertations from 311 undergraduate programs and 447 graduate programs are registered in TESIUNAM.

To aid scholarship in the field of religion, I analyzed the content of the database to identify the records dealing with Latin American religion. This paper presents the results of that analysis.

Features of the Database

TESIUNAM records include: author(s); dissertation title; place and date; number of pages; advisor; degree and major; university and school; record number; and call number.

The user can retrieve information by using one or several keywords in the following fields:

RANDOM (LIBRE): Retrieval by keyword searching
TITLE (TITULO): Retrieval by searching words in the title
AUTHOR (AUTOR): Retrieval by author(s) name
MAJOR (CARRERA): Retrieval by major field of study
DATE (AÑO): Retrieval by date of submission.
ADVISOR (ASESOR): Retrieval by name of supervising professor

CALL NUMBER (CLASIFICACION): Retrieval by local call number
RECORD NUMBER (MATRIZ): Retrieval by internal control number

These retrieval options can be used independently or in combination, and Boolean operators (*and*, *or*, and *not*) can be used in each case. Right truncation of words is performed by typing the sign $. The records retrieved can be printed or saved to a local file as a main card, a complete card catalog set, or a bibliographic record. Retrieved records can also be saved in ISO-ISIS format, which allows for the management of the data in the Microisis software, or SIABUC/ ASCII format which includes MARC tags. Other options are ISO2709 and LOGICAT formats.

Users may also access TESIUNAM on the World Wide Web by searching the OPAC of UNAM's General Direction for Libraries at <http:// www.dgbiblio.unam.mx/trihp.html>. Access points for retrieving information from the Web site are similar to the options available on the CD-ROM. There are three searching options:

(a)   author and title index;

(b)   random search of all indexes. The user can retrieve those records that include one word in all the fields integrating a record; search results can be limited by Boolean operators; word truncation is also possible;

(c)   keyword searches. Similar to the above option, a dissertation record may be retrieved by any word included in all the record fields.

Religion Searches

The richness of information included in the database and the variety of access points makes it an important resource for scholarly research. TESIUNAM contains useful information for scholars of Latin American religion. The main objective of this analysis was to determine the number of records dealing with religion. Several keywords were searched by using the RANDOM (LIBRE) option. Right truncation was used in most of the searches. Boolean operators, however, were not used since the objective was to find the greatest number of records. The keywords used in the searches were:

ATEISMO	DIOS$	JUDAISMO
ATEO$	DIVIN$	MARIA
BAUTIS$	ESCEPTICI$	MINISTRO$
BIBLIC$	ESPIRIT$	MISTIC$
BIEN	ETICA	MORAL
CANONICO	EVANGEL$	MORMON$
CATOLIC$	IGLESIA	PROTESTA$
CRIST$	JESUCRIS$	RACIONAL$
CULTO$	JESUS	RELIGIO$
		TEOLOG$

Table 1. Dissertations on Religion Recorded in the
TESIUNAM Database, by Keyword
(Number and Percentage)

Keyword	Number	Percentage
ATEISMO	2	0.2
ATEO$	1	0.1
BAUTIS$	11	1.2
BIBLIC$	1	1.0
BIEN	14	1.5
CANONICO	32	3.4
CATHOLIC$	68	7.2
CRIST$	68	7.2
CULTO$	29	3.1
DIOS$	33	3.5
DIVIN$	3	0.3
ESCEPTIC$	1	0.1
ESPIRIT$	74	7.8
ETICA	56	5.9
EVANGEL$	20	2.1
IGLESIA	173	18.3
JESUCRIS$	1	0.1
JESUS	13	1.4
JUDAISMO	1	0.1
MARIA	11	1.2
MINISTROS$	10	1.1
MISTIC$	13	1.4
MORAL	86	9.1
MORMON$	2	0.2
PROTESTA$	9	1.0
RACIONAL$	6	0.6
RELIGIO$	189	20.0
TEOLOG$	17	1.8
TOTAL	944	100.0

The search retrieved 944 records dealing with religion (see Table 1). Obviously, some records were retrieved in two different sets since they included two or more of those keywords. The largest number of records was retrieved by using the keywords RELIGIO$ and IGLESIA. Duplicate records were deleted. Table 2 shows that 42 percent of the records pertain to academic works submitted after 1990. Table 3 lists the dissertations according to university major. Almost a third of the dissertations were submitted by law students. The second largest group came from architecture. Mexican history suggests an explanation

Table 2. Dissertations on Religion Recorded in the
TESIUNAM Database, by Date
(Number and Percentage)

Date	Number	Percentage
Unknown	18	2.6
Before 1900	2	3.0
1900–1909	—	—
1910–1919	1	0.1
1920–1929	—	—
1930–1939	9	1.3
1940–1949	18	2.6
1950–1959	26	3.8
1960–1969	71	10.3
1970–1979	72	10.5
1980–1989	178	25.9
1990–	291	42.4
TOTAL	686	100.0

Table 3. Dissertations on Religion Recorded in the
TESIUNAM Database, by University Major
(Number and Percentage)

University Major	Number	Percentage
Architecture	130	19.0
Civil Engineering	18	2.6
Hispanic Language and Literature	14	2.0
History	56	8.2
Law	201	29.3
Pedagogy	14	2.0
Philosophy	101	14.7
Political Science and Public Administration	13	1.9
Psychology	19	1.9
Sociology	24	3.5
Other	96	3.5
TOTAL	686	100.0

for these results. Following his conquest of the Aztec empire, Hernán Cortés asked the sovereign of Spain, Juan Carlos I, for the right to evangelize the indigenous population. The evangelization was carried out by monks, not the clergy. The monastic brotherhoods built numerous churches and convents, accounting for the large number of studies of religious buildings.

In 1859 President Benito Juárez promulgated the Reform Laws, establishing the separation of church and state. Ecclesiastical goods were nationalized and the civil rights of the clergy restricted. The legal aspects of church-state relations and the civil rights of the clergy have been topics of controversy since that time and consequently the subject of numerous dissertations. Although most of the dissertations on religion are in the fields of architecture and law, a third group deals with philosophical aspects of religion.

TESIUNAM is a national database that supports scholarly research in diverse fields, including religion. Thanks to new electronic communications technologies and the Internet, religion scholars have access to an important database of dissertations in the field of religion emanating from Mexico's universities.

Religion in Brazil

12. The Use of Media by Jewish Communities in Brazil

Frida Garbati

The Jewish community in Brazil numbers approximately 200,000 persons. They live in São Paulo (90,000), Rio de Janeiro (60,000), and in small communities in the states of Rio Grande do Sul, Paraná, Minas Gerais, Bahia, Pernambuco, Pará, Amazonas, Rio Grande do Norte, Ceará, and Santa Catarina.

Jews have been in Brazil since its discovery, participating in the expedition of Pedro Alvares Cabral in 1500. The long arm of the Inquisition reached Brazil, persecuting Jews and sending them back to Portugal for trial. Jews also came with Prince Mauricio de Nassau, when the Dutch invaded Brazil's northeast region and established themselves in Recife between 1637 and 1644. Upon Nassau's expulsion, these Jews left and went north to New Amsterdam (New York).

The present Jewish community in Brazil developed from the beginning of the twentieth century, with mass immigration from Eastern Europe and later Holocaust survivors and other smaller groups, such as the Egyptians who came in 1956–1957 as a result of the Suez campaign. As they arrived, these newcomers slowly began organizing their community lives by establishing synagogues, financial aid and welfare programs, schools, and youth clubs. As the population grew, Jewish affinity groups formed based on communities, political parties, or even common ideology.

The thriving Jewish communities of Rio and São Paulo were concentrated in specific areas: Praça Onze in Rio and Bom Retiro in São Paulo. Today these are business areas, but in the 1920s they were both residential and commercial neighborhoods. A Jewish local press developed, which published some bilingual periodicals in Yiddish and Portuguese and others in only one language. They announced and described local events and social activities and opened their pages to debates between different ideologies. These titles were generally short-lived.

Serials

Rio de Janeiro's first monthly serial, *HaAmud, A Coluna: Órgão dos Interesses dos Israelitas no Brasil*, was published the first Friday of every month. The first issue (1916) stated the goals of the publication: "to explain, to clarify the ignorance about Jews and Judaism, present both in the press,

111

and in the population, in general; to correct these misconceptions, and to present the Jew as he is in his religious, social and political life." Only twelve issues were published.

In the 1920s several titles were published in Yiddish. In Rio de Janeiro, *Dos Iidische Vochenblat (O Semanário Israelita)* started in 1923, and in 1927 the title changed to *Brazilianer Iidische Presse (Imprensa Israelita Brasileira)*. In 1929, when journalist Aron Bergman purchased the publication, he changed the title to *Iidische Presse (Imprensa Israelita)*. The Portuguese title was *Diário Israelita* because it appeared five times a week and was sold at newsstands. It continued until the late 1980s. *Die Neie Velt (O Novo Mundo)* started in 1927. *Iidische Folkszeitung (Jornal Popular Israelita)* was published twice a week until Getúlio Vargas prohibited foreign-language publications during World War II. *Unzer Leben (Nossa Vida)* had a short life; only one issue and one special issue were published. *Kadima,* a handwritten and mimeographed periodical in Yiddish, was the house organ of the Kadima Youth Club, the first institution of its kind (1923). *Die Iugent (A Mocidade)* was published in 1928, as was *Die Onhoib (O Começo)*, a weekly of progressive Jews.

At the same time, other titles in Portuguese appeared: *Boletim do Azul-Branco Club* (1930) was the house organ of a youth club, Azul-Branco Club, the first organization to include both Ashkenazi and Sephardic members. Both *Illustração Israelita* and *Revista Israelita* circulated for short periods.

In the 1940s the following titles began publication: *A Voz Sionista* (1947), the house organ of the Brazilian Zionist Organization; *Aonde Vamos,* published by Aron Neuman; *Brazilianer Iidische Zeitung (Diário Israelita)*, published by Jacob Parnes and Milton Parnes; and *Jornal Israelita.*

Periodicals beginning in the 1950s and thereafter include *Menorah*, published by José Gomlevsky (1959); *Comentário*, published by Marcos Margulis; *Folha Israelita, Identidade,* and *Aleph* (1995).

São Paulo's first Jewish periodical, *Idiche Gezelschaftlicher und Naddels Bulletin (Boletim Social e Comercial Judaico)* appeared in 1928, issued by the organization Agudat Achim. It was followed by *Idische Velt (O Mundo Israelita)*; the *Folha da Manhã* in 1929 which had immigrant insertions; and *Folha Israelita,* in Yiddish. *São Paulo Iddische Zeitung (Jornal Judaico de São Paulo)* began in 1931 and continued until 1941, when foreign-language publications were prohibited by the Vargas regime. In 1932, *A Civilização* was published, followed by *Páginas Israelitas.*

During the 1940s two titles began publication: the weekly *Nossa Voz (Unzer Stimme)*, a bilingual publication representing the progressive group and lasting until the beginning of the military period (1964), and *Idische Press*, which later became *Der Naier Moment (O Novo Momento)* in 1950, appearing three times per week. In 1940 *Crônica Israelita* was published by Congregação

Israelita Paulista, becoming the precursor of *Resenha Judaica*, which is still published today. *Revista Brasil-Israel*, published by Bertha Wainer Kogan, continued until the early 1990s.

At present, the most important Jewish serials are published in São Paulo. Certainly the best title has been *Shalom,* which unfortunately was suspended in 1995. In its new phase, as a quarterly publication, each number pertained to a specific subject, such as Judeus da Bahia, A aventura sefaradi, and Golem. *Resenha Judaica* is undergoing changes as well. Oscar Nimitz, the former editor, is now the editor of the new *Tribuna Judaica. Sef@Rad Report* is the first Brazilian Jewish serial available on the Internet. Volume 3 of *Gerações/Brasil* was recently published and is also available on the Internet.

Other regions also had Jewish publications. Two titles were published in Porto Alegre as early as 1916: *Die Mentscheit (A Humanidade)* and *Die Kraft (A Força).* Manaus also had its Zionist-oriented *A Folha Israelita*, published by David José Israel during the 1940s and 1950s. In Curitiba, *O Macabeu* and *Jornal Israelita do Paraná* are published to date.

Television and Radio

In addition to print media, Jews started giving voice and face to their communities by broadcasting radio and television programs.

Programa Mosaico, in São Paulo, was broadcast from 1940 through 1982 and again from 1995 to the present. It was a daily, one-hour program, which included news from the Jewish Telegraph Agency, commentaries, traditional music, sports, cooking, medicine, and religious comments by rabbis. During World War II, it was a channel of communication for Holocaust survivors. Today it broadcasts 30 minutes a day, Monday through Friday, and includes news from Israel, traditional and modern Israeli music, and obituaries.

Rio has had several Jewish radio programs since the 1940s. *Seu Programa Israelita,* started by Jacob Parnes, began in 1941 at Rádio Club Fluminense and broadcasts three times a week. It was followed by *Hora Israelita Brasileira*, an hour-long program broadcast on Sundays by Parnes's son, Milton. *A Voz Israelita*, created by David Markus, aired daily in Yiddish from August 1955 until 1963 on Rádio Mundial. For a short period it was broadcast by Rádio Rio de Janeiro by Rádio Copacabana. When bomb threats were made against the radio station in 1981, the program was cancelled.

Porto Alegre has its *Hora Israelita* which dates to 1946. Curitiba started its *Hora Israelita do Paraná* in 1988. Directed by Ben Ami Saltz, the program includes interviews, local and Israel news, and Jewish traditional and Israeli music. Belo Horizonte recently began its *Hora Israelita.*

All previously mentioned radio programs before the 1980s were the result of individual initiative. But the bomb threat against Rádio Copacabana and the subsequent decision to remove *A Voz Israelita* from the station's schedule prompted the Jewish Federation of Rio (Federação Israelita do Estado do Rio de Janeiro, FIERJ) to take an active role in returning Jewish programming to the air.

The Federation elects a president every two years; all members of the community have the right to vote. Ronaldo Gomlevsky was elected president in 1984 on a platform to increase the political influence of the local Jewish community. Communication within the Jewish community and with the rest of society was a campaign issue. Gomlevsky's plans included publishing a weekly bulletin for all Jewish homes, reestablishing a radio program, and starting a television program. Within the first month of his chairmanship, *Diálogo em Comunidade* was aired, followed six months later by *Telex FIERJ* which reached 12,000 Jewish homes. The most significant innovation, *Comunidade na TV* (CNT), began broadcasting on November 4, 1985.

Diálogo em Comunidade was a 90-minute live radio program on Radio Bandeirantes, which aired between 1984 through 1988. Its programming ranged from interviews, debates, quizzes, music, and book reviews to a calendar of community events. FIERJ has a complete tape archive for this period. This was followed by *Som de Gerações* (1989–1990) and afterward by *Bom Dia Israel* (1990-91) on Rádio Imprensa. In 1992 the Jewish Federation, again under another period of Gomlevsky's leadership, broadcast five radio programs: *Diálogo em Comunidade* (same as the previous program), *Diálogo em Comunidade Musical* (music and schedule of events), *Debate em Comunidade* (live discussions on Brazilian social and political issues), *Diálogo na Noite* (live discussion with the Federation's president), and *Você Sabia Judaico* (information on Jews and Judaism and music).

These live programs had an important impact on the general population. They reached the Baixada Fluminense, a densely populated, lower-class area on the outskirts of Rio, where one finds much ignorance about Jews. The archives contain interesting correspondence from listeners. Again, these programs generally ceased with the election of the new president in 1994. The trend has once more reversed, and the emphasis is again on individual initiative. A new weekly program, *Shalom Israel,* produced by Shirley Nigri on Rádio Imprensa, is targeted at a young audience.

If radio gave a voice to the Jews, television gave them a face. The city of São Paulo was the pioneer of television programs. *Mosaico na TV* started in July 1961 and, according to the *Guiness Book of Records,* is the oldest Brazilian television program. Reaching an audience of 300,000 to 400,000, of mostly non-Jews, the program features news, interviews, music, contests, and commentaries by its director Francisco Gotthilf. Many well-known personalities have appeared on the program, such as David Ben-Gurion, Yitzhak

Rabin, Albert Sabin, Ed Koch (former mayor of New York City), Mikail Gorbachev, Pelé, and Brazilian president Fernando Henrique Cardoso. The program enjoys considerable credibility and is of interest to a non-Jewish audience because of its information on the Jewish people. At present it is broadcast every Sunday for 30 minutes on TV Gazeta/CNT.

Shalom, directed by Moyses Ackerman, was aired in the 1960s on TV Continental in Rio de Janeiro. *Shalom Brasil* began in 1995 as a 30-minute program in UHF (Rede Mulher) and now it is also available on cable TV for one hour on Sundays. The program includes Beit Chabad Rabbi Weitman in "The Rabbi Answers" and "Entrelinha," commentaries about Brazil and the world, interviews with prominent Jews in São Paulo, and Ashkenazi and Sephardic cookery. Since the program is received by parabolic antennas, it reaches all regions of Brazil. The director, Marcel Hollender, boasts about receiving a letter from a Jewish family in the state of Mato Grosso whose only link with Judaism is this program.

The Jewish Federation of Rio Grande do Sul has recently signed a contract with cable TV to start broadcasting a 30-minute program, *Kehila (Comunidade),* in June 1998.

Comunidade na TV (CTV) started as a 30-minute program, but within three months expanded to one hour on Sunday mornings on a commercial station and Tuesday evenings on cable TV. For the first time in Rio de Janeiro, it offers a continuous flow of information on Jewish traditions, values, religion, symbols, and customs. The telecast includes interviews with and information about Jewish intellectuals, artists, scholars, actors, writers, physicians, musicians, attorneys, politicians, sportsmen, and scientists—a virtual who's who. It also features information about the Federation's board meetings, events sponsored by Jewish organizations, Holocaust testimonies and observances, annual study missions to Israel, non-Jews (friends of the community), relations with black leadership, Israel, plays, exhibits, concerts, and Jewish cookery. Jewish holidays are always celebrated and explained, and Rabbis representing various movements provide a variety of points of view for the audience.

The practice of publicizing upcoming events and celebrations on television and showing them the following week when possible has led to a substantial increase in attendance at these events. The program also publicizes other information of interest such as free services offered by the Federation (an employment desk and distribution of medication for the needy) and promotes all six city Jewish schools at registration time.

Every two years, coinciding with the FIERJ elections, CTV is used for campaigning. Candidates for the Legislative Board have 30 seconds to introduce themselves and summarize their platform. Each candidate for the Executive is given three minutes every week until the election. This opportunity provides candidates with television time for as many as eight programs over a two-month period.

The Jewish Federation maintains copies of all programs in its video archive (PAL-M). An index will be compiled soon.

Comunidade na TV was created with the primary goal to open the Jewish community to Brazilian society. Jews have always been perceived as a closed, different group. It was time to bring down the walls by letting the general public into the Jewish community and openly discussing its history, issues, and special traditions and customs. This way Jews are seen as just another community, another segment of Brazilian society. The programs serve to diminish some of the ignorance that causes prejudice against Jews in Brazil.

A Hebrew proverb says, "There is no news under the sun" (Ein hadash tahat ha-shemesh). If we recall the goals of the first Jewish monthly published in Rio de Janeiro (1916), *HaAmud, A Coluna*, we see that Brazil still faces a similar situation of ignorance about Jews and Judaism. The hope is that a variety of television and radio programs in different cities will help make Jews better known and, most of all, understood and respected.

BIBLIOGRAPHY

Brumer, Anita. *Identidade em mudança: pesquisa sociológica sobre os judeus do Rio Grande do Sul.* Porto Alegre: Federação Israelita do Rio Grande do Sul, 1994.

Malamud, Samuel. *Do arquivo e da memória.* Rio de Janeiro: Bloch, 1983.

_____. *Documentário.* Rio de Janeiro: Imago Editora, 1992.

_____. *Recordando a Praça Onze.* Rio de Janeiro: Livraria Kosmos Editora, 1988.

Telex FIERJ. Various issues, 1985–1995.

Weltman, Henrique. *História dos judeus em São Paulo.* São Paulo: Expressão e Cultura, 1996.

Current Serials

Current serials published in the various Jewish communities in Brazil are listed below. The titles marked with a single asterisk are in the Library of Congress permanent collection and those marked with a double asterisk are part of Brazil's Popular Groups Microfilm Project. The frequency, when known, appears after the title. Most are house organs; others contain original articles and some translations, which vary from issue to issue of the same title. Telephone (T) and fax (F) numbers and e-mail (E) addresses are also included. All of the publications are distributed free of charge, unless a dollar amount appears at the end of citation.

The Abuhab's Family Newsletter (Irregular)
R. Capepuxis, 456
05452-030 São Paulo, SP
T: (011) 746-7732

Informa
Associação Israelita Brasileira
R. Rio Grande do Norte, 477
30130-130 Belo Horizonte, MG
T: (031) 224-2129

ASA: Judaísmo e Progressismo (Bimonthly)
Associação Scholem Aleichem
R. São Clemente, 15522600-001
Rio de Janeiro, RJ
T: (021) 246-1808
Also called *Boletim ASA.* Mostly original
articles and interviews covering Brazilian
social issues such as blacks, prejudice,
violence.

Beit Chabad (Monthly)
R. Chabad, 54/60
01417-030 São Paulo, SP
T: (011) 282-8711
F: 815-3805

Boletim Ar
Associação Religiosa Israelita
R. Gal. Severiano, 170
22290-040 Rio de Janeiro, RJ
T: (021) 295-6444
F: 542-6499

Boletim Informativo (Monthly)
Casa de Cultura Brasil-Israel
R. Novo Horizonte, 208
01244-020 São Paulo, SP
T: (011) 256-5155

Brasil-Israel: Parcerias e Perspectivas
(Annual)
Câmara Brasil-Israel de Comércio e Indústria
Av. Brig.Faria Lima, 1885/205
01463-900 São Paulo, SP
T: (011) 815-7788
F: 815-3653

Caderno Cultural Na'amat Brasil
Na'amat Brasil
Rua São Martinho, 48
01202-020 São Paulo, SP
T: (011) 67-5247

Chevra Kadisha Informa (Semiannual)
Rua Prates, 435
01121-000 São Paulo, SP
T. (011)228-9166
F: 229-1281

A Congregação
Religiosa Israelita
Rua General Severiano, 170
22290-040 Rio de Janeiro, RJ
T: (021) 295-6444
F: 542-6499

Corrente Wizo
WIZO
Rua Minas Gerais, 36
01244-010 São Paulo, SP
T: (011) 259-5264

Emda
R. Bahia, 408
01244-000 São Paulo, SP
T: 011-258-0741

O Estado da Sociedade (Irregular)
Universidade de São Paulo
Grupo de Pesquisa de Discriminação
Centro de Estudos Judaicos
R do Lago, 717 - Cidade Universitária
05508-900 São Paulo, SP
T/F: (011) 813-6528
Reports on discrimination in Brazil.

Fax FIERJ (Monthly)
Federação Israelita do Estado do Rio de
Janeiro
R. Buenos Aires, 68/15° andar
20070-020 Rio de Janeiro, RJ
T: (021) 242-4940
Formerly *Telex FIERJ*

FISESP Comunicação (Monthly)
Federação Israelita do Estado de São Paulo
R. Pinheiros, 498/5°
05422-000 São Paulo, SP
T: (011) 280-0111
F: 282-5785

Federação Israelita em Notícia
Federação Israelita do Estado do Rio Grande
do Sul
R. João Telles, 329
90035-121 Porto Alegre, RS
T: (051) 226-3256

Foco: Informativo Comunitário para as
Atualidades do Povo Judeu (Irregular)
Rio de Janeiro, RJ: Fundo Comunitário
Rua México, 90/7° andar
20031-141 Rio de Janeiro, RJ
T: (021) 532-4600

Folha Israelita Brasileira (Monthly)
Rua Prates, 209/103
01121-000 São Paulo, SP
T: (011) 228-3069

Gerações/Brasil (Quarterly)
Sociedade Brasileira de Genealogia Judaica
Rua Jardim Ivone, 17/23
041050- 020 São Paulo, SP
E: faiguen@ibm.net
http://www.lookup.com/homepages/82259/
sgjbpage.htm
Genealogy of Brazilian Jews and Brazilians of
Jewish descent, such as President Fernando
Henrique Cardoso.
Annual subscription $15

A Hebraica (Monthly)
Associação Brasileira A Hebraica
Rua Fidalga, 548/21
05432-000 São Paulo, SP
T: (011) 813-3068
F: 815-3805
Articles on club's history and activities; also
translations. Very good overview of Jewish
life in São Paulo.

O Hebreu (Monthly)
R. Cunha Gago, 158
05421-000 São Paulo, SP
T: (011) 870-1616
F: 816-1326
Annual subscription $ 50.00

Herança Judaica (Quarterly)
Editora B'nai B'rith
Rua Caçapava, 105
01448-010 São Paulo, SP
T: (011) 282-5844
Annual subscription $21.00

Hineini Comunidade Shalom (Monthly)
Rua Com. Zarzur, 568
04735-001 São Paulo, SP
T: (011) 247-2841

Iavnews (Irregular)
Colégio Iavne Beit Chinuch
Rua Pe. João Manuel, 727
01111-011 São Paulo, SP

Identidade (Bimonthly)
Renato Aizenman
Av. N.S. Copacabana, 1137/801
22070-010 Rio de Janeiro, RJ
T/F: (021) 287-1493 267-3290
E: identidade@ax.ibase.org.br
Translations from *The Jerusalem Report* and
Jerusalem Post. Some original articles by
Moacyr Scliar, Alberto Dines, Rabbi Nilton
Bonder, Gilberto Dimenstein, Boris Casoy.
Annual subscription $35

Informativo
Centro Israelita do Paraná
R. Mateus Leme, 1431
80530-010 Curitiba, PR
T: (041) 223-1380

Informativo Adolfo Bloch
Centro Cultural e Esportivo Adolfo Bloch
Av. Prof. Dulcidio Cardoso, 5000
22793-010 Rio de Janeiro, RJ
T: (021) 325-5111

Informativo CIB
Clube Israelita Brasileiro
R. Barata Ribeiro, 489
22040-000 Rio de Janeiro, RJ
T: (021) 257-1963

Informativo Shalom
Clube Monte Sinai
Rua. S.Francisco Xavier, 104
20550-012 Rio de Janeiro, RJ
T: (021) 284-9812

Informe B'nai B'rith (Monthly)
Editora B'nai B'rith
Rua Caçapava, 105
01448-010 São Paulo, SP
T: (011) 258-5844

Integração CONIB (Monthly)
Confederação Israelita do Brasil
Rua Consolação, 2223/81
01301-000 São Paulo, SP
T: (011) 258-8972
F: 258-6094
Reports on Jewish State Federations of Brazil.

Intercâmbio (Bimonthly)
Câmara Brasil-Israel de Comércio e Indústria
Av. Brig. Faria Lima, 1885
01463-900 São Paulo, SP
T: (011) 816-2912

*Israel: Revista de Atualidades Culturais,
Empresariais e Científicas* (Monthly)
R. Brig. Tobias, 118/3323
01032-000 São Paulo, SP
T: (011) 228-8760
E: cordeiro@originet.com.br
Annual subscription $55

*Jornal Israelita do Paraná: A Serviço da
Comunidade* (Monthly)
Editora Jornal Israelita do Paraná
Av. Cândido de Abre, 427/910
80530-903 Curitiba, PR
T: (041) 254-8155
E: yshuv@mps.com.br

Jornalik
Colégio Bialik
R. Simão Alvares, 680
05417-020 São Paulo, SP
T: (011) 816-7111

Judaísmo & Cultura: Kulanu
Caixa Postal 13818
01216-970 São Paulo, SP
E: http://www.net-ten.com.br/judaismo/

Kol News (Quarterly; internal distribution
only)
Divisão Feminina do Fundo Comunitário
R. Caçapava, 105/2°
01448-010 São Paulo, SP

*O Macabeu: Órgão Oficial da Comunidade
Israelita do Paraná* (Quarterly)
Federação Israelita do Paraná
R. Mateus Leme, 1431
80530-010 Curitiba, PR
T: (041) 338-7575

Max Nordau News
Colégio Hebrew Brasileiro Max Nordau
R. Prudente de Moraes, 1172
22040-042 Rio de Janeiro, RJ
T: (021) 287-1743

Menorah (Monthly)
Editora Menorah
Rua da Assembléia, 40/9°
20011-060 Rio de Janeiro, RJ
T: (021) 232-5889
Annual subscription $50

Morasha (Quarterly)
Congregação e Beneficência Sefardi Paulista
R. Dr. Veiga Filho. 547
01229-000 São Paulo, SP
E: morasha@ams.com.br
Most articles are translations and reports on
congregation's activities.

Nascente (Bimonthly)
Rua São Vicente de Paula, 276
01229-010 São Paulo, SP
T/F: (011) 826-7699

Pardes (Irregular)
Congregação Judaica Brasileira
Rua Prof,. Milward, 65
22611-070 Rio de Janeiro, RJ
T: (021) 493-5735

Peretz Informativo (Bimonthly)
Colégio I. L. Peretz
Rua Madre Cabrini, 175
04020-000 São Paulo, SP
T: (011) 5745-0131

Press Aleph (Bimonthly)
MW Comunicação Empresarial
R. Sen.Dantas, 75/2404
20031-201 Rio de Janeiro, RJ
T: (021) 232-7292
F: 252-0577
From n. 1-5, called *Aleph*. Rio de Janeiro
community activities.

Relatório Trienal
Congregação Israelita Paulista
R. Antonio Carlos, 653
01309-011 São Paulo, SP
T: (011) 256-7811

Renascença
Colégio Renascença
R. São Vicente de Paula, 659
04020-000 São Paulo, SP
T: (011) 824-0788

Resenha Judaica (Biweekly)
Empresa Jornalística Resenha Judaica Ltda.
R. Antonio Carlos, 582/5°
01309-001 São Paulo, SP
T: (011) 251-1351
F: 255-2806
Emphasis on São Paulo community; has
international correspondents.
Annual subscription $36

Sef@Rad Report (Bimonthly)
E: Sefarad@stbnet.com.br<http://
www.stbnet.com.br/hpf/sefarad>

Bilingual (Portuguese-English); the first
online Brazilian Jewish publication. First two
issues deal with Marranos and cryptojudaism;
contains book reviews.
Annual subscription $18 (Brazil); $25 (other
countries)

Tribuna Judaica (Two issues per month)
Nimitz & Rechtman Editores Ltda.
T. Tanabi, 299
05002-020 São Paulo, SP
T: (011) 871-3234
F: 3675-0072
E: tjudaica@uol.com.br
Annual subscription $36

UNIBES Informa
UNIBES
R. Rodolfo Miranda, 287
01121-010 São Paulo, SP
T: (011) 230-7300

WIZO Flash (Monthly)
WIZO
R. Minas Gerais, 36
01224-010 São Paulo, SP
T: (011) 256-3099

Television Programs

(As of June 1997)

Comunidade na TV (1985–)
Rio de Janeiro: Federação Israelita do Estado
do Rio de Janeiro
Sunday/Tuesday.
Sunday: CNT 9:00 a.m.-10:00 a.m.; Tuesday:
NET Cable TV 9:00 p.m.-10:00 p.m.

Kehila (1997–)
Porto Alegre: Federação Israelita do Rio
Grande do Sul
Weekly: Cable TV

Mosaico na TV (1961–)
São Paulo: Francisco Gotthilf, Director
Sunday: TV Gazeta: 1:00 p.m.–1:30 p.m.

Shalom Brasil (1995–)
São Paulo: Marcel Hollender, Director
Sunday: TV Mulher/NET cable TV:
7:00 p.m.–8:00 p.m.

Radio Programs

Hora Israelita (1948–)
Porto Alegre, RS: José Alpern, Director
Sunday. 1 ½ hours

A Hora Israelita (1997–)
Belo Horizonte, MG: Associação Israelita
Brasileira, Cláudio Rawicz, director
Sunday. Rádio Metropolitana

Hora Israelita do Paraná (1988–)
Curitiba, PR: Ben Ami Saltz, Director
Sunday, 1 hour

Mosaico no Rádio (1940–1982; 1995–)
São Paulo: Francisco Gotthilf, Director
Daily. (From 1940–1982 on Radio América
called *Hora Israelita*; thereafter *Programa
Mosaico*; 1995– Rádio Mundial; one-half
hour)

Shalom Israel (1997–)
Rio de Janeiro: Shirley Nigri, Director
E: shirley@infolink.com.br
Friday, one hour. Rádio Imprensa

13. A religião dos pioneiros norte-americanos no Brasil

Sonia T. Dias Gonçalves da Silva

Muito pouco se escreveu até hoje, tanto nos Estados Unidos como no Brasil, a respeito da imigração dos sulistas norte-americanos para o Brasil, logo após a Guerra Civil (1861–1865).

A escassez de publicações sobre esse assunto é sentida por historiadores dos dois países, como Eugene Harter, Vianna Moog e José Arthur Rios, pois nenhum livro foi publicado antes de 1960 especialmente sobre essa saída dos Confederados para formarem colônias em terras brasileiras. Coube a uma descendente direta de um dos pioneiros na região de Santa Bárbara, Judith MacNight Jones, resgatar a história oral e documentos para escrever e publicar, no Brasil, o livro *Soldado, descansa!* verdadeira bíblia sobre os primórdios dessa gente à procura de um novo lar em terras distantes.

Nem mesmo se sabe o número exato de sulistas que entraram no Brasil, divergindo esses dados entre 2.000 a 8.000 pessoas e alguns autores afirmando serem até 20.000 emigrados.

Histórico

A Guerra de Secessão castigou os Estados Unidos de 1861 a 1865. Segundo o historiador do protestantismo brasileiro, Émile-G. Léonard, não foi propriamente uma guerra civil, mas a oposição de duas civilizações e duas concepções de vida, com o triunfo de uma, industrial, sobre a outra, agrícola, e consequências sobre parte do mundo. Um reflexo dessas consequências aconteceu no Brasil, que passou a dever parte de seu desenvolvimento à vinda dos Confederados inconformados.

Enquanto o sul sofria os estragos da guerra, presenciando a invasão e o saque dos "carpetbaggers" e entrava na era da Reconstrução, algumas famílias Confederadas, desorientadas com a perda de suas terras e seus bens, pensavam em abandonar seus lares violados e emigrar para a América Latina. Tentativas são registradas pela história com saídas de sulistas para o México, América Central (Honduras e British Honduras) e América do Sul (Venezuela e Guiana).

Nessa época o Brasil passava por um período de progresso, após a vitória na guerra com o Paraguai e com a consolidação do espírito nacional. Também intensificou-se o movimento liberal na vida política, literária, religiosa e social. A liberalidade havia se iniciado com a vinda de Dom João VI e toda a Família Real, de Portugal para o Brasil, fugindo das tropas de Napoleão Bonaparte que ameaçavam invadir Portugal, em 1808. Com a elevação do Brasil a Reino Unido, deu-se a abertura dos portos e isso foi uma brecha para que estrangeiros, que ao país viessem ou que estivessem de passagem, pudessem praticar seus cultos.

O momento político era favorável a imigração devidos aos movimentos para a libertação dos negros escravos. Quando tal acontecesse já se antevia a escassez de mão-de-obra na lavoura. Havia, ainda, no Brasil, grupos interessados na vinda dos norte-americanos sulistas, como as autoridades ligadas à agricultura, que viam neles a possibilidade de viabilizar a cultura do algodão introduzindo novas técnicas de plantio. A oferta desse produto estava escassa no mercado mundial, porque, os Estados Unidos, grande plantador, teve as terras do sul saqueadas e incendiadas, ocasionando um declínio na produção mundial.

A imigração foi proporcionada por agentes estadunidenses—os mesmos que trataram da colonização do Oeste e pelo governo brasileiro, que abriu agências em New York e New Orleans para atender aos que quisessem emigrar. Os agentes eram intermediários entre os emigrados e os órgãos oficiais e o governo dava as passagens de navio e uma carta de apresentação. Agentes de emigração vieram ao Brasil para conhecerem as terras e condições do país. As levas de sulistas começaram a chegar em 1865 e continuaram até 1871. O auge foi no período de 1867 a 1868 e vieram entre 5.000 e 8.000 pessoas, alguns através de agência e outros por sua própria conta. Vinham profissionais liberais (dentistas, médicos, advogados, contadores), agricultores, aristocratas, pessoas da classe média, pobres, aventureiros e até mesmo 3 escravos e não somente sulistas, mas também "yankees" e europeus naturalizados norte-americanos. Ter a posse da terra por compra ou arrendamento era "conditio sine qua non" para o estabelecimento deles no Brasil. Procediam dos estados do Alabama, Georgia, Texas, Louisiana, South Carolina, Ohio, Virginia, Mississippi e Florida.

Foram formadas 7 colônias no Brasil, a saber (Figura 1):

— Em Santarém, no estado do Pará, região Amazônica, liderada pelo Major Langsford Hastings;

— Em Paranaguá, litoral do estado do Paraná, comandada pelo Doutor John Blue;

— No Lago Juparanã, no Rio Doce, no estado do Espírito Santo, encabeçada por Charles Gunter;

— Três colônias no Vale do Ribeira de Iguape, no litoral sul do estado de São Paulo, ao longo dos rios Itariri, Juquiá e Azeite, entre as cidades de Juquiá e Xiririca, lideradas pelo Reverendo Ballard Dunn, junto com os Coronéis Frank McMullan, William Bowen e Doutor James Gaston;

— Em Santa Bárbara, no interior do estado de São Paulo, única de caráter particular, cujas primeiras terras foram adquiridas pelo Coronel William Norris, que lá esteve em 1865, para conhecimento.

Figura 1. Colônias de americanos no Brasil na década de 60

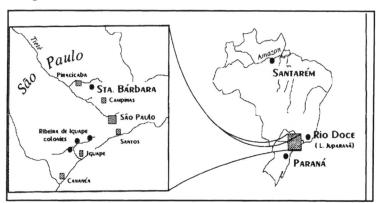

Fonte: C. B. Dawsey e J. M. Dawsey, *The Confederados: Old South Immigrants in Brazil* (Tuscaloosa: University of Alabama Press, 1995), p. 19.

Todas as 6 primeiramente citadas sucumbiram entre 1867 e 1869, quer pela morte de seu líder, como aconteceu em Santarém, quer pela dispersão ou mudança de seus membros para os centros urbanos mais próximos. As causas do fracasso, em geral, podem ser atribuídas ao isolamento dos colonos que viviam distantes dos centros urbanos, à falta de estradas para escoar a produção agrícola e demais infra-estrutura necessária, que o governo brasileiro prometeu fazer e não cumpriu.

A única colônia, de caráter particular, que progrediu foi a de Santa Bárbara, porque os sulistas trouxeram dinheiro e ouro e o local já era dotado de transporte, devido à economia cafeeira e estava situado bem próximo do centro urbano.

Muitos dos remanescentes das colônias fracassadas vieram juntar-se à família Norris em Santa Bárbara, fazendo esse núcleo ficar bem povoado.

A Vila de Santa Bárbara dos Toledos, hoje Santa Bárbara d'Oeste, situada a noroeste da cidade de São Paulo, entre Campinas e Vila Nova Constituição (hoje Piracicaba), distava 136 km da capital do estado. Sua economia baseava-se na agricultura, principalmente no plantio da cana-de-açúcar e na fabricação de seu derivado, a aguardente (conhecida também por cachaça ou pinga).

As regiões circunvizinhas de Campinas tinham as melhores terras, seu preço era acessível e contava com razoáveis meios de comunicação. A estrada de ferro que partia do porto de Santos chegava até a cidade de Jundiaí e esta distava 45 km de Campinas.

Cerca de 100 famílias se estabeleceram, entre os anos 1866 a 1868, em Santa Bárbara. Provinham, principalmente, dos estados de Alabama, Georgia,

Tennessee, Louisiana e Texas. Traziam alguns móveis e utensílios domésticos, sementes, animais e equipamentos agrícolas. Alguns possuiam dinheiro e aqui chegando trataram de adquirir terras. O Coronel Norris foi o primeiro a chegar ali e tinha trazido muito ouro e pode adquirir a Fazenda Machadinho, em 1866 e a seguir, mandou buscar sua família. A terra era boa e vermelha naquela região e as famílias se estabeleceram em 5 locais da Vila (Figura 2):

1. Na área próxima à Fazenda Machadinho, às margens do Ribeirão Quilombo, onde, em 1875, se construiu a estação ferroviária, depois conhecida como Estação, hoje o centro da cidade de Americana.
2. No bairro do Campo, próximo ao riacho Toledinho, na direção de Monte-Mór, onde se formou o Cemitério e depois foi erguida a Capela, situado entre Retiro e Estação.
3. No bairro Retiro, também denominado Bom Retiro, na direção de Capivari, do outro lado do riacho Toledinho, distando 12 km à sudoeste de Santa Bárbara;.
4. Na região do Funil, em direção à Limeira, até o Rio Piracicaba, ao norte de Santa Bárbara;
5. Na Vila de Santa Bárbara, ao longo da estrada para a Estação.

Figura 2. Americanos nos arredores de Santa Bárbara

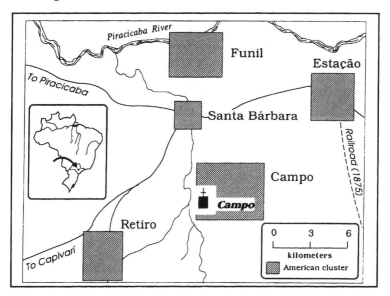

Fonte: C. B. Dawsey e J. M. Dawsey, *The Confederados: Old South Immigrants in Brazil* (Tuscaloosa: University of Alabama Press, 1995), p. 142.

As propriedades tinham cerca de 100 alqueires cada uma (2.420.000 metros quadrados). A terra dessa região era parecida com a do Alabama e, como logo após a chegada das famílias foi plantada, em pouco tempo foram feitas as colheitas e os produtos vendidos. Com o lucro do café, milho, algodão e cana se recuperou o dinheiro gasto com a compra das terras. (Vide Anexo 1.)

Como todas as famílias se dedicaram a agricultura, trouxeram a tecnologia usada no sul, como o arado de ponta de aço (steel-tipped plows) que mais tarde ficou conhecido como "arado americano" e técnicas no manejo de animais (Figura 3). Também disseminaram o uso do trole de rodas com arco de aço (trolley with steel-rimmed wheels) de 2 bancos e 4 assentos como meio de transporte e o carroção para o transporte dos produtos agrícolas em substituição ao carro de bois, pesado e lento que era usado no Brasil. Conseguiram grande produção de melancias, cujas sementes tinham vindo da Georgia e ainda não era conhecida no Brasil, a "cascavel da Georgia" (watermellon snake), que passou daí em diante a ser conhecida por mais de um século como "melancia de Santa Bárbara" e sua semente como "semente americana".

Figura 3. Santa Bárbara, municípios, vizinhos e fazendas

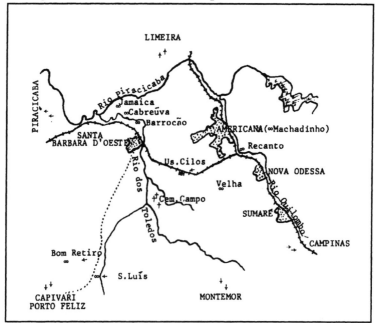

Fonte: Betty Antunes de Oliveira, *Centelha em restolho seco: uma contribuição para a história do trabalho batista no Brasil* (Rio de Janeiro: Editora da Autora, 1985), p. 3.

A máquina de costura, a lâmpada de querosene, a máquina descaroçadora de algodão, as vidraças nas janelas, os chaminés de tijolos, o fogão de ferro e o tear de fabricar seda fazem parte dos usos que os pioneiros trouxeram ao país e foram incorporados à cultura brasileira.

Como suas fazendas eram muito produtivas os americanos e seus filhos passaram a ser convidados para administrar fazendas e também dar treinamento a lavradores de outras regiões do país. A fazenda do Coronel Luís de Queiroz, em Piracicaba, foi administrada por vários americanos e se tornou uma fazenda modelo. Doada mais tarde para a Universidade de São Paulo, tornou-se a Escola Superior de Agricultura Luís de Queiroz, cujo curso de agronomia é o número 1 no "rank" da América Latina em sua especialidade.

Para escoamento da produção agrícola a Companhia Paulista de Estradas de Ferro construiu um ramal até a Fazenda Machadinho, nas terras do Coronel Norris, em 1875, distante 10 km de Santa Bárbara. Ao redor da Estação foi surgindo um pequeno comércio e foi sendo conhecido como Vila dos Americanos e depois Vila Americana, em 1890. Mais tarde Município de Vila Americana, em 1925 e finalmente Americana, em 1938.

Sem ser colônia organizada, o agrupamento de Santa Bárbara foi se tornando vila até chegar a ser a próspera cidade de Americana, hoje famoso parque industrial têxtil, com mais de 150.000 habitantes.

O cemitério

Os primeiros desafios foram grandes—o isolamento devido à distância entre as fazendas, a falta de escolas, a diferença do idioma, etc., mas com um fato inesperado os pioneiros não podiam nem sequer imaginar: onde enterrar seus mortos.

Até 1850, no Brasil, os defuntos eram enterrados dentro das igrejas—católicas, óbvio. Porém devido às mortes ocorridas por epidemias, foi proibido o sepultamento em recintos fechados, estabelecendo-se para isso os cemitérios públicos, criados pelas Câmaras Municipais. Haviam também os cemitérios particulares, fundados e mantidos pelas irmandades religiosas ou ordens terceiras, ao lado das igrejas. Segundo o costume romano as Câmaras Municipais mandavam benzer os cemitérios e os párocos pensaram ser seu direito não permitir o enterro de cadáveres não-católicos em tais propriedades municipais. O governo determinou então que neles fosse reservada uma área para sepultamento de acatólicos, mas nem todas as Câmaras cumpriram isso e em muitos municípios do interior não era raro se presenciar o triste espetáculo de se encontrarem fileiras de sepulturas de protestantes, judeus ou até mesmo de criancinhas falecidas sem batismo fora dos muros dos cemitérios, como acontecia em Vila da Constituição.

O primeiro falecimento na colônia Confederada foi de uma criança de 2 anos, neto de um dos pioneiros, em 1868 e seu corpo foi levado ao cemitério de

Santa Bárbara para o sepultamento. Mas lá chegando o pároco não permitiu o enterro por se tratar de criança não-católica. Um morador da cidade, de descendência alemã, penalizado com a situação daquele cadáver que ia e vinha em busca de uma autorização para ser enterrado, permitiu que o imunassem em seu quintal, pois já era tarde da noite. A ordem governamental ainda não havia chegado aos ouvidos daquele cura de Santa Bárbara.

A esposa do Coronel Thompson Oliver também faleceu, contaminada pelo bacilo da tuberculose e foi sepultada nas terras de sua própria fazenda, no Campo, no meio de um pasto para o gado, tendo sua sepultura uma cerca para que não fosse pisada. Era um local lindo, plano, cheio de árvores e à beira de um riacho. O Coronel foi permitindo que se enterrassem outros americanos ali e assim foi-se formando ali um cemitério. Depois a terra foi vendida aos Bookwalter e o cemitério continuou recebendo os restos mortais dos pioneiros e seus descendentes.

Em 1890 a Declaração dos Direitos, em seu artigo 72, parágrafo 5°, afirmava que os cemitérios passavam a ter caráter secular e seriam administrados pela autoridade municipal, ficando livre ao enterramento de pessoas pertencentes a qualquer seita religiosa.

Em 1921 a Prefeitura de Santa Bárbara resolveu legalizar a situação do Cemitério do Campo. Para tal, notificou os americanos que teriam que construir um muro fechando o local e colocar um portão trancado a chaves e também ter o Livro de Registro de Óbitos, com uma pessoa responsável pelo próprio.

Com o passar do tempo esse local não somente serviu para os sepultamentos mas para a reunião da colônia americana. Ao visitar o túmulo de seus mortos, aos domingos, a comunidade se encontrava, fazia suas orações, participava de um almoço comunitário, se inteirava das novidades, relembravam os casos dos pioneiros contados por seus pais e falavam de suas saudades.

O que mais chama a atenção são as incrições nas lápides, muitas com dizeres bíblicos, em inglês e símbolos maçônicos. Ligados à religião protestante, várias famílias deixaram gravados em sua última morada epitáfios que relembravam a continuidade da vida além da morte: "It shall not pass". Até hoje lá se fazem sepultamentos de descendentes dos pioneiros.

Possui hoje esse local cerca de 400 lápides, numa área de 2.000 m^2, no município de Santa Bárbara, de onde dista 12 km, tendo a mesma distância da cidade de Americana. Na entrada existe um gramado com árvores, onde há um galpão coberto, com mesas e cadeiras, para os almoços comunitários, uma casa para o zelador, uma capela e um obelisco comemorativo ao centenário da chegada dos imigrantes com os sobrenomes das 93 primeiras famílias.

A capela

Os primeiros tempos foram difíceis para os imigrantes cultuarem seu Deus e se reunirem para orar. Para tal os fiéis se agrupavam na sala das casas mais confortáveis, ou se durante um dia bonito, no quintal na sombra de uma árvore frondosa. Com o correr do tempo cada núcleo foi organizando seu próprio salão para os cultos.

As fazendas eram distantes umas das outras, não havia estradas ou caminhos bem conservados e os meios de transporte eram poucos. Sendo assim, as Escolas Dominicais e os cultos aconteciam a cada domingo, em cada um dos núcleos. As reuniões gerais ou especiais se realizavam quase sempre no Campo, contando com a presença de quase todos.

No ano de 1878, um mutirão realizado pelos americanos edifica a capela da comunidade, junto ao cemitério, simples e rústica, construída em madeira, com telhado de pequenas tábuas superpostas e amarradas ao madeiramento. Tinha dois degraus na frente, com dois pequenos quartos ao lado da entrada, um para guardarem os objetos da igreja e outro para as mulheres trocarem suas saias de montaria. O salão para os cultos tinha duas fileiras de bancos, uma para os homens e outra reservada às mulheres. Servia ela a todos os cultos, com pregações de ministros batistas, presbiterianos e metodistas. Mas todos a eles compareciam, pois os objetivos eram orar e cultuar a Deus e assim essa humilde construção tornou-se a primeira capela ecumênica no Brasil (Figura 4).

Uma das primeiras notícias sobre essa capela saiu publicada na Alemanha, em 1887. Uma educadora alemã, Ulla von Eck, que usou o pseudônimo Ina von Binzer, viveu no Brasil no período de 1881 a 1884 e morou com diversas famílias, ensinando seus filhos. Apesar de sua pouca idade—somente 22 anos—Ina fez importantíssimas observações sobre o modo de vida e condições sociais do país. Morou nas cercanias do Campo, numa fazenda e, tendo conhecido uma família de colonizadores norte-americanos, foi convidada a ir com eles, num domingo, à igreja. Descreve, com precisão de detalhes, a viagem a cavalo até a rústica capelinha, o edifício, as pessoas, o culto, etc. (Vide Anexo 2.)

Mais do que um local de oração a capela foi um ponto de reunião da comunidade. Os domingos eram todos passados no Campo. Alguns vinham a cavalo, outros de trole ou carroça ou mesmo a pé. As crianças brincavam, os jovens participavam de jogos ou conversavam, os homens falavam dos negócios e as mulheres, com retalhos, agulhas e linhas na mão costuravam seus "quilts" e ensinavam essa técnica a suas filhas. Na hora da merenda todos abriam suas cestas, onde estavam o frango frito à moda do Sul, os "biscuits", o pão de milho, a torta de frango, a manteiga fresca, a torta de maçã ou de noz pecan. E, como num picnic, o lanche era comunitário, tanto quanto o culto fora ecumênico.

Figura 4. A capela

Fonte: Judith MacKnight Jones, *Folhas esparsas* (São Paulo: João Scortecci Editora, 1996), p. 16.

A religião

A historiadora do metodismo no Brasil, Eula Kennedy Long, parafraseou o filósofo Pascal dizendo: "Se não fosse a ambição de Napoleão Bonaparte ao pretender invadir Portugal, a história do evangelho no Brasil teria sido outra". Antes da chegada da Família Real vir fugida para o Brasil, era mais fácil desembarca-rem no porto do Rio de Janeiro passageiros doentes de varíola ou lepra do que um judeu ou um protestante. Com a vinda de Dom João VI, em 1808, houve a abertura dos portos e ele se viu entre a cruz e a espada: deixar que estrangeiros—principalmente seus aliados ingleses—exercessem sua fé e ter que enfrentar a fú-ria da Igreja Católica, a religião oficial do país e praticada por seus patrícios portugueses que aqui residiam ou proibir a prática de cultos evangélicos e ter as tropas de Napoleão marchando nas portas de Portugal.

Quando os emigrados sulistas chegaram já havia algum trabalho evangéli-co iniciado no Brasil. Tentativas para a entrada das religiões protestantes tinham acontecido nos séculos XVI e XVII com as malogradas invasões de franceses huguenotes no Rio de Janeiro e holandeses em Pernambuco. No início do período imperial de Dom Pedro II surgiram as missões religiosas estrangeiras que deram força ao protestantismo brasileiro. Ao imperador não interessava a mensagem espiritual das igrejas que aqui se instalassem, mas sim em que elas poderiam servir, em que poderiam contribuir para melhoria na parte social. Ele também apreciava os missionários protestantes pelos seus conhecimentos, sua disciplina e pelos serviços práticos que eles poderiam prestar, conforme afirma Émile-G. Léonard. Sendo o monarca uma pessoa muito culta, confiava que, com a vinda de levas de imigrantes oriundos de países protestantes e civilizados, seu programa de colonização seria ousado e disso dependeria o futuro do país. Mas para ter sucesso precisava garantir a tais colonos a possibilidade de exercer sua fé, fazer seus cultos e educar seus filhos.

Na Vila de Santa Bárbara chegaram os primeiros missionários para atender as necessidades espirituais dos imigrantes. Pregavam em língua inglesa e os cultos reuniam somente os americanos. As igrejas construídas nessa época na Vila e nas colônias foram as primeiras em suas denominações no Brasil. Os imigrantes foram todos identificados como "protestantes", até mesmo algumas famílias católicas que vieram entre eles. O estigma era grande no país de religião católica para com os que professavam aquela fé, bastava se dizer a palavra "protestante" para apavorar as pessoas em certas cidades do interior. O povo acreditava que o demônio se apossava do corpo deles e que no interior de seus templos se faziam bruxarias.

Igreja e estado eram uma coisa só e a separação se deu pelo Decreto 119, de 1890, dando-se a todas as confissões religiosas a liberdade de culto e certas garantias para todos expressarem livremente seus ideais de fé.

Desde o tratado comercial firmado por Dom João VI com a Inglaterra foi permitida a construção de templos, desde que esse não tivesse torres e nem se assemelhassem com os edifícios das igrejas católicas.

A Constituição Imperial, de 24 de fevereiro de 1891, em seu artigo 5º, reafirmou a continuidade do catolicismo romano como religião oficial. Todas as outras podiam praticar cultos em residências particulares ou edifícios destinados a esse fim desde que não possuíssem forma exterior de igrejas, e, principalmente, não tivessem torres e nem sinos.

As missões que vieram para se instalar em Santa Bárbara deveriam atender necessidades espirituais dos pioneiros em língua inglesa mas tinham, também, como objetivo penetrar na cultura dominante de uma população católica e de língua portuguesa.

Os presbiterianos

Os sulistas já encontraram o presbiterianismo estabelecido no Brasil, nas províncias do Rio de Janeiro e São Paulo. Mas, nos Estados Unidos, dividida que estava essa fé entre norte e sul devido a Guerra Civil, foi ao Southern Presbyterian Mission que eles apelaram para pedir missionários para Santa Bárbara. A missão veio, mas por melhor conveniência, estabeleceu-se em

Campinas, com cerca de 20.000 habitantes e distante 60 km de suas casas, pois a cidade tinha clima moderado, mais população para levarem sua palavra evangélica, baixo custo-de-vida, proximidades do fim da ferrovia que vinha do porto de Santos e, principalmente, a possibilidade de trabalhar perto da Northern Presbyterian Mission, que já vinha atuando com sucesso. Também na província de São Paulo, dois pastores presbiterianos do sul já desenvolviam sua obra evangélica, os Reverendos Doutores James Baird e William Emerson, precedidos que foram pelo Reverendo Doutor James McFadden Gaston, que passara anos antes pregando e distribuindo sementes dessa fé.

Foram enviados ao Brasil os Reverendos George Nash Morton e Edward Lane, que, em setembro de 1869, iniciaram seu trabalho presbiteriano em Campinas. Morton e Lane fizeram trabalho notável no campo religioso e educacional e em 1870 já pregavam em português. Percorriam as cidades vizinhas, arregimentando ovelhas para o seu rebanho, inclusive iam a Santa Bárbara periodicamente e, em agosto desse ano, os imigrantes decidiram erguer uma capela, a Hopewell Church, que foi iniciada com 13 membros. Dois anos mais tarde já haviam duas igrejas presbiterianas em Santa Bárbara.

Os metodistas

O metodismo chegou ao Brasil em 1836, através dos Reverendos Justin Spaulding e Daniel Kidder, que foram precedidos pelo Reverendo Fountain Pitts no ano anterior, mas este somente viajou pelo Brasil e organizou, no Rio de Janeiro, uma certa "Sociedade Metodista".

Spaulding e Kidder intensificaram a divulgação das Escrituras, o primeiro deles na Côrte e o segundo viajando pelo interior, distribuindo Bíblias e incentivando a leitura dos livros da religião. Bom observador, preocupava-se Kidder em descrever a terra e os costumes. Voltando aos Estados Unidos, em 1840, publicou dois dos mais belos livros de viagens sobre o Brasil imperial: "Sketches of residence and travel in Brasil", em 2 volumes, sobre as províncias do Norte, onde retrata não somente a sociedade mas toda a vida brasileira. Juntou também suas notas de viagem às do ministro presbiteriano James Fletcher para publicar "Brazil and the Brazilians", que descreve, com fidelidade, as províncias de São Paulo e Rio de Janeiro.

Entre os sulistas emigrados havia um pregador leigo metodista, Reverendo Junius E. Newman, que durante a Guerra Civil servira de capelão nas forças confederadas. Tendo perdido tudo que possuía animou-se a buscar um novo lar em país distante, onde pudesse refazer, em paz, sua vida e propagar o Evangelho. Veio, em 1867, inicialmente para Niterói, mas depois juntou-se aos patrícios na Vila de Santa Bárbara e começou a pregar para os colonos americanos.

No terceiro domingo de agosto de 1871, sob sua liderança, com nove membros, foi fundada a Igreja Metodista Episcopal do Sul, numa casinha coberta de sapé, de chão de terra batida, abandonada à beira da estrada.

Foi grande e marcante o trabalho desse primeiro missionário na implantação definitiva do metodismo no Brasil bem como o suporte, dado pela Igreja Metodista Episcopal do Sul dos Estados Unidos, aos ministros que aqui vieram.

Os batistas

Em 10 de setembro de 1871 foi organizada a Primeira Igreja Batista no Brasil, em Santa Bárbara, sendo o reverendo Richard Radcliff seu fundador, somente para atender os imigrantes dessa colônia. Não se sabe o número exato de membros-fundadores, mas a historiadora batista Betty Antunes de Oliveira, também descendente dos pioneiros, diz terem sido 29 membros iniciais, provindos de 12 famílias.

No ano seguinte foi votado, na Junta de Richmond, um apelo dos pioneiros americanos pedindo um trabalho missionário no Brasil. Esse pedido não pode ser atendido mas esse pequeno rebanho não desanimou e, por mais 6 anos seguidos, reforçou suas súplicas à Junta, prometendo prover as necessidades e o sustento do pastor e contribuir em dinheiro para a Junta.

No primeiro domingo de 1879 foi organizada a Segunda Igreja Batista, a da Estação, assim denominada por ficar perto da linha férrea, com 12 membros, na Vila de Santa Bárbara, sob o comando de Pastor Elias Quillin.

Um general sulista, Alexander T. Hawthorne, que já estivera no Brasil, a convite de Dom Pedro II observando para estabelecer uma colônia de emigrados no sul da Bahia, intercedeu junto à Convenção Batista, em Kentucky, com a recomendação para que se instalasse, definitivamente, um trabalho de evangelização batista no Brasil. Relatava as razões para tal: governo justo e estável que recebe bem os imigrantes, povo cortês, liberal e hospitaleiro, clima ameno e solo fértil. O general foi nomeado Agente da Junta de Missões Estrangeiras no Texas e enviou o casal Bagby —Reverendo William e a esposa Anne Luther—que chegaram ao Brasil em março de 1881, indo para a colônia de Santa Bárbara. Lá chegando encontraram as duas pequenas igrejas fracas e quase abandonadas e passaram ao pastorado delas. Os 50 anos de trabalho desse casal foi notável, não somente em Santa Bárbara, mas também em todo território, para o estabelecimento da fé batista no país.

Os maçons

Embora não seja propriamente uma religião, a Maçonaria era atuante no Brasil, na época da chegada dos Confederados, principalmente na política e na cultura. Teve trabalho acentuado na proclamação da Independencia e nas relações internacionais. Dom Pedro II era maçom, bem como grande parte das autoridades dessa época, tais como o Barão do Rio Branco, José Bonifácio, o Marechal Deodoro da Fonseca, Rui Barbosa, etc.

Os próprios agentes da imigração que atuavam no Rio de Janeiro, os irmãos Charles e George Nathan, judeus ingleses que haviam residido em New

Orleans e se casado com as irmãs Goodman, do Alabama, eram maçons. Foram eles que informaram ao Coronel Norris onde estavam as melhores terras paulistas para o plantio.

O Ministro da Agricultura e Comércio do Brasil, Antonio Francisco de Paula Souza, também integrava a Maçonaria e foi ele um dos facilitadores, junto ao imperador, pela venda, a baixo custo, das terras aos sulistas.

Muitos eram os adeptos da Maçonaria entre os emigrados, tendo alguns sofrido perseguições em sua terra natal. O Coronel Norris, o líder da comunidade de Santa Bárbara, era maçom e foi Grão-Mestre na Grande Loja do Alabama, de 1861 a 1862, e seu filho Robert também fora membro da Loja de Fulton, Alabama.

De mentalidade americana, o protestantismo vigente na colônia admitiu os princípios básicos da Maçonaria: amor, fraternidade e caridade, e 16 emigrados, arregimentados pelo Coronel Norris, fundaram a "George Washington Lodge". A Loja obteve autorização do Grande Oriente do Brasil para seu funcionamento e foi a segunda no Brasil, de corporação profissional. Recebeu licença especial para trabalhar em língua inglesa e iniciou seus trabalhos em 1874 e dali três anos pode adotar integralmente o rito York. Seu primeiro Venerável foi o Coronel Norris e seu filho Robert sucedeu-o nessa responsabilidade. O livro "The History of Craft Masonry in Brazil" traz o retrato de onze de seus membros, com a data de 1810.

Seguindo os compromissos já adotados na Europa nos séculos XVI a XIX entre o Cristianismo e uma Maçonaria respeitadora da religião, essa Loja contava com batistas, metodistas e presbiterianos entre seus membros, inclusive dois pastores, um metodista e outro presbiteriano.

Os maçons sempre foram uma comunidade de posição privilegiada. Apegados à boa educação, tiveram também entre os imigrantes uma luta comum para o estabelecimento das escolas. Contribuindo com auxílio financeiro, chegaram a ter dois imóveis no centro de Santa Bárbara e permitiam que classes funcionassem em salões de suas Lojas, que se fizessem reuniões religiosas e até que servissem de centro para atividades sociais e festas. Também socorreram seus compatriotas de outras colônias estabelecidas na Amazônia e no litoral sul de São Paulo. O apelo, feito através de gestos, que significa "maçom em perigo", salvou muitas vidas de missionários propagandistas do protestantismo, na divulgação da fé, de situações difíceis e perigosas pelo interior do país.

Lutando com dificuldade, a Maçonaria teve importante papel na organização dessa comunidade de pessoas que vieram refazer suas vidas fora de seu torrão natal.

Os símbolos maçônicos que podem ser vistos nas lápides de suas sepulturas atestam que grande número de pioneiros fizeram parte da Loja George Washington.

As escolas

Impossível não associar o trabalho das igrejas protestantes a história do ensino no Brasil.

A vida escolar de muitas crianças vindas com os imigrantes foi interrompida e seus pais trataram logo de promover sua volta aos estudos. Em Santa Bárbara não havia escolas públicas e a maioria que havia na cidade eram escolas de cunho confessional católico.

Inicialmente coube às mães e irmãs mais velhas a tarefa de ensinar, em suas próprias casas, aos irmãos mais novos, para que completassem a instrução elementar. Os adolescentes tiveram que ajudar seus pais, os moços na lavoura e as moças nos serviços domésticos, pois pais e mães não estavam acostumbrados ao trabalho pesado, já que no Sul tinham escravos para isso. Foram poucos os que puderam voltar aos Estados Unidos para completar sua educação.

As famílias brasileiras mais abastadas dessa época contratavam professoras alemãs, inglesas ou francesas para residirem na casa—geralmente na fazenda, e ensinarem as matérias básicas aos seus filhos, bem como línguas e música. Com os americanos aconteceu o mesmo, as famílias com mais posses mandaram vir professoras americanas que ensinavam a educação básica, óbviamente em língua inglesa.

Foram surgindo, aos poucos, os chamados "colégios protestantes", que promoviam os valores da religião embutidos no ensino e divulgavam os trabalhos de sua fé. Essas escolas, devido aos constantes contatos com os Estados Unidos, adotavam os mesmos métodos de ensino aos filhos dos imigrantes. Tais métodos quebraram o monopólio existente nas práticas jesuíticas, introduzindo os estudos experimentais em substituição ao ensino puramente livresco, e também iniciando as classes mistas, as aulas em laboratórios, etc.

Todas elas, desde sua fundação, sempre tiveram alunos brasileiros e não-protestantes. Com o permanente contato dos descendentes com seus colegas brasileiros, eles iam cada vez se tornando mais abrasileirados e as escolas cada vez mais integradas na área educacional brasileira.

As escolas presbiterianas

Coube à Igreja Presbiteriana a primazia na instalação de escolas confessionais protestantes no Brasil. Segundo o historiador do presbiterianismo no Brasil, Júlio Andrade Ferreira, a primeira escola confessional presbiteriana de origem norte-americana a ser estabelecida na América do Sul foi o Colégio Internacional, na cidade de Campinas, em 1869, iniciando seu funcionamento em 1873, conforme Boanerges Ribeiro atesta.

Foi fundada pelos Ministros Doutores Edward Lane e George Morton e acolhia a mocidade de ambos os sexos. Grandes nomes da cultura paulista passaram por seus bancos escolares, entre eles o compositor de óperas Carlos Gomes, os políticos Júlio Mesquita, Paulo de Morais Barros, etc. Seu curso secundário preparava os alunos também para os exames dos cursos superiores. Esse Colégio chegou a ter 144 alunos, a maioria filhos da elite da zona Oeste paulista, cujos pais foram os baluartes do movimento republicano. Muitos desses jovens foram completar seus estudos universitários nos Estados Unidos.

O Reverendo Morton deixou a direção do Colégio em 1879 e no ano seguinte instalou o Colégio Morton, em São Paulo, por onde passaram nomes ilustres da burguesia paulistana, cujos pais ocupavam lugar de destaque na sociedade.

Eram as "Little Red School Houses" se impondo no cenário educacional brasileiro, seguindo a metodologia pedagógica da pátria-mãe de seus fundadores.

O Reverendo Lane continuou na direção do Colégio Internacional, auxiliado pelo Reverendo Dabney, até 1889 quando a epidemia de febre amarela atingiu seu auge na cidade de Campinas e as escolas todas tiveram que suspender suas atividades a fim de preservar a saúde dos alunos e professores. Com a morte do Reverendo Lane, em 1892, vitimado pela febre amarela, a escola foi definitivamente fechada em Campinas e transferida para a cidade de Lavras, no estado de Minas Gerais, com a criação do Instituto Evangélico, mais tarde denominado Instituto Gammon, sob a liderança do Pastor Samuel Gammon. Esta escola tornou-se, mais tarde, a pioneira no ensino agrícola no país, existe até hoje e é uma das mais famosas nessa área, transformada que foi em Universidade Federal.

Também coube a um dos pastores presbiterianos, o reverendo George Chamberlain, iniciar a Escola Americana em São Paulo, raiz do Mackenzie College, que veio revolucionar os métodos de ensino na época a ponto de uma de suas educadoras, Miss Marcia Brown, ser contratada pelo Governo de São Paulo para reformular o ensino primário. O Mackenzie, hoje Universidade, é uma das mais conceituadas do país, marcadamente na área do ensino de engenharia e direito.

As escolas metodistas

No ano de 1879 as duas filhas do Reverendo Junius Newman, Annie e Mary, abriram um colégio, com internato e externato, na cidade de Piracicaba. Mas, apesar dessa casa de ensino ter durado somente um ano, sua influência foi muito marcante.

Em 1881 a Igreja Metodista enviou para lá uma de suas educadoras, Miss Martha Watts, de inteligência e preparo fora do comum, aliados a uma consagração extraordinária ao magistério e ela, imediatamente, iniciou um educandário, o Colégio Piracicabano. Com somente uma aluna matriculada, o colégio conquistou a confiança das famílias progressistas da região e logo, em 1890, já era considerado um dos melhores estabelecimentos de ensino. Transformado em Universidade Metodista de Piracicaba (UNIMEP) em 1975, conta hoje com 11.000 alunos, distribuidos em 4 "campi" e 65 cursos de graduação e pós-graduação, alguns dos quais bem situados no "rank" nacional.

Em 1888, no Rio de Janeiro, construiu-se a Escola do Alto, confessional metodista, assim denominada por situar-se em cima de um morro e, pensava-se, imune à febre amarela, pois lá não havia águas paradas. Mas os mosquitos não demoraram a subir o morro e atacar alunos e professores, fazendo com que, em 1891, ela fosse transferida para Juiz de Fora, no estado de Minas Gerais e juntado ao Colégio Granbery. Esse tornou-se um dos mais afamados colégios do país. Também em Minas Gerais, na capital Belo Horizonte, em 1904, iniciaram-se os trabalhos do Colégio Isabela Hendrix, acolhendo somente meninas.

No final do século, em 1895, o Colégio Americano de Petrópolis abriu suas portas para um alunato vindo de famílias abastadas e de diplomatas, pois essa cidade serrana era a capital do estado do Rio de Janeiro e estava livre das epidemias de varíola e febre amarela. Durou até 1920, quando voltou para a cidade do Rio e tornou-se parte do Colégio Bennett, outra importante casa de ensino da rede particular brasileira.

Merecem ser citados os colégios metodistas de Ribeirão Preto e Santo Amaro, depois juntados em São Bernardo do Campo, que mantém a melhor escola de comunicação social do Brasil.

Muitos desses colégios iniciaram-se acolhendo alunos de um só sexo, mas depois tornaram-se mistos, para alunos de ambos os sexos.

Vale aqui dar um destaque a um colégio metodista que existiu em Taubaté, no Vale do Paraíba, estado de São Paulo. Iniciou suas atividades em 1890 e funcionou somente 4 anos e teve como aluno o escritor Monteiro Lobato. O Reverendo Kennedy foi seu professor e nunca poderia imaginar quão famoso seria esse seu aluno como um brilhante escritor da literatura infantil brasileira. A um amigo íntimo Lobato confidenciou que recebera inspiração para criar toda sua vasta obra infantil ao ouvir histórias bíblicas e lendas e mitos que esse seu professor narrava.

As escolas batistas

É difícil separar qualquer menção aos colégios protestantes do nome do casal Bagby— William e Anne Luther. Chegando ao Brasil em 1881 esses jovens missionários batistas, procedentes do Texas, pregaram em vários estados do nordeste e suleste para se estabelecer, em 1899, na cidade de São Paulo. Como o mais populoso e progressista estado brasileiro, contribuia mais para o Tesouro Nacional do que todos os outros juntos. A sua capital contava com população de 2.000.000 habitantes, 11.000 fábricas e uma multidão de estrangeiros que para ela imigraram. O casal adquiriu, de uma senhora presbiteriana, por US$ 3,000, o pequeno Colégio Progresso e o denominaram Colégio Batista. Nessa escola estudou o historiador Sérgio Buarque de Holanda que, numa entrevista a seu colega Richard Graham, da University of Texas, em 1982, declarou: "My kindergarten was run by an American lady, Mrs. Bagby". Isso, provavelmente, foi em 1907 ou 1908 e ele se lembrava de ir para a escola num carro puxado por 2 belos cavalos. Esse colégio tinha internato para crianças a partir de 6 anos. Existe até hoje e fica no bairro de Perdizes, na cidade de São Paulo.

A Fraternidade Descendência Americana

A Fraternidade Descendência Americana (FDA) foi fundada em 1954 e tem como objetivo a manutenção do patrimônio do Cemitério do Campo, divulgando-o por meio de palestras e pesquisas da história da imigração. Deve também estimular a amizade, a filantropia e a cooperação mútua entre seus descendentes. Disciplina os sepultamentos no Cemitério, permitindo somente a descendentes da colônia e seus cônjuges. Segundo o historiador Alcides Gussi, os objetivos dessa associação foram inspirados na Maçonaria. Seu emblema (Figura 5) é um triângulo azul sobre fundo branco, tendo na parte interna outro triângulo menor e, entre elas, as palavras Fraternidade Descendência Americana e, em seu centro, duas mãos que se entrelaçam num aperto.

Figura 5. Emblema da Fraternidade Descendência Americana

Fonte: Eugene C. Harter, *A colônia perdida da confederação: a emigração norte-americana para o Brasil após a Guerra de Secessão* (Rio de Janeiro: Nórdica, 1985), p. 94.

Coube a essa organização a iniciativa de fundar o Museu da Fraternidade nos anos 60, em um pequeno prédio construído dentro das terras do Cemitério. Vários acervos foram doados mas nos anos 80, com a criação do Museu da Imigração em Santa Bárbara d'Oeste, seus acervos foram transferidos para lá, onde é mantida uma exposição permanente, no segundo piso, sobre a imigração norte-americana.

A Fraternidade mantém reuniões trimestrais no Campo, onde há o culto ecumênico, o lanche comunitário e as conversas, geralmente, versam sobre as saudades de seus mortos e as lembranças das histórias das primeiras gerações. Seu funcionamento é como o de um clube e para tal mantém cadastradas mais de 300 famílias da 3ª e 4ª geracões que residem na região, no estado, no país e até nos Estados Unidos, para as quais envia correspondência. Ultimamente a Fraternidade realiza uma grande festa anual, no próprio do Cemitério, e também ministra cursos de culinária típica do sul e artesanato ("quilts" e bonecas) no Museu e publicou um livro com as receitas das comidas dos Confederados.

Conclusão

Os pioneiros norte-americanos no Brasil eram poucos, diante das muitas adversidades a serem vencidas. Mas uma a uma elas foram sendo sobrepujadas e os resultados conseguidos provam o que sua fé e perseverança puderam conquistar. Lutando contra um idioma desconhecido, costumes diferentes, distâncias geográficas e grupos heterogêneos a serem catequizados, os obstáculos foram sendo transpostos um a um.

Sem dúvida foi uma imigração nada expressiva perto das massas de europeus e depois asiáticos que ao país acorreram para fins de colonização. Mas o legado deixado em melhorias na agricultura, na religião e no ensino foram de valor incalculável.

Figura 6. Brazão da cidade de Americana

Fonte: C. B. Dawsey e J. M. Dawsey, eds., *The Confederados: Old South Immigrants in Brazil* (Tuscaloosa: University of Alabama Press, 1995), p. 174.

Figura 7. Localização das famílias em 1875

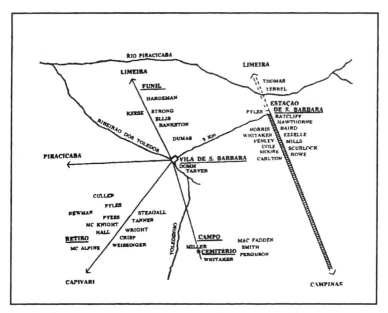

Fonte: Judith MacKnight Jones, *Soldado, descansa! uma epopéia norte-americana sob os céus do Brasil* (São Paulo: Jarde, 1967), p. 234.

As dádivas dos protestantes americanos, quer em dinheiro, esforços ou vidas para o serviço religioso e ao ensino, foi uma das contribuições mais úteis à historia do Brasil. A herança desses imigrantes está hoje incorporada à cultura brasileira e sente-se que são retribuídos através das homenagens a eles prestadas com nomes de ruas, praça, córrego, lagoa, bairros, nas cidades de Santa Bárbara e Americana. A própria cidade que leva o nome—Americana—já é uma homenagem a esses pioneiros e ela tem em seu brazão a bandeira confederada (Figura 6). O Museu da Imigração reconhece quão valioso foi essa contribuição e preserva e divulga os primeiros artefatos por eles trazidos e gerados, abrindo campo para pesquisa nesse assunto, dando a conhecer essa parte importante—e tão desconhecida—da história do Brasil.

Para finalizar, entendemos que a batalha desses Confederados foi vencida em sua terra natal, mas vencedora no trópico. A terra cultivada, as igrejas estabelecidas e as escolas fundadas foram a herança maior que esses pioneiros legaram em terras brasileiras. Cumprida sua missão, rendemos nossa homenagem a esses pioneiros (Figura 7), deixando aqui os versos gravados na lápide do avô paterno da historiadora-maior dos sulistas, Professora Judith MacKnight Jones, o pioneiro Napoleão Bonaparte McAlpine:

Soldier, rest! Thy warfare o'er	Soldado, descansa! Tua luta acabou
Sleep the sleep that knows no breaking	Dorme o sono eterno onde não há
Days of toil or nights of waking.	Dias de fadiga ou noites de vigília.

ANEXO 1

Nomes das primeiras famílias que chegaram em Santa Bárbara, segundo informações do pioneiro Thomas Steagall e outros.

Anderson	Dumas	Moncrief	Vaughn
Ayers	Ellis	Morre	Whitaker
Baird	Emerson	Morrison	Whitehead
Bankston	Ezelle	Newman	White
Barr	Ferguson	Norris	Waddell
Bazil	Freleigh	Northrup	Ward
Beasley	Gaston	Oliver	Watson
Bentley	Gates	Owen	Weissinger
Bookwalter	Gunter	Peacock	Wiggins
Boud	Hall	Perkins	Williamson
Broadnax	Hardeman	Pierce	Yancey
Brownlow	Harrison	Porter	
Bryant	Hogan	Prestridge	
Budd	Howard	Provost	
Buford	Howes	Ralston	
Cherry	Johnson	Reece	
Campbell	Jones	Richard	
Capps	Karnely	Russell	
Carlton	Keese	Shippy	
Carr	Kerr	Sampson	
Cole	Landers	Scurlock	
Colter	Lane	Seawright	
Crisp	Lang	Smith	
Cullen	Marchat	Steagall	
Currie	Mastiff	Strain	
Daniel	Mathews	Strong	
Daougherty	McDonald	Thorn	
Davis	McFadden	Thomas	
Demaret	McIntyre	Terrell	
Domm	McKnight	Towsend	
Drain	Miller	Trigg	
Dresback	Mills	Turner	

ANEXO 2

São Sebastião, 28 de julho de 1882

Querida e boa Grete.

Imagine como estou contente: existe aqui na vizinhança, uma fazenda de colonizadores norte-americanos, gente civilizada, portanto! Ninguém me tinha dito qualquer coisa a esse respeito mas hoje, eles vieram visitar-nos e nem calculam o que isso representa para mim.

Ach! Grete; apesar de muito amáveis, os Sousas não deixam de ser brasileiros; e a nós, estrangeiros, parecem sempre gente estranha, desprovidos de um certo senso de solidariedade que nos une, como hóspedes desta terra.

Além disso, a índole e a personalidade dos povos saxônicos despertam muito mais minha simpatia do que as dêstes latinos.

Só ao ouvir o som da língua inglesa respirei mais aliviada, sem levar em conta as atenções e gentilezas que Mr. Quimby e sua cunhada me dispensaram.

Mrs. Quimby ficara em casa com as crianças menores, mas a menina mais velha de 12 anos, veio a cavalo em companhia dos outros dois.

Estiveram aqui no sábado passado e de repente perguntaram-me:
- "Quer ir conosco amanhã à igreja?"
- "À igreja?" repeti admirada: "Onde?"
- "Oh! ainda não lhe contaram nada a respeito da nossa igreja? Não é de fato um edifício imponente mas, mesmo assim, podemos celebrar o nosso culto divino, cada terceiro domingo do mês. Venha conosco pernoitar em nossa casa e iremos até lá a cavalo, de manhã se quiser". Se queria! Naturalmente queria.

Selaram logo um cavalo e galopamos alegremente durante duas milhas até alcançar a fazenda de Mr. Quimby.

Agora já sei galopar com facilidade e Mr. Quimby tocou no meu ponto fraco quando me disse: - "You look as if you'd been born and bred on your horse".

Mrs. Quimby recebeu-me cordialmente, como hóspede desejada, e passamos o resto da tarde conversando, sentadas nas redes. Na manhã seguinte às nove horas, partia para a igreja uma cavalhada completa, tendo-se juntado a nós mais algumas senhoras e senhores.

Enquanto o caminho seguia através da fazenda não era mau, apesar de você não poder pensar que essa palavra "caminho" designe qualquer coisa além de um trilho, dando apenas para um animal de cada vez, em certos trechos, porém, tornava-se de tal forma intransitável, que na nossa terra teríamos retrocedido; mas os cavalos brasileiros não são mimados e, mesmo não estando ferrados, seguem seguros seu caminho, podendo-se confiar neles sossegadamente, até nos trechos mais difíceis.

Nosso grupinho apresentava-se imensamente pitoresco: os vestidos e chapéus claros das senhoras, os guarda-pós brancos dos homens, as grandes sombrinhas, também quase todas brancas, tudo isso alvejando e reluzindo sob um sol já quente demais, surgia aqui e desaparecia acolá, no meio das samambaias da altura de um homem, entre as quais os cavalos iam seguindo pelo atalho; em certo momento, ao atravessarmos um brejo tão grande que mais parecia um lago e onde os cavalos afundavam até a barriga, pudemos ver-nos todos refletidos na água, como um espelho.

Nunca tinha saído durante o dia a essa hora, porque em São Sebastião preferimos sempre o amanhecer ou a tardezinha para passear e devido a isso achava o sol desagradável demais. O caminho subia e descia, e até onde a vista alcançava não havia árvore nenhuma senão algumas raras e esguias palmeiras com suas copas graciosas, mas que não produziam nenhuma frescura, nem sombras pelo chão.

Assim conheci o abatimento que se apossa de nós após três horas de viagem a cavalo, debaixo do sol tropical: o calor ainda seria suportável; mas o pior era o dardejar direto dos raios do sol!

Parecia que todos sentiam o mesmo, porque a conversa foi esmorecendo, ficando cada vez mais monossilábica e por fim cessou por completo.

De repente, numa curva do caminho divisamos um edifício comprido feito de barro e coberto de palha.

- "Quem terá construído aqui no mato um celeiro tão distante de qualquer fazenda?" indaguei espantada.

- "Isso é a igreja" disse Mr. Quimby sorrindo, e nesse mesmo momento tomou por um atalho, ao lado da casa.

Minha impressão foi quase de assombro: - uma igreja, aquele paiol com paredes de barro esburacadas, telhado de palha e aberturas sem esquadrias que nem de longe se pareciam com janelas?

Mas minha dúvida não durou muito tempo: nossos companheiros chegavam, os homens, descendo dos cavalos, ajudavam-nos a apear dos nossos e depois prendiam os animais às árvores mais próximas do edifício.

Nesse instante, avisei outros cavalos e mulas com seus cavaleiros e cavaleiras; algumas senhoras já se achavam sentadas à sombra, daqui e dali, outras dirigiam-se para a igreja ou se aproximavam para cumprimentar Mr. Quimby e sua família.

-"How do you do?" ouvia-se de todos os lados, entremeados com o "How d'ye?" dos estados do sul. Trocaram-se depois as novidades, falando-se sobre todos os acontecimentos dessa região solitária, desde o último terceiro domingo do outro mês.

Um gole d'água na fonte mais próxima refrescou-nos e nos reanimou um pouco. Entramos na igreja depois de ter limpado os sapatos com uma vassoura colocada à entrada para esse fim; por alguns momentos, gozamos agradecidos daquele silêncio e da frescura, enquanto pouco a pouco ali se reuniam 50 ou 60 pessoas, todas, sem exceção, norte-americanos vindos de suas fazendas ou da colonia de Santa Bárbara.

Através de um grande buraco da parede de taipas, observava a cena lá fora, cada vez mais movimentada com a chegada de outras pessoas, os cavalos e mulas pastando sobre o capim, tendo como fundo as saias de montaria de variadas cores, que as senhoras tinham deixadas dependuradas nas árvores.

Pensava que nunca me vira sentada numa igreja como esta, enquanto atrás de mim uma jovem mamãe tentava acalmar o berreiro de seu último rebento, que naturalmente não estava gostando do passeio. Logo depois, veio sentar-se ao meu lado uma velhinha de cabelos alvos que eu já tinha observado através da minha parede quando ela chegou trotando alegremente na sua mula.

Em seguida, o pastor apareceu e o serviço divino começou. Um homem ainda moço e sem batina ou outra qualquer insígnia religiosa dirigiu-se para o altar de madeira (não havia púlpito) e apenas com o Novo Testamento na mão fez uma prédica linda e bem argumentada sobre a resposta de Cristo à pergunta do Batista: - "Éras tu que devias chegar, ou devemos esperar outro?"

Grete, era de converter qualquer pessoa.

Para nós, gente civilizada, era profundamente emocionante escutar as palavras da Bíblia que nos acostumáramos a associar às aulas de catecismo e aos lugares santificados de nossas igrejas, evocando-as inconscientemente dentro daquele ambiente, repetidas aqui, nessa cabana de barro, neste cenário tropical tão despido de exterioridades e de ornamentações sacras.

Mas elas soavam como em nossa terra, nem mais nem menos graves e solenes do que nas suntuosas catedrais, sob colunas altaneiras e estandartes coloridos.

Havia muito tempo que não entrava numa igreja, mas duvido que a missa mais brilhante na Basílica de São Pedro conseguisse despertar em nós a emoção deste serviço evangélico, numa cabana de taipas, num ponto perdido do sertão brasileiro.

A sensação da omnipotente presença do Deus Cristão e a prédica: - "Deus não mora nos templos construídos por mãos humanas", na sua impressionante grandeza, se impôs a todos nós e talvez até mesmo outros que não esperavam deixar-se dominar por essa emoção.

O calor sufocante havia abrandado e começou a soprar um vento leve; de repente, pela fresta da parede vi caírem grandes e espaçados pingos de chuva. Ai! as selas! A chuva aumentou logo e, diante disso, não houve outro remédio, senão o de recolhê-las com as saias para montar, abrigando-as na igreja, para evitar contrariedades durante a nossa volta.

Perto de 60 selas e umas trinta roupas de montaria foram colocadas a um canto da nave, e não pude deixar de sorrir ao pensar comigo mesma, o que não diriam numa capela, ou numa igreja européia, sobre esse fato que parecia aqui, tão natural.

A chuva cessou tão rapidamente como começara, e quando o serviço divino terminou e nós nos despedimos uns dos outros por um mês, as selas já podiam voltar aos seus lugares.

Ao retomar o caminho, sentíamos muito melhor disposição naquele ar fresco e sem poeira.

À noite, Mr. Quimby e sua cunhada trouxeram-me até São Sebastião prometendo vir buscar-me muito em breve.

Agora, aqui na porta está a velha e gorda Ana me chamando:

-"Chá, senhora!" Faço ponto final.

Escreva logo à sua elegante amazona, Ulla.

BIBLIOGRAFIA

Albino Bencostta, Marcus Levy. *"Ide por todo mundo": a província de São Paulo como campo de missão presbiteriana, 1869–1892.* Coleção Campiniana, 3. Campinas: Centro de Memória-UNICAMP e FAPESP, 1996.

Binzer, Ina von. *Alegrias e tristezas de uma educadora alemã no Brasil.* São Paulo: Anhembi, 1956. Publicado também sob o título: *Os meus romano: alegrias e tristezas de uma educadora alemã no Brasil.* 3 ed. Rio de Janeiro: Paz e Terra, 1982. (Pseudônimo de Ulla von Eck)

Costa, Ana Maria de Siqueira. "O destino [não] manifesto: 'we shall not pass'; os imigrantes norte-americanos no Brasil". São Paulo, 1985. Tese (Doutoramento), Universidade de São Paulo.

Crabtree, A.R. *Baptists in Brazil: A History of Southern Baptists' Greatest Mission Field.* Rio de Janeiro: Baptist Publishing House, 1953.

———. *História dos baptistas no Brasil até o anno de 1906.* Rio de Janeiro: Casa Publicadora Baptista, 1937.

Dawsey, John Cowart. "O espelho americano: americanos para brasileiro ver e Brazilians for Americans to See". *Impulso: Revista de Ciências Sociais* (Piracicaba) 6:12 (1993), 113–151.

Dawsey, Cyrus B., e James M. Dawsey, eds. *The Confederados: Old South Immigrants in Brazil.* Tuscaloosa: University of Alabama Press, 1995.

DeMuzio, Daniel Carr. "Confederate Descendants in Brazil". *Confederate Veteran* (julho–agosto 1991), 17–19.

Eisenberg, Peter Louis. *Guerra civil americana.* Tudo é história, 40. São Paulo: Brasiliense, 1982.

Ferreira, Júlio Andrade. *História da igreja presbiteriana do Brasi: em comemoração do seu Primeiro Centenário.* 2 volumes. São Paulo: Casa Editora Presbiteriana, 1960.

Gammon, Samuel Rhea. *The Evangelical Invasion of Brazil: A Half Century of Evangelical Missions in the Land of the Southern Cross.* Richmond, Va.: Presbyterian Committee of Publication, 1910.

Goldman, Frank P. "Três educadores norte-americanos no Brasil, 1860–1917". *ANHEMBI* 7 (26) 78 (maio 1957), 450–458.

———. *Os pioneiros norte-americanos no Brasil: educadores, sacerdotes, covos e reis.* Biblioteca Pioneira de Estudos Brasileiros. São Paulo: Pioneira, 1972.

Graham, Richard. "An Interview with Sérgio Buarque de Holanda". *Hispanic American Historical Review* 62:1 (fevereiro 1982), 3–17. Tradução: "Uma entrevista com Sérgio Buarque de Holanda". *Ciência e Cultura* 34:9 (setembro1982), 1175–1182.

Griggs, William Clark. *The Elusive Eden: Frank McMullan's Confederate Colony in Brazil.* Austin: University of Texas Press, 1987.

Gussi, Alcides Fernando. *Os norte-americanos (confederados) do Brasil: identidades no contexto transnacional.* Coleção Tempo & Memória, 2. Americana e Campinas: Prefeitura Municipal e Centro de Memória da UNICAMP, 1997.

———. "Identidades no contexto transnacional: lembranças e esquecimentos de ser brasileiro, norte-americano e confederado de Santa Bárbara d'Oeste e Americana". Dissertação (Mestrado). Universidade Estadual de Campinas, 1996.

Harrison, Helen Bagby. *Os Bagby no Brasil: uma contribuição para o estudo dos primórdios batistas em terras brasileiras*. Rio de Janeiro: Junta de Educação Religiosa e Publicações, 1987.

Harter, Eugene C. *A colônia perdida da confederação: a emigração norte-americana para o Brasil após a Guerra de Secessão*. Rio de Janeiro: Nórdica, 1985.

Hill, Laurence F. *Confederate Exodus to Latin America*. Austin: Texas State Historical Association, 1936.

Jones, Judith MacKnight. *Folhas esparsas*. São Paulo: João Scortecci Editora, 1996.

———. *Soldado, descansa! uma epopéia norte-americana sob os céus do Brasil*. São Paulo: Jarde, 1967.

Léonard, Émile-G. *O protestantismo brasileiro: estudo de eclesiologia e de história social*. 2 ed. Rio de Janeiro e São Paulo: Junta de Educação Religiosa e Publicações/ASTE, 1981.

Lessa, Benjamim Themudo. "Primórdios do trabalho protestante no Brasil". En *Ensaios Paulistas*, pp. 763–768 . São Paulo: Editora Anhambi, 1958.

Lessa, Vicente Themudo. *Annaes da Primeira Egreja Presbyteriana de São Paulo, 1863–1903: subsídios para a história do presbyterianismo brasileiro*. São Paulo, 1938.

Long, Eula Kennedy. *Do meu velho baú metodista*. São Paulo: Junta Geral de Educação Cristã da Igreja Metodista do Brasil, 1968.

Moog, Clodomiro Vianna. *Bandeirantes e pioneiro: paralelo entre duas culturas*. 7° ed. Rio de Janeiro: Civilização Brasileira, 1964.

Oliveira, Betty Antunes de. *Centelha em restolho seco: uma contribuição para a história do trabalho batista no Brasil*. Rio de Janeiro: Editora da Autora, 1985.

Ribeiro, Boanerges. *Protestantismo e cultura brasileira: aspectos culturais da implantação do protestantismo no Brasil*. São Paulo: Casa Editora Presbiteriana, 1981.

Rios, José Arthur. "Assimilation of Emigrants from the Old South in Brazil". *Social Forces* 26:1 (outubro 1947), 145–152.

Rocha, Isnard. *Histórias da história do metodismo no Brasli: em comemoração ao Primeiro Centenário da Implantação Definitiva do Metodismo no Brasil, 1867–1967*. São Bernardo do Campo: Imprensa Metodista, 1967.

———. *Pioneiros e bandeirantes do metodismo no Brasil: cem biografias, bispos, ministros, pregadores locais e leigos da Igreja Metodista do Brasil*. São Bernardo do Campo: Imprensa Metodista, 1967.

Smith, James Porter. *An Open Door in Brazil*. Richmond, Va.: Presbyterian Committee of Publication, 1925.

Tarsier, Pedro. *História das perseguições religiosas no Brasil*. São Paulo: Cultura Moderna, 1936.

Vieira, David Gueiros. "Some Protestant Missionary Letters Relating to the Religious Question in Brazil, 1872–1875". *Americas* (24 abril 1968), 337–353.

Weawer, Blanche Henry Clark. "Confederate Emigration to Brazil". *Journal of Southern History* 27:1 (fevereiro 1961), 33–53.

——. "Confederate Immigrants and Evangelical Churches in Brazil". *Journal of Southern History* 18:4 (novembro 1952), 446–468.

Religion in the
English-Speaking Caribbean

14. Changing Patterns of Denominational Affiliation in the Christian Church in Trinidad and Tobago

Margaret D. Rouse-Jones

The Republic of Trinidad and Tobago is a twin island state at the southern extremity of the Caribbean chain of islands. It achieved political independence in 1962. First colonized by Europeans (mainly Spanish, Dutch, and English), the islands were also home to descendants of Europeans (Spanish, French, and English), Africans, East Indians, Chinese, Syrian Lebanese, and Portuguese. Thus, the country is well known for its social, cultural, and ethnic diversity, which has also contributed to a complex pattern of religious life. Roman Catholicism, introduced by the Spanish in the sixteenth century, has remained the country's largest Christian denomination. Hindus are the second largest religious group, followed by Anglicans. Other Christian and Afro-Christian religions and Muslims constitute the other significant groups on the islands.

This paper examines the changing patterns of Christian denominational affiliation in Trinidad and Tobago for the period from 1946 to the 1990s.[1] The study considers the mainline denominations as well as the newer, independent fundamental Christian churches whose beliefs and practices are based in the teachings of the Holy Bible, but does not include reference to Afro-Christian groups that combine elements of Christianity with African religious traditions. It also looks at current trends in the Christian church scene such as the shift away from denominational patterns toward independent fellowships and congregations. Paradoxically, these independent ministries are actively seeking to form groups, networks, and associations, indicating a desire for unity.

The paper concludes with a bibliography of sources for the study of the Christian church in Trinidad and Tobago, an analysis of the research emphases as well as lacunae, and brief comments on the responsibility of librarians and other information providers to acquire and assure access to important materials. The bibliography was assembled mainly from the holdings at the West Indiana Collection at the Main Library, The University of the West Indies, St. Augustine. This collection constitutes the most extensive source of research resources on this subject.

The most significant development affecting the Christian church in Trinidad and Tobago over the last fifty years has been the growth of the

Pentecostal (including Charismatic) movement.[2] This movement, which began with a revival in Los Angeles in 1906, is the world's fastest growing Christian denomination—at a time when membership in most other denominations is declining.

Changing Patterns in Christian Church Affiliation

The history of the Christian church is "the story of the ongoing developmental process of putting the church back into the kind of divine order and structure which was manifested in the days of the early glory of the church in the Book of Acts."[3] There are five major movements in the restoration of the church:[4]

1. The Protestant Movement (1500) began with Martin Luther, who received the revelation of justification by faith (Romans 1:16–17). Great denominations evolved out of the ensuing conflict: Lutheran, Episcopal, and Presbyterian. It also spawned other leaders such as John Calvin and John Knox.

2. The Holiness/Evangelical Movement (1800) is identified primarily with John Wesley, the most outspoken exponent of the Holiness teaching, who saw the restoration of three main truths: sanctification, baptism by immersion, and divine healing. The Baptists, Methodists, Evangelicals, and Church of God are associated with this movement.

3. The Pentecostal Movement (1900) brought the restoration of the baptism in the Holy Spirit with the evidence of speaking in tongues. The Pentecostal Holiness Church, Assemblies of God, and United Pentecostal Church are among the main denominations that evolved from this movement.

4. The Latter Rain Movement (1948) brought to the church the reality and practice of lifting of hands with extended and melodious singing of praise and the deliberate praising of God in the dance, in contrast to the classical Pentecostal shout of praise and involuntary dancing in the spirit.

5. The Charismatic Movement (1960s), an extension of the Latter Rain Movement, represented the widespread evidence of all the truths which have been restored since the beginning of the period of the great restoration. "The Charismatic Movement broke open the hard shells of the established mainline Protestant and Catholic churches, sweeping many into the Kingdom of God."[5] Hamon classifies the Charismatic Movement into two main categories: the Denominational Basic-Charismatic and the Nondenominational Present-Truth Charismatic.

The Christian Church in Trinidad and Tobago

Census data pertaining to religious affiliation in Trinidad and Tobago for the period 1946–1990s shed light on the way the Christian church in Trinidad and Tobago is defined (Table 1). The data show the changing pattern of denominational affiliation in the Christian church and the growth of the Pentecostal movement. According to the 1946 census, 70.8 percent of the population was Christian, distributed among seven denominations—Roman Catholic, Anglican, Presbyterian, Wesleyan, Baptist, Moravian, and Seventh-day Adventist. An eighth category, "Other Christian," appears in the 1946 and 1960 censuses, accounting for 1.3 and 2.2 percent of the population, respectively. Pentecostals are not mentioned as a separate category; they were most likely counted among "Other Christians" in 1946.

Table 1. Religious Denominations in Trinidad and Tobago,
1946–1990

Denomination/Religion	As % of Total Population				
	1946	1960	1970	1980	1990
Roman Catholic	34.5	36.2	35.6	32.9	29.4
Anglican	24.2	21.1	18.1	14.7	10.9
Presbyterian	3.6	3.9	4.2	3.8	3.4
Wesleyan or Methodist	2.5	2.2	1.7	1.4	1.1
Baptist	2.2	2.2	0.72	2.4	3.0
Moravian	1.3	-	0.7	-	-
Seventh-day Adventist	1.2	1.5	1.8	2.5	3.7
Jehovah's Witness	-	0.46	-	0.8	1.3
Pentecostal	-	0.49	-	3.45	7.5
Church of God	-	-	0.54	-	-
Other Christian	1.3	2.2	-	-	-
Hindu	22.7	23.0	24.7	24.9	23.7
Muslim	5.8	6.0	6.25	6.0	5.8
Other Non-Christian	0.7	0.03	-	-	-
Other Not Stated	-	0.5	5.6	6.1	8.8
None	-	-	-	1.0	1.2
Total	100	99.8	99.9	99.9	98.8

Sources: Lloyd Braithwaite, *Social Stratification in Trinidad: A Preliminary Analysis* (Jamaica: Institute of Social and Economic Research, 1975; first published in 1953), p. 59; Trinidad and Tobago, Central Statistical Office, *Annual Statistical Digest, 1970, 1980, 1988, 1993,* "Population by Sex, Religion and Area," 1960, 1970, 1980, 1990. See also Margaret Rouse-Jones, "Changing Patterns of Denominational Affiliation in Trinidad and Tobago: An Exploratory Study," in S. Ryan, ed., *Social and Occupational Stratification in Contemporary Trinidad and Tobago* (St. Augustine, Trinidad: Institute of Social and Economic Research, The University of the West Indies, 1991), pp. 354–355.

According to the data in Table 1:

1. Roman Catholicism increased by about 2 percent between 1946 and 1960 and declined thereafter. By 1990 the percentage of the population that was Roman Catholic was lower than in 1946.

2. The percentage of Anglicans has also steadily declined: 24.2 percent in 1946; 21.1 percent in 1960; 18.1 percent in 1970; 14.7 percent in 1980; and 10.9 percent in 1990.

3. Presbyterians increased slightly in 1960 and 1970 and decreased slightly in 1980 and again in 1990. The percentage of Presbyterians in 1990 was less that it was fifty years before.

4. The Wesleyan/Methodist experience resembled that of the Anglicans; there was a decrease each year although it was not as dramatic.

5. The percentage of Seventh-day Adventists increased steadily over the fifty-year period: 1.2 percent (1946); 1.5 percent (1960); 1.8 (1970); 2.5 percent (1980); 3.7 percent (1990).

6. Jehovah's Witnesses also show an increase over the period: 0.46 percent (1960); 0.8 percent (1980); 1.3 percent (1990).

7. Pentecostals, as noted above, were not accounted for separately in the 1946 census. In 1960, they were less than 0.5 percent of the population. They are not represented in the 1970 census figures. In 1980 they constituted 3.45 percent.[6] However, the most dramatic change in the denominational pattern for the entire period is seen among the Pentecostals; between 1980 and 1990 the percentage of Pentecostals doubled.

As noted, among the more significant changes in the pattern of denominational affiliation are the decline of the Anglican Church and the increase in the number of Pentecostals. With respect to the latter, in 1980 the percentage of Pentecostals (3.45 percent) compared quite favorably with that of Presbyterians (3.81 percent) and exceeded that of the Wesleyan Methodists (1.4 percent), the Baptists (2.4 percent), and the Seventh-day Adventists (2.5 percent), all of whom, unlike the Pentecostals, had been separately identified in the 1946 census. For comparison, the percentage of Jehovah's Witnesses, who, like the Pentecostals, were not represented in 1946, like that of the Pentecostals, has constantly increased over the period under consideration. In 1960 they constituted 0.46, in 1980 0.8, and in 1990 1.3 percent, whereas Pentecostals increased from 0.49 percent, to 3.45 percent, to 7.5 percent in the same period of time.

Historical data indicate that by 1946 Pentecostals were making inroads into the religious fabric of Trinidad and Tobago society. The origins of the movement in Trinidad and Tobago may be traced back to 1920, with the arrival of the Jamieson family, Pentecostal missionaries who established the Woodbrook Pentecostal Church. In 1946 the Pentecostal Assemblies of the West Indies became a district of the Pentecostal Assemblies of Canada and the West Indies, and the West Indies School of Theology was founded for the training of pastors. Within the Pentecostal ambit came the Wilhelmsen family in 1953; they established the Open Bible Standard Churches. The New Testament Church of God was established in 1956 following the merger of a congregation of the Christian General Assembly with the New Testament Church of God (as distinct from the Church of God). In 1959 the International Pentecostal Assembly was formed as the result of an organization having split from the New Testament Church of God. In 1970 the Pentecostal United Holy Church of Trinidad and Tobago was incorporated. This was an offshoot of the United Holy Church of America which had been introduced into Trinidad and Tobago in 1950. All of these denominational groups have established congregations to varying degrees in the two islands.

There is also evidence, however, of dramatic increases within the last two decades in the number of independent Pentecostal or Charismatic churches.[7] Many of these are headed by pastors or elders who formerly belonged to the Pentecostal denominational groups (e.g., the Pentecostal Assemblies of the West Indies or the Open Bible Standard Churches). As indicated, these changes are not reflected in the census data. The adherents would most likely be represented as Pentecostal or "Other Not Stated" in the census data.

Until We All Reach Unity

The growth and development of the independent Pentecostal/Charismatic-type congregations in Trinidad and Tobago remains largely unstudied. A private source has drawn up a list that identifies twenty-one denominations and about seventy independent fellowships which have come into being in the last twenty years.[8] Another source mentions as many as 130 independent churches. It is worth noting as well that this phenomenon is also evident throughout Latin America. A recent report indicates that

> secular researchers calculate that 400 Latin Americans convert to evangelical Christianity every hour. . . . In Peru, a Protestant church is planted every eight hours. In Rio de Janeiro, one new congregation is born every day. . . .The fastest growth has been among Pentecostal and charismatic churches. Less than 2 percent of the Protestant population at the end of World War II were in Pentecostal churches. Today, about 66 percent of Latin American Protestants attend a Pentecostal church.[9]

The apparent fragmentation taking place within Christendom is in direct opposition to the doctrines of the Christian faith. The founder of the church, Jesus Christ, continually advocated unity among his followers. This was a consistent request when he prayed for what has evolved as the institution of the church:

Holy Father, protect them . . . so *that they may be one as we are one.* . . .
My prayer is not for them alone. I pray also for those who will believe in
me through their message, *that all of them may be one.* Father, just as you
are in me and I am in you . . . I have given them the glory that you gave
me, *that they may be one as we are one*: I in them and you in me. *May
they be brought to complete unity* to let the world know that you sent me
and have loved them even as you have loved me. (John 17:11, 20–23)
(Italics mine)

In the face of the move away from the traditional denominational patterns, however, there appears to be at the same time a coming together of the emerging
independent fellowships.

A *Time* magazine article refers to "post denominational Protestantism, a
religious movement that links thousands of U.S. churches in informal networks
outside the boundaries of mainline Protestant or evangelical denominations."[10]
In Trinidad and Tobago two such groupings, bringing together the independent
churches mentioned above, have emerged within the last decade. Although many
of the leaders of the independent churches came out of the denominational structure for a variety of reasons, there is a strong call for unity among them. One
such group of leaders of independent fellowships, while recognizing the independence of their congregations, felt it was necessary for them to unite in order
to assume an effective stance within the community. The group founded the Association of Independent Ministers (A.I.M.) in 1992. In a recent message, the
president expressed the view that the unification of independent ministers and
ministries under the umbrella of A.I.M. was not an impossible task. The membership of A.I.M. includes some one hundred ministers, representing 65 organizations and 130 nondenominational churches in Trinidad and Tobago.

The Association was established to address the need for an umbrella organization for autonomous assemblies and to create a forum where members
can gather in meetings, conventions, and associations. A.I.M. is also committed to fostering unity in the Body of Christ and eradicating the spirit of sectari-
anism and dissension through the propagation of the gospel of Jesus Christ. The
Association also recognizes that the church in general ought to make a positive
impact on the nation and influence the nonreligious sphere of societal activity.

Another interesting grouping of independent churches which has its base
in Trinidad and Tobago is the World Breakthrough Network (WBN), an association of some thirty individual ministers, ministries, churches, and church-
related organizations. The member organizations link their vision, resources,
products, and people in one unified purpose, while maintaining the essential
autonomy of their individual ministries. This grouping of independent churches
is important because of its international nature. Apart from the nine Trinidad
and Tobago churches, Barbados, Antigua, St. Kitts, St. Maarten, St. Vincent,

South Africa, United Kingdom, United States, Nigeria, Venezuela, Mexico, and Brazil are also represented in the World Breakthrough Network.

The church organization at the heart of this network is Elijah Centre. Established in 1990, it has grown considerably, "not only in numbers, but also in spiritual authority and vision." This fellowship adheres to all of the doctrines mentioned in the restoration movements described above. Its vision is also:

> To recognise and receive the foundation laying ministries of church apostles and prophets along with the other governmental office ministries of evangelists, pastors and teachers so that the house of the Lord may be established on a firm spiritual foundation and be brought to strength and maturity.[11]

The statement of faith includes a belief in the "full function of the five-fold ministry viz.: apostles, prophets, evangelists, pastors, teachers, given to perfect and equip saints (believers) so that they can enter into the work of their ministry." The original statement from which this tenet of faith is derived incorporates the idea that the unity of believers was the ultimate purpose for the five offices:

> It was he [Jesus Christ] who gave some to be apostles, some to be prophets, some to be evangelists, and some to be pastors and teachers, to prepare God's people for works of service so that the body of Christ may be built up *until we all reach unity* in the faith. . . .(Ephesians 4:11–13) (Italics mine)

The changing church scene in Trinidad and Tobago demonstrates an interesting paradox. There is, on the one hand, a movement away from the traditional denominational structures within which the Christian church operated toward an increase in the independent congregations. On the other hand, at the same time, these are turning to each other and striving for a unity which may seem incongruent with their natural existence and operation. The phenomenon is wide open for interpretation by sociologists, anthropologists, and others. However, to the adherent it may be an expression of the fulfillment of the Word of God, a mystery of the faith.

Bibliographic Resources

The following bibliography for the study of the Christian church in Trinidad and Tobago includes mainly materials held at the Main Library, The University of the West Indies, St. Augustine. Because the topic remains to be studied in greater depth, however, it presents many challenges to librarians and other providers of information resources.

A large percentage of the references are the outcome of the final year undergraduate course in the Faculty of Humanities and Education (formerly Arts and General Studies.) More than 80 percent (91 out of 115) of the citations are works undertaken as part of the university's Caribbean Studies Project[12] over the last twenty-five years. Although these undergraduate theses, in many cases the only piece of work on the subject, vary in quality, they continue to be used regularly, and the Library has had to assure their availability.

A review of the references also shows that Roman Catholics have been the most frequently researched group (50 studies), with particular emphasis on the church's influence in education. Other topics include: Charismatic renewal within Catholicism and especially the gift of prophecy; aspects of Marian theology; and religious orders, clergy, etc. (Benedictines, nuns of St. Joseph of Cluny, Carmelites).

Some studies cover specific periods in church history: for example, the pre-emancipation period; the period of intense trade union activity; the early years of British rule; and the period 1844–1870 when there was significant conflict with the Anglican Church.

The second most studied group, according to the bibliography, is the Canadian Mission/ Presbyterians. Most of the studies deal with the role of these missionaries in helping the East Indians, primarily indentured laborers, assimilate into society. As with the Roman Catholics, the theme of education has also been a focus of study as well, along with works on the role of women and the contribution of individual missionaries, such as John Morton and Kenneth Grant, and individual Presbyterian churches.

The Anglican Church, despite being the second largest Christian denomination, has not been the subject of much serious research. Two of the three Caribbean Studies Project theses on the Anglican Church look specifically at the brief period between 1844 and 1870, a time characterized by conflict between Anglicans and Roman Catholics, particularly in the area of education, which resulted in the disestablishment of the Anglican Church in 1870.

The Pentecostal and Evangelical groups (Church of God, Church of the Nazarene, Open Bible, Pentecostal Assemblies, Wesleyan Holiness) have also been the subject of work by undergraduate students of The University of the West Indies. These studies have begun to document the introduction, growth, and development of Pentecostalism in Trinidad and Tobago. For example, one study looks at the conversion of non-Christians (Hindus and Muslims) to Christianity since independence and notes that although the rapidly rising Pentecostal sects are drawing many members from the East Indian community to the faith, the majority of these Indians are coming from other Christian denominations.[13]

Pentecostals have also been the subject of anthropological research. One such study, by a researcher from Helsinki, examined religiosity of evangelical university students and raised issues relating to the acquisition of relevant information.[14]

On the subject of acquisition, most of the documentation for the study of the present-day Christian church in Trinidad and Tobago is still in the realm of gray literature. The brochures and pamphlets produced by the new independent churches are important sources for understanding the ongoing changes in the church. Information providers need to be vigilant in collecting these kinds of materials.

Churches on the Internet

A recent article in *Time* (December 16, 1996), commenting on "the signs of on-line religious activity," noted that religious organizations are using the new forms of electronic communication to improve their evangelization efforts. For example, some information about the Christian church in Trinidad and Tobago is available only on the Internet and in no other source. The Elijah Centre, mentioned above, has a fairly extensive Web site, which is maintained by "The Elijah Centre Technology Group." The Evangelical Churches of the West (such as Church of the Nazarene), Word of Life Faith Centre, Community Bible Church, and Kingsway Fellowship of Trinidad all have a significant Web presence.

To adequately serve the needs of scholars in the field of religion, libraries must pursue a proactive acquisitions policy, continuing to look to traditional sources while also collecting materials available only on the Internet or through other forms of electronic access.

NOTES

1. Several persons gave valuable assistance in the preparation of this paper. I should like to acknowledge their contribution because without it the paper would never have seen the light of day, as it was being written at the same time that I assumed responsibility as Campus Librarian at The Main Library, The University of the West Indies, St. Augustine. My sincere thanks go to the following persons: Elmelinda Lara, librarian in charge of the Social Sciences Division who searched the Internet and located relevant information; Graham Taylor, Systems Analyst who also searched the Internet for other Trinidad and Tobago Web sites and supplied information on the World Breakthrough Network; Juliet Chan Wing, computer operator at U.W.I. Library who searched the databases of West Indiana material and located materials in CARINDEX databases and in the database of the Caribbean Studies Project (CARST); Marlene Eversley searched the card catalogs and online public access catalog, located additional references, and prepared the bibliography; Gloria Baptiste and the staff in the West Indiana Division located material for consultation; Sherma Quamina-Wong Kang and Rabia Ramlogan assisted in the final preparation of the paper; Rev. Kenneth Ragoonath of Hospital Fellowship Ministry shared with me a list from his database of denominations and independent fellowships in Trinidad and Tobago; and Dr. Eric St. Cyr, pastor of Faith Revival Ministries, shared pamphlets and leaflets about the Association of Independent Ministers and other useful information. I would also like to express my appreciation for the constant encouragement and support given by my husband, Rupert Jones. Finally, and equally important, I thank Annette, Val, Paula, Karen, Nicole, little Sherma, Yolande, and Kathleen for their encouragement, moral support, and many prayers.

2. The term "Pentecostal" refers to those denominations and sects within Christianity that believe in and experience the Baptism of the Holy Spirit as it is described in the Biblical account of the 120 followers of Jesus Christ in the days following his death and resurrection. The disciples had been instructed to wait until they had been baptized with the Holy Ghost. This occurred on the feast day of Pentecost when it is reported that "they were all filled with the Holy Ghost, and began to speak with other tongues, as the Spirit gave them utterance" (Acts 2:4). Further evidence in the biblical record shows that other groups in the early church also had the same experience.

3. Noel Woodroffe, *Understanding God's Prophetic Move Today* (Trinidad: Elijah Ministries International, 1991), p. 7.

4. See Woodroffe, summarizing Hamon, *The Eternal Church* (Point Washington, Fla.: Christian International Publishers, 1981).

5. Woodroffe, p. 15.

6. Among the major non-Christian religions (Hindus and Muslims), the increases over the period were quite small. The Hindus showed a decrease between 1980 and 1990, as did the Muslims.

7. The Charismatic movement in Roman Catholicism in Trinidad and Tobago is treated in *The Fruitful Vine: The First Ten Years of Catholic Charismatic Renewal in Trinidad and Tobago: 1972–1982* (Arima, Trinidad and Tobago: National Service Team, Catholic Charismatic Renewal, 1983).

8. I am extremely grateful to Rev. Kenneth Ragoonath of Hospital Fellowship Ministry for sharing this list with me. Rev. Ragoonath has indicated that the list is not up to date.

9. "Latin America's Sweeping Revival," *Newsweek*, June 1996 [Internet version].

10. "Finding God on the Web," *Time,* December 16, 1966.

11. Elijah Centre: History and Purpose of the Assembly [www.elijahcentre.org].

12. The Caribbean Studies Project requires final-year students to prepare a paper, based on original research under faculty supervision, on a Caribbean-related topic (5,000–8,000 words).

13. See my "Changing Patterns of Denominational Affiliation in Trinidad and Tobago: An Exploratory Study," in Selwyn Ryan, ed., *Social and Occupational Stratification in Contemporary Trinidad and Tobago* (St. Augustine, Trinidad and Tobago: Institute of Social and Economic Research, The University of the West Indies, 1991), pp. 350–374.

14. In this particular instance the item was part of a collection donated to the library upon the death of a member of the faculty. The researcher had sent him a copy of the work.

BIBLIOGRAPHY

General

Broucek, David Roger. "Listening to the Church: The Perceptions of Trinidad Church Leaders Regarding the Educational Needs of Their Churches" [D. Miss. dissertation]. Deerfield, Ill.: Trinity Evangelical Divinity School, 1990.

Dayfoot, Arthur C. "Supplement to *The Shaping of the West Indian Church.*" Th.D. thesis, 1982. 1994.

Hamon, Bill. *The Eternal Church.* Point Washington, Fla.: Christian International Publishers, 1981.

Harricharan, J. T., Rev. *The Work of the Christian Churches among the East Indians in Trinidad during the Period of Indentureship, 1845–1917.* N.p., 1975.

Helander, Eila. "To Change and to Preserve: A Study of the Religiosity of Evangelical University Students and Graduates in Trinidad." *Annals of the Finnish Society for Missiology and Ecumenics,* 1986.

Maharaj, Esther. "Hindu and Muslim Conversion to Christianity in Trinidad since Independence." Caribbean Studies thesis, 1994.

Moore, Dennison. *Origins and Development of Racial Ideology in Trinidad: The Black View of the East Indian.* Tunapuna, Trinidad and Tobago: Chakra Publishing House, 1995.

Premdas, Ralph R. *Ethnic Conflict and Religion: The Christian Challenge of Reconciliation.* Notre Dame, Ind.: Joan B. Kroc Institute for International Peace Studies, University of Notre Dame, 1996.

Rouse-Jones, Margaret D. "Changing Patterns of Denominational Affiliation in Trinidad and Tobago: An Exploratory Study." In Selwyn Ryan, ed., *Social and Occupational Stratification in Contemporary Trinidad and Tobago.* St. Augustine, Trinidad and Tobago: Institute of Social and Economic Research, The University of the West Indies, 1991. Pp. 350–374.

Seeseran, E. B. Rosabelle. "Church and State in Education: Trinidad 1814–1870." M.A. thesis. St. Augustine, Trinidad and Tobago: The University of the West Indies, 1974.

Sitahal, Harold. "The Mission of the Church in Trinidad: An Examination of the Church's Work and Influence among the Descendants of the East Indians" [M. Th. Dissertation]. Montreal: McGill University, 1967.

Woodroffe, Noel. *Understanding God's Prophetic Move Today.* Tunapuna, Trinidad and Tobago: Elijah Ministries International, 1991.

African Methodist Episcopal Church

Whiskie, Wesley. "History of the African Methodist Episcopal (A.M.E.) Church in Trinidad and Tobago." Caribbean Studies thesis, 1996.

Anglicans

Caesar, Oris. "The Anglican Church as an Agent of Socialisation in Trinidad and Tobago." Caribbean Studies thesis, 1973.

Mathura, Rita. "History of the Anglican Church in Trinidad with Particular Reference to the Anglican-Catholic Conflict (1844–1870)." Caribbean Studies thesis, 1978.

Raymond, Wilcox A. "Relations between the Anglicans and Catholics in Nineteenth-Century Trinidad." Caribbean Studies thesis, 1973.

Baptists

Chatoor, Donna. "The Socio-Historical Development of the London Baptists in Trinidad." Caribbean Studies thesis, 1977.

Chaves, Ingrid. "A Study of the Historical Development of the Baptist Community of Trinidad." Caribbean Studies thesis, 1986.

Joseph, Eileen. "The Free Negro Settlements in Trinidad with Special Emphasis on the Baptists in the Six Company Villages of Ortoire and Savanna Grande." Caribbean Studies thesis, 1969.

Phillip, Ann M. "The History of the Fundamental Baptist Mission of Trinidad and Tobago." Caribbean Studies thesis, 1974.

Church of God

Drakes, Frank. "A Brief History of the Church of God in Trinidad and Tobago, 1906–1975." Caribbean Studies thesis, 1976.

Farrell, David. "Efforts by the 'Church of God' to Achieve Christian Unity in Trinidad and Tobago." Caribbean Studies thesis.

Church of the Nazarene

Brown, Pauline. "The History of the Church of the Nazarene in Trinidad and Tobago, 1966–1989." Caribbean Studies thesis, 1990.

Evangelical Churches

De Leon, Raphael. "Ritual Drama in the Evangelical Churches in Trinidad." Caribbean Studies thesis, 1991.

Helander, Eila. "To Change and to Preserve: A Study of the Religiosity of Evangelical University Students and Graduates in Trinidad." *Annals of the Finnish Society for Missiology and Ecumenics,* 1986.

Thomas, Wayne. "The History of the Evangelical Alliance Mission in Trinidad." Caribbean Studies thesis, 1977.

Open Bible Standard Church

Sinanan, Shobha. "The History and Development of Open Bible Standard Churches in Trinidad and Tobago." Caribbean Studies thesis, 1983.

Pentecostal Assemblies of the West Indies

Alexander, Colin. "Pentecostalism in Trinidad and Tobago: A History of the Churches in Trinidad and Tobago Which Are Affiliated to the Pentecostal Assemblies of the West Indies." Caribbean Studies thesis, 1975.

Drakes, Frankie Douglas. "Education for Leadership: An Historical Study of Major Problems of the Provision of Theological Training by Evangelical Churches in Trinidad and Tobago, 1946–1975." [M.A. Dissertation.] St. Augustine, Trinidad and Tobago: The University of the West Indies, 1986.

Glazier, Stephen D. "Pentecostal Exorcism and Modernization in Trinidad, West Indies." In Stephen D. Glazier, ed., *Perspectives on Pentecostalism: Case Studies from the Caribbean and Latin America.* Washington, D.C.: University Press of America, 1980. Pp. 67–80.

Gray, Germaine. "The Pentecostal Assemblies of the West Indies: Its History, Contribution and Impact upon West Indian Society, with Special Reference to Trinidad and Tobago." Caribbean Studies thesis, 1992.

Mohammed, Karen. "The Growth of the Pentecostal Movement in Trinidad." Caribbean Studies thesis, 1975.

Persad, Jannet. "A Comparative Study of Some Aspects of the Pentecostal and Presbyterian Churches in Trinidad." Caribbean Studies thesis, 1977.

Ramnarine, Debbie. "Four Decades of Pentecostalism in Trinidad: 1946–1986." Caribbean Studies thesis, 1987.

Rouse-Jones, Margaret D. "Changing Patterns of Denominational Affiliation in Trinidad and Tobago: An Exploratory Study." In Selwyn Ryan, ed., *Social and Occupational Stratification in Contemporary Trinidad and Tobago*. St. Augustine, Trinidad and Tobago: Institute of Social and Economic Research, The University of the West Indies, 1991. Pp. 350–374.

Soodan, Brenda. "A Survey of the Fundamentalist Evangelical Churches in Trinidad." Caribbean Studies thesis, 1974.

Taylor, Rollaton M. E. "The Attitude of Pentecostals to Alcohol and Drugs (Especially Marijuana) with Particular Reference to Woodbrook Pentecostal Church's Pattern." Caribbean Studies thesis, 1980.

Walker, Christopher Harlan. "Caribbean Charismatics: The Pentecostal Church as Community on the Island of Tobago." [Ph.D. Dissertation.] Chapel Hill: University of North Carolina, 1987.

Presbyterians

Bahadur, Catherine. "The Work and the Contribution of the Canadian Mission in Trinidad." Caribbean Studies thesis, 1973.

Bisnath, Edward. "The Canadian Mission to the Indians in Trinidad: A Historical Survey, 1868–1965." Caribbean Studies thesis.

Canadian Mission Council, Trinidad. *East Meets West in Trinidad*. Toronto: Young People's Missionary Education, 1934.

Doodnath, Samuel. *A Short History of the Early Presbyterian Church and the Indian Immigrant, 1845–1945*. [Trinidad]: S. Doodnath, [1984].

Dookhoo, Christian. "The Impact of the Presbyterian Church on Indian Women in Trinidad, 1900–1980." Caribbean Studies thesis, 1987.

Ganessingh, Neil. "An Historical Account of Canadian Mission Education in Trinidad." Caribbean Studies thesis.

Hamid, Idris. *A History of the Presbyterian Church in Trinidad 1868–1968: The Struggles of a Church in Colonial Captivity*. San Fernando, Trinidad and Tobago: St. Andrew's Theological College, 1980.

Kalloo, Kirk. "St. Andrews Theological College: The Evolution of Presbyterian Theological Education in Trinidad, 1892–1991." Caribbean Studies thesis, 1991.

Kasmally, Arlene Michelle. "A Brief History of the Guaico Pastoral Region of the Presbyterian Church of Trinidad and Tobago, with Special Reference to the Morton Memorial Church, 1868–1992." Caribbean Studies thesis, 1993.

Lachman, Roy B. "A Socio-Historical Account of the Role of the Presbyterian Church in Education in Trinidad." Caribbean Studies thesis, 1968.

Legge, Garth W. "The Report of a Preliminary Survey of the Presbyterian Church of Trinidad and Grenada: October 18–November 14, 1965."

Madhosingh, Christine A. "The Trinidad Presbyterian: The First Ten Years, 1904–1914." Caribbean Studies thesis, 1984.

Mahadeo, Marilyn. "The Role of the Presbyterian Church in the Education of East Indian Women of Trinidad." Caribbean Studies thesis, 1976.

Manraj, Nadine I. V. "The History of the Presbyterian Church in Trinidad and Its Role in the Society." Caribbean Studies thesis, 1993.

Mohipath, Rupertee. "The Role of Women in the Work of the Canadian Missionaries in Trinidad during the Last Century." Caribbean Studies thesis, 1976.

Mount, Graeme S. *Presbyterian Missions to Trinidad and Puerto Rico*. Hantsport, Nova Scotia: Lancelot Press, 1983.

Persad, Jannet. "A Comparative Study of Some Aspects of the Pentecostal and Presbyterian Churches in Trinidad." Caribbean Studies thesis, 1977.

Presbyterian Church in Trinidad and Grenada. *History of the San Juan/Santa Cruz Pastoral Change: National Centenary Celebrations, 1868–1968*. San Fernando, Trinidad and Tobago: [Presbyterian Church in Trinidad and Grenada], 1968.

Rameshwar, C. E. K. "The Role of the Presbyterian Church in Education in Trinidad, 1868–1917." Caribbean Studies thesis.

Ramlal, Victor Daniel. "The Contribution of Rev. Dr. Kenneth James Grant to the Development of the Canadian Mission among the East Indians in Trinidad." Caribbean Studies thesis, 1979.

Ramsewak, Gloria. "John Morton's Contribution to Education in Trinidad, 1868–1912." Caribbean Studies thesis, 1971.

Robinson, Lennard W. "The Work of the Presbyterians among the East Indian Community of Trinidad." Caribbean Studies thesis, 1969.

Sahadat, Joseph. "The Politics of the Presbyterian Church in Trinidad in Recent Times." Caribbean Studies thesis, 1979.

Samaroo, Brinsley. "The Canadian Presbyterian Mission to Trinidad." Paper presented to the 4th Conference of the Association of Caribbean Historians, Jamaica, 1972.

Samaroo, Brinsley. "Education as Socialisation: Form and Content in the Syllabus in the Canadian Missions Presbyterian School in Trinidad from the Late Century." Paper presented to the 15th Conference of the Association of Caribbean Historians, Jamaica, 1983.

Samaroo, Brinsley. "The Presbyterian Canadian Mission as an Agent of Integration in Trinidad during the 19th and Early 20th Centuries." St. Augustine, Trinidad and Tobago, 1972.

Sammy, David. "The Role of the Canadian Presbyterian Mission in the Establishment of Rural Education in Trinidad, 1868–1916." Caribbean Studies thesis, 1978.

Sharma, Rena Kamini. "Youth Involvement within the Presbyterian Church of Trinidad." Caribbean Studies thesis, 1977.

Tajudeen, Carol. "The Attitude of Sixth-Formers towards the Presbyterian Religion in San Fernando, Trinidad." Caribbean Studies thesis.

Teelucksingh, Jerome. "The Contribution of the Presbyterian Church to Education in Trinidad, 1868–1996." Caribbean Studies thesis, 1996.

Wajadally, Amerone. "The Role of the Presbyterian Church in the Development of Education in Trinidad." Caribbean Studies thesis.

Roman Catholics

Baptiste, Mary. "Youth Programmes Sponsored by the Catholic Charismatic Renewal in Trinidad and Tobago, 1978–1988: A Theological/Pastoral Appraisal." Caribbean Studies thesis, 1989.

Bernard, Jules. "The Role of the Catholics in Trinidad Education." Caribbean Studies thesis.

Birch, Ernest F. "The Development of the Roman Catholic Secondary School System in Trinidad and Tobago, 1872–1972." Caribbean Studies thesis, 1972.

Brunton-Kelly, Celeste Rose. "The Nuns of St. Joseph of Cluny and Teacher Education in Trinidad and Tobago." Caribbean Studies thesis, 1980.

Campbell, Carl C. "The Rebel Priest: Francis De Ridder and the Fight for Free Coloureds' Rights in Trinidad, 1825–1832." Paper presented to the 11th Conference of the Association of Caribbean Historians, Curaçao, 1979.

Campbell, John. "An Exploration into the Growth and Development of the Left in the Roman Catholic Church in Trinidad: The Case for a 'Local Theology'." Caribbean Studies thesis, 1993.

Carrington, M. "The Catholic Church in Trinidad and Local Labour, 1919–1937." Caribbean Studies thesis, 1996.

Charles, Jean. "The Catholic Church in Trinidad from Mid-Nineteenth Century." Caribbean Studies thesis, 1971.

Charles, Rose L. "The Problems of the Roman Catholic Church in the Existing Social, Political and Cultural Environment of Trinidad and Tobago." Caribbean Studies thesis, 1968.

Debi, Veda. "The Expansion of the Catholic Church in Trinidad, 1820–1838." Caribbean Studies thesis, 1975.

Dolabaille, Roma. "A Comparative Study of the Priestly Authority in Trinidad and Tobago." Caribbean Studies thesis, 1969.

Dougdeen, Karen. "Tierra de Gracia: A Study of the Marian Apparitions and Miracles at Betania, Venezuela, and Their Effects on Selected Members of the Catholic Community of Trinidad." Caribbean Studies thesis, 1994.

Dunne, James. "The Development of the Catholic Church in the Early Years of British Trinidad, 1797–1820." Caribbean Studies thesis.

Elias, George. "An Investigation of Some of the Factors That Are Responsible for the Estrangement of Roman Catholics from the Church in Trinidad." Caribbean Studies thesis, 1993.

Feheney, J. Matthew. "Catholic Education in Trinidad in the 19th Century." [M.A. Dissertation.] Mona, Kingston, Jamaica: The University of the West Indies, 1975.

The Fruitful Vine: The First Ten Years of Catholic Charismatic Renewal in Trinidad and Tobago: 1972–1982. Arima, Trinidad and Tobago: National Service Team, Catholic Charismatic Renewal, 1983.

Garcia, Bernard Alexander. "Spanish Missions in Trinidad." Caribbean Studies thesis.

Geofroy, Stephen. "Lay Ministry in the Roman Catholic Church in Trinidad in the Eighties: A Theological Evaluation." Caribbean Studies thesis, 1984.

George, Edwin A. "The Role of the Roman Catholic Church in Education in Trinidad and Tobago since the Mid-Nineteenth Century." Caribbean Studies thesis, 1972.

Gomes, Monica R. "The Role of the Catholic Church in Education in Trinidad and Tobago over the Past Century." Caribbean Studies thesis.

Graham, Roland. "The Myth and the Reality of Change in the Roman Catholic Church in Trinidad and Tobago (1956–1976)." Caribbean Studies thesis, 1977.

Guiseppi, Carlyle. "A History of the Catholic Youth Movement in Trinidad and Tobago from the Episcopacy of Archbishop Finbar Ryan to That of Archbishop Anthony Pantin." Caribbean Studies thesis, 1988.

Hee Houng, Thecla. "The Influence of the Roman Catholic Church in Education in Trinidad and Tobago during the Period 1800–1969, with Special Reference to the Years 1956–69." Caribbean Studies thesis, 1970.

Herbert, Patricia. "The Roman Catholic Church in Trinidad and Tobago in Transition from the 1960s to the Present." Caribbean Studies thesis, 1975.

Hoyte, Christopher. "The Impact of the Roman Catholic Religion on the Amerindians of Arima, Trinidad and Tobago: An Historico-Critical Account." Caribbean Studies thesis, 1991.

James, Cynthia A. "The Changing Education Role of the Roman Catholic Church in Trinidad and Tobago." Caribbean Studies thesis.

John, Jasmin Judy. "The Benedictines in the Caribbean with Special Reference to Trinidad and St. Lucia." Caribbean Studies thesis, 1982.

Joseph, Delia. "The Role of a Woman in the Catholic Church in Trinidad: A Case Study on Deborah De Rosia." Caribbean Studies thesis, 1993.

Kalloo, Koontie. "Marian Devotion: 20th Century, Trinidad." Caribbean Studies thesis, 1976.

Kelly, Patrick. "The Major Groups of Roman Catholic Clergy in Trinidad: Their Origin and Contemporary Involvement." Caribbean Studies thesis, 1977.

Marcano, Monica. "Understanding the Catholic Charismatic Renewal in Trinidad." Caribbean Studies thesis, 1980.

Martin, Ralph. *The Catholic Church at the End of an Age: What Is the Spirit Saying?* San Francisco: Ignatius Press, 1994.

Mason, Gabrielle Cita. "The Sisters of St. Joseph of Cluny in Trinidad, 1836–1895." Caribbean Studies thesis, 1977.

Mathura, Rita. "History of the Anglican Church in Trinidad with Particular Reference to the Anglican-Catholic Conflict (1844–1870)." Caribbean Studies thesis, 1978.

McPhillip, Lennox R. "The Catholic Church and the East Indian: 1845 to Present-Day Trinidad." Caribbean Studies thesis, 1977.

Moses, Michael Paul. "The Phenomenon Called Prophecy in the Catholic Charismatic Renewal in Trinidad." Caribbean Studies thesis, 1986.

Narine, Michael. "The Contribution of the Catholic Church to Education in Trinidad and Tobago (1836–1966)." Caribbean Studies thesis.

Pairaudeau, Madelane. "The Activities of the Carmelites of the English-Speaking Caribbean, with Special Reference to Trinidad and Tobago, from 1919 to the Present Time: A Theological Assessment." Caribbean Studies thesis, 1983.

Palmer, Ruth. "A Review of the Teaching of Religion in Catholic Schools in Trinidad and Tobago." Caribbean Studies thesis, 1970.

Pattron, Anand. "The Origin, Aims and Development of the Society of St. Vincent de Paul in Trinidad and Tobago." Caribbean Studies thesis, 1991.

Paul, Errol Clement. "The Roman Catholic Church's Attitude to Non-Legal Unions in Trinidad Today: A Critical Analysis of the Non-Legal Union from a Religious Standpoint." Caribbean Studies thesis, 1976.

Pereira, Christian. "The Background to the Appointment of Rev. Fr. Louis Gonin, O.P. as Fourth Archbishop of Port of Spain." Caribbean Studies thesis, 1976.

Pereira, John. "Benedictine Initiatives in Secondary Education in South Trinidad, 1930–1968." Caribbean Studies thesis, 1992.

Peters, Jimmy. "A Critical Exploration of the Spirituality of the Diocesan Clergy of Trinidad and Tobago." Caribbean Studies thesis, 1988.

Raymond, Wilcox A. "Relations between the Anglicans and Catholics in Nineteenth-Century Trinidad." Caribbean Studies thesis, 1973.

Reefer, Paulette. "Women in Charismatic Communities in Trinidad and Tobago." Caribbean Studies thesis, 1989.

Roberts, Callistus C. "A Survey and Evaluation of Two Roman Catholic (Christian) Religious Education Programmes in Trinidad and Jamaica since 1971." Caribbean Studies thesis, 1975.

Spence, Kenneth. "The Object of Exorcism as Understood by Three Roman Catholic Exorcists in Trinidad and Tobago: A Theological Appraisal." Caribbean Studies thesis.

Stephens, Joanne. "The Changing Perspective of the Roman Catholic Church towards Music Used in the Liturgy in Trinidad." Caribbean Studies thesis, 1984.

Swaratsingh, Kennedy J. "Priorities in Roman Catholic Parish Ministry: A Survey of All Full-Time Personnel Engaged in Parish Ministry in the Roman Catholic Church of Trinidad and Tobago." Caribbean Studies thesis, 1990.

Yearwood, Jacqueline. "A History of Point Fortin Roman Catholic Church, 1946–1993." Caribbean Studies thesis, 1993.

Wesleyan Holiness

Kirton, Rhoda. "The Wesleyan Holiness Church of Trinidad: A Study of Its Historical Development." Caribbean Studies thesis, 1977.

15. An Evaluation of Bibliographical Materials of Nontraditional Religions in Jamaica: Revival and Rastafari

Dorothy M. Palmer

This paper examines the two religions that are indigenous to the Caribbean island of Jamaica—Revival and Rastafari—and reviews their early development, structure, organization, and impact on Jamaican society as shown by bibliographic sources.

Religion has been an important ingredient in the lives of Caribbean people dating back to slavery when Africans used the guise of religion for meeting and planning activities. In Jamaica worship and affiliation to the "traditional" churches (Anglican, Roman Catholic, Presbyterian, Methodist, and to a certain extent Baptist) were determined by skin pigmentation and by class (Bisnauth 1995). The membership of the other religious bodies (Revival/Pocomania, Spiritual Baptists, and Pentecostals Rastafari among others) came primarily from the lower classes.

Revival

In comparison to the Rastafari, the resource material on Revival is sparse. This lack of research does not, however, lessen the important impact that Revival has had on the society. The discussion of Revival here includes the Pocomania movement since both are part of the same movement and it is difficult to differentiate between them. Pocomania believers use rum and ganja (marijuana), and they place more emphasis on singing and "spiritual dancing." They use witchcraft to a greater extent, adopt more extreme techniques of healing, and exhibit more emotional instability among their members (Simpson 1953).

Revival got its name from the "Great Revival of 1860–1861." Toward the end of the eighteenth century "there was a religious revival in England which led to Nonconformist missionaries being sent to Jamaica" (Besson and Chevannes 1996). The result was that Baptists successfully converted slaves. Black preachers such as George Lisle and Moses Baker formed the Native Baptist Movement, which served the "organizational interests of the slaves as well as spiritual guides of the flock" (Chevannes 1971, 1975). It is not a coincidence that "in the 1860's Native Baptist beliefs, reinforced by the Myalist Revival of the 1840's and 1850's and by the religion of the post-emancipation African indentured immigrants, contributed to and controlled the Great Evangelical Revival" (Besson 1976).

Alexander Bedward (1859–1930) was important in the movement and built up a large following during his thirty-year ministry. Bedward began his public ministry in the late 1890s, baptizing converts and demonstrating his curative powers by using "consecrated water" from the Mona River to heal. People from all over the island came to his "balm yard" for healing. His popularity was also evident in the words to a popular song:

> Dip dem Bedward, dip dem
> Dip dem iina healing stream
> dip them sweet but not too deep
> dip dem fi cure bad feelin.

Bedward was feared by the whites and after leading a march to the city was arrested and confined to a lunatic asylum (Chevannes 1971).

Recent statistics on Revival show a decline in membership, and the national census does not include this group because the numbers are so small (Besson 1996). Seaga, commenting on the data, believes they do not reflect the true strength of the Revival movement. Believers are not willing to declare membership in the group because of the "low prestige value within a dominant code of values." The Christian middle class views Revivalists, usually from the working class, as "superstitious, pagan, comical in ritual behavior and tolerant of dishonesty" (Seaga 1969).

Each group has a leader, post-holders, and floor members. The leader, the central figure of authority, tends to be autocratic and is usually the only one who exercises disciplinary action toward a member (Simpson 1956).

Revivalists believe in spirits, angels, protectors, and messengers. They believe that a person is protected by a guardian spirit. God, the Creator, is at the apex of the belief system and resides in the sky. He controls the elements such as lightning and thunder. He is, however, far away. Jesus, in contrast, is a good spirit who is always near and is therefore frequently called upon. Other good spirits include the "Lamb" and the "Dove." The bad spirits are Satan and other fallen angels (Chevannes 1995; Simpson 1956).

Each person is believed to have a shadow, which remains behind after death. The shadow of a good person is not visible, but a bad person's shadow is. Evil spirits look and act as they did in life and may even be seen to be wearing the same clothes.

There are different types of ritual in Revival, including prayer meetings, street meetings, and rituals for specific purposes such as feasting tables, altars, and baths. Prayer meetings are multifunctional and include spiritual indoctrination, discussion of functions to take place, and the general worship of the supernatural powers. Street meetings are usually held to solicit new members and to expound on the Scriptures. Rituals for specific purposes include thanksgiving for a special event, baptism, death, consecration, and so on. During this time the important cutting of the table takes place. The table usually includes fruits, candles, food, and flowers, which are distributed to those present with some items set aside for the spirits after the candles are lit (Seaga 1969).

Some symbols have special meanings. Water, for example, is important in all ceremonies. Glasses of water are usually placed on the altar and table and are used to summon the spirits. Consecrated water is used during baptism, may also be sprinkled on the floor of a church during a service, and is also used for healing (Simpson 1956; Seaga 1969).

A red flag is waved at the beginning of the ceremony to get rid of the evil spirits. Swords and machetes serve the same purpose. A whistle is also blown to warn spirits that the meeting is about to begin or to stop the singing and restore order. The drum is also an important musical instrument in the worship activities. The Bible is a sacred book, used for ceremonial activities, especially the reading of the Old Testament.

Healing is an important activity in the Revival religion. Chevannes (1995) describes healing "as an art which applies not only to the physical and mental illnesses but to the social ills as well." The importance of the balm yard can not be overemphasized since this is the central place for all activities. The use of special plants, barks, roots, and ganja are central to the healing.

Besson suggests that "Revival not only remains embedded in the island's peasant culture . . . but is undergoing transformation in keeping with the new modern context." The change is seen in the evolution of the structure of the Revival from small individual groups to churches and dioceses. These changes are reflected in the names of the churches. They are no longer called bands but Apostolic, and the leaders are called pastors or bishops. The membership now comprises more younger middle-class converts but continues to be dominated by females in both the urban and rural areas (Besson 1996; Chevannes 1995).

Rastafari

Rastafari is difficult to define. The following quotations suggest the complexity of the movement. "The Rasta and all that he represents is a symbol, a dialectical representation of contradictions of a society and indeed of an entire epoch of history"(Owens 1976). Nettleford says that "some are committed to a political and military struggle, others revivalist in orientation and origin, some quietest but all deeply involved with poverty and deprivation that was their climate of concern."

Several factors contribute to the interest in Rastas: the "impact of the Rastafari on the social and political life in Jamaica," the association with ganja at a time when Western countries are concerned with problems associated with it, the influence of migration to Great Britain and the United States, and of course reggae music (Chevannes 1977).

The early Rastafarians were concerned with economic hardship, racial discrimination, and repatriation to Africa. Much of the organizational structure and ritual resembled Revival. The groups were small and fragmented but tended to be democratic and subject to individualism. The organizational structure included a president, vice president, chairman, and secretary. Two systems seemed to operate in tandem—one tending to the "Spiritual needs and the other to matters pertaining to the state" (Simpson).

Neither beards, long uncombed locks, nor ganja was allowed. There was actually an aversion to smoking in public meeting. (Today ganja is the focus of ritual smoking.) Cultural life was based on the ritual celebrations such as the anniversary of the coronation of Haile Selassie on November 15, 1953, or Emancipation Day, August 1. The latter was a holiday in Jamaica until 1962 when the country gained independence and will be observed again beginning in 1997.

During the early period middle-class Jamaicans viewed the Rastafari, who were mainly from the lower classes, with contempt, believing they were "hooligans, psychopaths and dangerous criminals" (Simpson).

Prophets, tellers of the future, are sacred in religious organizations. The Rastas have two such prophets:

(1) Alexander Bedward, who, it is believed, attempted to fly to heaven and was tried and placed in a mental hospital where he died.

(2) Marcus Garvey, who founded the Universal Negro Improvement Association in the United States and proclaimed black nationalism, Africa for the Africans, and "one God, one aim, one destiny." Garvey said, "Look to Africa, when a black king shall be crowned for the day of deliverance is near." According to Garvey, the repatriation to Africa was to occur in the 1960s. He is still regarded as the major prophet among the Rastafari.

Certain events are important to Rastafari and some are regarded as the fulfillment of prophecy. One occurred in November 1930, when Ras Tafari was crowned Emperor Haile Sellassie, "King of Kings and Lord of Lords, and the Conquering Lion of the Tribe of Judah." Biblical Revelation (5:2, 5) was used to substantiate this fulfillment of prophecy:

> And I saw a strong angel proclaiming with a loud voice, "who is worthy to open the Book, and to loose the seals there of?" ... And one of the elders saith unto me "weep not: behold, the Lion of Judah, the Root of David hath prevailed to open the Book and to loose the seven spirits of God sent forth into all the earth."

The invasion of Ethiopia by the Italians was also fulfillment of Revelation (19:19). "And I saw the Beast and the Kings of the earth, and their armies, gathered together to make war against him that sat on the horse, against his army." In 1941, with the Emperor's return to Ethiopia, Revelation (19:20) was fulfilled. "And the Beast was taken, and with him the false prophet that wrought miracles before him, with which he deceived them that had the mark of the Beast and them that worshiped his image. These both were cast alive into a lake of fire with brimstone."

Several individuals had an early influence on the movement. Leonard P. Howell was the first person to preach the divinity of Rastafari in Kingston. He spoke an African language and was credited with writing *The Promised Key*, a basic Rastafari text published in Ghana about 1930. He also lived in the United States where he encountered black and white racism. In 1933 the Jamaican newspaper *Daily Gleaner* reported that Howell was selling photographs of the Emperor Haile Selassie and was telling purchasers that the photograph was their passport to Ethiopia. He spent time in jail for sedition (Smith).

Another important figure in the movement was Joseph Nathaniel Hibbert. Born in 1894, he migrated to Costa Rica in 1911 and joined the Ancient Mystic Order of Ethiopia, a Masonic society of which he became a Master Mason. On his return to Jamaica in 1931 he began to preach the doctrine of Haile Selassie.

A third important figure was H. Archibald Dunkley, a seaman on the Atlantic Fruit Company's boats. He quit his job in 1930 and studied the Bible for two and a half years to determine whether Haile Selassie was the Messiah whom Garvey prophesied. In 1933 he started preaching Ras Tafari as the King of Kings.

The movement has two basic beliefs: Rastafari is the living God, and salvation can come to the black man only through repatriation to Africa. The Rastafarians believe that Emperor Haile Selassie is the living God, the returned Messiah, and the representative of God the Father. Selassie means "Power of the Trinity." They believe that blacks are the true Israelites of the House of David and that the Emperor is the Lion of Judah and descended from King Solomon and the Queen of Sheba. It is believed that the Bible is a holy book, the true word of God. The average Rastafari knows the Bible and is willing to discuss the Bible anytime. The "Book of the Maccabees," not found in the King James version of the Bible, is also treasured.

Ganja is used by some of the members especially during ceremonial rituals. The Rastas have tried to persuade the government to legalize ganja, but without success. They cite Biblical support for its use: Genesis (3:18) states ". . . thou shalt eat the herb of the field"; Exodus (10:12) commands to "eat every herb of the land"; and Psalms (104:14) counsels, "He causeth the grass to grow for the cattle, and herb for the service of men" (Barrett 1988). Some people use ganja for therapeutic reasons, and others to keep away illness.

Babylon, an important concept in the Rastafari movement, is thought to include the state and the church as well as other institutions. Babylon symbolizes powerful forces that work against God and the people. Owens describes it as a "whole complex of institutions which conspire to keep the black man enslaved in the Western world and which attempt to subjugate coloured people."

Babylon at the local level includes the church and its members as well as the police. Religious ministers are considered the "Antichrists" who are "agents for the mental enslavement of the Blackman." The suggestion that the local police are part of Babylon has been reinforced in songs that show the dislike of the police.

Rome is considered the center of the Western world as well as a system of thought and behavior. It is the headquarters of the church and state union and is believed to have ruled mankind over the last two centuries. Rome is not only a specific place but also a general cultural pattern in which persons are trapped even when they are away from the city. The expression "out in Rome" suggests that a person has finally rejected the idols of society and recognizes the true God (Owens).

Ethiopia is important to the Rastafari because it is considered to be the prepared place for Israel and the heaven of the black. The Rastas also use the green, yellow, and red Ethiopian flag. Green represents the pastures of Africa, yellow the wealth of the land, and red the church. The concept of Ethiopianism reinforces the theory that religious teaching outside of the established churches will bring political pressure on behalf of social change (Barrett 1977; Nettleford 1979, 1976; Owens 1976).

The diet of the Rastafarians is very strict. They do not eat pork and most are strict vegetarians. They eat small fish, usually the "sprat." Salt and processed oils are forbidden. Fruits and fruit juices are used.

Language is an important means of communicating in any culture. It can be verbal or nonverbal and involves the use of symbols. Nettleford (1978) stresses the importance of language in culture: "Social protest manifests itself in language change. For defiance of society includes defiance of its language." The Rastafari have created their own language, which manifests itself in speech, dress, and symbols. Analyzing the speech pattern of the Rastafari, Pollard (1994) attributes its close relationship to the Jamaican Creole to the socioeconomic conditions of the urban poor. Pollard (1994) summarizes the language of the Rastafari: "It is evident that the whole stance of protest, of revolt in word, is evident and is attributed to the resentment of English as the language of colonialism."

Women are treated with respect but they have a submissive role. According to an elder: "A woman is the minister of home affairs and health, the husband the minister of foreign affairs and defense" (Chevannes). Rowe (1980) associates the position of women in Rastafari with the negative aspects of certain women in the Bible: Eve the temptress; Sarah, who posed as her husband's sister to safeguard his life; and Rachel and Leah, sisters who vied with each other for their husband's attention. The male is responsible for shielding the woman and guiding her away from sin. Women are seen as impure and must be prevented from corrupting men.

Since the 1970s change has been occurring as women are being allowed to become involved in some activities. In the 1980s, the Golden Jubilee for all Rastas, the question of the "daughters and their abilities and place in Rastafari" was raised, but the answer was that man is still the head. Judy Mowatt describes what the role of the women should be: "We know as Rasta queens and sisters that a woman is just as important as a man in the sight of God. . . . We are equal because whatever is revealed to a man is revealed to a woman." The ska, popular around the time of Jamaica's independence in 1962, has been attributed to the innovations of Count Ossie and the late Don Drummond, one of Jamaica's finest trombonist, who were both influenced by the Rastafari movement. The ska developed into reggae and is part of Jamaica's national heritage. Reggae music includes names like Toots and the Maytals, Jimmy Cliff, Peter Tosh, Bob Marley, and the Wailers. Reggae music has challenged the leaders and members of the society. The lyrics show rage, crying, or rejoicing. Barrett expressed it this way: "Reggae is expression, entertaining, revolutionary, and filled with Rastafarian symbolism."

Conclusion

Religion can impede social change or help to produce it. Religion helps to maintain the status quo. Changes in religion result from changes in the wider society. Religion can be seen as the central institution to the tradition of resistance, whether through force or symbolic forms such as language, folk tale, and proverb, or through creative alternative institutions (Chevannes 1995).

Jamaica has a history of social upheaval most of which has been brought about by groups on the fringes of society. Ethiopianism reinforces the idea that religious teaching outside the established churches will bring political pressure on behalf of social change (Barrett 1977). Since the 1960s the Rastafari have been a force to recognize.

BIBLIOGRAPHY

This bibliography has been compiled from the holdings of the University of the West Indies Library, Mona, and the National Library of Jamaica. Both published and unpublished documents are included. Although the publications on the Rastafari are numerous, only a few can be regarded as contributing to any new knowledge.

Ahkell, Jah. 1981. *Rasta: Emperor Haile Selassie and the Rastafarians.* Port of Spain: Black Starliner.

Albuquerque, Klaus de. 1976. "Millenarian Movements and the Politics of Liberation: The Rastafarians of Jamaica." Ph.D. diss., Blacksbury, Virginia.

——. 1980. "Rastafarians and Cultural Identity in the Caribbean." *Revista/Review Interamericana* 10 (2), 230–247.

Alleyne, Mervyn C. 1988. *Roots of Jamaican Culture.* London: Pluto.

Barrett, Leonard E. 1973. "Portrait of a Jamaican Healer: African Medical Lore in the Caribbean." *Caribbean Quarterly* 19 (3), 6–19.

——. 1977. *The Rastafarians: The Dreadlocks of Jamaica.* Kingston, Jamaica: Sangster's Book Stores Ltd. in Association with Heinemann Educational Books.

——. 1978. "African Roots in Jamaican Indigenous Religion." *Journal of Religious Thought* 35 (1), 7–26.

——. 1979. "Rastafarianism as a Life-Style." *Presence in Multi-Ethnic Canada.* Ed. Vincent D'Oyley. Vancouver.

——. 1988. *The Rastafarians: Sounds of Cultural Dissonance.* Revised and updated edition. Boston: Beacon Press.

Beckwith, Martha Warren. 1923. "Some Religious Cults in Jamaica." *American Journal of Psychology* 34 (1), 32-45.

Besson, Jean, and Barry Chevannes. 1996. "The Continuity-Creativity Debate: The Case of Revival." *New West Indian Guide* 70 (3–4), 209–228.

Bilby, Kenneth M. 1983. "Black Thoughts from the Caribbean: Ideology at Home and Abroad." *New West Indian Guide* 57 (3–4), 201–214.

Birhan, Iyaivata Farika. 1983. *Jah Is I Shepherd.* San Jose, Calif.: Rastafari Roots/ Redemption; Repatriation Unlimited.

Birhan, Iyawta Farika. 1981 *Fari iyaric: An Introduction into Rastafari Speech.* Illus. by Ras J. Tesfa. San Jose, Calif.: Queen Omega News Communication Unltd Co.

Bisnauth, Dale. 1995. "Cultural Dimensions of West Indian Development: Religion and Philosophy." *Bulletin of Eastern Caribbean Affairs* 20 (4), 1–6

Bishton, Derek. 1986. *Blackheart Man: A Journey into Rasta.* London: Chatto & Windus.

Bones, Jah. 1982. "Rastafari Literature and Authorship: A Critique." *West Indian Digest* 9 (90), 28–34.

Boot, Adrian, and Michael Thomas. 1976. *Jamaica: Babylon on a Thin Wire.* London: Thames & Hudson.

Boot, Adrian, and Vivien Goldman. 1982. *Bob Marley: Soul Rebel, Natural Mystic.* New York: St. Martin's Press.

Bowen, Wentworth E. 1971. "Rastafarianism and the New Society. " *Savacou* 5, 41–50.

Boyne, Ian. 1983. "Jamaica: Breaking Barriers between Churches and Rastafarians." *One World* 86, 3–4.

Braithwaite, Edward K. 1978. "Kumina: The Spirit of African Survival in Jamaica." *Jamaica Journal* 42, 45–63.

Breiner, Laurence A. 1985. "The English Bible in Jamaican Rastafarianism." *Journal of Religious Thought* 42 (2), 30–43.

Brooks, A. A. 1917. *History of Bedwardism: The Jamaican Native Baptist Free Church.* Kingston: The Gleaner Co.

Brown, Samuel. 1966. "Treatise on the Rastafari Movement." *Caribbean Studies* 6 (1), 39–40.

Byfield, Rev. [Bevis]. 1978 "Rastas Have Lessons for Jamaica's Transformation." *Caribbean Contact* 5(10), 16.

Callender, Jean A., comp. 1986. *African Survivals in Caribbean Religion: A Select Bibliography.* Cave Hill, Barbados: University of the West Indies.

Callam, Neville G. 1980. "Invitation to Docility: Defusing the Rastafarian Challenge." *Caribbean Journal of Religious Studies* 3 (2), 28–48.

Campbell, Horace. 1979. "The Rastafari Intervention: An Enquiry into the Culture of Rastafari— from Garvey to Rodney." Paper presented to the Society of Caribbean Studies Conference, School of Social Sciences, University of Sussex, Falmer, Brighton.

——. 1987. *Rasta and Resistance: From Marcus Garvey to Walter Rodney.* Trenton, N.J.: African World Press.

——. 1980. "Rastafari: Culture of Resistance." *Race and Class* 22 (1), 1–22.

Cashmore, Ernest. 1977. "The Rastaman Cometh." *New Society* 41 (777), 382–384.

——. 1979. *Rastaman: The Rastafarian Movement in England.* London: Allen & Unwin.

——. 1984. *The Rastafarians.* Foreword by Lord Searman; appendix by Jah Bones. London: Minority Rights Group.

Catholic Commission for Racial Justice (Great Britain). 1982. *Rastafarians in Jamaica and Britain.* London: C.C.R.J.

Chevannes, Barry [Alston Barrington]. 1970. "Healing the Nation: Rastafari Exorcism of the Ideology of Racism in Jamaica." *Caribbean Quarterly* 36 (1–2), 59–84.

——. 1971a. "Jamaican Lower Class Religion: Struggles against Oppression." Ph.D. diss., University of the West Indies, Mona.

——. 1971b. "Revival and Black Struggle." *Savacou* 5, 27–39.

——. 1976. "The Repairer of the Breach: Reverend Claudius Henry and Jamaican Society." *Ethnicity in the Americas.* Ed. Frances Henry. The Hague: Mouton. Pp. 263–268.

——. 1977a. "Era of Dreadlocks." Paper read at the Conference on the Africa Diaspora, Hampton Institute, Virginia.

——. 1977b. "The Literature of Rastafari." *Social and Economic Studies* 26 (2), 239–262.

——. 1978a. "Rastafarianism and Class Struggle: The Search for a Methodology." *Methodology and Change: Problems of Applied Social Science Research Techniques.* Ed. Louis Lindsay. Kingston: [N.p.]. Pp. 244–271.

——. 1978b. "Revivalism: A Disappearing Religion." *Caribbean Quarterly* 24 (3–4), 1–17.

——. 1979. "Social and Ideological Origins of the Rastafarian Movement in Jamaica." Ph.D. diss., Columbia University.

——. 1981. "The Rastafari and the Urban Youth." *Perspectives on Jamaica in the Seventies.* Eds. Carl Stone and Aggrey Brown. Kingston.

———. 1983. "Some Notes on African Religious Survivals in the Caribbean." *Caribbean Journal of Religious Studies* 5 (2), 18–28.

———. 1990. "Rastafari, towards a New Approach." *New West Indian Guide* 64 (3–4), 127–148.

———. 1991a. "The Dreadlocks Rastafari." *African Creative Expressions of the Divine.* Ed. Kortright; by Davis and Elias Farajaje—Jones: Howard University, School of Divinity. Pp. 37–52.

———. 1991b. "The Rastafari of Jamaica." *When Prophets Die: The Post Charismatic Fate of New Religious Movements.* Ed. Timothy Miller. Albany: State University of New York Press. Pp. 135–147.

———. 1995a. "The Rastafari Abroad." *America's Alternative Religions.* Ed. Timothy Miller. Albany: State University of New York Press. Pp. 297–303.

———. 1995b. *Rastafari and Other African-Caribbean World Views.* London: MacMillan Press.

———. 1995c. *Rastafari: Roots and Ideology.* New York: Syracuse University.

Clarke, Peter. 1986. *Black Paradise: The Rastafarian Movement.* Wellingborough, Northants: Aquarian Press.

Clarke, Sebastian. 1980. *Jah Music: The Evolution of the Popular Jamaican Song.* London: Heinemann Educational.

Cumper, George Edward. 1979. *The Potential of Ras Tafarianism as a Modern National Religion.* [N.p.: The Author.]

Davis, Stephen. 1977. *Reggae Bloodlines: In Search of the Music and Culture of Jamaica.* Garden City, N.Y.: Anchor Press.

De Albuquerque, Klaus. 1979. "The Future of the Rastafarian Movement." *Caribbean Review* 8 (4), 22–25, 44–46.

———. 1980. "Rastafarian and Cultural Identity in the Caribbean." *Revista Interamericana* 10 (2), 230–247.

Dijk, Frank Jan Van. 1988. "The Twelve Tribes of Israel: Rasta and the Middle Class." *New West Indian Guide* 62 (1–2), 1–26.

———. 1995. "Sociological Means, Colonial Reactions to the Radicalization of Rastafari in Jamaica, 1956." *New West Indian Guide* 64 (1–2), 67–101.

Ebanks, Margaret. 1981. *The Rastafarian Cookbook : Ital Recipes.* Kingston, [Jamaica]: Antilles Book Co.

Elkins, W. F. 1977. *Street Preachers, Faithhealers and Herb Doctors in Jamaica, 1890–1925.* New York: Revisionist Press.

Erskine, Noel Leo. 1978. "Black Religion and Identity: A Jamaican Perspective." Ph.D. diss., United Theological Seminary in New York.

Eyre, L. Alan. 1985. "Biblical Symbolism and the Role of Fantasy Geography among the Rastafarians of Jamaica." *Journal of Geography* 84 (2), 144–148.

Faith, Karlene. 1990. "One Love-One heart Destiny, a Report on the Rastafarian Movement in Jamaica." *Cargo Cults and Millenarian Movements: Transoceanic*

Comparison of New Religious Movements. Ed. G. W. Trompf: Moulton De Gruyter. Pp. 295–341.

Forsythe, Dennis. 1980. "West Indian Culture through the Prism of Rastafarianism." *Caribbean Quarterly* 26 (4), 62 – 81.

———. 1985. *Rastafari: For the Healing of the Nation.* Kingston: Zaika Publications.

Friday, Michael. 1983. "A Comparison of 'Dharma' and 'Dread' as Determinants of Ethical Standards." *Caribbean Journal of Religious Studies* 5 (2), 29–37.

Galloway, Ernestine Royals. 1981. "Religious Beliefs and Practices of Maroon Children of Jamaica." Ph.D. diss., New York University.

Garrison, Len. [N.d.] *Back to Africa: The Idea of the Return and Structural Migration as a Response to Cultural and Economic Deprivation of the Jamaican Society.* [N.p.]

Garrison, Len. 1973. "Out of Exile: A Study of the Historical Development of the Rastafari Movement in Jamaican Society, 1922–1972." Ph.D. diss., Ruskin College, Oxford University.

———. 1975. "Rastafarians: Protest Movement in Jamaica." *Afras Review* 1 (1) 10–13.

———. 1976. "Rastafarians: Journey Out of Exile." *Afras Review* 1 (2).

———. 1985. *Beyond Babylon: Collection of Poems (1972–82).* London: Black Star Pub.

Gradussov, Alex. 1969. "Kapo: Cult Leader, Sculptor, Painter." *Jamaica Journal* 3 (2), 46–51.

Guiton, Derek. 1985. "Seeing Ras Rastafari Plain, a Phenomenological Viewpoint." *British Journal of Educational Studies* 33 (3), 262–277.

Hebdige, Dick. *Reggae, Rastas and Rudies: Style and the Subversion of Form.* Birmingham, England: Centre for Contemporary Cultural Studies.

———. *Subculture: The Meaning of Style.* London: Methuen.

Hill, Robert. 1983. "Leonard P. Howell and Millenarian Visions in Early Rastafari." *Jamaica Journal* 16 (1), 24–39.

Hogg, Donald William. 1966. "Statement of a Ras Tafari Leader." *Caribbean Studies* 6 (1), 37–38.

———. 1967. "Jamaican Religions: A Study in Variations." Ph.D. diss., Yale University.

Homiak, John. 1985. "The 'Ancients of Days' Seated Black: Eldership, Oral Tradition and Ritual in Rastafari Culture." Ph.D. diss., Brandeis University.

———. 1994. "Rastafari Voices Reach Ethiopia." *American Anthropologist* 96 (4), 958–963.

Hughes, Roger. 1979. "Jamaica: The Rastafari Movement; A Bibliographical Essay." *Assistant Librarian* 72 (7–8), 104, 106–109.

Jackson, Michael. 1980. "Rastafarianism." *Theology* 83, 26–34.

Kerridge, Roy. 1985. "Fall of the Rastaman." *The Spectator* 254 (8166), 14–15.

Kitzinger, Sheila. 1969. "Protest and Mysticism: The Rastafari Cult in Jamaica." *Journal for the Scientific Study of Religion* 8 (2), 240–262.

———. 1971. "The Rastafarian Brethren of Jamaica." *Peoples and Cultures of the Caribbean: An Anthropological Reader.* Ed. Michael M. Harowitz. New York: Natural History Press. Pp. 580–588.

Lake, Obiagele. 1994. "The Many Voices of Rastafarian Women: Sexual Subordination in the Midst of Liberation." *New West Indian Guide* 68 (3–4), 235–237.

Laternari, Vittorio. 1971. "Religious Movements in Jamaica." *Black Society in the New World.* Ed. Richard Frucht. New York: Random House. Pp. 308–312.

Lee, Barbara Makeda. 1982. *Rastafari: The New Creation.* 3d ed. London: Jamaica Media Productions.

Lewis, William F. 1986. "The Rastafari: Millennial Cultists or Unregenerate Peasants." *Peasant Studies* 14 (1), 5–26.

A Look at the Black Struggle in Jamaica. 1969. [Kingston]: Black House Pubs.

McPherson, Everton S. P. 1991. *Rastafari and Politics: Sixty Years of a Developing Cultural Ideology; A Sociology of Development Perspective.* Frankfield, Jamaica: Black International Iyahbinghi Press.

Mais, Roger. 1974. *Brotherman.* London: Heinemann.

Miles, Robert. 1978. *Between Two Cultures: The Case of Rastafarianism.* Bristol: S. R. R. C. Research Unit on Ethnic Relations.

Moore, Joseph G., and George E. Simpson. 1957/58. "A Comparative Study of Acculturation in Morant Bay and West Kingston, Jamaica." *Abstract of Zaire* 9–10 (Nov.–Dec.), 979–1019; 11 (1958), 66–87.

Morrish, Ivor. 1982. *Obeah, Christ and Rastaman: Jamaica and Its Religion.* Greenwood, S.C.: Attic Press.

Mulvaney, Rebekah Michele. 1992. *Rastafari and Reggae: A Dictionary and Source Book.* New York: Greenwood Press.

Nagashima, Yoshiko S. 1984. *Rastafarian Music in Contemporary Jamaica: A Study of Socioreligious Music of the Rastafarian Movement in Jamaica.* Tokyo: Institute for the Study of Languages and Cultures of Asia and Africa.

Nettleford, Rex. 1969. "Pocomania in Dance-Theatre." *Jamaica Journal* 3 (2), 21–24.

———. 1970. "African Redemption: The Rastafari and the Wider Society, 1959–1969." *Mirror Mirror: Identity, Race and Protest in Jamaica.* [Kingston]: Collins and Sangster. Pp. 39–111.

———. 1976. "Introduction." In Joseph Owens, *Dread: The Rastafarians of Jamaica.* Kingston, Jamaica: Sangster.

———. 1977. "The Rastafarians of Jamaica: A Prophetic Presence in Plantation America." Paper presented at the Second World Black and African Festival of Arts and Culture (FESTAC).

———. 1979. *Caribbean Cultural Identity: The Case of Jamaica.* Los Angeles: UCLA Center for Afro- Caribbean Studies, University of California.

New Religious Movements and Rapid Social Change. 1986. Ed. James A. Beckford . London: Sage.

New York. Police Dept. 1985. "Rasta Crime: A Confidential Report." *Caribbean Review* 14 (1), 12–15, 39–40.

Nicholas, Tracy, and Bill Sparrow. 1979. *Rastafari: A Way of Life.* Garden City, N.Y.: Anchor Books.

'No Locks' S. B. G. Which Way Dreadlocks? 1979. Kingston, Jamaica: A Christian Press.

Norris, Katrin. 1962. "The Call of Africa." *Jamaica: The Search for an Identity.* Ed. Katrin Norris. London: University Press. Pp. 43–60.

Owens, Joseph. 1973. "The Rastafarians of Jamaica." *Troubling of the Waters.* Ed. Idris Hamid. San Fernando, Trinidad. Pp. 165–170.

———. 1975. "Literature on the Rastafari: 1955–1974; A Review." *Savacou* 11–12 (Sept.), 86–105, 113–114.

———. 1976. *Dread: The Rastafarians of Jamaica.* Kingston: Sangster.

———. 1978. "Rasta, Christ, and Marx." *Caribbean Contact* 6 (7), 2, 19.

Patterson, Horace Orlando. 1964. *The Children of Sisyphus.* London: New Authors.

———. 1964. "Rastafari: The Cult of the Outcasts." *New Society* 4 (111), 15–17.

Plummer, John. 1978. *Movement of Jah People.* London: Press Gang.

Pollard, Velma. 1980. "Dread Talk—The Speech of the Rastafarian in Jamaica." *Caribbean Quarterly* 26 (4), 32– 41.

———. 1994. *Dread Talk: The Language of Rastafari.* Jamaica: Canoe Press.

Post, Ken. 1970. "The Bible as Ideology: Ethiopianism in Jamaica, 1930–38." *West African Perspectives.* Ed. Christopher H. Allen and R. W. Johnson. Cambridge: University Press. Pp. 185–207.

Rastafari and Other African-Caribbean Worldviews. 1995. Ed. Barry Chevannes. Houndmills, Basingstoke: McMillan.

Rastafari Movement Association. 1976. *Rasta, a Modern Antique.* Kingston: R. M. A.

Rodney, Walter. 1969. *The Groundings with My Brothers.* London: Bogle-L'Ouverture Pubs.

Rowe, Maureen. 1980. "The Woman in Rastafari." *Caribbean Quarterly* 26 (4), 13–21.

Ryle, John. 1981. "Rastaman in the Promised Land." *New Society* 24–31 (Dec.), 535–537.

Savishinsky, Neil J. 1994. "Transnational Popular Culture and the Global Spread of the Jamaica Rastafarian Movement." *New West Indian Guide* 68 (3–4), 259–281.

Segal, Aaron. 1983. "The Land of Look Behind: A Film about Reggae and Rastafarianism." *Caribbean Review* 12 (2), 36–37.

Seaga, Edward. 1969. "Revival Cults in Jamaica: Notes towards Sociology of Religion." *Jamaica Journal* 3 (2), 3–13.

———. 1973. "The Rastafarian Movement: Its Influence Belies Its Numbers." *Encore, The Monthly Magazine* 2 (9), 58–61.

Semaj, Leachim T. 1980a. "Race and Identity and Children of the African Diaspora: Contributions of Rastafari." *Caribe* 4 (4), 15–18.

———. 1980b. "Rastafari: From Religion to Social Theory." *Caribbean Quarterly* 26 (4), 22–31.

———. 1985. "Inside Rasta: The Future of a Religious Movement." *Caribbean Review* 14 (1), 8–11, 37–40.

Shibata, Yoshiko. 1981. "Rastafarian Music in Jamaica: Its Historical and Cultural Significance as a Study of Socio-Religious Music in Culturology of Area Studies." Thesis, University of Toikuba, Japan.

Simpson, George Eaton. 1955a. "Culture Change and Reintegration Found in the Cults of West Kingston, Jamaica." *Proceedings of the American Philosophical Society* 9 (2), 89–92.

——. 1955b. "Jamaica Cult Music." *Social and Economic Studies* 4 (2), 133–149.

——. 1955c. "The Ras Tafari Movement in Jamaica: A Study of Race and Class Conflict." *Social Forces* 34 (2), 167–171.

——. 1956. "Jamaican Revivalist Cults." *Social and Economic Studies* 5 (4). [Whole issue.]

——. 1960. "The Acculturative Process in Jamaican Revivalism." *Men and Cultures: Selected Papers of the Fifth International Congress of Anthropological and Ethnological Sciences, Philadelphia , September 1–9 , 1956.* Ed. Anthony F.C. Wallace. Philadelphia: University of Pennsylvania Press. Pp. 332–341.

——. 1970. "The Ras Tafari Movement in Jamaica in Its Millennial Aspect." *Millennial Dreams in Action.* Ed. Sylvia L. Thrupp. New York: Schocken Books. Pp. 160–165.

——. 1980. *Religious Cults of the Caribbean: Trinidad, Jamaica and Haiti.* Rio Piedras: Institute of Caribbean Studies, University of Puerto Rico.

——. 1985. "Religion and Justice: Some Reflections on the Rastafari Movement." *Phylon* 46 (4), 286–291.

Smith, M. G., Roy Augier, and Rex Nettleford. 1968. *The Rastafari Movement in Kingston, Jamaica.* Mona: Institute of Social and Economic Research, University of the West Indies.

Stewart, Robert J. 1992. *Religion and Society in Post-Emancipation Jamaica.* Knoxville, Tenn.: The University Press.

Sunshine, Catherine A. 1985. "Rastafarianism . . . and the Search for Freedom in Black Religion." *The Caribbean: Survival and Sovereignty.* Washington, D.C.: Ecumenical Program for Inter-American Communication and Action (EPICA). Pp. 40–41.

Tafari, I. Jabulani. 1980. "The Rastafari: Successors of Marcus Garvey." *Caribbean Quarterly* 26 (4), 1–12.

Thomas, Michael. 1976. "Jamaica at War: The Rastas Are Coming!" *Rolling Stone* 12 (Aug.), 32–36.

Thomas, Michael, and Adrian Boot. 1982. *Jah Revenge: Babylon Revisited.* London: Eel Pie Pub.

Troyna, Barry. 1978. *Rastafarianism, Reggae and Racism.* Derby: National Association of Multi-Racial Education.

Turner, Terisa E. 1991. "Women, Rastafari and New Society, Caribbean and East African Roots of a Popular Movement against Structural Adjustment." *Labor, Capital and Society* 24 (1), 66–89.

Walters, Anita M. 1985. *Race, Class and Political Symbols: Rastafari and Reggae in Jamaican Politics.* New Brunswick, N.J.: Transaction Books.

Warner-Lewis, Maureen. 1993. "African Continuities in the Rastafari Belief System." *Caribbean Quarterly* 39 (3–4), 108–122.

Watson, G. Llewellyn. 1973. "Social Structure and Social Movements: The Black Muslims in the U.S.A. and the Ras-Tafarians in Jamaica." *British Journal of Sociology* 24 (2), 188–204.

——. 1974. "Patterns of Black Protest in Jamaica: The Case of the Ras-Tafarians." *Journal of Black Studies* 4 (3), 329–343.

White, Timothy. 1983. *Catch a Fire: The Life of Bob Marley.* 1st ed. New York: Holt, Rinehart & Winston.

Williams, Chris Ahkell. [1980?] *Rasta: Emperor Haile Selassie and the Rastafarians.* Trinidad: Black Starliner.

Williams, Kathy M. 1981. *The Rastafarians.* London: Ward Lock Educational.

Witvliet, Theo. 1985. "Theology in the Caribbean and the Rastafarian Movement." *A Place in the Sun: Liberation Theology in the Third World.* Maryknoll, N.Y.: Orbis Books. Pp. 102–117.

Yawney, Carole D. 1976. "Remnants of All Nations: Rastafarian Attitudes to Race and Nationality." *Ethnicity in the Americas.* Ed. Frances Henry. The Hague: Mouton. Pp. 231–262.

——. 1978. "Irons in Babylon: The Rastafarians of Jamaica as a Visionary Movement." Ph.D. diss., McGill University.

——. 1979. *Dread Wasteland: Rastafari Ritual in West Kingston, Jamaica.* Greeley: University of Northern Colorado, Museum of Anthropology.

Afro-Brazilian Religions

16. Forbidden Love: The Turbulent Relationship between the Roman Catholic Church and African Brazilian Religion

Mike Weems

Let me take the reader to Salvador, the capital of the northeastern state of Bahia in Brazil. The city itself is often called Bahia as well, which is an abbreviation for the name of the large bay that spreads out before it: Bahia de Todos os Santos, All Saints' Bay. The Cidade Alta, the Upper City, rises on a cliff above the Lower City, which sits at the edge of the bay. The view of the bay is magnificent from the cliff-edge of the Cidade Alta. This section of town also contains the Pelourinho (Little Whipping Post), the cobblestoned former slave market and present-day tourist center with its churches, bars, souvenir shops, and jewelry stores. Unfortunately, the bay cannot easily be seen from there. The smell of urine often wafts through the streets of the Pelourinho, especially in the morning. Swarms of hawkers selling necklaces, maps, and Senhor de Bonfim ribbons descend like mosquitoes on hapless tourists.

Bad smells and hawkers are left behind when one walks onto the sacred precincts of the Igreja da Nossa Senhora do Rosário dos Pretos, the Church of Our Lady of the Rosary of the Blacks, which is painted pastel blue on the outside and is shady and cool inside. It is a small (by Baroque standards) but beautiful edifice built by slaves for slaves. It is also a central point for both the black Catholic community and a tourist must-see; a donation is requested from visitors who enter the chapel.

Panoramas made with blue and white tile line the lower part of one wall. Statues are placed symmetrically on either side of the altar, giving the chapel an orderly, formal air. The most important images are discernable by position and size: a large white Madonna dominates the chapel, flanked on both sides by two male black saints, one of them cradling a white baby Jesus in his arms.

The sacristy, the more relaxed yet still formal room behind the chapel, is where guests are greeted and the clergy meet before and after Mass. There is a large table and chairs made of fine wood, portraits of high-ranking black clergy, statues of saints, and a small plaster image of a black woman, dressed in white, with blues eyes and fitted with a muzzle that is strapped around her head. This is Anastácia, purportedly a Bantu princess who refused to acknowledge her place as a slave and was punished with a metal gag, a heavy metal collar around her neck, and shackles. She is revered as a saint in popular Catholicism, but the church has yet to canonize her. This, however, does not prevent the curator from giving visitors holy cards with a picture of Anastácia and a prayer that she intercede before the Most High on the petitioner's behalf. He also has small posters of her. The cards and posters are *gratis*, free of charge.

Although she was Catholic, Anastácia can not be canonized, I was told, because she had not given up the beliefs of her African ancestors before she died. Her suffering, the injustices inflicted upon her, the Christian way in which she forgave her persecutors, and the way in which she bore her cross without complaint are not enough, even in 1997, to wash away the taint of possible African religious error. In the global competition for Catholic sainthood, Anastácia can not make the cut. Her presence might send the wrong message.

Yet, in the Church of Our Lady of the Blacks, Anastácia has a place, even a shrine. In a small courtyard behind the church, there is a large niche with offerings to Anastácia on the back wall and a black metal stand for votive candles burned in her honor. Every Monday, people regularly come to this shrine with candles, flowers, and small images of things, such as houses, dolls, and body parts. They pray to Anastácia for the necessities of this life, both the mundane (house payments) and the miraculous (cure for illnesses). The candle stand has white wax all over it, and the niche is crowded with little images. It is a popular, well-used shrine.

A place has been made for Anastácia, but in the back of the church, away from the chapel and the presence of the Catholic Holy of Holies, the Blessed Sacrament. She can come in, but only around the back, not through the front door, so to speak.

The official exclusion of the African from the Roman in Catholicism, however, is not so apparent in the traditions of popular or folk Catholicism, which are manifested throughout the city of Salvador at key moments in the yearly calendar of festivals. The rules of segregation tend to loosen and at times disappear, such as during the procession for the Festa da Lavagem do Senhor de Bonfim (the Feast of the Washing of the Lord of the Good Ending), which takes place in early January and begins in the Lower City, Cidade Baixa, a stone's throw from the bay at the Church of the Conception, and ends seven kilometers away at the steps of the all-white Church of Our Lord of the Good Ending. African Brazilian women, dressed in white, walk and dance their way down a preset, police-protected route, along with what appears to be well over a million people. When they reach their destination, they pour water on the steps of the church from flower-filled vases they have carried on their heads for seven kilometers. Then they scrub the steps with brooms. The steps are washed in honor of both Our Lord Jesus and Our Lord Oxala, an African Yoruba deity. Other Yoruba deities show up as well, manifesting themselves in some of those women who go into trance in front of the church, literally in front of God and everybody. Later in the year, on Good Friday, many Bahians prepare a traditional dinner of African-Bahian dishes which is eaten between noon and mid-afternoon, the hours commemorating Jesus' time on the cross. This meal is the *axexe*, the feast for the honored dead, and it is held during the time of day on Good Friday when many Catholics refrain from eating at all. In September, a feast is held for children, who are represented by the Catholic martyrs Cosmas and Damian. These martyrs are popularly represented as young twins and can also represent the Ibeji or Sacred Twins of the Yoruba tradition. Images of Cosmas and Damian are common in Bahia and they are always portrayed as Europeans, but there are times when their African identity is given away. It is not unusual to find a third, smaller figure standing between them. This is Doum, the name given to a child born after twins who is also important in the Yoruba tradition. As far as I know, there is no such association with the child born after twins in the Portuguese tradition. Whenever Cosmas, Damian, and Doum appear together, they are Africans as well, no matter how white they may appear.

This is the reality of Catholicism in Bahia: much of it is African, no matter how this African-ness is sent around the back by calling it "quaint," a "survival," or, less tactfully, "wrong." A common academic term for this religious form with a strong multicultural heritage is *syncretism*, the blending of religions by communities caught between two or more systems of belief. This term is most often used with non-Christian religions blending with Christianity. It often implies a confusion of irreconcilable traditions, a hodgepodge of beliefs and practices thrown together by people who do not have a deep understanding of any one tradition. "Syncretism" can be used as a way to academically send African Brazilian Catholicism around to the back door in comparison to more acceptable, less confused forms of religion.

Because of this implication, I will use the language of the Bahian anthropologist Vivaldo da Costa Lima. In reference to *catolicismo popular*, Lima states that "I spoke of identification, in symbolic equivalence, not in syncretism."[1] That phenomenon in Bahia which has been called "syncretism" does not necessarily collapse different systems together; in fact, the opposite often occurs. Symbols and names open up and expand to multiple meanings. As Lima says, it is beyond ambivalency—it is *plurivalency*.[2]

The richness and sophistication of this plurivalency is the result of an ugly, shameful beginning. There is a long history of violation, deceit, secret rendezvous, and passion between European and African communities in Brazil. This story of forbidden love begins with a program (or, more appropriately, a *pogrom*) of systematized brutality and cultural rape inflicted upon Africans by the Portuguese, to which the officials of the Catholic Church reluctantly turned a blind eye. The violation started with the forced migration of millions of people from Africa to the New World. Those Africans were coerced into accepting the religion of their kidnappers, often with little or no instruction in that religion.

There is serious doubt that any real campaign for the true conversion of the slaves initially occurred. In other words, the marriage of the Church of Bahia's large African community as Christ's spiritual bride never took place for the majority of her constituents. Because they were kidnapped by Catholics, they became Catholics by law. In too many cases, their new status as slaves, the violation itself, *was* the wedding ceremony.

The Church of Rome was initially against the slave trade. Those who participated in this enterprise were threatened with excommunication, but the threats did no good. Rather than lose whole regions of the Americas, the church leadership compromised its moral position and refocused on slaves as potential Christians. But the religious education of the slaves was not a major priority for their masters, and at times those masters encouraged the Africans to keep their traditional beliefs.

Those Africans and their descendants were reluctant to forget their first loves, different deities from all over black Africa, from regions as diverse as modern-day Senegal, Togo, Benin, Ghana, Ivory Coast, Nigeria, Congo, Angola, Mozambique, and Zanzibar. African religious practices were at times officially tolerated by the Bahian authorities despite Catholic censure because they were seen as a means to keep the slaves from uniting. Ancient animosities between neighboring African peoples were kept alive by the cultivation of different ethnic religions.

There were also Muslims among them who created secret schools to teach the Qur'an and their own African language through Arabic script.[3] Multiethnic Muslim revolts, however, eventually led to the death of Islam in Brazil, thus eliminating a serious rival for the religious affections of slaves in Bahia.[4] Of all the religions brought over by Africans, only Islam by itself could unify the slaves from various peoples. Islam is also a religion which historically could not coexist for long within a Catholic cultural matrix. Other religions, however, could do so, but only by resorting to deceit and secret rendezvous with their deities.

The strong Catholic tenets of Portuguese society made it virtually impossible for the slaves to keep from becoming Catholic, at least in outward appearance. I am referring to popular or folk Catholicism, which, for many Catholic communities (including the Portuguese), enjoyed considerable independence from Vatican guidelines, especially in the lay people's relationships with the saints. The slave traders, for example, had patron saints to protect their ships and increase their profits. The flexible relationship between the lay community and the community of saints was passed on to the slaves through the seasonal feast days and day-to-day practices which permeated the lives of Portuguese Brazilians.

It was within this context of popular Catholicism that Africans and their descendants kept alive various forms of African religion. Different African deities were venerated by associating them with Catholic saints who could be utilized without fear of censure from the masters, the priests, or the Inquisition. This in turn led to new interpretations about the nature of those saints in their triple function as official representatives of the church, unofficial miracle workers for the needs of the common believers, and silent, trustworthy witnesses to secret rendezvous between Africans and their beloved deities.

The anthropologist and photographer Pierre Verger states that "These same saints, who had protected the interests of slave traders and the lives of a portion of the Black cargo, had the good sense to examine their consciences, which resulted in a change of position: they then protected the slaves, helping them to fool their masters."[5] Indeed, it appears that, from what scant evidence survives about African slave cultures in Brazil, the saints represented both European and African spiritual beings. Officially, only the Catholic deity and saints could be praised, so that any public religious ceremony had to be dedicated to them, or appear to be so. Acts of devotion had to center around Catholic images, from crosses to plaster saints. From the close association that still exists today between the images of certain saints and African deities, we can surmise that the worship of African deities went underground. The African deities were hidden, as it were, behind the saints.

This, however, does not mean that it was all a facade, that the Africans were only pretending to venerate the Catholic saints, or that the saints became "confused" with the deities. What it means is that the Africans found a way through the saints to preserve their religious heritage. I refer to the success of popular Catholicism in the African Brazilian community today, which is not the result of ignorance or a mere mask. It would be presumptuous to assume that the Africans and their descendants did not have respect for the Catholic saints or their spiritual powers. But the Africans discovered that these same saints, when acting as "gateways" to the deities, did not seem to mind being liaisons. If the Catholic saints had not approved of their role in African worship, would they not have put a stop to it? Likewise, the African deities did not seem to mind the presence of the saints. African Brazilians used one tradition to support the other without seeking the approval of Catholic ecclesiastical authorities. The only authorities whose approval was necessary, the saints and the deities, appeared to accept and support the situation.

There is a principle which is shared in both popular or folk Catholicism and African Brazilian religion: things can be negotiated with or without an official priesthood, including *who* is venerated and *how*, resulting in religious practices that incorporate both Catholic and African elements. This arrangement has been problematic for the Catholic hierarchy for centuries, and with the development of an official and public priesthood in certain African religious denominations, the close association of the saints and deities in this negotiation is the center of a fairly new controversy. Some leaders of these African denominations, such as Mother Stella of Oxossi, call for the separation of the African from the Catholic in order to make those denominations more African. During her term as the leader of the prestigious House of Axe Opo Afonjá, images of the saints have been removed from positions of honor and no association between the saints and deities is acknowledged. There is still, however, a large white cross on the grounds of Axe Opo Afonjá, formerly known as O Centro da Santa Cruz (the Holy Cross Center) de Axe Opo Afonjá.

But some of the oldest and most traditional centers of African worship continue the association and keep the statues. They reject the idea that they would necessarily be more African by becoming less Catholic. Anthropologist Júlio Braga (who is also a leader in the African religious community) feels that it is not necessary to demand the separation of the Catholic from the African, although in his own house, the House of Axeloya, there are no images of the saints.[6]

The position of the Catholic Church in Salvador today concerning African Brazilian religions appears to be one of evasion. The church refuses to officially recognize the existence of African Brazilian religious communities as legitimate communities in their own right. This includes the influential and highly organized Houses of Candomblé, such as the Gantois, Casa Branca, and the aforementioned Axe Opo Afonjá. A warning has been issued recently to the clergy by the church leadership in Bahia that even public interfaith dialogue would be dangerous and should be avoided.[7]

Yet, unofficially, contact has been made on many levels, including the initiation of the late French priest François l'Espinay into the Candomblé House of Ile Axe Opo Aganju, a move that was acceptable to his superiors. I use the term "acceptable" because I can find no records saying that they actually gave him *permission*. Rather, they did not *prevent* him from doing so, nor does it appear that they ordered him to recant his allegiance to the House after he had joined. Individual priests and nuns have reached out to the African Brazilian religious community, but the leaders of the church are not yet ready to go beyond individual or unofficial encounters.

The saints and the deities, however, are not bound by restrictions imposed by Catholic or African religious leaders. In Salvador, not far from the commercial district, Mass is held every Monday afternoon at the Church of Saint Lazarus. In modern Catholicism there is no longer a Saint Lazarus; along with Saint Christopher and others, he is no longer on the official list of saints. But the people who attend this church are not ready to give up their beloved leper-saint just because the Roman Catholic hierarchy says so. I have heard that the Mass is said by the Igreja Católica Brasileira, the Brazilian Catholic Church, an organization of dubious repute that will conduct Catholic ceremonies which are not sanctioned by the Roman Catholic Church. At the same time as the Mass, a ceremony in honor of Omolu, the Yoruba deity of pestilence, is held in front of the church. White-clad priestesses wait on the steps of Saint Lazarus to bless people with popcorn (a food sacred to Omolu), which lies, freshly popped, at the foot of a large metal cross. I have also seen a priestess bless a car with popcorn. Donations are accepted both inside and in front of the church.

A real motivator for the continuation of this forbidden love for both Roman Catholicism and African religion is money. There is a tourist market for so-called religious syncretism. One example can be found in the town of Cachoeira, a few miles outside of Salvador. Cachoeira is the home of an African Catholic sisterhood, the Irmandade da Nossa Senhora da Boa Morte (the Sisterhood of Our Lady of the Good Death). This sisterhood is composed of elderly African Brazilian women who carry prestige in the African Catholic community as both members of a locally (and historically) important Catholic organization and as practitioners of African religion. They are also Cachoeira's biggest tourist draw, and a modern visitors' center has been built in town to showcase the sisterhood.

Let us return to Salvador proper and the Festa da Lavagem do Senhor de Bonfim. Besides being both an African and a Catholic ceremony, this celebration brings in thousands of tourists and their money, as they flock to the ornate Catholic churches (creating a source of revenue for the church and the state of Bahia) and the lavish Candomblé festivals (resulting, often indirectly, in a source of revenue for the African Brazilian community and the state).

Although the official stance of the Catholic Church is that the faithful should be "monogamous" and follow only Catholic doctrine and practice, tolerance is generally the rule. Those in the Candomblé community who want to eliminate Catholic elements do not insist, however, that people choose one religion or the other. The reformers do not have a problem with members having allegiance to both Catholicism and Candomblé, as long as they do not "mix" the two in rituals or their understanding of the deities. But both sides have to contend with the fact that the hearts of many Bahians are big enough to love both the deities and the saints, and that this love does not seek out differences but tends to see the sacred as the sacred, no matter what form it takes.

NOTES

1. "Festa e religião no centro histórico," *Afro-Asia* (1995), p. 73.

2. Ibid., p. 74.

3. The Haussa Muslims in Brazil wrote in Haussa using the Arabic alphabet. Raimundo Nina Rodrigues, *Os Africanos no Brasil*, 4th ed. (São Paulo: Companhia Editora Nacional, 1976), p. 140.

    4.   Roger Bastide, *African Religions of Brazil* (Baltimore: Johns Hopkins University Press, 1978), p. 153.

    5.   Pierre Fatumbi Verger, *Orixás* (Bahia: Corrupio-FACEBA, 1981), p. 25.

    6.   Interviews with Mother Stella and Júlio Braga, Salvador, April 1996.

    7.   Interview with Father Colin McLean, Order of the Columbans, Salvador, March 1997.

17. El papel de la mujer en el candomblé

Malgorzata Oleszkiewicz

> From the beginning, the Creator-God put women in charge of all the good things on earth. Without their sanction, no healing can take place, rain cannot fall, plants cannot bear fruits and children cannot come into the world.[1]
>
> Olodumaré dio el poder a las mujeres; el hombre, solo, nada podrá hacer en ausencia de ellas.[2]

Al caminar por las calles de Salvador, Bahia, lo primero que llama nuestra atención es el carácter africano de la ciudad. Este carácter se nota en las *bahianas* vestidas en sus blancos trajes tradicionales vendiendo *acarajé* y *abará*, en los frecuentes toques de tambores y desfiles dancísticos, en los nombres de las instituciones y negocios, y en los mercados callejeros llenos de actividad. La población que presenta diferentes mezclas es predominantemente negra y mulata, y aunque las estadísticas indiquen un 75% de población de origen africano, se dice que no hay persona que no tenga sangre africana en Bahia.

Este carácter africano se hace mucho más patente si nos adentramos en la esencia de la ciudad, sus raíces espirituales y culturales, presentes en el candomblé. El candomblé es una religión afro-brasileña desarrollada en la segunda mitad del siglo XVIII y el siglo XIX por esclavos de la región yoruba (parte de lo que hoy es Nigeria y Benin). Después de la llegada al Nuevo Mundo, las creencias africanas tuvieron que ser camufladas y disfrazadas con elementos católicos para así poder ser aceptadas por los colonizadores. De esta manera nació el sincretismo religioso, donde elementos de la religión católica y la africana se mezclan. Este fenómeno ocurrió en todas las regiones donde hubo diferentes influencias, como Haití, Trinidad, Cuba y Brasil. Sin embargo, mientras en Cuba este sincretismo es muy fuerte hasta hoy día, en el Brasil hay una creciente reafricanización del candomblé y más que de sincretismo se habla de religiones alternadas.[3] El término sincretismo se reserva para cultos que incluyen conscientemente las influencias de tradiciones muy variadas, como la umbanda, y es el candomblé la religión considerada más "pura" en cuanto a sus raíces africanas.

En este trabajo me propongo discutir el rol del elemento más importante en el candomblé —la mujer afro-brasileña— y su interdependencia con la

sociedad más amplia en el nordeste del Brasil. Mi propósito es escudriñar la
visión estereotipada de ésta únicamente como víctima de abuso racial, sexual y
de clase y demostrar que existen espacios donde la mujer afro-brasileña se apro-
pia de su poder y lo ejerce.

Ya en 1947, la antropóloga norteamericana Ruth Landes, hasta hoy día la
única en publicar un libro sobre las mujeres en Bahia, escribe:

> . . . stability is provided by black women. And the women have everything:
> they have the temples, the religion, the priestly offices, the bearing and
> rearing of children, and opportunities for self-support. (Landes 1994:147)

A través de los años, otros autores como Edison Carneiro (1948), Melville
Herskovits (1957), Vivaldo da Costa Lima (1977) y Klaas Woortmann (1987),
confirman la tesis sobre la matrifocalidad de la vida en Bahia, especialmente
en lo que se refiere a las clases bajas de ascendencia africana. Esto significa que
en el norte y el nordeste del Brasil, las mujeres negras, especialmente las mayores, tienen el poder en la esfera religiosa y doméstica, tanto como en el mercado informal. Hay que resaltar que esta situación es el reverso de lo que
acontece en las clases media y alta, donde las mujeres siguen siendo subyuga-
das tanto en la esfera política y económica, como en la doméstica y la religiosa.
¿A qué se debe tan notable reversión? Para responder a esta pregunta, tenemos
que examinar la tradición religiosa y la cosmovisión yoruba, así como la situación social después de la llegada de los esclavos al Nuevo Mundo y su conexión
con las costumbres africanas.

Según el mito yoruba de la creación del mundo, Odùduwà o Oòduà aparece como la "diosa suprema del mundo" o "eterna y coexistente con Dios".
Ella es la compañera de Obàtálá, con el cual constituye la unión de la tierra y
del cielo en forma de una gran güira o calabaza (Verger 1992:31–34).[4] En otro
mito, Odù recibe el poder del pájaro eyè y la calabaza elèye, la señora del pájaro. Olodumaré o Dios supremo le dice que ella será ìyá won, la madre de todos
los seres humanos. Odù exagera su poder y lo pierde en favor de los hombres;
sin embargo, las mujeres siguen controlando ese poder (Verger 1992:25–28).

En la tradición yoruba se cree que las mujeres, especialmente las mayores, poseen el poder aje. Se las llama awon iya wa "nuestras madres", ìyámì
"mi madre" e ìyá àgbà "vieja y sabia" (Drewal y Drewal 1990:9). Este poder
puede ser protector o destructor y por eso en Africa estas madres ancestrales
son aplacadas y homenajeadas durante los festivales Gèlèdé. Según Margaret y
Henry Drewal (1990:xv) el significado etimológico de la palabra Gèlèdé es el
siguiente: gè significa "to soothe, to placate, to pet or coddle"; èlè "refers to a
woman's private parts, those that symbolize women's secrets and their life-giving
powers" y dè "connotes 'to soften with care or gentleness.'" El festival Gèlèdé
es "an artistic expression of a pan-Yoruba belief: that women, primarily elderly

women, possess certain extraordinary power equal to or greater than that of the gods and ancestors." They are called "our mothers," "the gods of society," and "owners of the world" (Drewal y Drewal 1990:xv).

Juana Elbein dos Santos indica que en Bahia el festival Gèlèdé, relacionado con la sociedad femenina del mismo nombre, se realizaba hasta la muerte de Maria Júlia Figueiredo, Omóníké, una *ìyá-làse*, o celadora del *axé*,[5] del más antiguo *terreiro nagô* (yoruba) de Bahia, Ilé Iyá-Nàsó. Este festival tenía lugar cada ocho de diciembre, el mismo día que hasta hoy es celebrada la Virgen de la Inmaculada Concepción, "la patrona de Bahia", identificada con el *orixá* Oxum, la madre protectora de la gestación. Hoy día, el poder de las *ìyá-mi* o "nuestras madres" está conservado en las *iabas* u *orixás* femeninos del candomblé, tales como Oxum, Iemanjá, Nana, Oya y Ewa. Todas ellas son *ìyá-elèye*, poseedoras de la calabaza o güira con el pájaro dentro, símbolo de su poder. Otro *orixá* femenino, Oba, encabeza la sociedad secreta femenina, E'léékò, de la cual en el Brasil hoy día se sabe muy poco (Elbein dos Santos 1993:114–117).

Las *ìyá-mi* son símbolos de la fecundidad y su poder de gestación es simbolizado por una gran calabaza huevo-vientre, dentro de la cual se encuentra un pájaro. Hoy día varias de las *iabas* u *orixás* femeninos llevan un *abebé* o abanico ritual con la imagen de un pájaro (Iyá-mi Agbá). Los festivales de Gèlèdé se realizan en Africa para propiciar estas fuerzas y apaciguar el enorme poder de las *ìyá-mi* (Elbein dos Santos 1993:117). En los *terreiros* del Brasil se realiza hasta hoy día el padê, un ritual de restitución del poder genitor femenino (Iyá-mi Agbá).

La creencia en el gran poder femenino, representado por las *iabas*, también se refleja en la estructura de los *terreiros* o comunidades de culto del candomblé. La mayoría de los *terreiros* es dirigida por una *iyalorixá* o *mãe-de-santo*, sacerdotisa suprema con un poder casi absoluto.[6] Su nombre *iaôrixá* significa "esposa del orixá" (Costa Lima 1982:92). Ella designa a una *iyá kêkêrê* o *mãe pequena*, que le ayuda en las principales funciones del *terreiro*. La *iyalorixá* "pone la navaja en la cabeza" o inicia a las *iaôs* o *filhas-de-santo*. Una *iaô* o "esposa más joven", después de una ceremonia realizada a los siete años de iniciada, pasa a la categoría *ébomin* que le permitiría formar su propio *terreiro*, si esta fuera la voluntad de los *orixás*. También hay otra importante categoría de mujeres —las *ékédes*. Son iniciadas que no "reciben santo"—no entran en trance— y ayudan a las *filhas-de-santo* cuando éstas son poseídas por los *orixás*. Otras funciones, como la preparación de las comidas rituales para los *orixás*, son también realizadas por mujeres. La *iyá bassê* es una persona mayor encargada de la comida sacrificial y ofrendas que dirige las actividades de la cocina. Tanto la *iyalorixá* como la *iyabassê* debe ser una mujer mayor que demuestra experiencia, paciencia y equilibrio. La palabra *iyábassê* viene del yoruba *iyágbà-sê*, *iabá-sê*, lo cual significa "vieja que cocina" (Costa Lima 1992:101).

La *mãe-de-santo* o *iyalorixá* es la intermediaria de la fuerza mística de los *orixás* o dioses. Establece la comunicación y consagra e interpreta la voluntad de los "santos". Hoy día en el Brasil ella también está a cargo de la adivinación con los caracoles o *búzios*, ya que la función masculina del *babalaô*, que persiste en la región yoruba de Africa y otros lugares influenciados por ella, como Cuba, en el Brasil prácticamente ha desaparecido. Además, la *iyalorixá* dirige toda la actividad de la casa de culto, como las ceremonias públicas y privadas, la disciplina, la economía, los mecanismos de promoción y la asistencia espiritual y material a la *familia-de-santo* o grupo de personas asociadas a la comunidad del candomblé (Costa Lima 1977:119). Es una persona que por su función especial de intermediaria con los *orixás* y como guardiana de la fuerza espiritual y de la tradición, es receptora del mayor respeto. Las *iaôs* o "esposas más jóvenes" de los *orixás* son las iniciadas que entran en trance durante las ceremonias. Al incorporar a sus respectivos *orixás* ayudan a traer la fuerza espiritual y vital, *axé*, a la tierra.

La función principal de los hombres en un *terreiro* es la de *ogã*. El *ogã* para ser "confirmado" tiene que pasar por una iniciación pero, en comparación con las *filhas-de-santo* o *iaôs*, los *ogãs* son sólo "parcialmente iniciados". Entre los *ogãs* confirmados, la *iyalorixá* escoge al *pêjigã* o "señor del altar", al *axôgún* o sacrificador de animales y al *alabê* o director de los tambores sagrados. Los *ogãs* son protectores que proveen prestigio y apoyo financiero al *terreiro* y ayudan en la organización de las ceremonias. Por eso generalmente su función es exterior a la religión. Según Edison Carneiro en su ya clásico estudio de 1948, *Candomblés da Bahia*, "las mujeres detienen todas las funciones permanentes del candomblé, mientras que a los hombres se les reservan apenas las temporarias u honoríficas. . . . Esta división de la jerarquía parece confirmar la opinión de que el candomblé es un oficio de mujer . . ." (1991:116, 117).

Hay también casas de candomblé dirigidas por hombres, los *babalorixás* o *pais-de-santo*, pero esto no ocurre en los candomblés más tradicionales. De los siete *terreiros* que he frecuentado en Salvador en el verano de 1996, sólo uno era dirigido por un *pai-de-santo*.[7] Aunque muchas casas inician a *filhos-de-santo* hombres, esto no ocurre en los candomblés más antiguos, como Engenho Velho o Casa Branca, u ortodoxos como el *terreiro* Ilê Asé Orisanlá J'Omin, principal objeto de mis pesquisas en Bahia. Según Carneiro (1991:115), "Por lo menos en teoría el *filho* tiene los mismos privilegios que la *filha*. Pero, en realidad, su posición es muy inferior. Los candomblés más antiguos de Bahia no hacen santo de un hombre".

Es sabido que tanto los *pais-de-santo* como los *filhos-de-santo* u hombres que incorporan a los *orixás*, son casi todos homosexuales. De acuerdo a las pesquisas de Vivaldo da Costa Lima, entre las 136 casas de candomblé estudiadas, 34 eran dirigidas por *pais-de-santo*, de los cuales 28 eran "confesadamente" o "notoriamente" homosexuales (1977:171). Esto está relacionado con el hecho de que para ser poseída por un *orixá*, la persona tiene que adoptar simbólicamente el rol femenino. El iniciado o iniciada es el "caballo" al cual cabalga el santo u *orixá* durante la posesión. Este acto de posesión por el *orixá* tiene una analogía con el acto sexual. Aunque el sexo mítico de los dioses puede ser masculino, femenino o andrógino, en el acto de posesión los dioses son estructuralmente masculinos y los iniciados —femeninos. Así los iniciados, sean mujeres u hombres, al ser montados por los *orixás*, asumen el papel femenino en las ceremonias religiosas. Este hecho está confirmado por sus ropas y sus peinados. También los sacerdotes yoruba-africanos siempre son mujeres u hombres travestidos que usan las vestimentas nupciales del siglo XIX (Matory 1988:222-223). Quiero agregar que Peter Fry, en su libro *Para inglês ver* (1982), polemiza con la posición de Ruth Landes según la cual el *bicha* u homosexual es sólo una pálida imitación de mujer. Según Fry, en el *bicha* se juntan ciertos aspectos clave de los papeles masculinos y femeninos que son manipulados en su propio beneficio. Por ejemplo, le es más fácil al homosexual que a la mujer bregar con la policía o con la justicia (Fry 1982:76).

También Matory explica la función del hombre en los rituales yorubas del norte y del nordeste del Brasil, donde la tradición patrilineal es mucho más débil que en el sur, en Cuba y en Puerto Rico. En el Brasil, el comportamiento sexual es considerado tradicionalmente en categorías de actividad y pasividad y no de hetero u homosexualidad. Los hombres activos (*homens*) que penetran a mujeres o *bichas* (homosexuales pasivos) son los que "comen" y los *bichas* y mujeres son los que "dan". El hecho de penetrar a un hombre o a una mujer no afecta la identidad social del hombre (Matory 1988:226–227).

¿Tiene este reparto de roles dentro de la religión algún correspondiente en la situación económica y social de las mujeres y los hombres en Bahia? Como dije anteriormente, en el sistema social dominante en el Brasil, las mujeres, los africanos y los homosexuales siguen siendo subyugados al poder de los hombres blancos de clases altas, que son la fuerza activa política y económicamente. Sin embargo, si miramos la situación entre las clases bajas de descendencia africana en el norte y el nordeste, tanto a nivel religioso como laico, notaremos que hay un reverso de esta situación. Aquí son las mujeres afro-brasileñas mayores las que tienen el poder. ¿Cómo explicar tan notable reversión?

Sabemos que durante la esclavitud novomundista, la institución de la familia entre los africanos fue bruscamente desintegrada. El hombre de ascendencia africana no podía mantener un status de proveedor en el cual se apoyaría su poder. Además, las familias fueron divididas y los que llegaban eran principalmente personas solas. Al liberarse de la esclavitud, fue más fácil para las mujeres que para los hombres obtener empleo en servicios domésticos o como vendedoras en las calles y los mercados. En consecuencia, las mujeres de clases bajas hasta hoy día tienden a tener compañeros transitorios o hasta varios a la vez, pues ninguno es capaz de mantener y proveer estabilidad a la familia (Woortmann 1987:145). Como las mujeres trabajan, tienen sus propios ingresos y como sus hijos son con frecuencia de diferentes padres, la familia es matrilineal y los hijos reciben el apellido de la madre. Las hijas se valoran más que los hijos (Woortmann 1987:105) y la familia frecuentemente se compone de varias generaciones de mujeres. Igual que en el candomblé, ellas constituyen el elemento estable en la familia y su poder aumenta con el tiempo.

Esta situación también tiene relación con el sistema de poligamia en el Africa occidental, donde un hombre puede estar casado con varias mujeres que habitan con sus respectivos hijos en el mismo caserío. Estas mujeres gozan de poder en asuntos domésticos, lo cual frecuentemente se extiende a su independencia en el exterior. Esto se debe a que son comerciantes muy activas y frecuentemente llegan a acumular más riqueza que sus maridos.[8] En Bahia, este sistema poligínico persiste de una forma no oficial, con la diferencia de que las mujeres viven en diferentes casas. Esta situación refuerza el énfasis matrilineal del parentesco y la independencia de las mujeres.

En el norte y el nordeste del Brasil es notable la interdependencia entre el candomblé y las otras esferas de la vida social. El sistema simbólico de género de los cultos afro-brasileños, donde la base de la distinción es la "actividad" o la "pasividad" del individuo, ha sido adoptado por la sociedad más amplia, creando las categorías de *homen* y de *bicha*. Por otra parte, las circunstancias socioeconómicas han tenido impacto en la estructura y la práctica de los cultos, dando una notable preponderancia a las mujeres —las sacerdotisas del *axé*. Gracias al candomblé, dos grupos marginalizados y desprovistos de poder en la sociedad dominante, las mujeres mayores y los homosexuales, ambos de origen africano y de clases bajas, encuentran respeto y poder. El contexto del candomblé eleva las vidas de sus adeptos de una situación de marginalidad y miseria a una de riqueza espiritual y muchas veces también material, gracias a la armonía que se introduce en sus vidas. El atractivo del candomblé reside en estar en contacto con la fuerza espiritual y cósmica *axé* que se renueva constantemente durante los rituales, la posesión y el compartir de las comidas sagradas. Gracias a esta fuerza, los adeptos reciben dirección y apoyo espiritual de los *orixás*, compañerismo y protección de la comunidad y éxtasis de la posesión relacionado con la belleza visual, la música y la danza. Es un gozo tanto para el espíritu como para los sentidos, porque los dioses no son algo alejado y abstracto. Descienden a la tierra para guiar y proteger a sus adeptos y por eso siempre necesitan ser adorados.

Gracias a estos atractivos, el candomblé está dejando de ser una religión de africanos de clases bajas. Cada vez más blancos de clase media y alta e incluso personalidades de la vida pública se le están integrando. De una religión marginal perseguida por la policía hasta los años 80, el candomblé se está convirtiendo en un espacio prestigioso, reconocido e integrado por cada vez más artistas, intelectuales y extranjeros. Eso está ocurriendo gracias a la dedicación de las mujeres negras, sacerdotisas mediadoras del *axé*. También se está elevando el prestigio y el poder de la mujer afro-brasileña en la sociedad más amplia, cuando ésta se proyecta publicando libros y entrevistas e interviniendo en encuentros y congresos. Quizás mediante estas nuevas formas de proyección, la sociedad oficial será forzada a reconocer la importancia y el poder de la mujer afro-brasileña, sustento de los hombres y de los dioses.

NOTAS

1.   Testimonio recogido por Rowland Abiodun en la región yoruba central y oriental, citado en Drewal y Drewal (1990:9).

2.   Del "Mito da criação do pano de Egum", citado en Verger (1992:27). Esta y las subsiguientes traducciones de citas del portugués y del inglés son mías.

3.   Juana Elbein dos Santos, entrevista personal, 5 de agosto de 1996.

4.   Este mismo mito también fue recogido en Cuba por Teodoro Díaz Fabelo en su *Lengua de santeros Güiné Gongorí* (1956:164).

5.   *Axé* es la fuerza vital y mística de los *orixás* a la vez que el lugar de culto o *terreiro* del candomblé.

6.   En el año 1977, Vivaldo da Costa Lima reporta que, en una muestra de 136 casas de candomblé en Bahia, 102 eran dirigidas por mujeres y 34 por hombres. Esto constituye un 75% de casas dirigidas por mujeres, mientras que en la investigación de Edison Carneiro en los años 40, el porcentaje era un poco más del 50% de *iyalorixás* en los 67 *terreiros* registrados (Costa Lima 1977:55).

7.   Me refiero a las siguientes casas de tradición nagô: Ilê Asé Opô Afonjá, Casa Branca, Menininha do Gantois, Ilê Asé Opô Aganjú, Ilê Asé Orisanlá J'Omin, la casa de tradición angola de mae Bebé y una casa de caboclo.

8.   Drewal y Drewal (1990:10).

BIBLIOGRAFIA MINIMA

Carneiro, Edison. 1991. *Candomblés da Bahia.* Río de Janeiro: Civilizaçao Brasileira, 1948.

Costa Lima, Vivaldo da. 1977. "A família-de-santo nos candomblés Jeje-Nagôs da Bahia: um estudo de relações intra-grupais". Tesis de maestría, Universidade Federal da Bahia.

——. 1982. "Organização do grupo de candomblé: estratificação, senioridade e hierarquia". *Bandeira de Aairá.* São Paulo: Nobel.

Cros Sandoval, Mercedes. 1975. *La religión afro-cubana.* Madrid: Playor.

Díaz Fabelo, Teodoro. 1956. *Lengua de santeros Güiné Gongorí.* La Habana.

Drewal, Henry John, and Margaret Thompson Drewal. 1990. *Gèlèdé: Art and Female Power among the Yoruba.* Bloomington: Indiana University Press.

Elbein dos Santos, Juana. 1993. *Os Nàgô e a morte*. Petrópolis: Vozes, 1975.

Fry, Peter. 1982. *Para inglês ver*. Río de Janeiro: Zahar Editores.

Iyá-mi Agbá Mito e Metamorfose das Maes Nagô. Video. Prod. Sociedade de Estudos da Cultura Negra no Brasil. Dir. Juana Elbein dos Santos. 55 min.

Landes, Ruth. *The City of Women*. 1994. Albuquerque: University of New Mexico Press, 1947.

Matory, James Lorand. 1988. "Homens montados: homossexualidade e simbolismo da possessão nas religiões afro-brasileiras". *Escravidão e invenção da liberdade: estudos sobre o negro no Brasil*. João José Reis, ed. São Paulo: Brasiliense. Pp. 215–231.

Sáenz de Tejada. 1997. "Raza y género en la narrativa femenina afro-brasileña". *Revista de Crítica Literaria Latinoamericana* 46:269–285.

Staal, Parvati Jeannette. 1992. "Women, Food, Sex and Survival in Candomblé: An Interpretive Analysis of an African-Brazilian Religion in Bahia, Brazil". Ph.D. diss., University of California, Los Angeles. Ann Arbor: UMI, 1992. 9301561.

Verger, Pierre. 1992. "Esplendor e decadência do culto de Iyàmi Osòròngà 'Minha Mae a Feiticeira' entre os Iorubas". *Artigos Tomo I*. São Paulo: Corrupio. Pp. 5–91.

Woortmann, Klaas. 1987. *A família das mulheres*. Río de Janeiro: Tempo Brasileiro.

18. The Power of Axé: Trends and Sources in Afro-Brazilian Religious Studies

Eileen Oliver

> Macumba is like a powerful family which protects you, which is always there, always present, and in whose heart you have a place. You no longer feel abandoned or alone. Things become simpler, more obvious. And soon, absurd as it may seem, everything begins to go better: work, romantic or psychological problems, everything improves or is resolved . . . you can't just call it magic. There is no explanation. All you can do is observe what happens. . . .[1]

This paper is a result of several years of bibliographic research on Afro-Brazilian religions. I began the study at the Memorial Library at the University of Wisconsin, Madison, which houses an extensive Brazilian collection. Other libraries invaluable to my research were the Benson Latin American Collection at the University of Texas at Austin and the Library of Congress. The bibliographic sources include both scholarly and popular literature, much of it published in Brazil. Increasingly, however, scholars from a variety of fields and from many countries are adding to our awareness of the unique and universal character of Afro-Brazilian religions.

The history of Afro-Brazilian religions begins with the slaves brought to Brazil. Despite separation from their African homelands and the often harsh conditions they faced in Brazil, the slaves and their descendants managed not only to retain much of their African culture but also to influence Brazilian culture—its food, dance, music, and religion. Afro-Brazilian religions share several traits: belief in *axé*, the life-giving spiritual force that emanates from individuals in trance, spiritual entities, and nature; belief in spiritual entities, including Catholic saints, African *orixás* or gods, native Indian spirits *(caboclos),* and the spirits of Afro-Brazilian slaves *(pretos-velhos);* use of possession trance, during which communication with spiritual entities takes place; and a variety of rituals and ceremonies which can include elaborate initiation rites, music, dancing, herbal baths, and various food offerings to spiritual entities.

Afro-Brazilian religions are not centralized. Each spiritual center, often referred to as a *terreiro,* has its own leader, the *mãe* or *pai-de-santo.* This leader is responsible for the material and spiritual well-being of the other members, who in turn are expected to contribute to the success of the terreiro.

Many members of an Afro-Brazilian religion also consider themselves Catholics, and for these individuals, there is no conflict of interest in participating in more than one religion.

Any review of the literature on Afro-Brazilian religions must begin with Nina Rodrigues, a native Brazilian who was born in Maranhão in 1862, studied forensic medicine in Bahia, and died in Paris in 1906. As Roger Bastide noted, "We must stress the work of Nina Rodrigues because all subsequent research developed out of it."[2] Writing at the beginning of the century, Rodrigues noted that Bahia was perhaps the only province in Brazil where one could still study African blacks. Rodrigues's goal in studying this group was to contribute to the "scientific" knowledge of blacks in Brazil.[3] Prior to Rodrigues, few had deemed the Africans in Brazil worthy of any such "scientific" study, and no one had attempted to undertake such a task.

In his works, the most important of which include *O animismo fetichista dos negros bahianos* and *Os africanos no Brasil*, Rodrigues proposed an interpretation of African religions in Brazil within the framework of clinical psychology. He argued that hysteria was prevalent among blacks, as well as whites, and concluded that all African religious celebrations took the form of induced somnambulism. Rodrigues believed that the "weak" intellectual development of the "primitive" Negro, combined with the nervous exhaustion produced by initiation ceremonies, provoked hysteria. This led him to conclude that African religion represented a pathological phenomenon.[4]

In *O animismo fetichista dos negros bahianos* Rodrigues sought to provide an unbiased description of African religion and religious practices present in Brazil, and in *Os africanos no Brasil* he attempted a historical account of Brazilian slaves, as well as a psychological study of the African religious sentiment. This latter endeavor was particularly important to the author, for he believed that African social psychology affected the formation of the national population. He also believed that multiple and varied manifestations of religious sentiment provide the best means for assessing a people's mental condition.[5]

Many of Rodrigues's findings continued to be accepted by anthropologists, sociologists, and other scholars and popular writers throughout the early twentieth century. These include his discovery of religious syncretism between African deities and Catholic saints and the supposed cultural superiority of the Sudanese blacks over the Bantu peoples. Rodrigues believed that this superiority accounted for the heavy Yoruba influence in Bahian candomblés. Likewise, Rodrigues attested to the "incontestable superiority" of black religion over that of the indigenous peoples.[6] Rodrigues's methodology of looking for "African survivals" in Brazil continued throughout the century, and helped support his theories and those of others about the "purity" of Yoruba-influenced candomblés, compared with the religions of other "nations" or ethnically affiliated groups in Brazil.

Rodrigues was deeply concerned with the effects of racial mixing in Brazil. He had no doubt that eventually, through the process of acculturation by Brazilian European races, the black race would be subsumed, but worried what effects this would have on the nation as a whole. He therefore went to great lengths to prove that not all black African groups brought to the Americas as slaves were equal. For example, he distinguished between the *camitas* (Hamites), whom he considered to be a branch of the white race and, in his mind, possessing a superior culture, and pure black Africans. While he wrote that few camitas were brought to Brazil, he noted that many *mestiços* with camita blood were indeed introduced into Brazil.

While Rodrigues staunchly argued against police persecution of African religious practices in Brazil, and while he sought to educate others on the culturally advanced state of much of African religion, mythology, and the arts, he remained a man of his times. The final chapter of *Os africanos no Brasil*, titled "The Psychological Remains of Criminality in Brazilian Blacks," discusses the consequences of the coexistence in society of races in different stages of moral and juridical evolution. He labeled the type of crimes that blacks contributed to as "ethnic criminality" and explained that they were due to African religious beliefs, the African "eye for an eye" mentality, and the African belief that one is not responsible for crimes committed against individuals outside of one's community.[7]

The best-known student of Nina Rodrigues, also a doctor of forensic medicine, was Artur Ramos. His research interests lay in psychiatry and ethnology. In the early 1920s he, along with his friend Jorge Amado, made many visits to Candomblé terreiros in Salvador. Both were interested in revealing the "mystery of the mythical world" of black Bahians.[8] Jorge Amado would later write many novels into which he incorporated themes of Afro-Brazilian life. In 1931 Ramos presented a paper at a medical conference titled "The Psychological Problem of Curandeirismo" which was the result of his observations made in the Candomblé terreiros. He continued to investigate the use of religious practices to cure physical illnesses and published many articles on this subject.[9]

Like Nina Rodrigues, Ramos examined cultural survivals of Africa in Brazil, but extended the geographical focus of this work to include Rio de Janeiro where various Afro-Brazilian religions, often labeled as Macumba and believed to be of Bantu origin, were practiced. Also, like Rodrigues, Ramos believed that the candomblés of Bahia, along with some xangôs in the North, had better preserved their African (Sudanese) origins, and he noted that they should not be confused with the Macumba terreiros of Rio de Janeiro.[10]

Ramos believed that in most "primitive" African religions, magic and religion were inseparable; the priest served as magician, diviner, and healer. When Africans were transplanted to Brazil, however, contact with more "advanced" religions led them to make a distinction between religion and magic. The former involves a priest and prayers, while the latter, referred to as *feitiçaria* or witch-craft, involves subjugating supernatural forces to one's will, often to deliber-ately harm an individual or individuals. Many of Ramos's works focused on feitiçaria-inspired crimes and typify the thinking of many medical practitioners of the early twentieth century. Ramos distinguished between the true pai-de-santo whose role was that of priest, and the *feiticeiro* or witch doctor. Perhaps because of this kind of distinction, Roger Bastide wrote that Ramos's greatest contribution to the study of Afro-Brazilian religions was his anti-racism, his anti-ethnocentrism, and his substitution of the principle of "cultural relativity" for the notion of superior and inferior cultures.[11]

Edison Carneiro, a contemporary of Artur Ramos, was an Afro-Bahian born in 1912 in Salvador. Carneiro became interested in Afro-Brazilian studies in the early 1930s, encouraged perhaps by his father, Antônio Joaquim de Souza Carneiro, who had published works on Afro-Brazilian folklore. Carneiro stud-ied black life in Bahia from 1933 to 1939 and published several books and nu-merous articles in Brazilian journals. His two principal works, published in 1936 and 1937, are *Religiões negras: notas de etnografia religiosas* and *Negros bantus: notas de etnografia religiosa e de folclore*. In the latter work Carneiro found that many Bantu beliefs and liturgy in "mixed" *candomblés de caboclo* were similar to Yoruba-influenced candomblés. Carneiro also wrote on the Bantu contributions to Brazilian culture which included the musical form samba, the Angolan martial art of *capoeira,* and various festivals. In his work *Candomblés da Bahia*, published in 1948, Carneiro noted that increasingly men without of-ficial training were becoming spiritual leaders of candomblés. Even so, he found that the hierarchical division of spiritual power in these terreiros remained within the female domain, as each center continued to be a domestic, familial organi-zation, far removed from the daily activities of the outside world.[12]

Roger Bastide considered the highpoint of the 1930s to be the three con-ferences held in Recife, Bahia, and Belo Horizonte in 1934, 1937, and 1939 in which Edison Carneiro, Artur Ramos, Jorge Amado, Gilberto Freyre, and many other scholars from a variety of disciplines participated. Edison Carneiro left Bahia in 1939 for Rio de Janeiro, and according to Waldir Freitas Oliveira it was only in 1959 with the founding of the Centro de Estudos Afro-Orientais da Universidade Federal da Bahia that Afro-Bahian studies resumed.[13]

In 1938 Ruth Landes, a doctoral graduate in anthropology from Colum-bia University, arrived in Brazil to study relations between the black and white population. Shortly after her arrival Landes changed the focus of her work to study the role of women in Bahian Candomblé. Her constant guide, compan-ion, and means of access into the world of Candomblé was Edison Carneiro. The result of Landes's studies was her book *The City of Women*, published in

1947 and translated into Portuguese in 1967. Roger Bastide was alone among his contemporaries in praising this work.[14] There were several reasons for this: many felt that Landes's personal relationship with Carneiro had compromised her anthropology; Landes's writing style was subjective and decidedly unscientific (today it would be called "new" or "experimental" ethnography); and, most important for the field of Afro-Brazilian religious studies, Landes's focus on race and gender was unconventional and therefore the target of criticism in the 1930s and 1940s. Today, of course, these themes play an important role in postcolonial and feminist anthropology.[15] The reissue of *The City of Women* in 1994 demonstrates its importance. As an introduction to the Afro-Bahian world of the 1930s, Landes's work has no equal.

Roger Bastide (1898–1974), a native of France, conducted research and taught in Brazil for twenty years. Like his compatriot, the famous photographer and ethnographer Pierre Verger, Bastide not only studied Afro-Brazilian cults but also became intimately involved with them. Both obtained the prestigious position of *ogã* in Bahian candomblés, and therefore were responsible for the material well-being of their terreiro, as well as serving as liaisons to the outside community.

During the course of his stay in Brazil, Bastide came to believe that blacks must become aware of their need to create an Afro-Brazilian anthropology based on their own experience and to reject foreign theories that falsify the true significance of the Afro-Brazilian religious experience.[16] He was very enthusiastic about the works of Deoscoredes M. dos Santos and his wife, Juana Elbein dos Santos, both Candomblé priests and therefore privy to the life and beliefs of their religion as no outsider could ever be.

Bastide rejected the strict division of the social sciences into isolated fields of study. He advocated the use of social anthropology, combined with cultural anthropology and psychology, as a means of understanding the persistence of Afro-Brazilian religions. Bastide also believed that one could not study a group, in this case Brazilian blacks, without examining their relationship to outside groups, including whites, Brazil as a whole, and the rest of the world.[17]

In one of his best known works, *The African Religions of Brazil: Toward a Sociology of the Interpenetration of Civilizations,* Bastide argued that syncretism was too simple an explanation for the Afro-Brazilian cults that emerged among blacks in Brazil. He wrote that creative efforts on the part of Afro-Brazilians to adjust to new economic, social, and political situations, along with collective memory, resulted in the many cults found in Brazil today. In a later work, *African Civilizations in the New World,*[18] Bastide seems to contradict his previous theory when he suggests, on the one hand, that Afro-Brazilian religions are "preserved" rather than living religions in that they fight cultural erosion by refusing to progress in any direction. On the other hand, he finds that Macumba or Umbanda spiritualism is a "live" religion. In a later article, "The Present Status of Afro-American Research in Latin America,"[19] Bastide returns to his original argument by suggesting that future research make clear that black culture is not rigid, but rather a living culture, capable of constant creation, a culture that plays an important role in global society.

Later scholars, however, have found much to criticize in Bastide's work. Maria Cavalcanti questioned Bastide's belief that Umbanda, because of its emphasis on the individual over the collective, does not have the "subtle philosophy" that Bastide attributed to Candomblé. She also rejects Bastide's belief in a unified future for Umbanda. She argues that individualism and competition between terreiros continues and the heterogeneous nature of Umbanda is stronger than ever, as is its popularity. Contrary to Bastide, Cavalcanti argues that Umbanda's characteristics of heterogeneity and fluidity are compatible with the existence of a structured, symbolic system.[20]

Beatriz Góis Dantas has reexamined the idea of African, and especially Nagô (a Brazilian term for Yoruba), "pureness" within Candomblé. She argues that elite intellectuals, such as Raimundo Nina Rodrigues and later Roger Bastide, propagated the belief that Nagô cults are more "pure" than other forms of Candomblé, and that Nagô practitioners sided with these intellectual "authorities," originally to receive protection from the police and the church, and later as a means of validating their religion at the expense of others.[21] Like Dantas, David Hess agrees that Bastide tended to view all Afro-Brazilian religions from the point of view of Yoruba, Bahian Candomblé. Hess also argues against two of Bastide's major assumptions concerning Umbanda and Quimbanda magic— the incoherence of and the discontinuity between these two religions. His examination of some popular "how to" manuals reveals that Umbanda and Quimbanda appear to be "aspects or tendencies of a single system" which "represents a coherent series of transformations which can be plotted out along a series of mutually related codes." Despite the many arguments against some of Bastide's theories, however, Hess writes that "the broader contours of [Bastide's] sociology of Afro-American religion—particularly his linkage of religious ideologies to issues of domination in the broader society—will probably remain untouched as the key elements of his work."[22]

In his *Aguas do rei* Ordep José Serra argues against Dantas's theory that Nagôs and intellectuals conspired against other non-Nagô cults in an effort to elevate their own candomblés. He also rejects her suggestion that anthropologists and other intellectuals influenced the beliefs and practices of Nagô candomblés. Serra finds that while many Candomblé leaders read the works of anthropologists, these works were and remain too superficial to be used as liturgical guides. Further, he argues against the assertion by Dantas and Júlio Bacelar that Candomblé members' concern with their African heritage, orthodoxy, and pureness of ritual practices is a recent phenomenon brought about by the studies by intellectuals.[23]

Most scholarly work on religions other than Bahian Candomblé, Rio de Janeiro Macumba, and São Paulo and Rio de Janeiro Umbanda are more recent and include the religions of Xangô and Jurema in the state of Pernambuco, Tambor de Mina and Nagô in the state of Maranhão, and Pajelança, also known as Catimbó, and Batuque in Brazil's northern and central regions.[24] José Jorge de Carvalho has studied the role of Jurema in the lives of Recife's poorest residents. He describes the irreverent, sexual, and violent behavior found in Jurema public sessions as a subtle and sophisticated means of relating with and extracting power from the spiritual world. This behavior, which is rejected in Xangô, Umbanda Branca, Spiritism, and Catholicism, also allows participants to break with the established model of behavior at the sacred level.[25]

Scholars of Tambor de Mina, an Afro-Brazilian religion of mostly Dahomean origins practiced in the state of Maranhão, include, among others, Maria Amália Pereira Barreto, Mundicarmo Maria Rocha Ferretti, and Sérgio Figueiredo Ferretti. The last of these has written on the differences between Bahian Candomblé and Tambor de Mina, as well as the differences among the various Tambor terreiros. He attributes these differences to influence from various "nations" or ethnic groups of slaves brought to this state, as well as to Amerindian and Umbanda influences. Ferretti also examines why Tambor mythology differs from that of Nagô candomblés, Haiti, and the ancient kingdom of Dahomey. He finds this is due to the long period of isolation from other Africans and African descendants by Maranhão blacks. Ferretti argues that Tambor de Mina is based on a fragmented mythology in which the past and the present are mixed and reinvented in a ritualized and sacred context, and that these fragments serve to maintain the force of Tambor's rites and myths.[26]

René Ribeiro, a student of Roger Bastide, wrote one of the first detailed descriptions of the internal activities of Recife Xangôs. His work, *Cultos afro-brasileiros do Recife: um estudo do ajustamento social*, examines the bilateral nature of the acculturation process between Brazil's Afro-Brazilian and Luso-European cultures. He found that neither culture imposed itself on or replaced the other. Rather the two permeated each other, resulting in a new configuration which, not being fundamentally different, was structurally and functionally distinct from the two original systems. He also concluded that possession trance, by providing intimacy with the supernatural world, liberation from psychological tensions, and approval from other group members, provided psychological support in confronting everyday problems. This analysis of possession trance as a socially approved and healing state was a far cry from Nina Rodrigues's theory of induced somnambulism.[27]

More recently, Rita Laura Segato has examined the roles of parenthood, personality, sexuality, and myths within Xangô. She finds that within Xangô cults of Nagô tradition there exists a systematic attempt to liberate biologically determined categories of parenthood, personality, and sexuality, as well as to remove the institution of marriage as a pivotal position in society. Segato writes that these attitudes and behaviors can be traced back to Xangô members' slave heritage, during which period the above social structures were systematically destroyed. She also finds that Xangô myths exhibit no sign of ethics in the Weberian sense, but rather a political, Machiavellian ethic in which rules are separated from morals, and that these practical rules are a result of the experience of a people deprived of political expression in their lives.[28]

Earlier in this century Ruth Landes was criticized by many of her contemporaries for her observations of homosexuality and the dominant role of women in Candomblé. Recently, others have resumed this line of questioning and confirmed many of Landes's observations. Peter Fry has examined the relationship between male homosexuality and Afro-Brazilian cults in Belém do Pará and has found that some terreiros serve as a social niche for homosexual men where they may interact with one another and others in a congenial setting, and where they may acquire prestige and status as pais-de-santo. He notes that Afro-Brazilian cults are associated with homosexuals of both sexes more in the north and northeast of Brazil than in the industrialized southern cities. He posits that this is due to the less "restrictive" nature of the correct roles of men and women in the south.[29] James Lorand Matory has investigated the similarities of cosmic ideas between Afro-Brazilian religions and those of the Yoruba in Nigeria. He concluded that in popular Brazilian thought and in Yoruba symbolism of cosmic relations, *bichas* (homosexual men) and women are the "normal" depositories of divine power, and in the role of priest/medium heterosexual men would be considered "deviates."[30]

Afro-Brazilian religions have long ceased to be the chosen religion of Afro-Brazilians only. While these religions continue to offer a sense of community and prestige to those marginalized groups who lack these attributes in the public domain (such as women and the poor), they offer much more. Brazilians and foreigners from all backgrounds have added to the growth of these religions. Umbanda in particular continues to spread not only throughout Brazil, but into neighboring countries as well, and, like Santería, it has even arrived in the United States.

Rita Laura Segato has investigated Umbanda's rapid expansion in Argentina. She notes that while Umbanda can be considered a means of "whitening," dissolving, and absorbing black culture in Brazil, it is also an important source of the reinstallation of plurality and black culture in Argentina. For in the latter country, Afro-Brazilian religions have allowed the reintroduction of a symbolic repertory which permits one to ethnically construct, differentiate, and reestablish oneself in a country where ethnic individuality is discouraged and repressed.[31]

Future research in Afro-Brazilian religions will no doubt continue to take on a larger geographical focus and explore new themes, as Brazilian and other societies struggle to adapt to a changing and increasingly converging world. Maria-José, a Rio de Janeiro mãe-de-santo, eloquently expresses the inclusiveness of Afro-Brazilian religion when she says that it

> takes care of its followers from birth to death. It prevents the faithful from ever being alone, and it supports them at all times, against all adversaries. It can operate anywhere, under any circumstances. It excludes no one. All of us can be its children.[32]

NOTES

1. Serge Bramly, *Macumba: The Teachings of Maria-José, Mother of the Gods*, trans. Meg Bogin (New York: St. Martin's Press, 1977), p. 9.

2. Roger Bastide, *The African Religions of Brazil: Toward a Sociology of the Interpenetration of Civilizations*, trans. Helen Sebba (Baltimore: John Hopkins University Press, 1978), p. 19.

3. Raimundo Nina Rodrigues, *Os africanos no Brasil: revisão e prefácio de Homero Pires; notas biobibliográficas de Fernando Sales*, 4th ed. Brasiliana, vol. 9 (São Paulo: Nacional, 1976), pp. 17–18.

4. Bastide, *African Religions*, pp. 20–21.

5. Rodrigues, *Os africanos*, p. 121.

6. Ibid., p. 221.

7. Ibid., pp. 273–275.

8. Waldir Freitas Oliveira and Vivaldo da Costa Lima, eds., *Cartas de Edison Carneiro a Artur Ramos: de 4 de janeiro de 1936 a 6 de dezembro de 1938*, Baianada, 5 (São Paulo: Corrupio, 1987), p. 23.

9. Ibid., p. 24.

10. Ibid., pp. 92–93.

11. Bastide, *African Religions*, p. 21.

12. Edison Carneiro, *Candomblés da Bahia*, 5th ed. (Rio de Janeiro: Civilização Brasileira, 1977), p. 117.

13. Waldir Freitas Oliveira, "Os estudos africanistas na Bahia dos anos 30," in Oliveira and Lima, *Cartas de Edison Carneiro*, p. 32.

14. Sally Cole, "Introduction: Ruth Landes in Brazil," in Ruth Landes, *The City of Women* (Albuquerque: University of New Mexico Press, 1994), p. xxi.

15. Ibid., p. xxiv.

16. Roger Bastide, "The Present Status of Afro-American Research in Latin America," *Daedalus* 103 (1974), 113.

17. Ibid., p. 114.

18. Roger Bastide, *African Civilizations in the New World*, trans. Peter Green, Torchbook Library Edition (New York: Harper and Row, 1971).

19. Bastide, "Present Status of Afro-American Research," p. 116.

20. Maria Laura Viveiros de Castro Cavalcanti, "Origens, para que as quero: questões para uma investigação sobre a umbanda," *Religião e Sociedade* 13 (July 1986), 97, 99–100.

21. Beatriz Góis Dantas, "Repensando a pureza nagô," *Religião e Sociedade* 8 (July 1982), 15–20.

22. David J. Hess, "Umbanda and Quimbanda Magic in Brazil: Rethinking Aspects of Bastide's Work," *Archives de Sciences Sociales des Religions* 79 (July–September 1992), 150–151.

23. Ordep Serra, *Aguas do rei* (Rio de Janeiro: Vozes, 1995).

24. Yvonne Maggie, "Afro-Brazilian Religions," *The Encyclopedia of Religion* (New York: Macmillan, 1987), p. 102.

25. José Jorge de Carvalho, "Violência e caos na experiência religiosa," *Religião e Sociedade* 15 (1989), 8–33, and "Jurema," in *Sinais dos tempos: diversidade religiosa no Brasil,* ed. Leilah Landim, Cadernos do ISER, no. 23 (Rio de Janeiro: ISER, 1990), pp. 131–138.

26. Sérgio Figueiredo Ferretti, "Religiões de origem africana no Maranhão," in *Culturas africanas: documentos da reunião de peritos sobre "As sobrevivências das tradições religiosas africanas nas Caraíbas e na América Latina"* (N.p.: UNESCO, 1985), pp. 156–172, and "Voduns da casa das minas," in *Meu sinal está no teu corpo: escritos sobre a religião dos orixás,* ed. Carlos Eugênio Marcondes de Moura (São Paulo: EDICON/EDUSP, 1989), pp. 178–200.

27. René Ribeiro, *Cultos afro-brasileiros do Recife: um estudo do ajustamento social,* 2d ed. Série Estudos e Pesquisas, 7 (Recife: Instituto Joaquim Nabuco de Pesquisas Sociais, 1978).

28. Rita Laura Segato, "A Folk Theory of Personality Types: Gods and Their Symbolic Representation by Members of the Shango Cult in Recife, Brazil" (Ph.D. diss., The Queen's University of Belfast, 1984); "Iemanjá em familia: mito e valores cívicos no xangô de Recife," *Anuário Antropológico* 87 (1990), 145-190; *Ciudadania, por que no? Estado y sociedade no Brasil à luz dum discurso religioso afro-brasileiro,* Série Antropologia, no. 132 (Brasília, D.F.: Universidade de Brasília, Instituto de Ciências Humanas, Departamento de Antropologia, 1992).

29. Peter Fry, "Male Homosexuality and Spirit Possession in Brazil," in *The Many Faces of Homosexuality: Anthropological Approaches to Homosexual Behavior,* ed. Evelyn Blackwood (New York: Harrington Park Press, 1986), pp. 137–153.

30. James Lorand Matory, "Homens montados: homossexualidade e simbolismo da possessão nas religiões afro-brasileiras," in *Escravidão e invenção da liberdade: estudos sobre o negro no Brasil,* ed. João José Reis (São Paulo: Editora Brasiliense, 1988), pp. 215–231.

31. Rita Laura Segato, *Uma vocação de minoria: a expansão dos cultos afro-brasileiros na Argentina como processo de re-etnicização,* Série Antropologia, no. 99 (Brasília, D.F.: Fundação Universidade de Brasília, 1990).

32. Bramly, *Macumba,* p. 159.

Religious Syncretism and the
Latin American Indian

19. Transculturación y sincretismo religioso en la poesía quechua colonial

Angel Esteban

El fenómeno antropológico que tuvo lugar con el encuentro de las culturas europeas y precolombinas, al menos en el ámbito hispánico, debe calificarse como *transculturación*, superando el de *aculturación*, que simplifica la realidad histórica y resulta, en ocasiones, ambiguo.[1] Fue el cubano Fernando Ortiz quien aclaró las diferencias en 1940, al afirmar que

> el vocablo *transculturación* expresa mejor las diferentes fases del proceso transitivo de una cultura a otra, porque éste no consiste solamente en adquirir una cultura, que es lo que en rigor indica la voz anglo-americana *aculturación*, sino que el proceso implica también necesariamente la pérdida o desarraigo de una cultura precedente, lo que pudiera decirse una parcial desculturación y, además, significa la consiguiente creación de los nuevos fenómenos culturales que pudieran denominarse *neoculturación*.[2]

Si queremos dar una respuesta válida para los interrogantes que se plantean hoy sobre las características de la propia idiosincrasia en la cultura peruana, es necesario observar el proceso desde la perspectiva del concepto de transculturación, el cual, en palabras de Angel Rama, revela

> resistencia a considerar la cultura propia, tradicional, que recibe el impacto externo que habrá de modificarla, como una entidad meramente pasiva o incluso inferior, destinada a las mayores pérdidas, sin ninguna clase de respuesta creadora. Al contrario, el concepto se elabora sobre una doble comprobación: por una parte registra que la cultura presente de la comunidad latinoamericana (que es un producto transculturado y en permanente evolución) está compuesta de valores idiosincrásicos, los que pueden reconocerse actuando desde fechas remotas; por otra parte corrobora la energía creadora que la mueve, haciéndola muy distinta de un simple agregado de normas, comportamientos, creencias y objetos culturales, pues se trata de una fuerza que actúa con desenvoltura tanto sobre su herencia particular, según las situaciones propias de su desarrollo, como de las aportaciones que le vienen de fuera. Es justamente esa capacidad para elaborar con originalidad, aun en difíciles circunstancias históricas, la que demuestra que pertenece a una sociedad viva y creadora, rasgos que pueden manifestarse en cualquier punto del territorio que ocupa aunque preferentemente se los encuentre nítidos en las capas recónditas de las regiones internas.[3]

Desde los primeros momentos de la conquista y la colonización existe en el territorio andino una situación favorable para la configuración paulatina de un sincretismo religioso y cultural, manifestado en las costumbres y canalizado en cierta medida por la riqueza espiritual del mundo del arte, en todas sus modalidades. Los incas habían adoptado la costumbre de tomar, sin excesivos reparos, elementos culturales y religiosos de los pueblos que iban conquistando, incorporándolos a su sistema, siempre que se respetara el ápice de la pirámide donde se instalaba su principal divinidad.[4] Una vez asimilados esos elementos, la memoria colectiva que pasaba de generación en generación olvidaba el origen de la cultura precedente de la época *purunpacha* (es decir, tiempo de las poblaciones desiertas o bárbaras) y hacía suyo el préstamo.[5] Esa versatilidad hizo de la incaica una civilización abierta y flexible, en cierta medida permeable, aunque con algunas costumbres muy arraigadas e indeclinables, como el culto a los muertos, el valor de las *huacas* o diversos aspectos de la religión popular. Por esta razón, y por la semejanza real de algunos principios relativos a creencias y prácticas con la religión de los conquistadores, cronistas como el Inca Garcilaso o Guamán Poma de Ayala llegaron a afirmar que los incas estuvieron mejor preparados que otros pueblos precolombinos para asimilar los cambios que llegaron en el siglo XVI. Ahora bien, no debe olvidarse que tanto Garcilaso como Ayala participan de una situación híbrida. Su visión no es la de los vencidos. Por sus venas corre sangre indígena pero su mentalidad ya no es precolombina, sino *mestiza*, al decir de Martí. El sincretismo etnológico va acompañado del sincretismo ideológico. Su formación inicial ya es cristiana, su mentalidad de base también, y los elementos culturales oscilan entre la visión americana y la europea, la lengua quechua y la española. Y si la lengua es una cosmovisión, todos los objetos que pasen a través de ella quedarán contaminados por un modo concreto de interpretar la realidad. Todo esto se da independientemente de los motivos, ocultos o expresos, que llevaron a los autores a escribir sus crónicas, por otro lado bien conocidos. La crónica es el género literario que mejor expone y demuestra la realidad del mestizaje desde el primer momento, porque, independientemente de los motivaciones, raza, procedencia y carácter del autor, un mundo que ya no es ni español ni indígena se avizora desde el discurso del cronista. Afirma Porras Barrenechea que se trata de un

> crisol en el que, por obra del impulso misionero y humanitario de la metrópoli, se funden esencias de los dos pueblos, bajo el signo cristiano y español. El hombre educado en la cultura occidental concibe y vuelve a pensar en la historia inaprehensible del alma primitiva, conforme a las normas de su propia e insólita experiencia. En sus manos el Imperio Incaico se occidentaliza, inconscientemente, en tanto que el cronista se indianiza, a menudo, y prende en amor por las cosas de la tierra. Fundidas las dos

razas y las dos culturas, con sus ideas y sentimientos disímiles, el cronista, que las acepta y las incorpora a su sentimiento nuevo del Perú, es ya mestizo espiritual y pronto lo será por sangre y nacimiento.[6]

La poesía que vamos a estudiar, y el conjunto de textos en prosa que complementan el mundo ofrecido por los versos, pertenece esencialmente a uno de los corpus más completos de literatura quechua: el que ofrece Edmundo Bendezú en el volumen 78 de la Biblioteca Ayacucho.[7] Es decir, incluimos en este trabajo las traducciones de obras anteriores a la llegada de los españoles, recogidas por autores posteriores y vertidas al español por ellos mismos, y obras escritas en el período colonial, fundamentalmente por indígenas o mestizos, traducidas en un arco temporal que va desde los momentos cercanos a su composición hasta nuestro siglo, como son las de José María Arguedas, Jesús Lara, Edmundo Bendezú, Farfán, Meneses, etc. Los cronistas que han recuperado textos imprescindibles para conocer la cultura quechua son: Juan de Betanzos (su crónica es de 1551), Pedro Sarmiento de Gamboa (1572), Cristóbal de Molina el Cuzqueño (1573), Blas Valera (1578), Guamán Poma de Ayala (1585), el Inca Garcilaso (1593), Francisco de Avila (1598) y Juan de Santacruz Pachacuti (1613). Para entender bien el sentido de su obra, conviene hacer las siguientes observaciones:

1. Con excepción de Sarmiento, que tuvo un intérprete, todos conocen a la perfección el quechua.

2. La mayoría de los escritores traducen teniendo en cuenta la primacía de la civilización europea sobre la indígena. Es decir, su punto de vista está más cerca del colonizador que del colonizado, y en ocasiones se falsea el sentido original del texto, se cristianiza o adapta a una mentalidad sincretizada. Esto ocurre en ocasiones hasta en los textos que hacen referencia a la época precolonial.

3. El grado de fidelidad a la historia depende no sólo de la traducción de los textos en quechua, sino también de la veracidad de los datos aportados por el documento escrito, que a su vez avala los datos que durante cientos de años han ido pasando de generación en generación. Sólo en la época colonial se fijan mediante la escritura de documentos. La distancia, por ejemplo, entre las fuentes de Garcilaso y Sarmiento, es abismal pues, mientras el primero se basó principalmente en la exposición oral de los *ayllus* o familias incas, Sarmiento tomó contacto con grupos que simpatizaban con la política de Toledo, que pretendía, oficialmente, destruir la cultura inca, incluso la religión, haciendo de este propósito una cuestión de estado, secular, organizada, y sin tener en cuenta el contenido respetuoso con el problema indígena de la bula *Sublimis Deus*, que había sido promulgada por el Papa Pablo III antes del mandato de Toledo, y de la que el virrey hizo caso omiso.

4. La literatura quechua es fundamentalmente oral, y en el momento en que empieza a ponerse por escrito, la memoria colectiva reconoce al menos la historia de los últimos cuatrocientos años,[8] que son los que se han podido reconstruir con cierta fidelidad.[9]

5. Es necesario aludir al concepto de *sujeto* para determinar la función del elemento que produce esa literatura, con el fin de aclarar de qué tipo de autor se trata. En el caso que nos ocupa, estamos ante una realidad autorial escindida o complementaria. La función creativa, al tratarse de literatura oral, es anónima y colectiva, pues "el depositario de la memoria oral se identifica con la voz de toda la cultura quechua".[10] El transcriptor, sin embargo, especialista de la escritura, es el que pone el nombre propio a la obra, atribuyéndole en ocasiones la voz de un yo occidental. Ahora bien, la transcripción no mantiene, como podría suponerse, absolutamente distanciados a los dos sujetos, por su función específica, sino que el segundo, en el momento de elegir el tipo de discurso que va a transcribir, ya ha comprometido parte de su dirección ideológica. El transcriptor no es un mercenario, un empleado a sueldo, sino un sujeto que contiene ya elementos de una mentalidad sincretizada.

6. Esta literatura es distinta a la escrita directamente en español en la misma época, es decir, lo que sería la literatura *oficial*, con unos rasgos que apenas la diferencian en lo esencial de la literatura producida en la Península. Literatura generalmente aportada por españoles emigrados, en la que con menor propiedad puede aplicarse el concepto de sincretismo que estamos manejando.

La cristianización del Nuevo Mundo obedeció a un plan acorde con la mentalidad del conquistador. El occidente cristiano, consciente de su papel instrumental en el proyecto salvador universal, iniciado por Jesucristo y los Apóstoles, no dudó en aplicarse para convertir a ese vasto territorio que, probablemente, no tenía noticia de la Buena Nueva. Los métodos variaron según las regiones, personas y momentos de la convivencia entre las dos culturas. Mientras algunos pensaban que la verdad primaba sobre el respeto a la libertad —casi siempre aquellos que poseían el poder político y ejecutivo— la mayor parte de los religiosos eran partidarios de la convivencia pacífica y la transformación paulatina, mediante la explicación, la información y el ejemplo. A principios del siglo XVI, los dominicos del Perú deseaban la utilización extensiva de la persuasión en vez de la represión,[11] la voluntaria adhesión del indígena, y una oposición radical a los métodos integracionales de Toledo. Uno de los soportes teóricos más importantes con el que contaron los defensores del sincretismo y el respeto fue el libro de José de Acosta, *De Natura Novi Orbis libri duo et de promulgatione Evangelii apud barbaros sive De procuranda*

Indorum salute libri Sex, de 1588, alegato continuado dos años más tarde en la *Historia natural y moral de las Indias*, cuyos capítulos V y VI intentarán demostrar que se pueden mantener, adaptándolas, las principales manifestaciones de la herencia cultural indígena, si bien es cierto que los elementos idolátricos esenciales, que no coinciden con la doctrina cristiana, deben ser eliminados con el tiempo. En este sentido, la literatura cobra un valor especial, porque se convierte en un instrumento indirecto, más fácilmente aceptable que el rigor de la doctrina fría, de manual catequético, y es además el vehículo que transporta la vivencia y el sentimiento, que son las verdades sinceras del hombre, frente al carácter hipotético, teórico, de la enunciación de unos principios.

La primera idea que sale al paso en la consideración de este mestizaje es la de la existencia de una divinidad y sus características. Toda religión tiene su punto de apoyo básico en la realidad de uno o varios dioses. De ahí deriva toda la cosmogonía, cosmología, teología, filosofía y moral de los súbditos de esa religión. La divinidad aparece en la mayoría de los poemas rescatados de la literatura oral y, por supuesto, ocupará un espacio importante en la poesía colonial. Los incas abrigaron la concepción de un dios trascendente, por encima del mundo, creador de él. Ya en el *Tahuantisuyo*, durante la época imperial, los pueblos vencidos se incorporaban al imperio con los mismos deberes y derechos, conservando sus dioses, lengua y costumbres, pero con la condición de aprender la lengua oficial del imperio y reconocer un dios supremo. Hay por tanto, una especie de monoteísmo subyacente a esta jerarquía de divinidades. No obstante, también la poesía nos da cuenta de la coexistencia de monoteísmos diferentes —que no de politeísmo, aunque lo hubo— conviviendo en cierta armonía, sobre la base de la cuestión del linaje o el *ayllu* (familia). El poema titulado "Canción" lo pone de manifiesto con estas palabras:

> Tu eres noble del Cuzco,
> yo soy noble de Colla.
> Juntos beberemos
> y comeremos
> y conversaremos
> sin que nadie intervenga.
> Yo soy de los que usan
> asiento de plata,
> tú, de los que lo usan de oro.
> Tú eres de los que adoran
> a Viracocha, preceptor del mundo,
> yo soy de los que adoran al Sol.[12]

Es Pachacútec, el segundo emperador desde la unificación del Imperio, el que reconoce una entidad divina más alta que el Sol, con todos atributos de poder y espiritualidad propios de una divinidad trascendente: Wirakocha, quien, según la tradición inca, ayuda al Imperio en un momento delicado, cuando los Chancas están a punto de conquistar la capital. Su nombre completo tiene cinco vocablos APU KON TITI WIRA KOCHA, que significan: Señor Supremo (Apu) de todo lo creado (Titi), el fuego (Kon), la tierra (Wira) y el agua (Kocha). Además de las crónicas que recogen el relato de la creación, de las que la más completa es la *Suma narración de los Incas*, de Juan de Betanzos, son muerosísimos los poemas dedicados a la divinidad, en los que se destaca sobre todo el poder creador, la omnipotencia, el señorío sobre el universo, su paternidad, el gobierno providente del mundo, etc. Aunque todos estos aspectos son independientes de la religión cristiana y los poemas fueron compuestos antes de la llegada de los españoles, las concomitancias con la religión del conquistador son numerosas. El tipo de lenguaje utilizado en la traducción de los textos, que acerca las coincidencias teológicas, es, en ocasiones, el primer síntoma de ese sincretismo que, en muchas de las crónicas y, abiertamente en la poesía colonial, va a producirse de un modo claro. En el himno más antiguo de la literatura inca, titulado "Wiraqocha" y atribuido a Manco Capac, el primer Inca, se denomina a Wirakocha "señor del origen", "supremo juez", "enorme creador", y se ponen en su boca palabras similares a las del Génesis para describir la creación de la primera pareja: "sea esto hombre,/sea esto mujer".[13] En otros poemas se le llama "Creador de la tierra, de hombres procreador" (6), "Señor Todopoderoso" (7), "Aquél que rige/los mares extendidos/en el alto cielo/y en la tierra" (7), "el modelador" (9), "Hacedor" (10, 11, 13, 14, 15), "Señor del génesis" (12), "soberano Dios" (15), "soberano Padre" (15), "señor de la creación" (17), "origen del universo" (25), etc.

Hay un grupo de denominaciones que se acercan al concepto de Providencia y manifiestan una alta concepción de la divinidad como principio no sólo original sino también conservador, paternal, celoso de su obra. En el poema "Principio de mundo" el *amauta* reza así a su Hacedor, como portavoz de todos los hombres: "guárdalos y vivan sanos y salvos,/sin peligro y en paz" (10). Este himno, registrado por Cristóbal de Molina El Cuzqueño, está incluido en el *Symbolo Catholico Indiano* de 1598 y tomado por Teodoro Meneses para la catequización de los indígenas. En otro himno parecido y también utilizado por la tradición cristiana, el *amauta* había finalizado con una coda que es traducida por Cristóbal de Molina en 1573 de este modo: "y éstos/a quienes deste el ser,/ guárdalos,/y tenlos de tu mano,/para secula sin fin" (11). En estas oraciones recogidas por El Cuzqueño son frecuentes también las consideraciones de tipo moral, útiles para la predicación cristiana, como la del himno cuarto, en el que se pide al "dichosísimo y venturosísimo Hacedor" que los hombres "vivan sanos y salvos/con sus hijos y descendientes,/andando por camino derecho,/sin pensar en malas cosas" (11–12). Por eso, son frecuentes calificativos como "Padre, conductor del mundo" o "gobierno del mundo, dios" (21), "conductor del hombre" (22), etc. En el *haylle* (canto de triunfo) sagrado "Tijsi Viracocha", texto conocidísimo en la tradición quechua, se invoca a la divinidad como génesis del universo y se concluye con una estrofa de aceptación rendida a la voluntad del creador:

> Que tu mano magnánima
> siempre se extienda
> y que tu sempiterna voluntad
> sea la única que florezca. (25)

Si comparamos estos textos con aquellos que se escriben en la época colonial, observamos semejanzas y diferencias: aparece un lenguaje común, unas invocaciones parecidas, como "Tú, el hacedor del Sol, el embellecedor de la Luna",[14] "Tú, que cuentas todo lo contable y existente", "el rededor de la tierra y el mundo celeste sostienes, y ordenas que gire y se vuelva", "Tu poderoso ser sopla los vientos" (141), "nuestro infalible Señor", "viviente Dios" (143), "Señor Todopoderoso" (144), "mi Dios, mi Hacedor, mi Salvador", "Excelsa Hermosura" (145); sin embargo, las diferencias son mayores, aunque más sutiles, más escondidas, incitando, en algunas ocasiones, a la confusión, mezcla o sincretismo de credos, si bien queda claro que cualquier contaminación mutua debe salvaguardar intactos los principios fundamentales de la religión católica. El poema "Escucha", del *Directorio espiritual en la lengua española y quichua, general del Inca, compuesto por el Padre Pablo de Prado*, del siglo XVII, expone las mismas ideas, ya conocidas, sobre la existencia de Dios y su gobierno providente y todopoderoso en relación con el hombre pero, sutilmente, evita las mayúsculas al referirse a Dios o el Padre, porque es el mismo Dios el que habla. Al variar el punto de vista—en los poemas de la época anterior siempre es el hombre quien se dirige a Dios para pedirle cosas, darle gracias, pedirle misericordia o adorarle—, la demostración de la existencia de Dios es más evidente, pues Él sale al encuentro del hombre y se pone a su altura. Además, después de decirle que ha creado al hombre, y que ha creado todas las cosas para su disfrute y aprovechamiento, comience a enumerar algunos de los elementos concretos que le ha dado, típicos de la cultura peruana: la flor amarilla de *chinchircoma*, la roja de *huayarcuma*, y la blanca del *hamancay* (133), realidades que ya habían sido objeto de enumeración en poemas precolombinos como "Canción lacerante" (*Cicllallay:* mi hermosa flor azul; plumaje amarillo de la flor de chinchircoma [16]) o "La canción de la sombra" (la flor amarilla y roja del *chihuanhuay*; el lirio del *amancay* [17]). En otras composiciones, sin embargo, no hay diferencias reseñables ni en los elementos del poema, ni en el estilo de la narración, ni en el punto de vista. Es el caso de la "Plegaria del amanecer", un largo poema en prosa, recogido por el Padre Jorge A. Lira, donde los elementos referidos a la divinidad y su relación con el mundo podrían pertenecer tanto a la tradición incaica anterior a la llegada de los españoles como a la época colonial, exceptuando una leve alusión final a los ángeles, que clarifica el sentido del texto. Hay, por último, un grupo de composiciones abiertamente católicas, como "Despedida de Jesús", "Yo, tu pobre", "Hermosa doncella", "A la Virgen", "Chuchulaya", "Endecha a la Virgen", "El encuentro fina", "Eternamente viviente Dios", "Muerte inminente", "Consumación", etc., en las que, sin ambages, aparecen Jesucristo, la Virgen María, los ángeles, la idea del Cielo después de la muerte, el pecado como ofensa a la divinidad, el juicio final, y fragmentos de la historia de la salvación, casi siempre relacionados con la pasión, muerte y resurrección de Jesucristo.

Tienen especial relevancia, más en la poesía precolombina que en la colonial, el grupo de expresiones utilizadas para separar la creación del hombre y la mujer con el fin de diferenciar los sexos. Aparecen en poemas como "Exorcismo": "aquél que ordena:/Este sea varón,/ésta sea mujer" (7); "Principio del mundo": "diste ser y valor a los hombres,/y con decir sea éste hombre,/y ésta sea mujer,/hiciste, formaste y pintaste/a los hombres y a las mujeres" (10), o "Wiraqocha": "Sea esto hombre,/sea esto mujer" (5). En algún poema dedicado a la reflexión sobre la muerte, como "Consumación", se distingue del siguiente modo: "Ya viejo, ya vieja,/aquí un joven, allá una muchacha;/todos acabamos en frío cadáver" (147). Creación y muerte, origen y destino, son los principales enigmas de cualquier filosofía o teología. Los primeros cronistas, al recuperar la historia del pueblo inca, recogen los primeros mitos sobre la procedencia y el inicio de su civilización. Garcilaso y Guamán Poma de Ayala son los más explícitos, y complementan los escasos datos que nos ofrecen los poemas. Esos "hombre y mujer", primeramente creados y de los que descienden los incas, son Adán y Eva, como expresa Ayala en varios momentos de su crónica. Cuando refiere en 1585 a la leyenda de Manco Capac, conecta el texto bíblico con las relaciones orales aprendidas de la tradición quechua:

> La primera historia del primer rey inca, que fue de los legítimos descendientes de Adaneva y multiplico de Noé, y de la primera gente de Uariuiracocha Runa y de Uari Runa y de Purun Runa y de Auca Runa; de aquí, salió el poderoso Inca Tócay Cápac, Pinau Cápac, primer inca. . . . Hasta que comenzó a reinar la madre y mujer de Manco Cápac Inca. (47–48)

El pasaje más representativo al respecto es el que cuenta por extenso el mito de la creación de los indios, donde la confusión entre la historia mítica inca y el relato del Antiguo Testamento es total, estableciendo relaciones que traspasan el origen adánico y la conocida historia del diluvio, común por otro lado a tradiciones de todo el orbe. Después de las paráfrasis del comienzo del Génesis, la relación se estrecha con el profeta Habacuc:

> Como el profeta Abacuch decían así a grandes voces: "¡Señor: hasta cuándo clamaré y no me oirás y daré voces y no me responderás!"[15] "¡*Cápac*

(Señor) *haycacamam caparisac mana oyariuanquicho! ¡Cayariptipas mana hay niuanquicho!"* Con estas palabras adoraban al criador, con la poca sombra que tenían y no adoraban a los ídolos, demonios *uacas.* Comenzaron a trabajar, arar, como su padre Adán. (148)

Seguidamente, se justifica que, al llegar los españoles, aquellos habitantes del territorio colonizado no recordaran sus orígenes vetero-testamentarios y llamaran al único Dios Viracocha, reconociendo también su ley, a pesar de haber perdido la noción de la existencia de las tablas que Dios entregó a Moisés. Afirma que tuvieron "una sombrilla del conocimiento del criador" (149), que no idolatraban, que llamaron al diluvio *uno yaco pacha cuti*, que "vivían sin pleito y sin pendencia ni tenían mala vida" (149). Son, finalmente, comparados a los profetas Isaías y Salomón. El resto del capítulo lo dedica Ayala a enriquecer la tesis lascasiana de la bondad natural de los indios, aplicándola de modo eminente a los incas. Esto probaría varios supuestos:

1. Que los indios —los incas, en este caso— son hombres con alma, lo mismo que los europeos.
2. Que los incas son una cultura superior a otros grupos indígenas, menos civilizados.
3. Que sólo existe un Dios, que es el mismo para los cristianos y para los incas, aunque durante muchos siglos se haya llamado de modo diferente.
4. Que existe una ley natural, inscrita por Dios en los corazones de todos los hombres, la cual, oscurecida por el pecado, necesita en ocasiones de profetas o enviados para revelarse a un pueblo o colectividad.

Tiene mucho interés la doctrina de estos cronistas —no sólo de Ayala— sobre la función profética o reveladora de ciertos elementos, tanto divinos como humanos. En algún momento Garcilaso utiliza el término escolástico de *causas segundas* (*Comentarios Reales de los Incas*, Libro segundo, capítulo XXVII). Describiendo la poesía de los incas y su historia, comenta:

> Los incas poetas los compusieron (los versos) filosofando las causas segundas que Dios puso en la región del aire para los truenos, relámpagos y rayos, y para el granizar, nevar y llover, todo lo cual dan a entender en los versos, como se verá. Hiciéronlos conforme a una fábula que tuvieron, que es la que sigue. Dicen que el Hacedor puso en el cielo una doncella, hija de un rey, que tiene un cántaro lleno de agua para derramarla cuando la tierra ha menester, y que un hermano de ella le quiebra a sus tiempos, y que del golpe se causan los truenos, relámpagos y rayos. . . . Dicen que el granizar, llover y nevar lo hace la doncella . . . , dicen que un Inca poeta y astrólogo hizo y dijo los versos loando las excelencias y virtudes de la dama, y que Dios se las había dado para que con ellas hiciese bien a las criaturas de la tierra.

El poema a que se refiere lo cita a continuación, y es también recogido en la edición citada de *La literatura quechua* de Bendezú (29) bajo el título "Hermosa doncella". También relata Garcilaso que la fábula y los versos fueron encontrados e interpretados por el Padre Blas Valera, fuente que puede contrastar y corroborar con lo que él mismo había oído en sus *niñeces* de labios de algunos familiares. El concepto de *causa segunda* va a ser de gran utilidad para Garcilaso y Ayala en su defensa de la civilización incaica y de su catolicismo. En la *Suma Teológica* 1–2, q.19, 4c, se habla de ella como una causa real pero dependiente de la primera, que en cualquier caso es Dios. "Causa prima plus influit quam secunda" afirma S. Tomás de Aquino, para concluir: "Operatio causae secudae semper fudatur super operationem causae primae et praesupponit eam". Es decir, que la causa segunda es la ayuda de la que se vale Dios para manifestarse en el mundo. La fábula de la hermosa doncella es un modo de explicar la existencia de fenómenos atmosféricos aludiendo a causas segundas, pero tiene más interés el esfuerzo de Ayala y Garcilaso en aplicar ese concepto al funcionamiento positivo de la civilización inca. Con ello se justifica la cristianización del Perú, ya que esa buena disposición no es otra cosa que un "cristianismo de base escondido" hasta la llegada de los españoles. En el capítulo XV del primer libro de los *Comentarios Reales de los Incas*, Garcilaso asegura que en los primeros tiempos los incas vivían de un modo salvaje, sin tener noticia de la *ley natural*. Pero Dios les envió un "lucero del alba", el Inca, que les dio noticia de ella para que cuando llegaran los españoles los hallasen "no tan salvajes, sino más dóciles para recibir le fe católica, y la enseñanza y doctrina de nuestra santa madre la iglesia romana, como después acá la han recibido". Esta función, sin forzar el sentido del texto, es similar a la que tienen los profetas y, sobre todo, Jesucristo, en la tradición cristiana. Los contenidos, además, se adecúan perfectamente al mensaje trasmitido por unos y otros: Garcilaso habla de leyes que trae el Inca para que sepan es mucho más explícito con la concreción que el cristianismo hace de la ley natural en los diez mandamientos. En su texto sobre el mito de la creación de los indios asegura que en la tercera edad desde que Noé escapó del diluvio, los indios "comenzaron a hacer ropa hilada y tejida *auasca* (en urdimbre) y de *cunbe* y otras policías y galanterías" (150), "tuvieron mandamiento y ley", "no se mataban ni reñían", "adoraron al criador", "no entremetían idolatrías", "no se halló adúltera ni había puta ni puto", "se casaban vírgenes" (151).

Aparte de la justificación religiosa, hay otro propósito que aflora al final de esta enumeración. Las Casas pretendía defender a los indígenas frente a los abusos de los colonos, y por eso su texto *Historia de las Indias*, capítulo CXCVIII, habla de una gobernación *naturalísima* de los indígenas precolombinos, de una *bondad natural*, que no sabía lo que era "hurto, ni adulterio, ni fuerza que hombre hiciese a mujer alguna, ni otra vileza, ni que dijese a otro injuria de palabra u menos de obra". Es decir, la ley natural para Las Casas,

evidenciada en el comportamiento de los indígenas, se correspondía exactamente
con los diez mandamientos. Pues bien, en Ayala esta defensa de la dignidad del
indígena es más contundente, porque lo que Las Casas deja intuido, en el peruano es una declaración formal: el indígena ha sido, en muchas ocasiones, superior al europeo, pues ha cumplido *naturalmente* la ley de Dios mientras el
cristiano, que ha dispuesto de unas *causas segundas* continuadas y cualificadas
durante siglos, parece que ha olvidado su cumplimiento. Éstas son las palabras
de Guamán Poma:

> Mirad cristianos lectores, mirad, esta gente del tercer hombre, que fueron
> amantes con su ley y ordenanzas antiguas, de conocimiento de dios y criador,
> aunque no le fueron enseñados. Tenían los diez mandamientos y buena obra
> de misericordia y limosna y caridad entre ellos . . . , jamás dejan a la ley y
> de hacer sus oraciones al dios del cielo *pachacámac;*[16] . . . y jamás mezclaban
> cosas de idolatrías y mentiras. . . . Mira cristiano lector, aprenden de esta
> bárbara, que aquella sombra de conocer al criador no fue poco; y así, procura
> de mezclar con la ley de dios para su santo servicio. (152)

Son muchos más los elementos que demuestran una rápida transculturación al hilo de las realidades de tipo espiritual manifestadas en los textos poéticos y en las crónicas. El demonio de los cristianos es encontrado por
todos los cronistas en el clásico *Zupay* peruano, cuyas referencias más antiguas
son de 1550.[17] El séptimo himno de Sallqamaywa opone la maldad de ese ser a
la bondad, poder y providencia de Viracocha. Cuando comparamos este poema
antiguo a ejemplos de la poesía colonial, como "Eternamente viviente Dios" o
"El encuentro final", donde también hay alusiones al demonio, encontramos un
sistema de pensamiento similar, que completa el de las crónicas. De un modo
similar, se hablará del infierno (156), de la existencia entre los incas de una especie de "sacramentos de palabra", naturales, desde los más remotos tiempos,
como el bautismo o el matrimonio (154), de ciertas fiestas que se hacen coinci-
dir con las cristianas, como la de Chaupiñamca,[18] que se asimila a la del Corpus Christi (120), del paso de los apóstoles Santo Tomás (sobre todo) y San
Bartolomé por América,[19] etc.

Hasta aquí los datos que aporta la literatura quechua de la época. Sabemos,
sin embargo, que los lazos establecidos en los textos ni son tan pacíficos como
semejan, ni las concomitancias son tan obvias, ni el proceso de transculturación
tan natural. Se sabe, por ejemplo, que en 1559 los dominicos habían destruido
unos tres mil ídolos. Ayala dirá adelante que nunca existieron, y que Albornoz,
en el transcurso de su campaña por la zona sur, había dejado fuera de circulación
al menos ocho mil. En cuanto a hechiceros y otros tipos de brujería, Arriaga esti-
maba que hacia 1620 ocupaban una parte nada despreciable de la población peruana.[20] Los indígenas, a pesar de nacer ya en un ámbito cristiano, mantenían por
tradición ciertas prácticas de culto a las *huacas* naturales: montañas, ríos,

manantiales, etc. Los jesuitas, poco después de llegar al Perú, hacia 1570, se sombran de los aspectos idolátricos del sincretismo. El Padre Bartolomé Hernández, por ejemplo, escribe una carta el 19 de abril de 1572 al Consejo de Indias, en la que exclama: "Están como los moros de Granada y . . . sólo tienen el nombre de cristiano y las ceremonias exteriores".[21] Si bien algunos de estos testimonios son exagerados pues, como dice Duviols, los que los redactaban "podrían tener interés en magnificar el peligro" de contaminación, lo cierto es que por esas fechas "subsisten (continúa el historiador francés) creencias y manifestaciones religiosas indígenas coexistentes con las prácticas católicas y esto nos induce más al análisis de las modalidades de coexistencia de los dos rituales, que a una conclusión terminante, ya que no cabe duda de que las religiones autóctonas fueron profunda y diversamente modificadas".[22] En este sentido, algunos comentaristas de la época ven una actitud positiva en los datos que aporta el sincretismo, porque virrey Toledo, uno de los extirpadores más combativos, comprende la situación del indígena en una carta dirigida al rey, del 20 de marzo de 1573, cuando escribe que nada más hacerse cristianos vuelven a sus *huacas*, "aunque no por eso piensan que dexan nuestra fe y religión cristiana".[23] Y Baltasar Ramírez da esta explicación, atendiendo al mismo fenómeno: "No son tan idólatras como solían ser ni son christianos como deseamos y así coxeando con entrambos pies acuden a lo uno y a lo otro".[24] La historia del sincretismo y la transculturación, que comenzó inevitablemente cuando los españoles decidieron quedarse en la tierra y hacer allí una morada estable, no ha terminado después de cinco siglos, como lo demuestran los fenómenos culturales de mestizaje que continúan hoy dejando su huella, para enriquecer una de las culturas más atractivas que ha dado nuestro ya casi extinto milenio.

NOTAS

1. Gonzalo Aguirre Beltrán, en su obra *El proceso de aculturación* (México: UNAM, 1957), distingue entre ad-culturación (unión o contacto de culturas) y ab-culturación (separación de culturas, rechazo). Pierre Duviols lo utiliza constantemente para referirse al tema que nos ocupa: la incidencia de la cultura hispánica en el territorio incaico. Su punto de vista es siempre el mismo: la política religiosa y cultural española, encaminada a la extirpación de las religiones andinas, influyó decisivamente en su proceso de *aculturación*. (En *La destrucción de las religiones andinas* [México: UNAM, 1977]).

2. Fernando Ortiz, *Contrapunto cubano del tabaco y del azúcar* (Caracas: Biblioteca Ayacucho, 1978), p. 86.

3. Angel Rama, *Transculturación narrativa en América Latina* (México: Siglo XXI, 1982), pp. 33–34.

4. Luis E. Valcarcel, *Etnohistoria del Perú Antiguo* (Lima: Universidad de San Marcos, 1959), pp. 138–139.

5. Raúl Porras Barrenechea, *Mito, tradición e historia del Perú* (Lima: Ediciones Retablo de Papel, 1973), p. 34.

6. Ibid., p. 54.

7. Edmundo Bendezú Aybar, *Literatura quechua* (Caracas: Biblioteca Ayacucho, 1980).

8. Porras Barrenechea, *Mito,* p. 35, y Bendezú, *Literatura quechua,* p. xx de la introducción.

9. No es éste el momento de entrar en la discusión acerca del sentido del término *literatura* como discurso escrito, texto concreto, y mucho menos sobre el hipotético carácter literario de los *quipus,* generalmente utilizados para registrar datos sencillos, materia básica para que el *quipucamayoc* confeccionara el cantar oportuno. Garcilaso llegó a decir, incluso, que el "ñudo dice el número, mas no la palabra" (Abraham Arias-Larretta, *Literaturas aborígenes de América,* 9ª ed. [Buenos Aires: Editorial Indoamericana, 1968], pp. 99 y ss); aunque Arturo Capdevila, *Los Incas* (Buenos Aires: Labor, 1937), asegura que "No era tan solo el quipus un auxiliar nemotécnico: contenía una escritura completa. ¿Y quién dudaría de que estos nudos, nuditos e hilillos atados, sean tan capaces como nuestros signos ortográficos de una perfecta equivalencia fonética?" Cfr. también Bendezú, *Literatura quechua,* pp. xv y ss. de la introducción, y Porras Barrenechea, *Mito,* pp. 22 y ss. Estas son las palabras de Bendezú: "el problema central reside en saber si el concepto de literatura requiere, para su formulación, del concepto de letra. Etimológicamente no hay duda que es así; y, desde el punto de vista de las literaturas escritas que conocemos en el mundo también es así. Pero esta formulación adolece de un etnocentrismo que excluye a grandes segmentos de la población mundial y también a los períodos más largos de la historia del hombre sobre la tierra. Esta exclusión es un grave despovo que se hace a la humanidad, aun reconociendo que el refinamiento tecnológico de la escritura significó un rápido avance de la ciencia y de la filosofía en el mundo occidental, porque creó una cultura basada en el libro, al que las mayorías nunca tuvieron acceso; cultura que arrogantemente desdeña la experiencia de la raza humana acumulada sin escritura fonética durante milenios. . . . El etnocentrismo occidental funciona también para el tradicional concepto de historia, según el cual la verdadera historia comienza con la escritura y el resto es pre-historia. Cuando se aplica este concepto a las culturas prehispánicas del Perú, resulta el absurdo de que la historia, en esta parte del mundo, comienza con los cronistas españoles. . . . Así, el período más importante, es decir de algunos miles de años, del desarrollo del hombre en este continente quedaría excluido del campo de la historia". Seguidamente propone Bendezú una solución basada en la obra de Charles F. Hockett, *Curso de lingüística moderna* (Buenos Aires: Editorial Universitaria, 1971), donde se da una definición de literatura que no excluye ninguna sociedad humana, consistente en ciertos discursos, breves o largos, que los miembros de la sociedad concuerdan en valorar positivamente y en cuya repetición periódica, en forma esencialmente idéntica, todos ellos insisten.

10. Julio E. Noriega, "La poesía quechua escrita: una forma de resistencia cultural indígena", *Cuadernos Hispanoamericanos* 523 (1992), 82.

11. Duviols, *La destrucción,* p. 424.

12. Traducido por Jesús Lara en 1968 y perteneciente al texto original de Sallqamaywa. Bendezú, *Literatura quechua,* p. 31.

13. Ibid., p. 5. A partir de ahora, las citas relativas a los poemas y las crónicas se realizarán sobre la base de esta edición, con el número de página dentro del texto, entre paréntesis.

14. Recordemos que Viracocha fue, durante mucho tiempo, una divinidad no superior al Sol y la Luna, ya que en el altar mayor del templo del Cuzco (Inti Huasi) estaban colocadas por encima, en el lugar más alto, las imágenes de esos dos astros fundamentales, y más abajo los demás astros, en una suerte de mapa celeste en el que se reflejaba la estructura religiosa de los Incas. Sólo después del triunfo sobre los Chancas Viracocha comenzó a ocupar un lugar más alto. Por ello, expresiones como ésta tienen un significado más profundo que la simple exaltación de la divinidad y, en el caso de los cristianos que escriben en quechua conociendo la historia anterior, su aparición expresa está claramente intencionada.

15. Es, precisamente, el comienzo del Libro de Habacuc, el segundo versículo del primer capítulo, que consiste en la transcripción de un oráculo, pasaje conocido en la tradición judeo-cristiana.

16.   Véase que aquí aparece el nombre de *pachacámac* y no el de Viracocha para nombrar a la divinidad. El Inca Garcilaso da cuenta de ello en el libro II, capítulo 2º de sus *Comentarios Reales de los Incas*, señalando que la élite del Cuzco había llegado a un conocimiento natural de Dios adorándolo bajo ese nombre: "Decían que era el que daba vida al universo y la sustentaba, pero que no le conocían porque no le habían visto, y que por esto no le hacían templos ni le hacían sacrificios, mas que lo adoraban en su corazón (esto es, mentalmente) y le tenían por Dios no conocido". El poema precolombino titulado "Pachacámac" llama a esa divinidad "Padre: señor de la creación", y le pide: "Vierte tus aguas/para tus pobres,/para tus hombres" (17-18). Más información sobre el papel creador de esta divinidad en la cultura incaica en Peter Eeckhout, "El creador y el adivino. A propósito de Pachacamac, Dios precolombino de la costa central de Perú, côte centrale du Perou", *Revista Española de Antropología Americana* 23 (1993), 135-152.

17.   Duviols, *La destrucción*, pp. 38 y ss.

18.   Diosa relacionada con la creación de los hombres, cuya historia se cuenta por extenso en el texto de Francisco de Avila, de finales del siglo XVI.

19.   Fernández de Oviedo, en su *Historia General y Natural de las Indias*, I, VII, t. I, p. 30, de 1535, ya escribe: "Digo que en aquestras nuestras Indias, justo es que se tenga e afirme que fue predicada en ellas la verdad evangélica". Aunque el texto no es del todo elocuente, esta información se ha de contrastar con la de Las Casas, quien refiere a una tradición según la cual los primeros españoles que pisaron Yucatán habrían encontrado cruces cristianas al llegar allí, y que los indios de su diócesis de Chiapas hacía mucho tiempo que adoraban a las tres personas de Santísima Trinidad bajo los nombres de Icona, Bacab y Echuac, siendo Chibirias el nombre de la mujer que trajo al mundo a Bacab. La primera noticia de la presencia de Santo Tomás la da también Las Casas, asegurando que había huellas de su paso por Brasil. A mitad del XVI ya se relaciona, por asimilación fonética, la divinidad guaraní Pay Zumé con el apóstol incrédulo. La primera alusión de la evangelización del Perú por Tomás es de 1548, y en los años 50 adquiere un vigor más pronunciado, gracias a los escritos sobre la evangelización de Cieza, Betanzos, Cristóbal de Molina y, en los 70, de Sarmiento de Gamboa. Duviols, *La destrucción*, pp. 56 y ss. Para la *Nueva Corónica . . .* de Guamán Poma, sin embargo, fue San Bartolomé el primer apóstol que evangelizó el Perú, que dejó la cruz de Carabuco para conmemorar las victorias que cosechó contra el demonio con el fin de liberar al hechicero Anti, y convertirlo posteriormente. Con respecto a la figura del apóstol Santiago, también introducido en una época temprana y difundido copiosamente por todo el territorio hispanoamericano, consultar José Ramón Mariño Ferro, "Santiago en el altiplano de Bolivia", *Cuadernos de Estudios Gallegos* 33:98 (1982), 559-567.

20.   Pablo Arriaga, *La extirpación de la idolatría en el Perú*, 1621 (Lima: CLDRHP, 1920), t. I, p. 73. Consultar también, para el tema específico de la brujería, Iris Gareis, "Brujos y brujas en el antiguo Perú: apariencia y realidad en las fuentes históricas", *Revista de India* 53:198 (1993), 583-613.

21.   Duviols, *La destrucción,* p. 432.

22.   Ibid., p. 433.

23.   Ibid., p. 436. Consultar también Luis Millones, *Mesianismo e idolatría en los Andes Centrales* (Buenos Aires: Fundación Simón Rodríguez, 1989).

24.   Herman Trimborn, *Quellen Zur Kulturgeschichte des präkolumbischen Amerika* (Stuttgart, 1936), p. 24. Algunos ejemplos concretos sobre el sincretismo aplicado a la religión popular pueden consultarse en la obra de Jesús Contreras Hernández, "Sibsistencia y ritual en Chinchero (Perú)", *Boletín Americanista* 25:33 (1983), 195-222.

20. Manifestaciones de fondo y forma en la religión prehispánica y la católica

Elsa Barberena B.

El choque de las culturas indígenas con las europeas produjo los diferentes grados de nuestro mestizaje o de nuestra identidad plural. No es posible encasillar a los países bajo el rubro de Latinoamérica o Iberoamérica porque formamos una sociedad plural. A la pluralidad cultural de los indígenas se sumó la pluralidad también cultural de una España recién liberada del yugo árabe, que se hallaba pasando del feudalismo al Renacimiento.

Octavio Paz y Edmundo O'Gorman sostienen que nuestro pasado contiene tres entidades históricas estrechamente vinculadas. Primero la conocida con el nombre del Imperio Mexica; segundo el virreinato de la Nueva España; y tercero la nación mexicana. Sin embargo es una continuidad rota, son más bien superposiciones. En lugar de concebir la historia de México como un proceso lineal, deberíamos verla como una yuxtaposición de sociedades distintas. Las superposiciones son sobre el mundo precolombino vencido, no muerto. Se construyó una sociedad distinta, Nueva España, que alcanzó su apogeo en el siglo XVIII y que, a su vez, fue derrotada en las guerras civiles de la primera mitad del siglo XIX. Jean Meyer (1989) nos dice que recordemos que "América es plural en la unidad de vocación que se le atribuye, que es cambiante en la permanencia que se le supone, que es, en fin, al mismo tiempo mosaico y continente".

Muchos de los elementos constitutivos del mundo prehispánico reaparecen en Nueva España; esos mismos elementos y otros propios de Nueva España son parte del México moderno. Lo que ocurre en el siglo XVII colonial, salvadas las distancias morales y de tiempo, nos dice Sergio Fernández, es análogo al XX mexicano. No aprendemos o traicionamos nuestro pasado histórico. De la Nueva España, que nos separan siglos, no parecen alejarnos segundos: el hambre, la marginación de los indios, las nuevas relaciones entre iglesia y estado, la corrupción, el analfabetismo, la ignorancia política.

Por otra parte elementos del mundo prehispánico y de Nueva España constituyen el México moderno, entre ellos la religión y la cultura. Este documento trata el elemento de la religión en sus manifestaciones de fondo y forma en la religión prehispánica y la católica. Entre éstas están los dioses, el paraíso, el infierno, el fuego, el calendario, los ángeles y la tierra prometida.

La colonización de los ingleses fue una empresa privada. Fundaron sus comunidades para escapar de una ortodoxia de la religión; su objetivo era la libertad religiosa. La conquista de los españoles fue una empresa imperial: la cruz, la espada y la corona; la establecieron para la conversión de los nativos y su objetivo era extender la religión.

Todo cambió en el mundo indígena con la llegada de los españoles. Al terminar la conquista de Tenochtitlan, los aztecas vieron transformar su mundo de manera radical: sus creencias religiosas, sus valores morales y su manera de vivir fueron puestos en duda por los europeos. No obstante los sistemas de valores de las religiones prehispánica y católica eran religiosos, tanto en el centro ceremonial como en el templo, la pintura y la escultura estaban al servicio de la arquitectura religiosa.

Los recién llegados sacerdotes, primero los misioneros y luego los seglares, en su afán de catequizar adaptaron sus construcciones a las costumbres precolombinas: amplios atrios y capillas abiertas o de indios. La evangelización era masiva y tenía que ser a cielo abierto, como en los centros ceremoniales aztecas. Este afán les impuso cierta tolerancia en cuanto a la inclusión de símbolos o glifos precolombinos en los relieves ornamentales labrados por los indios. Ejemplo: la Capilla Real de Cholula, Puebla.

El culto católico le da preferencia a los espacios internos y el precolombino a los externos o públicos. Las imágenes de dioses, emperadores y héroes eran antropomórficamente similares al hombre común en el mundo precolombino, mientras que en la colonia los santos tenían la misma fisonomía de los españoles, pero distinta a la de los indios.

En las culturas precolombinas estaba reglamentado el uso de los ornamentos y de las joyas. En la Contrarreforma era necesario usarlos para deslumbrar a los feligreses y persuadirlos de la vitalidad del catolicismo. Con los incas el empleo del oro era símbolo del sol, su máxima deidad; en la Nueva España lo era de nobleza y divinidad.

La simbología de los colores existía en la Europa medieval y en el mundo precolombino. La parafernalia de símbolos que rodeaba y tipificaba a cada deidad en los murales y códices mesoamericanos se encontraba también en la colonia, con los ángeles, la Virgen y la imagen de Dios Padre.

A la colonia le tomó un tiempo largo pasar de la coexistencia de dos estéticas, la feudal ibérica y la precolombina, al mestizaje ibérico. A fines del siglo XVII comenzó el inicio y acentuación del mestizaje estético que continúa hasta nuestra época. En sus inicios, la colonia no pudo tener ningún proyecto estético propio: los frailes tomaron las formas renacentistas las precolombinas con un espíritu feudal, mientras los indígenas utilizaron las feudales con espíritu precolombino o insertaron en las manifestaciones católicas sus efigies paganas.

La arquitectura precolombina tenía poco que ofrecer en cuanto a los espacios internos, aunque sí muchísimo en los públicos. La imponencia espacial era signo de la omnipotencia divina. La evangelización masiva generó las capillas abiertas o de indios, como la arquitectura típica de la colonia en cuanto a sus espacios. Pero no llegó a la majestad ni a la belleza de los centros ceremoniales prehispánicos.

Un motivo que se repite constantemente en la historia religiosa de los grupos indígenas es la erección de un santuario en honor de su patrono o divinidad protectora, como primer acto de la colonización de un nuevo territorio. Ejemplo: el santuario al dios Huitzilopochtli que se convirtió en el Gran Templo de los aztecas. En Tenochtitlan había más de ochenta templos sin contar los estantes para cráneos, las escuelas de sacerdotes y otras instalaciones relativas al culto. El Códice Florentino contiene una valiosa enumeración de estos edificios.

La arquitectura barroca muestra rasgos locales. La profusión agorofóbica del barroco tuvo antecedentes en los relieves ornamentales y en los murales con imágenes humanas del mundo precolombino. El feligrés transitaba los espacios generosos en altura y tenía la impresión que éstos lo rodeaban. La imponencia espacial era signo de omnipotencia divina. De este modo el indígena revivía la expansión espacial de los centros ceremoniales de sus antepasados. Se repite la situación de erigir templos en honor de los patronos.

El proyecto feudal y el precolombino se caracterizaban por acentuar el plano pragmático de las imágenes o sea, sus efectos en el receptor. En esto es oportuno pensar en las palabras de Santo Tomás: "Lo importante no es que el artista no opere bien, sino cree una obra que opere bien". Lo que importa es la utilidad de las obras de arte y su participación en las necesidades del hombre.

La imagen era información y no espectáculo, así como la religiosa era rito y no espectáculo. Lo ingenuo no es un elemento que se da por ignorancia sino porque se opera desde otras culturas: la precolombina y colonial.

La pintura sigue en la colonia la tradición precolombina de la figura comunicativa provista de una predominante línea activa tanto en los códices anteriores a la colonia, como en los confeccionados durante el siglo de la conquista. Las proporciones y la falta de perspectiva central van a ser las características del dibujo popular a través de los siglos. La predominante línea activa se encuentra en los murales de lxmiquilpan, Metztitlan, Culhuacan y Actopan, algunos con elementos aztecas.

Pintar como los españoles era la máxima aspiración de los pintores nativos. En las iglesias coloniales las pinturas parecen zozobrar en medio de un océano de ornamentos. No fue evidente la inserción de elementos autóctonos en las pinturas como lo fue en los relieves líticos de las iglesias. La elevada demanda de cuadros religiosos en el siglo XVII impuso la industrialización de la

pintura y con ella se fueron introduciendo elementos de factura y trazos inge-
nuos, más otros de la visión y estética precolombinas.

Si las pinturas trataban de conservar puro su europeísmo, las cruces y los
relieves mostraban rasgos precolombinos. La piedra era labrada por indígenas
y éstos revelaban sus orígenes en las figuras ornamentales en un estilo llamado
tequitqui.

El profesor español, José Moreno Villa, propuso el calificativo de *tequitqui*
para designar el estilo de la ornamentación escultórica de la arquitectura del siglo
XVI en México, nacida al ponerse en contacto el español con el indígena, cada
uno con sus tradiciones y su manera de sentir. La participación del artista americano, nos dice Marta Fernández (1988), no fue sólo como mano de obra, sino
como artista creador o recreador. Constantino Reyes Valerio encontró 121 motivos prehispánicos en 166 edificios del siglo XVI en pintura y escultura.

Xavier Moyssén (1967) nos dice que la representación de la Crucifixión
fue permitida cuando la evangelización del país quedó cimentada con cierta fir-
meza, o lo que es lo mismo una vez que triunfó sobre los viejos cultos idolátricos
la religión cristiana. Las primeras representaciones de la cruz fueron puramente simbólicas, sin la presencia del cuerpo de Jesucristo.

El realismo de los cristos mexicanos es un legado de la escultura española, y en él los indios se sintieron plenamente identificados. El historiador Raúl
Flores Guerrero los relaciona con el culto prehispánico dada a Xipe-Totec, el
desollado. Diversas interpretaciones se han elaborado por la reiteración constante de la presencia dramática de la sangre y su coincidencia con las viejas prácticas religiosas de los indígenas. No obstante Moyssén las califica de
superficiales, a la vez que afirma que quizá quienes sostienen tales puntos de
vista les asista la razón y se reserva el derecho de opinar sobre un problema que
es demasiado complejo.

Entre las fuentes para el estudio de la religión mesoamericana están:
· el arte y la arquitectura
· los manuscritos precolombinos que contienen las tradiciones rituales,
  proféticas, históricas y genealógicas de diferentes ciudades-estados
· los códices del tiempo posterior a la conquista
· las fuentes textuales basadas en tradiciones indígenas figurativas y orales
· las historias escritas por miembros de la aristocracia azteca
· los relatos de españoles que fueron testigos oculares de ciertos sucesos,
  por ejemplo, las cartas de Cortés al rey de España
· la historia detallada y descripciones de ritos escritos por clérigos como
  Diego Durán, Motolinía y Bernardino de Sahagún, que investigaron a
  fondo la religión azteca

Los dioses

Alfonso Caso (1986) menciona que el temor y la esperanza son los padres de los dioses. El hombre colocado ante la naturaleza que le asombra y anonada al sentir su propia pequeñez, ante fuerzas que no entiende ni puede dominar pero cuyos efectos dañosos o propicios sufre, proyecta su asombro, su temor y su esperanza fuera de su alma y, como no puede entender ni mandar, teme y ama, es decir adora. Por eso los dioses prehispánicos han sido hechos a imagen y semejanza del hombre, mientras que en la religión católica el hombre ha sido creado a imagen y semejanza de Dios.

En la religión prehispánica la Pareja Divina Suprema expulsó del cielo a sus hijos por un pecado que cometieron; los dioses desterrados vivieron intensas aventuras en su nueva morada, adoptando con frecuencia las formas de hombres o animales. La Pareja Divina Suprema lanza del cielo a sus arrogantes hijos por su pretensión de ser adorados y quedan en el mundo para dar origen y estar al cuidado de un grupo humano.

Los dioses poblaban los más altos niveles celestes (13) o el mundo inferior (9); eran además creadores de la gran maquinaria del cosmos por la cual fluían sus fuerzas, y los regentes de las distintas partes que componían la maquinaria; tienen el don de ubicuidad. Ejemplo: Xololtl podía encontrarse sobre el horizonte como ser venusino, o como esencia de los ajolotes o en el interior de cada una de sus imágenes de piedra o de barro.

Los dioses tenían la facultad de mostrarse como unidades de la dualidad masculino-femenino y la unión de todos los dioses en una sola persona, el Dios Unitario, suma de todos los poderes cósmicos: llamado Pijetao entre los zapotecos, Hunab Ku entre los mayas o Tloque Nahuaque entre los nahuas.

Ometeotl y Omecihuatl, los dueños de la vida, crean por un lado los dioses activos, llenos de ardor, astrales, creadores, fundadores, guerreros, en movimiento; por otro lado las diosas más bien pasivas, ligadas al hogar y a la tierra, telúricas, nocturnas, dueñas de la sexualidad y de la fecundidad-fertilidad.

Hoy en día estas oposiciones siguen vigentes en Tecospa polarizadas entre Dios y Guadalupe. En el cerro del Tepeyac existían dos deidades femeninas esculpidas sobre la pared rocosa que Alfonso Caso identificó como Chalchiuhtlicue y Tonatzin o Chimecoatl.

Fray Bernardino de Sahagún menciona que en el Tepeyac se adoraba a Tonatzin, la Madre de los dioses. Fray Juan de Torquemada cita en cuatro párrafos a Tepeyacac, lugar donde se adoraba a Tonan que quiere decir nuestra madre. Jacinto de la Serna menciona que su fiesta principal era del 19 de diciembre al 7 de enero.

El Códice de Teotenatzin, documento dibujado en la primera mitad del siglo XVII sobre papel europeo, representa a la diosa Teotenantzin o Tenatzin (la venerable madre de alguien) o Teonantzin (la venerable madre de dios). De acuerdo a este códice las esculturas de las deidades femeninas, ahora desaparecidas, todavía se encontraban en 1743 en el cerro del Tepeyac. En este lugar se venera hasta el día de hoy a la Virgen de Guadalupe que es la madre de Dios.

Para los católicos Dios es el que es de modo absoluto y que por tanto existe en todo lugar y todo tiempo. Puede aparecer en una hora determinada de una vida humana como fue mediante la encarnación del Hijo de Dios. En el Evangelio de San Juan (14:25–26) se dice que el Hijo de Dios, el Señor Jesús, antes de morir les dijo a sus discípulos: "Yo les he hablar mientras estaba con ustedes. En adelante, el Espíritu Santo, Intérprete que el Padre les enviará en mi nombre, les va a enseñar todas las cosas y les recordará todas mis palabras".

La misión del Espíritu Santo está siempre unida y ordenada a la del Hijo. El Espíritu Santo fue enviado para santificar el seno de la Virgen María y fecundarla por obra divina, él que es el Señor que da la vida, haciendo que ella conciba al Hijo eterno del Padre en una humanidad tomada de la suya.

Según el Códice Florentino, Coatlicue, la dama en hábito de serpiente y madre de Huitzilopochtli, quedó encinta al caer sobre el suelo del templo de Coatepec un plumón, que ella se apresuró a recoger y poner en su seno.

El paraíso

Para los aztecas lo que determina el lugar al que va el alma después de la muerte no es la conducta en esta vida, sino principalmente el género de muerte y la ocupación que en vida tuvo el difunto.

Al paraíso oriental o "casa del Sol" van los guerreros que murieron en el combate o en la piedra de los sacrificios; acompañan al Sol en jardines llenos de flores, en los que repiten el simulacro de sus luchas. Cuando bajan a la tierra después de cuatro años, se transforman en colibríes y otras aves de plumajes abigarrados y se alimentan con el néctar de las flores.

Al paraíso occidental van las mujeres muertas en parto. Cuando bajan a la tierra lo hacen de noche y son entonces fantasmas espantables y del mal agüero principalmente para las mujeres y los niños. Llevan por cabeza una calavera y con manos y pies provistos de garras. Son las "mujeres diosas" y antes de transformarse en diosas tienen un gran poder mágico.

Los que mueren ahogados o por rayo o por lepra, o de alguna otra enfermedad que se consideraba relacionada con los dioses del agua, van al Tlalocan, el paraíso de Tlaloc, que queda al sur, el lugar de la fertilidad, donde crece toda clase de árboles frutales y abunda el maíz y la chía.

Tepantitla —en nahuatl, lugar de paredones— es probablemente uno de los sitios teotihuacanos más famosos ya que es aquí donde se encuentra uno de los murales mejor conocidos del arte teotihuacano, el llamado Tlalocan o Paraíso de Tlaloc, por Alfonso Caso en 1942. Este autor se basa en fuentes documentales del posclásico y de la época colonial que narran el sitio al que iban las almas de los seres humanos cuando morían de cierto tipo de enfermedades.

El paraíso se representa con una composición poblada de pequeños seres humanos, aparentemente todos del sexo masculino, en un despliegue febril de actividades; algunos, posiblemente, están relacionados con la práctica de curaciones; otros aparecen en un juego de pelota, algunos más nadando, cazando mariposas o cantando como parece sugerir la vírgula florida que sale de la boca. Encontramos una marcada proliferación de plantas, insectos, animalitos, ojos, torrentes de agua y hasta, posiblemente, representaciones de prácticas agrícolas.

Vemos, de igual modo, plantas como maíz y cacao. La deidad central de la composición, dividida en franjas horizontales, es Tlaloc de cuyas manos salen unas gotas de agua. En la parte media de la composición las escenas recuerdan las descripciones de los placeres que disfrutan quienes llegan al paraíso.

Esto se puede relacionar con la escritura del Génesis que nos presenta el paraíso en la imagen de un jardín o parque en el que hay aguas frescas que fluyen inagotablemente, árboles que dan sombra, animales de muchas especies. Todo eso es imagen y significa el mundo.

En el Génesis (2:8–9, 15) se dice, "El Señor Dios plantó un jardín en el Edén hacia Oriente y puso allí al hombre al que había formado. Y el Señor Dios hizo crecer del suelo toda clase de árboles, de hermoso aspecto y buenos para comer; y el árbol de la vida en medio del jardín, y el árbol del conocimiento, del bien y del mal . . .".

Este paraíso es algo totalmente diverso de lo que se dice desde el punto de vista naturalista, o romántico, o despreciador, o concupiscente. Este paraíso era el mundo que Dios había querido realmente; el segundo mundo que había de surgir constantemente del encuentro del hombre con el primer mundo creado también por Dios. Y en él debía tener lugar y ser producido todo cuanto se llama vida humana: conocimiento y comunidad, realización y arte; pero en gracia, verdad, pureza y obediencia.

Esta situación no estaba asegurada sino puesta aprueba. Aquí no hay ninguna seguridad, pues ésta inmediatamente destruiría la libertad. La obra de Dios la había puesto en manos del hombre, confiado en él para que la conservase con gloria y realizase en ella un trabajo que perseguiría la obra de Dios. Pero el hombre traicionó esa confianza, con el intento de quitarle a Dios su mundo de las manos.

El infierno

En el mundo prehispánico, los que no han sido elegidos por el Sol o por Tlaloc van simplemente al Mictlán, que queda al norte, y ahí las almas padecen una serie de pruebas mágicas al pasar por los infiernos. Son nueve los lugares en donde las almas sufren antes de alcanzar, a los cuatro años, el descanso definitivo.

En primer lugar para llegar al Mictlán tienen que pasar por un caudaloso río, con la ayuda de un perro de color leonado; en segundo lugar el alma tiene que pasar entre dos montañas que se juntan; en tercer lugar por una montaña de obsidiana; en cuarto lugar por donde sopla un viento helado, que corta como si llevara navajas de obsidiana; después por donde flotan las banderas; el sexto lugar es un lugar en que se flecha; en el séptimo infierno están las fieras que comen los corazones; en el octavo se pasa por estrechos lugares entre piedras; y en el noveno y último descansan o desaparecen las almas.

Los amuletos mágicos con que se solía enterrar a los muertos, entre los aztecas, tenían por objeto ayudar a éstos en su última etapa, el Mictlán o noveno estrato de los infiernos, a lograr la paz eterna que ansiaban.

Para el camino se les daba un jarrillo con agua; los papeles les servían para atravesar por las sierras que se juntan; quemaban los atavíos que habían usado los difuntos durante su vida, para que no tuvieran frío al cruzar por donde el viento sopla; les ponían una cuenta de jade en la boca para que les sirviera de corazón y quizás para dejarla en prenda en el séptimo infierno, donde las fieras devoraban los corazones de los hombres. Por último les daban ciertos objetos valiosos para que los entregaran a Mictlantechuhtli, el señor de los infiernos.

La enseñanza de la Iglesia Católica afirma la existencia del infierno y su eternidad. Las almas de los que mueren en estado de pecado mortal descienden a los infiernos inmediatamente después de la muerte y allí sufren las penas del infierno, "el fuego eterno". La pena principal del infierno consiste en la separación eterna de Dios en quien únicamente puede tener el hombre la vida y la felicidad para las que ha sido creado y a las que aspira.

Los católicos usan medallas y reliquias de los santos como apoyo y protección durante la vida, y muchas veces también las acompañan a su muerte.

El fuego

Según la leyenda precolombina, fue una pareja, un hombre y una mujer, que inventaron el fuego y cuando lo hubieron hecho, se dedicaron a asar pescados para comerlos; pero los dioses se indignaron por la osadía que habían tenido al descubrir el fuego sin su consentimiento, y les cortaron las cabezas convirtiéndolos en perros.

Como en la mitología griega, el hombre audaz que es capaz de apoderarse del fuego, que significa el poder humano, sin el consentimiento de los dioses, tiene que ser castigado por ellos; paga con su vida la osadía de pensar que los hombres se bastan a sí mismos para resolver sus problemas.

En la época precolombina la fiesta del fuego nuevo se iniciaba con un apagón de todas las hogueras que ardían en templos y casas. El mundo quedaba envuelto en una penumbra universal como en la época que precedió a la creación. En la primera madrugada del siglo —de 52 anos— los sacerdotes encendían el fuego nuevo y lo traspasaban a los pobladores del reino. Así se escenificaba el ciclo de destrucción y renacimiento del cosmos.

En el rito católico durante la ceremonia del fuego nuevo, el sábado de gloria, se bendice y enciende el cirio pascual que simboliza a Cristo resucitado. Cristo es el Señor del tiempo, su principio y su cumplimiento: cada año, cada día y cada momento son abarcados por su Encarnación y su Resurrección, para que de este modo encontrarse de nuevo en la plenitud de los tiempos.

El calendario

En el mundo prehispánico existían el calendario ritual de 260 días y el solar de 360 días seguidos de otros cinco días considerados "peligrosos" o de mal agüero. El calendario ritual era el vigente para los natalicios de las deidades protectoras de la colectividad, tanto la propia como las cercanas. El calendario solar determinaba las principales fiestas en honor de los dioses de la guerra, el Sol, la lluvia y la fecundidad.

En el Concilio de Nicea (año 325) del mundo cristiano todas las iglesias se pusieron de acuerdo para que la Pascua cristiana fuese celebrado el domingo que sigue al plenilunio (14 del mes de Nisán) después del equinoccio de primavera. La reforma del calendario en Occidente (llamado "gregoriano", por el nombre del Papa Gregorio XIII, el año 1582) introdujo un desfase de varios días con el calendario oriental. Las iglesias occidentales y orientales buscan hoy un acuerdo, para llegar de nuevo a celebrar en una fecha común el día de la Resurrección del Señor. Al igual que en el mundo precolombino el calendario sirve para las principales fiestas de Jesucristo, el Espíritu Santo, la Virgen y los santos.

En el México moderno están vigentes las dos formas vivenciales en la concepción del tiempo: la temporalidad de larga duración y cíclica del mundo indígena y la temporalidad lineal, histórica, establecida por los europeos. En la mentalidad cíclica el tiempo vuelve sobre sí mismo al acabar un ciclo y llegar otro nuevo. El tiempo concebido como una línea va del pasado al futuro.

Como ejemplo de esta vivencia y de acuerdo al calendario azteca, el 20 abril de 1997 en el Museo Nacional de Antropología veneraron a la tierra —Tonantzin Coatlicue— mediante danzas prehispánicas. Grupos de estos danzantes danzan con cierta regularidad en los atrios de la Basílica de Guadalupe y en la Catedral. Su misión es convencer a la tierra que a pesar de todo el cemento que el hombre le ha puesto, los seres humanos la aman y le agradecen que les proporcione el alimento. Por esto hay que venerarla, consentirla y generar toda la energía posible para estar en armonía con ella.

Los ángeles

De acuerdo a la religión católica las verdades de la angelología (doctrina de los ángeles) eclesiástica no son verdades de la fe de primer orden; de hecho forman parte desde el principio del depósito de la fe. La iglesia guardiana auténtica del depósito de la fe e intérprete legal de la revelación divina confirma la existencia de los espíritus celestiales llamados "ángeles" en la Sagrada Escritura.

La palabra ángel proviene del griego "angelos" o sea, del latín "angelus", de donde fue tomada por las lenguas romanas y germánicas; significaba originalmente "enviado" o "mensajero"; corresponde al hebreo "malak" que se deriva de la raíz enviar. En el Antiguo Testamento hebraico aparece la palabra 217 veces.

En sentido teológico, los ángeles son seres espirituales dotados de inteligencia y libre voluntad creados por Dios de la nada, al inicio de los tiempos para su propio servicio y como una ayuda para los hombres. La iglesia ha afirmado que podemos y debemos creer en la existencia y actividad de los ángeles, de los buenos y también de los malos.

La Sagrada Escritura acentúa en diversos pasajes que el número de los ángeles es inmenso; repetidamente los compara con un ejército. Por otra parte cada ángel es un fenómeno único, una especie por sí; no existen dos ángeles de la misma especie. El ángel de la guarda que proviene del coro angelical más inferior, es asignado a cada hombre desde su nacimiento.

De igual manera, el nahual del México prehispánico significó el doble, o personalidad de cada hombre; también la divinidad propia del día del Tonalamatl que asistía a la persona por todo el tiempo de su existencia; un ser vivo, de especie no humana, asociado con el recién nacido en el momento de su nacimiento.

En tiempos modernos, el nahual es más bien un hechicero que tiene la facultad de transformarse en bestia de muy variadas especies (mamíferos, aves, reptiles, etc.). En esta bestia sufre y hace lo que en su propia figura haría y sufriría y todo lo que a estas bestias acontece le sobreviene a él en su forma humana. El fin de estos modos de transformación es casi siempre de intenciones perjudicantes y casi nunca de intenciones benévolas.

Dios reveló a los ángeles el misterio de la encarnación prevista da la segunda persona de la Santísima Trinidad, con la exigencia de reconocer al Dios hombre como su rey y a su Madre virginal como su reina. El resultado de esta prueba de los ángeles fue que una parte se sometió a Dios en un acto perfecto de amor y obediencia humilde, alcanzando la visión beatífica de la gloria de Dios, y la otra, liderada por Lucifer, se rebeló contra El en un pecado de soberbia, y son los espíritus malignos que causan daño.

La tierra prometida

Los mexicas creían haber sido elegidos por Huitzilopochtli, quien los había sacado de Aztlán, su tierra original, para conducirlos a través de una ardua peregrinación hasta la tierra prometida, en donde los convirtió en el pueblo más poderoso de la tierra; a cambio les demandó obediencia ciega y la obligación de construir oratorios para ofrendar al Sol su alimento divino: la sangre y los corazones de los guerreros capturados en la guerra.

En el libro del Exodo (6:6–8) se lee, "Yo soy el Señor, les quitaré de encima las caras de los egipcios, los libraré de su esclavitud, los rescataré con brazo extendido y haciendo justicia solemne. Los adoptaré como pueblo mío y seré su Dios; para que sepan que soy el Señor, su Dios, el que les quita de encima las cargas de los egipcios, los llevaré a la tierra que prometí con juramento a Abrahán, Issac y Jacob, y se las daré en posesión. Yo, el Señor".

Conclusiones

Las religiones son productos estéticos porque en sus mitos, magias y ritos operan diferentes categorías estéticas y porque vienen acompañadas de acciones, danzas, imágenes y objetos estéticos. Los bienes estéticos estaban al servicio de la religión lo mismo para el hombre precolombino y el feudal europeo; unos y otros eran profundamente religiosos.

El catolicismo medieval de los españoles y las manifestaciones mágico-religiosas indígenas tuvieron muchos puntos de contacto. Estos fueron incorporándose en los ritos y mitos católicos y en otros casos estos fueron interpretados por la mentalidad mágica de los indígenas.

El alma popular se adueñó del catolicismo y comenzó a insertar en sus ritos elementos precolombinos. Se gestan diferentes mestizajes, los que fueron evolucionando a lo largo de la colonia y de la república, hasta llegar a la actual cultura popular.

El mestizaje estético se fue diversificando e incrementando, mientras iban disminuyendo en cantidad y calidad lo ibérico y lo precolombino puros, sin desaparecer hasta hoy.

BIBLIOGRAFIA

Acha, Juan. 1993. *Las culturas estéticas de América Latina*. México: UNAM, Coordinación de Humanidades.

Caso, Alfonso. 1986. *El Pueblo del Sol*. Figuras de Miguel Covarrubias. México: Fondo de Cultura Económica.

Catecismo de la Iglesia Católica. 1992. 2d ed. Madrid: Asociación de Editores del Catecismo.

Dorta, Enrique Marco. 1979. "Consideraciones en torno al llamado estilo tequitqui". En *La dicotomía entre arte culto y arte popular*. Coloquio Internacional de Zacatecas. México: Instituto de Investigaciones Estéticas, UNAM. Pp. 135–161.

ELSA BARBERENA B.

Eliade, Mircea. 1996. *Historia de las creencias y de las ideas religiosas: desde la época de los descubrimientos hasta nuestros días*. Barcelona: Herder.

Fernández, Martha. 1988. "Arte tequitqui y arte mestizo: el artista americano". En *Simpatías y diferencias: relaciones del arte mexicano con el de América Latina*. X Coloquio Internacional de Historia del Arte del Instituto de Investigaciones Estéticas. Estudios de Arte y Estética, 28. México: Instituto de Investigaciones Estéticas, UNAM.

González Torres, Xololtl. 1995. "El sacrificio humano entre los mexicas". *Arqueología Mexicana* 3 (15), 5–6.

Guardini, Romano. 1989. *El Espíritu del Dios viviente*. Bogotá: Ediciones Paulinas.

_____. 1965. *Meditaciones teológicas*. Cristianismo y Hombre Actual, 71. Madrid: Ediciones Cristiandad.

Guitton, Jean. 1967. *Diálogos con Pablo VI*. Cristianismo y Hombre Actual, 80. Madrid: Ediciones Cristiandad.

Holbock, Ferdinand. 1995. *Unidos con los ángeles y los santos*. México.

Meyer, Jean. 1989. *Historia de los cristianos en América Latina*. México: Vuelta.

Moyssén, Xavier. 1967. *México angustia de sus cristos*. México: Instituto Nacional de Antropología e Historia.

Quirk, Robert E. 1973. *The Mexican Revolution and the Catholic Church*. Bloomington: Indiana University Press.

The Library of Congress and
Global Resources

21. The Library of Congress Brazil Field Office: Past Accomplishments and New Challenges

Pamela Howard-Reguindin

The establishment in 1962 of the overseas acquisitions and cataloging programs of the Library of Congress (LC) marked an innovative approach to foreign acquisitions and signaled the Library's commitment to obtaining elusive foreign publications in all fields of scholarly research. There are currently six overseas offices: Kenya, Pakistan, India, Indonesia, Egypt, and Brazil. In recent years, acquisitions by these offices have averaged some 250,000 pieces per year with participant libraries receiving an additional 500,000 items annually.

The Rio de Janeiro office, like the Nairobi, Kenya, office, opened in 1966 as a National Program for Acquisitions and Cataloging office serving LC for Brazilian publications. In 1986 responsibility for collecting from Uruguay was added; the Cooperative Acquisitions Program (CAP) for serials was initiated in 1990.

The Rio de Janeiro office staff comprises fifteen Brazilian employees—five acquisitions librarians, three cataloging librarians, and seven support staff; a half-time acquisitions position is based in São Paulo. The staff is responsible for collecting and cataloging books and other materials from Brazil and Uruguay for the Library of Congress, the National Library of Medicine (NLM), and the National Agriculture Library (NAL). The office is located in the U.S. consulate in Rio de Janeiro, with a beautiful view of Sugarloaf Hill.

In addition to collecting for LC, NLM, and NAL, the Rio office (like the five other overseas offices) also operates the Cooperative Acquisitions Program for obtaining periodicals for approximately 45 American and European libraries. In all, some 1,100 Brazilian subscriptions are placed annually for these universities, on a cost-recovery basis so as not to adversely affect Uncle Sam's ever shrinking pockets.

Over the years, the office has become recognized throughout Brazil and the international academic community for its comprehensiveness in collecting and excellence in processing Brazilian and Uruguayan materials. Among its accomplishments are several special microfilm projects including the filming of several Brazilian newspapers in conjunction with the Brazilian National Library and the Brazil's Popular Groups pamphlet and poster collection, which contains a considerable amount of material dealing with religious activities in

Brazil. The National Library newspaper filming has been temporarily suspended, but I am assured that more raw film is on order from LC to film the *Jornal do Brasil, Estado de São Paulo, Tribuna de Imprensa, Jornal do Comércio,* and the *Gazeta Mercantil* for 1994 through 1997.

The major event in 1997 was the celebration of the thirtieth anniversary of the Rio office. A reception was held in March in the consulate, which was subsidized to a large extent by private donations. The lively crowd of 150 guests included exchange partners, consulate colleagues, former employees, and dignitaries. Invited speakers were Winston Tabb, Associate Librarian of Congress; Dr. Georgette Dorn from the Hispanic Division; the acclaimed author and president of the Brazilian Academy of Letters, Dr. Nélida Piñón; the director of the Getúlio Vargas Foundation, Dr. Celina Amaral do Peixoto; José Mindlin, industrialist, philanthropist, and bibliophile extraordinaire; the chief of staff of the National Library of Brazil, Marta de Senna; and Ann Hartness of the University of Texas, who spoke on behalf of the Cooperative Acquisitions Program participants and the Seminar on the Acquisition of Latin American Library Materials (SALALM). A brochure was produced for the event. We thank those who wrote letters of support that were included in the brochure. We also express appreciation to book dealers Susan Bach, Ltd. and Linardi y Risso for their special contributions to the festivities—financial support in one case and a lovely commemorative plaque in the other.

For seventeen years, 1975–1992, the office produced an accessions list which was delivered to over 500 institutions worldwide. The list was used by bibliographers, scholars, and book dealers to verify Brazilian publications and confirm the latest publications available. This list ceased publication in 1992 for lack of adequate funding and staffing. The list from the India office ceased with the last issue for 1996. It is hoped that Web sites will be created to provide the same information, albeit not necessarily for posterity.

Over the years, as the office has moved from place to place (from outside the consulate to inside the building on many different floors) the amount of documents sent to the Library steadily increased until 1994, when it peaked at about 39,000 items. Since then, we have reduced our intake. This past year, our intake for Brazil was down by 12 percent and nearly 10 percent for Uruguay. As the budget shrinks, as staff is "rightsized," and Library collecting guidelines change, it is perhaps ironic that we should take pride in and receive kudos for reducing the level of intake.

This situation has created our first challenge: to maintain the high quality and depth of the research collection with an ever decreasing staff and funds. Of immediate concern is the assessment by the General Accounting Office with respect to the Cooperative Acquisitions Program. Though LC is authorized by Congress to run the Cooperative Acquisitions Program, the General Accounting

Office has determined that LC is not authorized to spend the administrative fees collected from the CAP participants and that this money should be returned to the U.S. Treasury. If LC's Overseas Operations Division is not authorized to use these fees solely to cover the costs of the program, the program will not survive. In late March Congress did authorize LC to redirect some of its Congressionally appropriated funds to the Cooperative Acquisitions Program, which saved the program for this fiscal year. The Library requested from Congress the authorization to establish a "revolving" fund, which will enable us to spend the administrative fees to cover the direct costs of the program. Library officials continue to work toward resolving this issue and have notified Congressional oversight staff that LC will reluctantly be forced to discontinue CAP at the end of this fiscal year if the legislation is not passed.

An increase in the service charge by the Department of State's International Cooperative Administrative Support Services (formerly FAAS—Foreign Affairs Administrative Support) presents another challenge. In any overseas mission there are certain functions which, for bureaucratic reasons, are either usually or can only be performed by the Department of State. Examples are payroll for Brazilian staff, cashiering for payments made to dealers, dealing with customs for large-sized purchases, and contracting. For many years, all government agencies with offices overseas have signed agreements to reimburse the Department of State for those services. Starting with fiscal year 1998, the Department of State is radically changing the rules for reimbursement, which will significantly increase the costs for these services. As a result, the already high cost of doing business in Brazil, "o custo brasil" as it is known in the business world, will increase. It will be a challenge to control the general office costs as well as the cost of the Cooperative Acquisitions Program.

There is periodic discussion about whether the mission should move out of the old embassy/consulate building. It appears that this may occur in about two years. If so, LC will have to decide whether the office should be accommodated in the same facilities as other agencies or elsewhere; the latter might be cheaper.

The installation of a local area network in the Rio office is taking time. LC Jakarta already has an intranet and prototype Web site providing access to its acquisition files and serials check-in software for participant subscriptions. The Rio office lags behind, but the goal is to establish a local area network, an intranet, and a Web presence, probably as part of an Overseas Operations Division Web site.

This year Guyana, French Guiana, and Suriname will be added to the Rio office portfolio. To my knowledge Suriname has not been visited by an LC employee, and Terry Peet was the last LC employee to visit Guyana and French Guiana, in 1991 and 1992, respectively. I will be visiting there in late August or early September to acquire materials and to set up exchange programs. I will write a trip report and distribute it to anyone interested.

It is my hope that the Rio office will serve the Library of Congress and the broader academic community for the next thirty years, so that the Library can continue to obtain and preserve the best intellectual production of Brazil, Uruguay, French Guiana, Guyana, and Suriname.

22. Pushing the Envelope: Beyond Acquisitions

Terry C. Peet

On October 1, 1997, the Directorate of Acquisitions and Support Services of the Library of Congress (LC) will be reorganized after several years of intensive planning. The three acquisition divisions dedicated exclusively to either purchase, non-purchase, or overseas acquisitions will be restructured to form three geographically oriented divisions: the Anglo-American area, the European and Latin American areas, and the African and Asian areas. The new configuration will allow each division and its component units to concentrate on total acquisitions from a particular geographic area regardless of method (i.e., purchase, gift, exchange).

Planning for this wholesale realignment began in April 1978 when the Hispanic Acquisitions Project was created. In November 1981 the project became permanent under the rubric Hispanic Acquisitions Program. For the three-year period between its inception and formalization, the Hispanic Acquisitions Program was under the guidance of the Director of Acquisitions where it enjoyed a considerable degree of autonomy. After November 1981, despite its administrative re-placement into the Exchange and Gift Division, the autonomy remained essentially untouched and undiminished.

With considerable hindsight, it is now apparent that the assignment of responsibility for the acquisitions of all types of materials, by any means, from Iberia, Latin America, and the Caribbean inevitably led to an empowerment of the program that was perhaps in part unintended, certainly unforeseen. It also opened opportunities that augmented many more acquisition strategy possibilities.

The reorganization of acquisitions in the Hispanic area unleashed a torrent of activism unknown to acquisition areas either in the Library of Congress or in perhaps most other libraries. The activism took shape in the following ways.

Acquisitions Decisions

Decisions on the method of acquisition (purchase, gift, exchange) were made within the new unit. As we created a coordinated, integrated acquisitions environment, the staff slowly began to realize the extent of the authority it had been granted. Attempts to alter the traditional dichotomy of purchase and non-purchase were halting, but as we gained our sea legs we realized that we could experiment based on conditions that varied greatly from one region or country to another. For example, exchanges with most government bodies in Paraguay and Bolivia were so difficult and time-consuming that it quickly became apparent that a commercial dealer would be more effective. Conversely, in Chile, Spain, Portugal, and much of the English-speaking Caribbean, exchanges were more easily developed and successfully sustained, and we were able to reduce considerably the quantity of purchases in those areas. We tailored custom approval plans to specific countries, a concept not practiced in LC before. We had full view of all acquisitions and were able to eliminate duplication of effort, reduce labor-intensive strategies, and uncover gaps that had been missed. We therefore reduced acquisitions by eliminating duplication only to increase acquisitions by filling in gaps.

Negotiating Authority

Under the reorganization, we had full authority to negotiate exchange arrangements and approval plans. Under the old regime this authority was divided between two acquisition divisions that often behaved as competing brothers. The mere fact that two or more staff members were handling acquisitions by different modes for the same area, despite any informal lines of communication, led inevitably to an uncoordinated approach for all acquisitions from a particular area. Under the new regime, an acquisitions specialist handling Mexico became familiar with all publishing and methods of acquisition for that area. A possible area of duplication or an oversight or gap that might not otherwise be identified was now subject to closer scrutiny by the acquisitions specialist.

Recommending Authority

The authority to recommend a title for acquisition has been a contentious issue within the Library. Recommending authority does not include authority to select the title for retention somewhere in the Library's collections. Unlike most libraries, LC strictly observes the distinction between recommendation (pre-acquisition) and selection (post-acquisition). By design and practice, the recommending authority granted the coordinator and the specialists in the Hispanic Acquisitions Project in November 1981 had been restricted to current monographs only for practical reasons. Often, either because of time constraints or because of the acquisitions specialist's familiarity with the material offered in lists or catalogs, the acquisitions specialist, in one fell swoop, recommended, searched, and ordered current monograph titles. Needless to say, the restructure streamlined the process and shortened the time line by weeks, if not months.

Selection Authority

Selection, the process of reviewing incoming materials, ordered or unsolicited, involves making two decisions about each piece. The first is whether the material is desired for the collections or elsewhere, i.e., whether it is in scope based on the corpus of Collection Policy Statements the Library of Congress has drafted over the years and revises from time to time. The second decision is the manner of treatment, and in the case of cataloging, the cataloging priority and the manner of cataloging, such as individual, minimum level, collection level, and so on. Functioning as selection officer, the acquisitions specialist becomes the collection developer. There is and always will be inherent tension in the relationship between the acquisitions specialist/selection officer and recommending officials as long as the two functions are not performed by the same person. The tension is beneficial, though not understood, especially in its effect on collection development.

Collection development has taken an unfortunate turn in the Library. There is no longer an office for collection development that oversees the general development of the collections. This office was eliminated in favor of a collection development activity dispersed among more than 250 staff members, some of whom are recommending officials, some are acquisitions specialists/selection officers, and some are both. The problem with the new scheme is that there is little uniformity of approach. Each recommending officer, even those within the same area studies, takes a different approach. Some ignore collection policy statements. In those cases, the selection officer mitigates the effects of excesses in either direction—too little or too much—so that collecting is not only balanced but is also carried out according to collection policies.

Recommending officers provide critical and indispensable input for acquisitions specialists/selection officers. In the case of retrospective and special format materials, the acquisitions specialist must defer to the expertise of the recommending official. In matters dealing with contemporary materials, the deference is subtle and cautionary. The ability of the recommending officials to apply or even to understand collection policies varies greatly. In some instances expertise clouds judgment about what is appropriate for the collections; occasionally experts are too narrowly focused. Their complaint about some incoming materials may be personal and inconsistent with collection policies. The role of the acquisitions specialist as selection officer is to be the great leveler, the balancer, the one who takes all concerns into account. For example, a scholarly work in Spanish on Byzantine studies published by the Centro de Estudios Bizantinos y Neo-Helénicos in Santiago de Chile was rejected by a recommending officer, but restored by the acquisitions specialist acting in the capacity of selection officer. The acquisitions specialist is a generalist whose concern is the acquisition of material according to collection policies, not according to a narrow focus of interest, expertise in a particular field, prejudice, or preconception. A good selection officer listens to and carefully considers the opinions of the recommending official

and makes a final decision based on what is best for the Library. The instances
of intractable disagreements are rare indeed. The understandable tension between the recommending official or subject matter expert and the selection
officer or generalist is healthy.

Encouraging Buyouts

On the surface, any activity undertaken to secure the buyout of one firm
by another is totally inappropriate. However, assume for a moment that an owner
of a firm expresses an interest in retiring, for example, and that firm is the only
one purveying materials from a particular geographic area. A survival instinct
springs into action and we suggest and actively encourage a purchase of the firm
by another in order to preserve acquisitions from that particular area.

Bookdealer Relations

We have become aggressively involved in encouraging vendors to enter new geographic areas. A good example occurred many years ago. During
a seven-year period we dealt with three different native bookdealer firms and
found all seriously wanting. In desperation we called a bookdealer from another country and encouraged that vendor to provide service for us as he was
in his own country.

Similarly, in some countries, notably Belize and Andorra, we have invited
non-dealers to enter the market, have taught them how to prepare lists and in-
voices, and have even given them guidelines on profit margins and pricing techniques. In one instance, the individual was willing to provide the service at cost;
eventually, with some effort, we convinced the dealer to build in some profit
margin lest he tire quickly of his efforts on our behalf.

USMARC Vendor Records

The concept that bookdealers would provide bibliographic records of titles
sold to customers in MARC format for use by libraries in creating their online
acquisition records (variously called preliminary cataloging, initial bibliographic
control, or acquisition process information file) has been adopted by at least
twelve vendors in the Hispanic area and is now growing among European
bookdealers. The benefits are obvious. Creating records in MARC format stan-
dardizes the records, enables client libraries to place more materials faster under bibliographic control with equal or less staff, and nearly eliminates the
possibility of unwanted duplication and expenditure. Bibliographic control must
be considered de rigueur the last step in acquisitions; if you don't know you
have a title even though you bought it, you don't have it. I'm proud of the fact
that the first three bookdealers to provide MARC records for the Library of Congress were Hispanic, the fourth was Italian, and the next seven were Hispanic.

The Hispanic area led the way in this development, and other libraries are responding to the availability of vendor-supplied MARC records.

Bookdealer Partnerships

Most bookdealers supplying major academic libraries, besides trying to make a living, fall into one or more of the follow categories:

a. they are bibliophiles;
b. they have substantial academic background, some having earned doctorates;
c. they are interested in placing their country's publications in major First World libraries and take pride in their efforts toward that end.

I have found that bookdealers will bend over backward to obtain something on their client's behalf.

Whenever I mention I am in acquisitions many immediately imagine some library technician in a cramped corner office typing orders or processing incoming materials. To be sure, we do this, but for us at the Library of Congress, acquisitions is definitely collection development. We negotiate agreements, assume recommending and selection responsibilities, and make decisions on funding and staffing allocation. In terms of the university acquisitions unit, we are somewhere between acquisitioners, bibliographers, and specialists. Call us what you want, it makes no difference; see what we do and how we do it. No matter how you slice it, the Hispanic Acquisitions Program (9 staff, covering 41 countries, bringing in 105,000 items annually, and performing preliminary cataloging of 14,000 of its 21,000 monograph intake), without the fabled Rio office, is indisputably the largest acquisitions program for Hispanic materials anywhere.

23. Back to the Future: An Immodest Proposal

Terry C. Peet

In the fall of 1993 Duke University, with financial support from the Andrew W. Mellon Foundation, convened a conference to discuss a plan prepared by the Association of Research Libraries (ARL) to develop a network-based, distributed program for coordinated collection development of Latin American and Caribbean materials among U.S. and Canadian research libraries. The plan focused on foreign acquisitions and outlined a system in which participating research libraries would share responsibilities for collecting Latin American and Caribbean imprint publications. The goal was to restore a broad range of significant research publications to national collections of books, serials, and other formats.

The ARL project has been largely limited to the sphere of participating libraries. There is a need to examine the feasibility of creating a similar network-based, distributed program for collection development in the commercial sector. In light of diminishing budgets and reduced staffs, we need to explore all possible avenues of distributed responsibility not only to maintain the programs we have instituted over the past two or three decades but also to expand and improve those programs.

Beginning with the first overture in mid-1993, more than a dozen major Latin American and Spanish bookdealers have taken on the responsibility of providing bibliographic records in USMARC format for their client libraries. This effort, first proposed by the Hispanic Acquisitions Section with the generous and indispensable assistance of the Network Development and MARC Standards Office, is now being imitated in other parts of the world. Thanks to the availability of electronic technology, free enterprise has been able to adopt this new network-based, distributed program. The result has been more rapid delivery of available preliminary records and reduced inputting time and effort in libraries where staff shortages abound. For the Hispanic Acquisitions Section, this development has been a godsend without which we would have fallen hopelessly behind in bibliographic control of new monographic acquisitions.

Enough about USMARC. What I want to discuss is newspapers. Newspapers from abroad are expensive, occupy enormous amounts of space, are time-consuming to prepare for filming, and require many hours to film. Many years ago, the Library of Congress made a commitment to filming for the American library community a vast number of newspapers. At present, in Latin America, the Caribbean, and Iberia, this amounts to 57 titles. Worldwide the number is 340 (61 domestic and 279 foreign). No other institution anywhere has such an enormous responsibility in the area of filming. Only a few years ago the Library had eight newspaper processors dedicated to preparing newspapers for filming— now there are only two, one of whom is on light duty. A few years ago the Library had 41 cameras busy filming newspapers and other materials in its Photoduplication Service, but 20 of those cameras are now idle with no one to operate them. The Library is no longer able, with its reduced budget, to do all it did before.

The responsibility for preserving foreign newspapers needs to be shared. I would encourage commercial ventures, including bookdealers, many of whom are already subscription vendors, to seriously consider the possibility of creating microfilming centers within their establishments. Such centers would obtain the print copies of contemporary newspapers and would organize, film, and deliver them to their client libraries on a timely, frequent basis. I emphasize the words contemporary, timely, and frequent. Contemporary means today's newspaper edition, not a run from the 1950s or the nineteenth century. Timely means delivery of microfilm within two months of publication. The January and February issues of *El Mercurio* (Santiago de Chile), for example, would be filmed by late March of a given year and shipped to client libraries in early April. Frequent means at least every three months depending on the size or bulk of the newspaper. The bulkier the newspaper the more frequent its filming and delivery.

The rationale behind contemporary, timely, and frequent is to eliminate the temptation to acquire a print copy, thereby saving 80 percent of the subscription cost (which is attributable to transportation) and freeing up space in libraries' newspaper decks. At present, the library is spending $1,100 per print newspaper subscription and more for subsequent microfilming. Under the suggested plan, the library would be able to allocate some of its savings from canceled print subscriptions to immediate microfilm subscriptions.

The Library has already begun preliminary discussions toward this end. The Library of Congress and the Biblioteca Nacional de Chile signed an agreement at the Department of State to explore a cooperative microfilming project of contemporary newspapers from the Cono Sur (Chile, Argentina, Paraguay). The Library of Congress is prepared as part of its contribution to the project to be situated in the Biblioteca Nacional de Chile to provide the raw microfilm, technical training in LC, and other technical expertise including the possible loan of one of its idle cameras.

In a different way the Library has also had preliminary discussions with Editorial Inca, headquartered in Cochabamba, Bolivia, and Miami, Florida. This venture would include newspapers from Bolivia, Peru, Ecuador, Colombia, and Venezuela, areas already covered by the "Inca empire." Legal hurdles and details have yet to be worked out. The microfilming center could be established in Miami. Similarly, we hope that some way can be found to locate one of LC's idle cameras in the Rio office to cover titles from Brazil, Uruguay, and the Guyanas.

Of course, every library will probably want to retain print subscriptions for a few key newspapers, but most could be discarded in favor of microfilm only if such microfilm can be produced and delivered on a timely and frequent basis.

Other technologies such as scanning and storing on compact disks are not suitable for immediate retention of whole text. With doubts about the longevity of CD-ROM and talk about new technologies to replace scanning and CD-ROM by the first decade of the new century, perhaps we should rely on the older, proven technology of microfilm for future conservation.

The best part of this proposal is not that it makes sense, if we have the will to put it into action. The best part is that the intended executors of future conservation are a group of business people who have wonderfully agile minds, are well educated people of letters in their own right, are anxious to promote the world of learning and research, and have demonstrated at every turn their willingness to venture into new areas of service. These people are our colleagues at the beginning of the acquisition stream, the bookdealers. It is my hope that they will welcome this proposal as an invitation to undertake not only a new and successful commercial venture but, more important, one that will preserve in situ their national history and patrimony.

24. Gabriel René Moreno, Bolivian Bibliographer

Nelly S. González

At the 38th Annual Meeting of the Seminar on the Acquisition of Latin American Materials (SALALM) in Guadalajara, Laurence Hallewell added a nice touch to the presentation of the José Toribio Medina Award by providing a comprehensive, yet concise description of Medina's contributions to the field of bibliography. He also noted that "José Toribio Medina y Zavala is not only the outstanding bibliographer for our own field of interest, but he has even been called 'The Greatest Bibliographer in Christendom.' " In his remarks, he demonstrated both why Medina should be so honored, and why we continue to recognize outstanding contributions to the field of bibliography with the award that bears his name.[1]

At the following year's (1994) Medina Award presentation, Laura Gutiérrez-Witt added a new dimension to the ceremony by honoring another Latin American bibliographer, the unforgettable Nettie Lee Benson. Her "Homage to Nettie Lee Benson" reviewed Benson's devotion to Latin American library collections; her efforts can be seen today in the Nettie Lee Benson Collection of the University of Texas at Austin.[2]

Continuing this tradition, this paper is about another great Latin American bibliographer, a Bolivian, Gabriel René Moreno. Moreno is to Bolivia what Medina is to Chile. Like Medina, he was a prolific writer, and his work was not limited to outstanding achievements in bibliography. Moreno was a master historian, sociologist, literary critic, and educator who had an important impact on Bolivians' understanding of themselves. His influence in each of these disciplines continues through re-editions and analyses of his works. Although he is one of a very few Bolivian bibliographers known to Latin American specialists in other countries, this tireless compiler and his enormous output deserve wider acclaim. His works will serve myriad scholars and specialists in Bolivian studies.

Major works by Moreno include *Biblioteca boliviana: Catálogo de la sección de libros y folletos* (first published in 1879 with supplements through 1908), *Biblioteca boliviana: Archivo de Mojos y Chiquitos* (1888), *Bibliotecta peruana* (a multivolume work which commenced publication in 1896), *Ultimos días coloniales en el Alto-Perú, Bolivia y Argentina: Notas biográficas y bibliográficas* (1896), *Bolivia y Peru: notas históricas y bibliográficas* (1901), and *Bolivia y Perú: Mas notas históricas y bibliográficas* (1905). Notable also are his numerous "folletos" including "Poetas bolivianos I: Biografía de Don Nestor Galindo" (1868), "Poetas bolivianos II: Biografía de Don Daniel Calvo" (1870), "Daza y las bases chilenas de 1879" (1881), and "El General Ballivián" (1895). These important works only scratch the surface of a long career of writing, criticism, and historical documentation during troubled times of war between Chile and Bolivia.

Guillermo Ovando Sanz (1996) provides insight into the multifaceted aspects of Moreno's working life. Born in Santa Cruz, Bolivia, in 1836, at age 19 Gabriel was sent by his father to Santiago, Chile, to study law. By age 23 he had formed a writing group, Círculo de los Amigos de las Letras; at age 28 he produced a catalog of the Instituto Nacional; and at age 32 was named successor to the outgoing director of the Biblioteca del Instituto, a position he held from 1868 until his death in 1908. Although he spent most of his life in Chile and Peru, his dedication to his native Bolivia can be seen in his work on Bolivian literature, poetry, and politics. A prolific writer, he produced 114 works over his lifetime and another 141 works have been written about him. Gabriel René Moreno deserves a place among the notable Latin American bibliographers.

Ovando Sanz identifies 97 important works by Moreno including books, pamphlets, and important articles in journals of the period, including *Revista del Pacífico*, *La Revista de Sud América*, *Revista de Santiago*, *Revista de Artes y Letras*, *Revista Chilena*, and *Revista de Buenos Aires*. There are also numerous works about Moreno and his contribution that assure the preservation of Bolivian bibliographic control. Ovando Sanz identifies 16 works specifically about Moreno, about 10 re-editions of his works, and more than 72 works referring to Moreno. Siles Guevara's comprehensive bibliography notes scholarly output by and about Moreno in the following categories:

Collaborations in journals	67
Pamphlets	8
Books	20
Prologues (for other authors)	2
Texts in collections	2
Translations	1
Anthologies (own)	1
Anthologies (with others)	3
Additions to his work	2
Bibliographies (about)	14
Criticism and biography	124
Unsigned works	11
Total	255

Gabriel René Moreno has never received the recognition he deserves in the United States, but there are many Latin American biographies of Moreno and a few bibliographies of his contribution to Chilean, Peruvian, and Bolivian history and bibliographic work. Humberto and José Vázquez-Machicado (1988) write of Moreno as the highest kind of man, a nonconformist and moral idealist in the style of Emerson, a patriot historiographer dedicated to Bolivia. Even though he lived during a difficult period of disputes between Chile and Bolivia and the subsequent War of the Pacific, his work never stopped. He was a superb bibliographer, historian, literary critic, and educator. Moreno's work deserves our attention.

Major Works by Gabriel René Moreno

Books

Biblioteca boliviana: Catálogo de la sección de libros y folletos. Santiago de Chile: Imprenta Gutenberg, 1879.

Biblioteca boliviana: Archivo de Mojos y Chiquitos. Santiago de Chile: Imprenta Gutenberg, 1888.

Bibliotecta peruana: Apuntes para un catálogo de impresos. Santiago de Chile: Imprenta Cervantes, 1896.

Ultimos días coloniales en el Alto-Perú, Bolivia y Argentina: Notas biográficas y bibliográficas. Santiago de Chile: Imprenta Cervantes, 1896.

Bolivia y Peru: Notas históricas y bibliográficas. Santiago de Chile: Imprenta Cervantes, 1901.

Bolivia y Perú: Mas notas históricas y bibliográficas. Santiago de Chile: Imprenta Litografía y Encuadernación, 1905.

Pamphlets

"Poetas bolivianos I: Biografia de Don Nestor Galindo." Santiago, Chile: Imprenta Nacional, 1868.

"Poetas bolivianos II: Biografia de Don Daniel Calvo." Santiago, Chile: Establecimiento tipográphico de El Independiente, 1870.

"Daza y las bases chilenas de 1879." Sucre, Bolivia: Tipografía del Progreso, 1881.

"El General Ballivián." Santiago de Chile, Imprenta Cervantes, 1895.

Selected List of Studies about Gabriel René Moreno

Condarco Morales, Ramiro. *Grandeza y soledad de Moreno.* La Paz, Bolivia: Universidad Mayor de San Andrés, 1971.

Ovando Sanz, Guillermo. *Gabriel René Moreno.* La Paz, Bolivia: Fundación Humberto Vázquez-Machicado, 1996.

Sanabria Fernández, Hernando, et al. *Estudios sobre Gabriel René Moreno: Homenaje al sesquicentenario del nacimiento de Gabriel René Moreno.*

Santa Cruz de la Sierra, Bolivia: Casa de la Cultura Raúl Otero Reiche, 1986.

Siles Guevara, Juan. *Gabriel René Moreno: Historiador boliviano.* La Paz, Bolivia: Editorial "Los Amigos del Libro," 1979.

Siles Guevara, Juan. *Contribución a la bibliografía de Gabriel René Moreno.* La Paz, Bolivia: Universidad Mayor de San Andrés, 1967.

Vázquez-Machicado, Humberto, and José Vázquez-Machicado. "Gabriel René Moreno." In *Obras Completas.* La Paz, Bolivia: Editorial Don Bosco, 1988. Vol. VI, pp. 1–126.

NOTES

1. Laurence Hallewell, "Medina and the Medina Award," *Technology, Environment, and Social Change,* edited by Patricia Noble (Albuquerque, N.M.: SALALM, 1995), p. 445.

2. Laura Gutiérrez-Witt, "Nettie Lee Benson, January 15, 1905–June 23,1993, a Personal Memoir," *Modernity and Tradition: The New Latin American and Caribbean Literature, 1956-1994,* edited by Nelly S. González (Austin: SALALM, 1996), pp. xix–xxv.

25. Diplomacy in the Service of the Arts: Manoel de Oliveira Lima and the Musical Materials at the Oliveira Lima Library

Marcelo Campos Hazan

The importance of the distinguished Brazilian historian, diplomat, journalist, professor, and bibliophile Manoel de Oliveira Lima (1867–1928) is understandably manifold. The writer of nearly twelve hundred essays and the presenter of more than seventy lectures, Oliveira Lima was a scholar of many subjects and an advocate of many causes. This paper discusses his career from a musicological point of view and examines his musical legacy preserved in the Oliveira Lima Library.

It should be noted from the outset that music was not among Oliveira Lima's primary interests or talents. The eminent anthropologist Gilberto Freyre (1900–1987), a friend since the age of sixteen and also a biographer, did not believe that he was an enthusiast, stating that his art of preference was actually painting.[1] In his own memoirs, Oliveira Lima recalled having had a strong aptitude for historical subjects from an early age, but never a gift for "music and singing."[2] The Brazilian diplomat also had a declared preference for the theater over opera[3] and he is in fact the author of one historical play, *O Secretario d'El-Rey*, the only fiction work of his vast output.[4] This notwithstanding, Oliveira Lima grew accustomed to the opera from an early age and became an assiduous operagoer at the Teatro São Carlos during his student years and early diplomatic career in Lisbon. Oliveira Lima's theatrical experiences are well depicted in his memoirs, in which he refers to several important turn-of-the-century singers such as the celebrated tenor Francesco Tamagno (1850–1905), the creator of the title role in Giuseppe Verdi's (1813–1901) *Otello*, and the legendary soprano Adelina Patti (1843–1919), the most highly rewarded singer in opera history.[5]

As a scholar, Oliveira Lima did venture on occasion into topics of a musicological nature; the chapter "As Solenidades da Corte" from *Dom João VI no Brasil*,[6] for example, contains useful information on the musical establishment of King Dom João VI (1767–1826). However, Oliveira Lima's writings on music pale in comparison to his contributions as a diplomat. In 1907, upon his assignment to the position of Plenipotentiary in Belgium, Oliveira Lima set forth an ambitious program with the specific intent of promoting Brazilian cultural values abroad. Lectures such as "Machado de Assis [1839–1908] et son Oeuvre Littéraire," presented at the Sorbonne on April 3, 1909,[7] received great

critical acclaim and contributed to his eventual recognition as "intellectual am-
bassador of Brazil." As a result of this success, he received an invitation to represent the country in the III Congress of the International Musical Society that
was held in Vienna, on the occasion of the centennial of Joseph Haydn's (1732–
1809) death. There, on May 28, 1909, Oliveira Lima presented a historical 35-
minute lecture titled "La musique au Brésil: Au point de vue historique."[8] It is
significant that his presentation was illustrated with the actual performance of
various Brazilian compositions, for this probably represented the first instance
in which the music of the great colonial master José Maurício Nunes Garcia
was ever performed to a modern European audience.

However, Vienna only anticipated a greater recognition that was still to come.
On April 4, 1910, Oliveira Lima presented the lecture "La Conquête du Brésil"
for the solemn session of the Royal Geographical Society of Belgium. The occasion was especially important since it marked the first public appearance of King
Albert I (1875–1934) after the official period of mourning for the death of his
father, King Leopold II (1835–1909). As in Vienna, Oliveira Lima strove to make
music an integral part of the *soirée*, and works by Nunes Garcia, Antônio Carlos
Gomes (1836–1896), and Alberto Nepomuceno (1864–1920) were performed to
the great acclaim of the Belgian public and press. Weeks later, on April 22, the
Brazilian diplomat would showcase once again the music of his country, promoting a benefit concert for the flood victims of France and Belgium in which works
by Carlos Gomes (1836–1896), Manuel Joaquim de Macedo (1847–1925), and
Henrique Oswald (1852–1931) were successfully performed.

After his fruitful five-year appointment in Belgium, Oliveira Lima retired
from the diplomatic corps to pursue an academic career, settling definitively in
Washington, D.C. in 1920. He taught international law at Catholic University
of America, became a member of the exclusive Kosmos Club, and actively supported the Latin American music concerts promoted by the Pan American Union
at the time. On February 5, 1924, he inaugurated the Manoel de Oliveira Lima
Library, which remains to this day the outstanding repository of his impressive
personal collection of tens of thousands of books, manuscripts, and objects of
art. The music at the Oliveira Lima Library was not systematically acquired,
consisting largely of pieces that previously belonged either to the founder or to
his beloved wife, Flora, an amateur pianist. From Oliveira Lima's numerous
diplomatic missions we find several versions of Francisco Manuel da Silva's
(1795–1865) Brazilian national anthem. Much orchestral music from his lectures and concerts survives, including several compositions by Leopoldo Miguéz
(1850–1902), from whom the library owns a full score of his well-known *Hymno
da Proclamação da República*, bearing the composer's own signature.

The bulk of the musical collection, however, consists of piano sheet music. Much of it reflects the popularity of such early nationalism exponents as

the brothers Luiz (1861–1934) and Alexandre Levy (1864–1892), Ernesto Nazareth (1863–1934), and Alberto Nepomuceno (1864–1920). There are also a number of vocal selections from famous operas, as well as fashionable arrangements for piano solo based on operatic themes. Foremost among these works stands a handsomely bound *Grande Fantaisie* on a theme from Verdi's *Il Trovatore* by a Gennaro Perrelli, which originally belonged to none other than the Emperor Dom Pedro II (1825–1891) himself.[9]

The Oliveira Lima Library also houses a rich collection of thousands of missives that includes letters from personalities such as President James Monroe (1758–1831), Simón Bolívar (1783–1830), and Victor Hugo (1802–1885),[10] and Oliveira Lima's correspondence with Alberto Nepomuceno, Manuel Joaquim de Macedo, and other music notables mentioned earlier is therein preserved as well.[11] Finally, not to be overlooked among the many important iconographical pieces at the Oliveira Lima Library is a striking photograph of an aged Carlos Gomes taken in Washington, D.C. in 1893,[12] during the composer's visit to the United States on the occasion of the Columbian International Exhibit in Chicago.

Beyond their musicological interest, these miscellaneous items stand today as reminders of Oliveira Lima's pioneering efforts toward the international recognition of Brazilian music. No doubt, Oliveira Lima's accomplishments are true examples of how much can be achieved when the ones who hold high places are endowed with a love for the arts and the vision to promote them.

NOTES

1. Gilberto Freyre, *Oliveira Lima, Don Quixote Gordo* (Recife: Universidade Federal da Paraiba, Imprensa Universitária, 1968), p. 79.

2. Manoel de Oliveira Lima, *Memórias, Estas Minhas Reminiscencias*, with a foreword by Gilberto Freyre, Coleção Documentos Brasileiros (Rio de Janeiro: Livraria José Olympio Editôra, 1937; reprint, with a new foreword by Fernando da Cruz Gouvêa, Coleção Pernambucana, Recife: Governo de Pernambuco, Secretaria de Turismo, Cultura e Esportes, Fundação do Patrimonio Artístico e Histórico de Pernambuco, Diretoria de Assuntos Culturais, 1986), p. 12 (page references are to first edition).

3. See ibid., pp. 40–41.

4. Manoel de Oliveira Lima, *O Secretario d'El-Rey* (Rio de Janeiro: Livraria Garnier, 1904).

5. Oliveira Lima, *Memórias,* p. 42.

6. Manoel de Oliveira Lima, "As Solenidades da Corte," in *Dom João VI no Brasil, 1808–1821*, 2 vols. (Rio de Janeiro: Typ. Jornal do Commercio, 1909; 2d ed. with a foreword by Octavio Tarquínio de Sousa, Rio de Janeiro: Livraria José Olympio Editôra, 1945; 3rd ed. with a foreword by Wilson Martins, Rio de Janeiro: Topbooks, 1996), pp. 605–622 (page references are to third edition).

7. The address is published in Manoel de Oliveira Lima, "Machado de Assis et son Oeuvre Littéraire," in *Machado de Assis*, with a foreword by Anatole France (Paris: Louis-Michaud Editeur, 1909), pp. 19–85. A version in Portuguese by Oliveira Lima is available in *O Estado de São Paulo*, May 9, 1909.

8.   The lecture is recorded in Manoel de Oliveira Lima, "La musique au Brésil. Au point de vue historique," in *III Kongress der Internationalen Musik Gesellschaft* (Vienna: Artaria & C.; Leipzig: Breitkopf & Härtel, 1909), pp. 443–446; *L'Independance Belge* (Brussels), June 15, 1909; and *Courrier du Brésil* (Paris), May 27, 1909. A version in Portuguese by Oliveira Lima is found in both *Jornal do Comércio* (Rio de Janeiro) and *O Estado de São Paulo*, June 13, 1909. A version in Spanish, with translation by Eduardo Sánchez de Fuentes, is published in *Boleín Musical de la Habana* 2, no. 18 (November 1910), 1–2.

9.   The cover is green and ornamented in gold, displaying a frame that wraps a crown with the initials D. P. II (royal arms). The frontispiece, also decorated in gold, bears the following inscription: "This work was composed and published to be respectfully dedicated and offered to his majesty by GP, pianist of his majesty King Luiz of Portugal and Knight of the sundry orders" ("Cet ouvrage a été composé et edité pour être respectueusement dédié et offert a sa majesté par GP pianeste de sa majesté Dom Luiz Roi de Portugal et Chevalier de plusieurs ordres").

10.   See Godfrey F. Ferris, "Names of the Correspondents with Dr. Manuel [*sic*] de Oliveira Lima, 1884–1928," 1938, typescript, The Manoel de Oliveira Lima Library, Washington, D.C.

11.   See Manoel S. Cardozo, "A Guide to the Manuscripts in the Lima Library, The Catholic University of America Washington, D.C.," *Handbook of Latin American Studies* 6 (1940), 471–504.

12.   See *Rare Brazilian Photographs from the Oliveira Lima Library. Art Gallery of the Brazilian-American Institute. June 10 to July 18* (Washington, D.C.: n.p., 1977), and Museu da Imagem e do Som, *Fotografias Raras da Biblioteca Oliveira Lima. MIS julho–agosto/81* (São Paulo: Fundação Padre Anchieta, 1981).

26. Preservation Microfilming of the Colección Lafragua in the Biblioteca Nacional de México

Carl Deal

The Colección Lafragua in the Biblioteca Nacional de México is among the most prestigious collections held by that venerable institution. Its preservation is one of the most significant projects to be undertaken by the Latin American Microform Project (LAMP) with a foreign institution, and it followed the signing of a *convenio* with the Biblioteca Nacional in 1993.[1] Scholars from around the world supported this binational effort, the third project undertaken by LAMP with a Latin American national library.[2] The project was completed in the fall of 1997 and included 236 rolls of microfilm. Requests for purchase or interlibrary loan may be directed to the Center for Research Libraries in Chicago where the materials are housed.

The project was initiated by scholars from Princeton University. Negotiations between a LAMP representative in Mexico and the administration of the Biblioteca Nacional resulted in the preparation of a joint grant proposal. The project was funded in August 1995 by Fideicomiso para la Cultura México/USA, a binational commission supported by the Rockefeller Foundation, the Fundación Cultural Bancomer, and the Fondo Nacional para la Cultura y las Artes.

LAMP's commitment of $100,000 was matched by Fideicomiso, and the Biblioteca Nacional has contributed to the funding and has underwritten major staff and administrative costs. The project was completed four years after the signing of the *convenio*.[3]

The Biblioteca Nacional was interested in this project because of the collection's historical contents and value as an important part of the Mexican national patrimony. Many scholars and librarians consider it one of the most important collections held by the Biblioteca Nacional. This is evident from letters of support by scholars from Canada, England, Mexico, and the United States that accompanied the grant proposal to Fideicomiso. Dr. Carlos Marichal in citing the rarity and diversity of its contents identified it as possibly the most important collection for the study of the intellectual and political history of Mexico in the first half of the nineteenth century. Prof. Rodney D. Anderson described it as "irreplaceable for the study of the post colonial history of Mexico." Prof.

John H. Coatsworth stated, "Preserving the Lafragua Collection on microfilm is not only of crucial importance to historical scholarship on Mexico, but it is also vital for the conservation of a truly priceless element of Mexico's national patrimony." Prof. Timothy E. Anna in comparing the Colección Lafragua with holdings at the University of California, Berkeley Library and with the Sutro Collection of the California State Library states, "The Lafragua Collection is the largest and most complete, and since collecting it originally was the work of one of 19th century Mexico's most significant statesmen, it has a wholeness no other collection can equal." Prof. Alan Knight was delighted over the possibility that the collection would be preserved and made available to graduate students from the Latin American program at the University of Oxford. Prof. Charles Hale, who used the collection for two books, urged, "All measures must be taken to preserve the collection" further noting that it has high value to the world of historical scholarship on nineteenth-century Mexico.

The diversity of the contents of the collection to which Dr. Marichal referred is readily seen in the four bibliographic guides that have been prepared at the Biblioteca Nacional and published by the Instituto de Investigaciones Bibliográficos.[4] Dr. Nettie Lee Benson, an early president of the Seminar on the Acquisition of Latin American Library Materials (SALALM) and longtime director of the Benson Latin American Collection at the University of Texas, is acknowledged by Lucina Moreno Valle for her help in forming the appendix that contains lists of the Poder Legislativo from 1821 to 1853. The guides are arranged in chronological order and extensively indexed with complete bibliographic entries for the 1,580 volumes in the Colección Lafragua. Each entry is consistent in format and includes an abstract. To the delight of scholars, most of the abstracts are extensive, especially in the guides produced by Meza Oliver and Olivera López.

Types of materials in the collection include manuscripts; municipal, state, and national official publications, many of which appear in the *Gaceta del Gobierno de México*; ecclesiastical publications like sermons, pastoral letters, funeral orations, religious proclamations; eulogistic and commemorative poetry; royal decrees; letters; laws; maps; medical treatises; newspapers and articles from newspapers; patriotic discourses and political pamphlets; and reprints from some foreign publications, particularly from Spain and Cuba. Most of the material bears directly upon Mexico, Mexicans, and events in Mexico.

Of the 1,580 volumes in the collection, 452 are collections of sermons bound in vellum. Although the exact number of titles to be microfilmed will not be known until the end of the project, the three presently published guides include 9,089 titles: 627 for the period of 1800–1810; 1,840 for the period of 1811–1821; and 6,622 for the period of 1821–1853. The number of titles to appear in the guide in preparation for the years in 1854–1875 will augment this amount considerably, since materials published after 1875 and into the 1920s also are included. An author/title index to the four guides on CD-ROM is being considered by the Biblioteca Nacional.

A second reason to preserve this collection is the prominence of the Mexican scholar José María Lafragua, who assembled the collection and gave it to the Biblioteca Nacional. He was the first director of the Biblioteca Nacional and spent a lifetime collecting the materials he later donated to that library. The excellent Advertencia by Ernesto de la Torre Villar and the Prefacio by Lucina Moreno Valle in the first volume of this bibliographic quartet contain a brief biographical essay on Lafragua and information on the collection he assembled. From these one learns that Lafragua was a man of his times, concerned about the future of his country, its culture, and its economic, social, and political development.

Lafragua was born in Puebla in 1913, where he graduated in law in 1935 from the Colegio Carolino de Puebla. He became a member of the Partido Federalista and, tireless in his dedication to public service, served as minister of foreign relations in the liberal administrations of Comonfort, Juárez, and Lerdo de Tejada. Torre Villar credits him with the elaboration of the Código Civil and the Código de Procedimientos Civiles, as well as important collaboration on the Código Penal. Scarcely four years after the formation of the Biblioteca Nacional in 1871, Lafragua donated the major part of his private library, now known as the Colección Lafragua, to the National Library and a second and smaller part to the Colegio del Estado de Puebla.[5]

The collaboration between LAMP and the Biblioteca Nacional to film this collection also involves the Center for Research Libraries in Chicago (CRL); TYMSA, the commercial microfilm company producing the original silver halide films in Mexico; and Micro Media Imaging Systems in New York, where service copies for both CRL and the Biblioteca Nacional are being produced. Since no company producing acceptable 35 mm microfilm to meet the project's standards could be identified, producing a 16 mm film with an experienced company was acceptable to both parties. Also, the costs for producing 16 mm film were considerably less.

Problems of technology and standards had to be settled. For example, the question of the acceptability of a 16 mm film was questioned. The Hemeroteca Nacional has 35 mm cameras and other modern equipment, as well as competent and experienced staff who are accustomed to meeting ANSI requirements. Nevertheless, it was totally committed to its own work and unable to do the filming.

Copies on 16 mm microfilm of items from the Lafragua Collection that previously had been produced by TYMSA were reviewed and approved by LAMP. However, guaranteeing that ANSI standards would be maintained throughout the project demanded constant review. As a result, the technician in charge of the microfilming laboratory at the Hemeroteca Nacional was assigned to review and generally oversee the filming by TYMSA.

Shipments of twenty-five rolls of the original silver halide film were forwarded as they were completed from the Biblioteca Nacional to Micro Media Imaging Systems in New York City. There, a silver service and diazo copy were produced for both CRL and the Biblioteca Nacional before the original was returned to the Biblioteca Nacional. Producing copies in the United States proved to be more cost-effective. Limiting shipments to a total of twenty-five rolls prevented exorbitant unanticipated costs that would result in the loss of a larger shipment.

The Biblioteca Nacional did not have experience with a preservation project of this type, but it did have the administrative staff and personnel who were able to embark on a new endeavor. The amount of staff time assigned by the Biblioteca Nacional has been considerable, and the quality control to meet ANSI standards has been stringently maintained. Because of the rarity of the material and the need to maintain quality control on a daily basis, the project required that TYMSA set up its camera in the Biblioteca Nacional.

In agreeing upon standards, consideration was given to those of the Research Libraries Group (RLG). However, they were unnecessarily stringent and the ANSI requirements were deemed adequate. The familiarity with ANSI standards by technicians in Mexico also made them attractive. Since this is a preservation project of an important collection, LAMP suggested that the original silver negative be sent for storage and service to National Underground Storage Inc. in Boyers, Pennsylvania. However, the climate-controlled underground vault where the collection is now housed at the Biblioteca Nacional was deemed preferable.

Finally, the decision on film targets for each roll of film required some study. This was especially important since RLG standards were not being followed. Agreement was reached to include those required by the ANSI standards as well as others designed for this project. Targets for checking resolution, listing the titles on each role, and identifying ownership and copyright are among those that are being used.

In conclusion, this project is a model that LAMP and other organizations might apply with foreign institutions. Its advantages are that it imposes international ANSI standards for microfilming, provides an attractive package for seeking matching funds, and depends upon staff participation from the partner institution at no cost to LAMP. Most important, the material being filmed is under bibliographic control with four published guides, and the project assigns the actual administration and quality control of the filming to the institution that owns the material. The establishment of a formal relationship through an official *convenio* and a successful initial project also may lead to future cooperation in new preservation filming and to exchanges for microfilms owned by each institution. Finally, establishing close relationships with national libraries and other prestigious cultural agencies can also facilitate new projects with other institutions in a particular country.

A problem LAMP has experienced has been the identification of institutions abroad that have the funds, access to equipment, desire, and administrative and technical expertise to carry out cooperative projects. The Lafragua project has been successful because it had the institutional commitment, resources, and characteristics of the model described above. The original grant proposal was prepared at the Biblioteca Nacional by its coordinator, Dr. Judith Licea de Arenas. It has been administered in a superior manner by the present coordinator, Lic. Marcela Uribe, and it enjoys the full support of the director of the Instituto de Investigaciones Bibliográficos, Dr. José G. Moreno de Alba.[6]

LAMP should consider extending its cooperation with foreign organizations and publishers in the field. It should prepare a sample model *convenio* for institutional cooperation and a form letter requesting permission to film a particular serial or newspaper. This form letter would help members of LAMP institutions, already in the field for other reasons, secure a publisher's permission to film a particular title. The sample *convenio* could be used in expediting cooperative projects with institutions requiring formal agreements before projects can be undertaken. It is recognized that representation of LAMP in the field would require some coordination with CRL and with LAMP to ensure that the materials and projects have prior approval of the organization.

NOTES

1.   One of six foreign area microfilm preservation projects administered by the Center for Research Libraries (CRL) in Chicago, Illinois, LAMP has 38 dues-paying members.

2.   The first project was with the Biblioteca Nacional in Rio de Janeiro. It has expanded and received support from the Mellon Foundation to digitize the films from this cooperative effort. The digitization project includes the annual reports of federal ministries and presidential messages from 1890 to 1933, as well as the annual reports of the governors and presidents of the Brazilian states covering the period 1833–1930. The second project in Chile was more modest and filmed early years of the Chilean magazine *Arcella*.

3.   Cooperative projects like this often can not be undertaken without formal agreements (*convenios*). These agreements have to meet legal and other bureaucratic requirements. Once instituted, they facilitate continuing cooperation and avoid the need to renegotiate a new institutional agreement for each project.

4.   Lucina Moreno Valle, *Catálogo de la Colección Lafragua de la Biblioteca Nacional de México, 1821–1853,* Instituto de Investigaciones Bibliográficas, Biblioteca Nacional de México, Série: GUIAS 2 (México: UNAM, Instituto de Investigaciones Bibliográficas, 1975); Rocío Meza Oliver and Luis Olivera López, *Catálogo de la Colección Lafragua de la Biblioteca Nacional de México 1800–1810,* Instituto de Investigaciones Bibliográficas, Biblioteca Nacional de México,

Série: Guias (México: UNAM, Instituto de Investigaciones Bibliográficas, 1993); Rocío Meza Oliver and Luis Olivera López, *Catálogo de la Colección Lafragua de la Biblioteca Nacional de México, 1811–1821,* Instituto de Investigaciones Bibliográficas, Biblioteca Nacional de México, Série: Guias (México: UNAM, Instituto de Investigaciones Bibliográficas, 1996); Rocío Meza Oliver and Luis Olivera López, *Catálogo de la Colección Lafragua de la Biblioteca Nacional de México, 1854–1875,* Instituto de Investigaciones Bibliográficos, Biblioteca Nacional de México, Série: Guias (México: UNAM, in press).

5.   The collection that corresponded to the state of Puebla today is housed in the Biblioteca Lafragua on the campus of the Benemérita Universidad Autónoma de Puebla (BUAP). Unfortunately, as noted by Torre Villar, a major portion is missing. An assessment of the collection for preservation was undertaken by Dr. Dan Hazen in 1993. A current grant from Fideicomiso to BUAP for work toward the collection's preservation is not related to the LAMP/Biblioteca Nacional project.

6.   It is worth noting that the Biblioteca Nacional and the Hemeroteca Nacional are both administered by a coordinator and are under the single administration of the Instituto de Investigaciones Bibliográficos and its director, who in turn comes under the jurisdiction of the rector of the Universidad Nacional Autónoma de México (UNAM).

Contributors

Carlos Alberto Acuña Ramos, Pontificia Universidad Católica de Perú

Elsa Barberena B., Universidad Nacional Autónoma de México

Donna A. Canevari de Paredes, University of Saskatchewan, Canada

Edward L. Cleary, Providence College

Carl Deal, University of Illinois

Georgette M. Dorn, Hispanic Division, Library of Congress

Angel Esteban, Universidad de Granada, Granada, Spain

Frida Garbati, Library of Congress, Rio de Janeiro Office

Virginia Garrard-Burnett, University of Texas at Austin

Nelly S. González, University of Illinois

Marcelo Campos Hazan, The Catholic University of America

Pamela Howard-Reguindin, Library of Congress, Rio de Janeiro Office

Karen Lindvall-Larson, University of California, San Diego

Filiberto Felipe Martínez-Arellano, Universidad Nacional Autónoma de México, Centro Universitario de Investigaciones Bibliotecológicas

Malgorzata Oleszkiewicz, University of Texas at San Antonio

Eileen Oliver, Kent University

Dorothy M. Palmer, The University of The West Indies–Mona, Jamaica

Eudoxio Paredes-Ruiz, University of Saskatchewan, Canada

Terry C. Peet, Library of Congress

Margaret D. Rouse-Jones, The University of The West Indies–St. Augustine, Trinidad and Tobago

Rubén Ruiz Guerra, CCyDEL, Universidad Nacional Autónoma de México

JACK A. SIGGINS, George Washington University

SONIA T. DIAS GONÇALVES DA SILVA, UNICAMP–Brazil

RAFAEL E. TARRAGÓ, University of Minnesota

MIKE WEEMS, Ohio State University

Conference Program

Saturday, May 17, 1997

9:00 A.M.–1:00 P.M.	Committee Meetings
2:00–3:00 P.M.	**Inaugural Session**

Opening
Mark L. Grover
SALALM President
Brigham Young University
Minute of silence in remembrance of *Donald S. Wisdom*
and *W. David Rozkuszka*

Thomas S. Cohen
Curator, Oliveira Lima Library, The Catholic University
of America

Saul Sosnowski
Director, Latin American Studies Center, University of
Maryland, College Park

Georgette Dorn
Chief, Hispanic Division, Library of Congress

Angela Kinney
President, Hispanic Cultural Society, Library of Congress

José Toribio Medina
Award
Nelly S. González
University of Illinois

Welcome and
Announcements
Terry C. Peet
Local Arrangements
Library of Congress

Sunday, May 18, 1997

10:00 A.M.–6:00 P.M.	Committee Meetings
7:00–10:00 P.M.	Libreros' reception at the Organization of American States

Monday, May 19, 1997

The Catholic University of America

10:00–11:00 A.M.   **General Session**
Introduction: *Mark L. Grover,* Brigham Young University
Rapporteur: *Bartley A. Burk,* University of Notre Dame

Edward Cleary, Providence College
"The Catholic Church in Latin America"

11:00 A.M.–12:00   **Panel: Liberation Theology**
Moderator: *Joseph C. Holub,* University of Pennsylvania
Rapporteur: *Sandra Pike Raichel,* Literatura de Vientos
Tropicales/México Norte

Phillip Berryman, Temple University
"Liberation Theology: What Now?"

Thomas E. Quigley, U.S. Catholic Conference
"Liberation Theology: What Now? II"

12:00–1:00 P.M.   **Panel: Portuguese and Brazilian Books, Manuscripts,
and Paintings in the Oliveira Lima Library**
Moderator: *A. J. R. Russell-Wood,* Johns Hopkins University
Rapporteur: *Pamela Howard-Reguindin,* Library of
Congress Field Office, Rio de Janeiro

Thomas Cohen, The Catholic University of America
"Rare Books in the Oliveira Lima Library"

José Neistein, Brazilian-American Cultural Institute
"Manoel de Oliveira Lima: The Historian as Art Collector"

Marcelo Campos Hazan, The Catholic University of America
"Diplomacy in the Service of the Arts: Manoel de
Oliveira Lima and His Music Collection"

María Angela Leal, The Catholic University of America
"Cataloging Luso-Brazilian Materials in the Oliveira
Lima Library"

The Library of Congress

3:00–4:00 P.M.   **Panel: The Library of Congress and Global Resources**
Moderator: *Georgette Dorn,* Library of Congress
Rapporteur: *Mich Nelson*

Anunciada Colón de Carvajal, Fundación Histórica Tavera,
Madrid
"Proyectos de la Fundación Histórica Tavera en el ámbito
de la edición digital"

Pamela Howard-Reguindin, Library of Congress Field Office, Rio de Janeiro
"The LC Brazil Field Office: Past Accomplishments and New Challenges"

Terry C. Peet, Library of Congress
"Pushing the Envelope: Beyond Acquisitions"

4:00–5:00 P.M. **Panel: Take Two Steps Backforward: Preservation into the 21st Century**
Moderator: *John R. Hébert,* Library of Congress
Rapporteur: *Nancy L. Hallock,* University of Pittsburgh

POLICY AND TECHNIQUES
Ann Seibert, Library of Congress
"Policy and Techniques of Preservation in the Library of Congress and Recommendations for Future Acquisitions"

Amparo Torres, Library of Congress
"Outreach Programs, Preservation: Interns, *Apoyo,* Publications"

ACQUISITIONS
Terry C. Peet, Library of Congress
"Back to the Future: An Immodest Proposal"

HISTORICAL DOCUMENTS
John R. Hébert, Library of Congress
"Historical Documents and Preservation: Use and Content; Diego Durán's *Historia, Huexotzinco Codex* (1531), and Ocharte's *Graduale*"

Workshop: Managing Internet Resources: A Latin Americanist Perspective
Moderator: *Tony Harvell,* University of San Diego
Rapporteur: *Sarah Landeryou,* University of Denver

David Seaman, University of Virginia
"Online Electronic Texts and the Humanities Scholar"

Paul Bary, Tulane University
"Providing Access to Electronic Texts in Latin American Studies: Practical Issues for the Reference Librarian"

Cecilia Sercan, Cornell University
"Metadata for Internet Resources: A Cataloger's Perspective"

Panel: Latin American Research Resources in the Washington Area
Moderator: *Barbara A. Tenenbaum,* Library of Congress
Rapporteur: *Tracy North,* Library of Congress

Virginia Newton, Columbus Library, Organization of
American States
"Treasures in the OAS Archives and the Columbus Library"

James Patrick Kiernan, Historian of the Organization of
American States
"Possibilities and Limitations for Using the Resources of
the OAS for Research"

Crystal K. Converse, Contributing Editor, *Handbook of
Latin American Studies*
"Finding Latin America: Exploring the National Archives"

5:30–7:30 P.M.   Reception, Hispanic Division, Library of Congress

Tuesday May 20, 1997

9:00–10:00 a.m.   **General Session**
                     Introduction: *Laura Gutiérrez-Witt,* University of Texas at
                     Austin
                     Rapporteur: *Darlene H. Waller,* University of Connecticut

                     Virginia Garrard-Burnett, University of Texas at Austin
                     "Protestantism in Latin America"

10:00–11:00 A.M.   **Session**
                     Introduction: *Peter S. Bushnell,* University of Florida
                     Rapporteur: *Molly E. Molloy,* New Mexico State University

                     The Rev. Juan A. Quevedo-Bosch, Priest-in-charge, San
                     Bernabé Anglican Hispanic Congregation, Toronto, Canada,
                     and Toronto School of Theology, University of Toronto
                     "Religión en Cuba hoy"

                     **Workshop: Political and Governmental Resources on
                     the Internet**
                     Moderator: *Joseph C. Holub,* University of Pennsylvania
                     Rapporteur: *Carla J. Dewey,* MINITEX Library Information
                     Network

                     David Block, Cornell University
                     Teresa Lara-Meloy, Political Database of the Americas

11:00 A.M.–12:00   **Panel: Catholicism and Politics in Latin America:
                     Examples of Their Mutual Influence**
                     Moderator: *Eudoxio Paredes-Ruiz,* University of
                     Saskatchewan, Canada
                     Rapporteur: *Mena Whitmore,* Pentagon Library

Jack Siggins, George Washington University
"José Martí: Political Philosophy and the Catholic Church"

Eudoxio Paredes-Ruiz, University of Saskatchewan, Canada
" 'Evita' vs. catolicismo argentino, 1945-1952"

Donna A. Canevari, University of Saskatchewan, Canada
"The Image and Mythology of Eva Perón: Saint or Sinner"

Panel: Resources for the Study of Religion in Latin America
Moderator: *Mina Jane Grothey,* University of New Mexico
Rapporteur: *Catherine R. Nelson,* University of California,
Santa Barbara

Gloria de Alfaro and *Yolanda Maloney,* University of Colorado
"Quo Vadis: Emerging Issues in Latin American Religious
Studies Collections"

Karen Lindvall-Larson, University of California, San Diego
"Documents of Religious Missions to Latin America:
Their Potential for Non-Religious Missions Research"

Panel: Religion in Mexico
Moderator: *Cecilia Puerto,* San Diego State University
Rapporteur: *Cecilia S. Sercan,* Cornell University

Rubén Ruiz Guerra, CCyDEL, Universidad Nacional
Autónoma de México
"Los protestantes mexicanos en la política: una perspectiva
histórica"

Filiberto F. Martinez-Arellano, Universidad Nacional
Autónoma de México, Centro Universitario de Investigaciones
Bibliotecológicas
"TESIUNAM: A Database for Supporting Scholarly Activities
Dealing with Religion"

2:00–3:00 P.M. **Panel: Judaism in Brazil**
Moderator: *Peter Johnson,* Princeton University
Rapporteur: *Thomas H. Marshall,* University of Arizona

Regina Igel, University of Maryland–College Park
"Where Is the Jewish Brazilian Past? The Challenges for
a Researcher"

Frida Garbati, Library of Congress, Rio de Janeiro Office
"The Use of Media by Jewish Communities in Brazil"

3:00–4:00 P.M. **Panel: Religion in the English-Speaking Caribbean**
Moderator: *Richard F. Phillips,* University of Florida
Rapporteur: *Peter S. Bushnell,* University of Florida

Margaret Rouse-Jones, The University of The West Indies–
St. Augustine
" 'Until We All Reach Unity . . .': An Overview of the
Changing Patterns and Bibliographic Resources on the
Christian Church in Trinidad and Tobago"

Dorothy Palmer, The University of The West Indies-Mona
"An Evaluation of Bibliographic Materials in Non-Traditional
Religions in Jamaica: Pocomania/Revivalists and Rastafarians"

Panel: Religious Thought and Practice in Latin America
Moderator: *Denise A. Hibay,* New York Public Library
Rapporteur: *Marian Goslinga,* Florida International University

Rafael E. Tarragó, University of Minnesota
"All Humankind Is One: Bibliographic Sources for Research
on Archbishop Claret and Racism in Nineteenth-Century Cuba"

Francisco Salvador, St. Vladimir Orthodox Theological
Seminary
"La iglesia ortodoxa en Chile"

**Workshop: Be a Host(ess) with the Most: Guidelines
for SALALM Local Arrangements Committees**
Moderator: *Gayle Williams,* University of Georgia
Rapporteur: *Laura Shedenhelm,* University of Georgia

Gayle Williams, University of Georgia Libraries
Laura Gutiérrez-Witt, University of Texas at Austin

4:00–5:00 P.M.   **Panel: Research and Bibliography of Afro-Latin Religions**
Moderator: *Marian Goslinga,* Florida International University
Rapporteur: *Patricia Vaught,* University North Carolina,
Chapel Hill

Eileen Oliver, University of Texas at San Antonio
"The Power of Axé: Trends and Sources in Afro-Brazilian
Religious Studies"

Sara Sánchez and *Diana Kirby,* University of Miami
"Cuban Santería: A Review of the Literature; An Annotated
Bibliography"

Panel: Protestants and Evangelicals in Latin America
Moderator: *Nelly S. González,* University of Illinois
Rapporteur: *Karen Lindvall-Larson,* University of California,
San Diego

Eileen Marie McLaughlin, Ohio University
"Protestantism in Puerto Rico: North America's Religious
Invasion"

Carlos Alberto Acuña Ramos, Pontificia Universidad Católica de Perú
"La iglesia evangélica en el Perú: una aproximación socio-política"

Panel: Confessions of a Bibliographer: Newly Acquired Inquisition Collections
Moderator: *Scott Van Jacob,* University of Notre Dame
Rapporteur: *Angela M. Carreño,* New York University

Scott Van Jacob, University of Notre Dame
Walter Brem, The Bancroft Library

8:00–10:00 P.M. Movies
Onward Christian Soldiers (First Run/Icarus Films)
A Quiet Revolution (The Cinema Guild)

Wednesday May 21, 1997

9:00–10:00 A.M. **General Session**
Introduction: *Mark L. Grover,* Brigham Young University
Rapporteur: *Mina Jane Grothey,* University of New Mexico

Joseph Murphy, Georgetown University
"African-Latin Religions into the Twenty-First Century"

10:00–11:00 A.M. **Panel: Brazilian Candomblé**
Moderator: *Carla J. Dewey,* University of Minnesota
Rapporteur: *Ana María Cobos,* Saddleback College

Mike Weems, Ohio State University
"Forbidden Love: The Turbulent Relationship between Roman Catholicism and African-Brazilian Religion"

Malgorzata Oleszkiewicz, University of Texas at San Antonio
"The Role of Women in Brazilian Candomblé"

Panel: Religious Syncretism and the Latin American Indian
Moderator: *Edmundo Flores,* Library of Congress
Rapporteur: *Tony A. Harvell,* University of San Diego

Edmundo Flores, Library of Congress
"Religious Conversion and Syncretism in Mesoamerica and Peru during the Sixteenth Century: A Study of Spiritual Conflict and Union in the Americas"

Angel Esteban, Universidad de Granada, Granada, Spain
"Mezcla religiosa y cultural: el sincretismo español y precolombino en la poesía hispanoamericana del Siglo de Oro"

Panel: Religion of the Immigrants
Moderator: *Ann Hartness,* University of Texas at Austin
Rapporteur: *Rachel Barreto-Edensword,* The Catholic
University of America

Georgette Dorn, Hispanic Division, Library of Congress
"The Mennonite Colonies of Paraguay and the Indigenous
Population"

Sonia T. D. Gonçalves da Silva, UNICAMP-Brazil
"A religião dos pioneiros norte-americanos no Brasil na região
de Santa Barbara d'Oeste, São Paulo, Brasil"

11:00 A.M.–12:30 P.M. **Town Meeting**
Moderator: *Mark L. Grover,* Brigham Young University
Rapporteur: *John B. Wright,* Brigham Young University

1:30–2:15 P.M.   **Closing Session and Business Meeting**